By Little and By Little

By Little and By Little

THE SELECTED WRITINGS

OF DOROTHY DAY

Edited and with an Introduction by

ROBERT ELLSBERG

Alfred A. Knopf   New York   1983

Grateful acknowledgment is made to the following for permission to reprint from
previously published material:

Commonweal magazine: Excerpts from "The Scandal of the Works of Mercy,"
"About Mary," and "We Plead Guilty" by Dorothy Day. Copyright © Commonweal Publishing Co., Inc. Reprinted by permission.

Harper & Row, Publishers: Specified excerpts, abridged and adapted, from *The
Long Loneliness: An Autobiography* by Dorothy Day. Copyright, 1952 by Harper
& Row, Publishers, Inc. Copyright renewed, 1980 by Tamar Teresa Hennessy. Re-
printed by permission of Harper & Row, Publishers, Inc. Specified excerpts, abrid-
ged and adapted, from *Loaves and Fishes* by Dorothy Day. Copyright © 1963 by
Dorothy Day. Reprinted by permission of Harper & Row, Publishers, Inc.

Templegate Publishers and Fides/Claretian: Excerpts from *Therese* by Dorothy Day.
Reprinted by permission.

Library of Congress Cataloging in Publication Data
Day, Dorothy, 1897–1980.
By little and by little.   Includes index.
1. Church and social problems—Catholic Church—Addresses, essays, lectures.
I. Ellsberg, Robert.   II. Title.
HN37.C3D358   1983   261.8'3   82-48887
ISBN 0-394-52499-3
ISBN 0-394-71432-6 (pbk.)

Manufactured in the United States of America
First Edition

Frontispiece: Dorothy Day, 1970 © Bob Fitch

Going to confession is hard. Writing a book is hard because you are "giving yourself away." But if you love, you want to give yourself. You write as you are impelled to write, about man and his problems, his relation to God and his fellows. You write about yourself because in the long run all man's problems are the same, his human needs of sustenance and love. . . . I am a journalist, not a biographer, not a *book* writer. The sustained effort of writing, of putting pen to paper so many hours a day when there are human beings around who need me, when there is sickness, and hunger, and sorrow, is a harrowingly painful job. I feel that I have done nothing well. But I have done what I could.

Dorothy Day, *The Long Loneliness*

Contents

Preface

The present volume is a selection of Dorothy Day's published work, spanning a period of over fifty years. Although the great majority of the pieces have been reprinted from *The Catholic Worker,* a number of other magazine articles are included, as well as selections from all her books. These latter (with the exception of an immature novel published in 1924) include *From Union Square to Rome* (1938), the first account of her conversion; *House of Hospitality* (1939), a chronicle of the early years of the Catholic Worker; *On Pilgrimage* (1948), the journal for a single year; *The Long Loneliness* (1952), an autobiography; *Therese* (1960), a life of St. Therese of Lisieux; and *Loaves and Fishes* (1963), her most extensive account of the Catholic Worker movement.

The organization of this material, a project which began soon after Dorothy's death in 1980, has posed a number of difficulties. Neither a purely chronological order nor a strict arrangement according to theme seemed adequate to convey the particular qualities of her writing: a unified vision imposed on a discursive style; a concern for the topical, rooted somewhere outside of time. Eventually, the material found its own organization. The result is a somewhat roundabout chronicle of a life, loosely organized by theme, with much backing up and jumping ahead. As in life, the issues and occasions tend to overlap. The only rule I have followed has been to observe, within each "chapter," the order in which individual pieces were written.

Nearly all the articles from *The Catholic Worker* have been edited in one way or another. The method and motive for this deserve some explanation.

Dorothy Day always considered herself more a diarist and journalist than a "book writer." All the time given to writing, and especially to careful revision and editing, impressed her as time stolen from other responsibilities—not simply publishing a newspaper, but caring for the extended Catholic Worker family that was so demanding of her attention. As Judith Gregory, one of the editors from the early sixties, recalls, "She once reproved me when I spoke of writing in some way that to her implied perfectionism; writing seemed to be for her above all to report."

She had much to report. In the fifties and sixties, Dorothy's column, typically, might fill half the eight pages of the paper. "On Pilgrimage," the title she finally settled on, defies easy classification: a single column might be part editorial, part meditation, part journal, part news of her wanderings, often combined with long quotations from books or summaries of retreats and conferences. It was a vehicle all her own, its style reflecting her belief in the sacramentality, the holy sublimity, of the everyday. Nevertheless, even her editors sometimes urged her to "get to the point." One of them once told her bluntly that her writing lacked logic. It was logical enough, she insisted. "I go from one paragraph to the next."

Such criticism was not as likely to be made of that work which represented her most careful and deliberate efforts. Her books often included articles originally printed in the *Worker*. The contrast between the edited and original versions is the best indication of the serious regard in which she held the craft of writing. In her own newspaper, with limited time and plenty of space to fill, there was little incentive to curb a natural tendency to digression and repetition. Part of this was deliberate. If something was worth saying, she believed, it was worth saying twice; in many cases her digressions served in some mysterious way to make her most important points. Yet it was also true, as is often the case with prolific writers, that her work was sometimes improved with a bit of tightening.

While Dorothy assumed overall responsibility for the paper, the actual editing was, for the most part, left to a succession of managing editors, a post I filled from 1976 to 1978. Speaking from personal experience, I can state that while these editors were given broad license, most of them tended to extreme caution in tampering with Dorothy's prose. Such caution did not always serve her well. Nevertheless, Dorothy regarded her own work with extraordinary detachment. She was rarely satisfied with her writing, but once an article was done she put it from mind and moved on to other things. This was, aside from being a necessity, a practical exercise in humility. I recall how often she would hand me her copy with a look of resignation, saying, "Here it is. Do what you want with it."

What I have wanted to do, in handling material from *The Catholic Worker,* is to select the most striking and characteristic examples of Dorothy's writing, and to present them in their most clear and effective form. At times, this has meant condensing a very long article. In other cases, particularly in selections from her column, "On Pilgrimage," only a specific portion of the original article has been used. Except in the case of selections from her books, breaks in the text have not been indicated.

In her articles, I have made occasional revisions of punctuation, grammar, and syntax, as these seemed indicated, and I have supplied a number of titles. I am confident that I have performed the job Dorothy would have done herself, or assigned to her editor: the work which must certainly be done in transposing her writing from *The Catholic Worker* to another context.

Many times I have wished I could consult Dorothy on one matter or another. I would have liked to ask whether she was the author of several unsigned articles I chose, in caution, not to use. I would have questioned her about the quotation which inspired the title of this book: "It is by little and by little that we are saved." It is a line she repeated quite frequently, sometimes attributing it to St. Paul, a likely enough source, though I can find no trace of it in any biblical concordance.

Fortunately, I have been well provided with willing advisers. Of the many persons who have offered encouragement and counsel in the preparation of this book, I would like to make special mention of Chuck Matthei, Peggy Schreiner, Robert Coles, George Abbott White, David Townsend, Jana Kiely, Jim Forest, and Rachelle Linner. Sally Fitzgerald read the manuscript and made invariably useful suggestions at every stage of this project. My mother provided an office in her home in the first summer of work. Phil Runkel, archivist of the Catholic Worker collection at Marquette University, responded with astonishing speed and helpfulness to all my questions and requests for material. I would also like to thank my editor at Knopf, Barbara Bristol, for all her initiative, patience, and consistently good judgment.

This work has been a continuation, at least in spirit, of the five years, 1975–80, I spent as part of the Catholic Worker community in New York. The many people I met in those years have given me a lasting example of faithfulness and friendship. I would especially like to thank Frank Donovan, Deane Mary Mowrer, Dan Mauk, Peggy Scherer, Eileen Egan, Anne Marie Fraser, Fritz Eichenberg, and Tamar Hennessy. This book would not have been possible without their support.

My thanks go as well to the editors of *The Catholic Worker* for the use of material originally printed there. (Anyone wishing information about the Catholic Worker movement should write to: The Catholic Worker, 36 East First Street, New York, N.Y. 10003.)

My deepest gratitude is to Dorothy Day. The opportunity to reflect on her life and words over these many months has been yet another one of her gifts to me. I recall the words of the Nicaraguan poet Ernesto Cardenal, on the death of Thomas Merton, which I read in *The Catholic Worker* before I ever knew her:

> Beloved is the time of pruning,
> All the kisses will be given that you could not give
> The pomegranates are in bloom
> All love is a rehearsal for death.

Cambridge   ROBERT ELLSBERG
September 1982

Introduction

When Dorothy Day was still a young girl, she determined that she would become a writer. Inspired by the class-conscious fiction of Jack London and Upton Sinclair, she dreamed of writing "such books that thousands upon thousands of readers would be convinced of the injustice of things as they were." In the end, she became a different kind of writer, and perhaps something more, so that the countless number of people who were touched by her words, as well as the example of her life, were led to reflect not only on the injustice at large in the world but on the even more mysterious depths of love. The difference reflected a change in her understanding of "things as they were." After her conversion in 1927, her vocations as a writer and a radical found their place within a larger vocation. That calling, according to Cardinal Suhard, the attempt in obedience to follow Christ, "does not consist in engaging in propaganda, nor even in stirring people up, but in being a living mystery. It means to live in such a way that one's life would not make sense if God did not exist."

St. Peter enjoined the followers of Christ to be ready always to "give reason for the faith and hope" within them. In the case of Dorothy Day, this resulted in something more than simple apologetics. For her, theological discourse was a matter of straight reportage. She lived in the presence of God, a God who had passed through creation and entered into our suffering flesh. Sin, grace, redemption—these were facts, apart from which our lives, our history, and the news of the daily press were incomprehensible abstractions. She wrote to give reason for a marriage of convictions that was a scandal and stumbling block to many: radical politics and traditional, conservative theology. Yet it was not what Dorothy Day wrote that was extraordinary, nor even what she believed, but the fact that there was absolutely no distinction between what she believed, what she wrote, and the manner in which she lived.

Such a life would have been instructive even had she never put a word on paper. In fact, she filled reams of paper with her words: half a dozen books and approximately 1,500 articles, essays, and reviews. Of the latter, most were published in *The Catholic Worker,* the paper she founded in

1933 and edited until her death forty-seven years later. Yet many of those
who now honor her memory have known little of that writing. Far more
numerous than her regular readers were those who simply took comfort in
the fact of her presence on the Bowery, living among the very poor,
speaking out against war and injustice, issuing her warnings and protests
(occasionally from jail), and giving proof, decade after decade, that the
Gospel could be lived.

She herself was reluctant to draw distinctions between "writing" and
"doing." "Each is an act," she once said. "Both can be part of a person's
response, an ethical response to the world." It is fortunate that so much
of that response is recorded in writing, and in a style which bears the vivid
impression of its author's personality. She remained always a most personal
writer, even when dealing with large and sometimes abstract issues. Perhaps
this was the reason her readers, and so many others only slightly acquainted
with her work, found it natural to call her, simply, "Dorothy."

It is difficult to appraise the legacy of such a life. One can note that her
spirit lives on in the Catholic Worker—both the newspaper with a circulation of 100,000 and the network of more than fifty communities across
the country, which continue to hold out a vision of a "society where it is
easier for people to be good." Countless thousands have been sheltered in
these "Houses of Hospitality"; millions of meals have been served. But
Dorothy attached little importance to such figures. Hospitality, she insisted,
meant more than serving a meal, offering a bed, or opening a door; it
meant opening one's heart to the needs of others.

In a statement of aims and purposes frequently reprinted in *The Catholic
Worker,* the goal of the movement is stated simply: "to realize in the
individual and society the expressed and implied teachings of Christ."
Dorothy understood the Incarnation to be an ongoing fact: God had once
and for all assumed our humanity, and we could not hope to know Him
without also turning to our neighbors in love. Such love was not merely a
passing glow, but something concrete and active. It meant extending
fellowship, sharing bread with the hungry, clothing the naked, standing
beside those who were outcast and persecuted.

The value of such a venture is not properly assessed in terms of profits
and losses. Objectively speaking, the Catholic Worker has aspired to a kind
of "holy folly." After fifty years, it has amassed no board of directors, no
foundation, no computerized mailing list. The newspaper, which is mailed
by hand, has never advertised. None of the staff has ever received a salary.
The sole fund-raising strategy, if one can call it that, has entailed the

occasional printing of an appeal in the paper, which sells today, as it always has, for a penny a copy.

It is likely that any responsible management consultant, invited to survey the organization of the movement, would issue a grim forecast on its future. And yet it has continued these many years, while so many other better-organized efforts have failed. From the beginning, Dorothy displayed a willful indifference to conventional business sense. If the work were to survive, she believed, it would have to be on the basis of something other than the wisdom of the world.

When Dorothy Day died in 1980, at the age of eighty-three, the historian David O'Brien, writing in *Commonweal,* called her "the most significant, interesting, and influential person in the history of American Catholicism." Such a statement is all the more extraordinary considering that it refers to someone who occupied no established position of authority, and whose views, after all, met with virtually universal rejection throughout most of her career.

She had spent her youth among socialists, anarchists, and Communists, and considered herself one of them. She had known the rootless bohemian life, the nights of bars and parties and unhappy love affairs. She had borne a child out of wedlock, and had soon thereafter shocked her "progressive" friends by her decision to enter the Roman Catholic Church. In their view, she had gone over to the church of wealth and power, the bastion of conservative prelates, so often in open alliance with the interests of the status quo. Dorothy did not try to deny these charges. But it was also, she believed, for all its sins, the church of the poor and the dispossessed, the church that was somehow the Body, in this world, of its crucified Saviour.

Part of what attracted Dorothy to Christianity was its theology of immanence, God's indwelling presence in the world. The injustice suffered by the poor had made her a radical. And in the Gospels she learned that God Himself had walked among the poor, had known hard work, exile, and the life of a wanderer. He had revealed Himself to those who were abused and unwanted, and had become one of them Himself, laying down His life, an enemy of Church and State alike.

In becoming a Catholic, Dorothy had not forsaken her political convictions. But what she found in the Gospels was an understanding of human liberation, a sense of community and solidarity much larger than politics alone could provide. To be both a radical and a Catholic did not mean that she inhabited an "underground" Church, distinct from the faith and practice of ordinary believers. Nor did it signify the kind of seductive idolatry that would identify the Kingdom of God with a particular movement or cause. It certainly did not mean that religious language was to be used to justify a secular agenda of power, influence, and results. It simply meant that she held the powers of this world, as she held herself, accountable to the word and commandment of God.

That commandment, as she understood it, entrusted us with a special responsibility for the vindication and defense of life. Dorothy responded to that obligation not only in its personal form of charity but in its most political form as well: challenging, resisting and obstructing the institutional forces which led to poverty and the waste of war. In all her activities, even as she marched on picket lines or went to jail, she was strengthened by a constant discipline of prayer: daily Mass, the rosary, at least two hours a day of meditation on Scripture. She called herself "a loyal and obedient daughter of the Church," and frequently repeated her offer to close down operations if ordered to do so by the Cardinal. The order never came. Who can say if someone in the Chancery didn't recall the words of Gamaliel in the Book of Acts: "If this teaching or movement is merely human, it will collapse of its own accord. But if it should be from God, you cannot defeat them, and you might actually find yourselves to be fighting against God!"

What then can be said of the meaning of Dorothy Day's life for her country and her Church? How one answers this question may depend somewhat on one's understanding of the word "saint." There continue to be individuals among us, of whom Mother Teresa of Calcutta is perhaps the most celebrated example, who serve to demonstrate in a secular age that holiness remains an attainable ideal. The heroic charity of such individuals receives nearly universal praise and is often cited as an inspiration. Dorothy Day, who practiced charity, but spoke of justice, remained in her life a more troubling figure. "Don't call me a saint," she used to say. "I don't want to be dismissed that easily." She was a "sign of contradiction," an example of a holiness not easily domesticated, and therefore, perhaps, an example of particular relevance for our time.

This is an age in which human beings live under the imminent possibility of self-annihilation. Dorothy Day suggested one form of the Christian vocation in such an age—to point a way back to life and sanity, and a way of living such as might, if it were widely practiced, provide a basis for the coming generation to survive. Without rejecting the institutional Church, Dorothy drew on the radical possibilities within its tradition. She called on the Church to recover its identity as an offense and mystery in the eyes of the world, a world that seeks its security in weapons and its identity in power and possessions. If Dorothy is remembered in a hundred years—if anyone is alive to remember her—it may well be because the Church will have assumed the prophetic witness which she embodied, and the definition of the word "Christian" expanded to embrace its original identity with "Peacemaker."

All Christians are called to be saints; so Dorothy believed. By that term, she meant to refer to the line of men and women who have reminded us of God, who, in their lives, enlarged the boundaries of human love, and bade us follow. It requires no great effort of imagination to picture Dorothy Day in their company.

* * *

She was born in Brooklyn on November 8, 1897, the third of five children in a lower-middle-class family of tenuous security. Her father was an itinerant sportswriter. After a brief residence in Oakland, which ended with the San Francisco earthquake, the Days settled in Chicago. There Dorothy was first exposed to the raw sights and smells of poverty. After an early period of childish piety, which saw her baptized in the Episcopal Church, Dorothy's interest in religion faded. In its stead, she embraced a new faith in the ideals of the social and political radicals whose promise to change the world—"not just to minister to the slaves," but "to do away with slavery"—seemed the most sensible response to social conditions. In 1914, as a freshman at the University of Illinois in Urbana, she made her first act of political commitment by joining the Socialist Party. It was mostly a symbolic gesture; she found the meetings dull, and attended few of them. After two years she chose to dispense with formal education altogether and set off eagerly for New York, there to embark on what seemed the more serious business of life.

Having settled on the career of a writer, she soon found a job that pleased her as a reporter for *The Call,* a Socialist daily, whose editorial staff represented a broad spectrum of warring radical factions. She herself had little interest in ideological disputes, but as it seemed important to declare a stand, she carried the red union card of the Industrial Workers of the World (I.W.W.), the radical syndicalists who looked forward to the day of "one big union" and the general strike that would bring the capitalist system to a halt. Finding lodging in an apartment on the Lower East Side, Dorothy immersed herself in the vibrant street life of the immigrant quarter, and set to work on her articles: interviews with Leon Trotsky and birth-control advocate Margaret Sanger, stories about strikes, picket lines, and evictions, all written in an indignant, occasionally tabloid style. On March 21, 1917, she joined the crowd in Madison Square Garden gathered to celebrate the February Revolution in Russia, and hailed what seemed in her youth the dawn of a new era.

A brief job with the Anti-Conscription League ended with the declaration of American entry into the First World War. There followed a position with *The Masses,* a lively and combative journal, whose staff included such figures as Floyd Dell, Max Eastman, and John Reed. *The Masses* had claimed for itself the task of disturbing the values and sensibilities of the bourgeois class, a goal that was evidently achieved—within months of Dorothy's arrival, the journal was suppressed by the government, and the editors indicted on charges of sedition.

Out of work, Dorothy responded impulsively to an invitation to join the ongoing protest of the suffragists in Washington. Arrested for attempting to picket the White House, she was sentenced with a group of distinguished women to a term of thirty days in Occoquan, a penitentiary legendary for its brutality. A hunger strike ensued, and the women were placed in solitary confinement. Afterward, the protest was considered a great success. Nevertheless, Dorothy truly suffered in her first frightening days of confinement, and she was surprised and somewhat embarrassed to find herself turning to the Bible for consolation.

Back in New York, she soon fell in with a new circle of bohemians and rebels, the "Village set," who congregated about the Provincetown Playhouse. During the cold winter of 1917–18, Dorothy was the inseparable companion of Eugene O'Neill. After rehearsals at the Playhouse, she, O'Neill, and the others would proceed to the back room of a saloon in the Village, nicknamed "The Hell Hole" by its patrons. It was there, amid the smoke and drink, that she first heard O'Neill offer a lugubrious rendition of Francis Thompson's poem "The Hound of Heaven." And often, after listening all night to one of O'Neill's gloomy monologues, she would guide him home and put him to bed, and then, in the first hours of dawn, drop into a back pew of St. Joseph's Church in the Village. It was warm and quiet, and she found herself comforted "by the lights and silence, the kneeling people and the atmosphere of worship." She was troubled by the disorder around her, and reacted, as she would throughout her life, with an instinct for reverence.

The suicide of a friend in January prompted her to break loose from this sad, careless circle. For a year she worked as a nurse trainee at King's County Hospital in Brooklyn. There she fell desperately in love with an older man, a writer, of a rather menacing charm. When the affair resulted in her becoming pregnant, Dorothy, hoping to forestall her inevitable abandonment, chose to have an abortion. It was a futile gesture, and the memory of this waste of life would remain with her always.

The years that followed were marked by loneliness and restless searching. She traveled, wrote, and held a succession of nondescript jobs. For a time, she lived in Chicago and worked on *The Liberator,* a Communist journal. While there she was arrested a second time, swept up in a Red Scare raid on an I.W.W. flophouse where she had spent the night. The police would not dignify her with a political charge. She was held as an "occupant of a disorderly house," i.e., a prostitute.

In the spring of 1924, Dorothy published a frankly autobiographical novel, *The Eleventh Virgin,* which she later reviled as "a very bad book." Whatever the merits of the work, the proceeds allowed her to buy a small bungalow on Staten Island in a colony of artists and radicals. With this move began a period which would later stand out in her memory as a time of "natural happiness." It was not a consistently happy time, but for a few short years, she knew something of the satisfactions of home and family life. She learned to see the beauty of the world, not just its strife and cruelty, and in her "natural happiness" came to believe in the possibility of a happiness beyond nature.

"The man I loved, with whom I entered into a common-law marriage, was an anarchist, an Englishman by descent, and a biologist," she wrote. He was Forster Batterham, an oddly placed figure in the literary circles in which she then moved. His interests, refreshingly enough, lay in the natural sciences, on which he could speak at length with authority and enthusiasm. Together, he and Dorothy fished in the bay, studied the stars, and collected specimens from the beach. Under his tutelage, Dorothy, who had spent her life in cities, discovered a new world around her. She began to "think and weigh things more." And she found herself once again reading the Bible and wanting to pray.

Forster found all talk of religion incomprehensible and distressing. He was a rationalist, delighted by nature, but scornful of man and the injustice of his institutions. Dorothy admired his integrity and the purity of his feelings. But there was a tension between their temperaments that went beyond her tentative move toward faith. She did not share his pessimism or extreme individualism. She remained basically hopeful, continuing to believe in the power of human beings to change the world as well as their lives.

In the summer of 1925, Dorothy realized that she was once again pregnant. It would be hard to exaggerate the significance of this event in her life. Unquestionably, her reaction was influenced by the memory of the child she had denied and lost. For a long time, she says, she had believed herself incapable of bearing a child. Now she felt herself entrusted once more with a part in the renewal of life, and in her joy and gratitude her first thoughts were of God. She was determined to have the child baptized a Catholic: "I knew that I was not going to have her foundering through many years as I had done, doubting and hesitating, undisciplined and amoral." She would give to her child what she did not, as yet, have the courage to claim for herself.

Tamar Teresa was born in March. With the help of one Sister Aloysius, a nun whom Dorothy had accosted on the beach, the child was baptized in July. Forster looked bitterly on all this activity, the ultimate destination of which was clear to both, though it remained unspoken. Dorothy was making her own hesitant way toward the Church of Rome, a move he could regard only as one of morbid escapism. A consistent anarchist and atheist, he would be married by neither Church nor State. He would have nothing to do with the Catholic Church, or with Dorothy if she were part of it. Sadly, she realized that "to become a Catholic would mean for me to give up a mate with whom I was much in love. It got to the point where it was the simple question of whether I chose God or man." Painfully, uncertainly, she chose God. A tense year passed, with frequent outbreaks of recrimination and remorse. But finally she insisted on a break. The next day she went to a church in Tottenville and received the Sacraments of the Church. She writes that she felt no particular joy at the time. It was simply something that had to be done.

It should be emphasized that in becoming a Catholic, Dorothy was not attracted by any aura of intellectual or aesthetic sophistication. She had read St. Augustine and the life of St. Teresa, but her formal theological training had been supervised by Sister Aloysius and the *Baltimore Catechism*. She was joining the Church of the masses, of immigrants, the Church, as her father put it to her scornfully, of "Irish cops and washerwomen." As a radical, she had been taught to regard these working people as noble champions of history to the extent that they heeded the wisdom of their self-appointed vanguard, and as exploited and opiated cattle insofar as they submitted to the superstitions of religion. But she had come to recognize in the families she saw at Mass other qualities which she lacked and envied: a sense of life in its wholeness and holiness, of transcendence, order, and obedience. The latter, she had once thought, was a word to be scorned. But now "I had reached the point where I wanted to obey. . . . I was tired of following the devices and desires of my own heart, of doing what I wanted to do, what my desires told me I wanted to do, which always seemed to lead me astray."

Yet on the day she became a Catholic, she suffered a sense of double loss. Besides the pain of leaving the man she loved, there was also the feeling of having rejected the cause of "the workers, the poor of the world, with whom Christ spent His life." For if the Church was the home of the poor, it was also, scandalously, the home of power and privilege. She was working at the time for the Anti-Imperialist League, a Communist affiliate, and her conversion struck many of her friends and colleagues as a terrible betrayal. As for herself, she did not believe she was abandoning her previous commitments. She had acted on the faith that to choose God before everything could not ultimately be a choice against life, justice, or peace. So she entered the wilderness, trusting that God would somehow turn her confusion to His purposes.

That confusion remained with her for the next five years, as she struggled to raise her child alone on the occasional wages of a free-lance writer. She was confident of her act of faith, but still uncertain whether there was not more she was being called to do. In December 1932, she was in Washington, D.C., covering the Hunger March of the Unemployed, organized by her old Communist friends. The march represented a crisis point in her search. Watching this procession of ragged men, transformed by a sense of purpose and an ideal of justice, she was moved to go to the National Shrine of the Immaculate Conception, and there offer up a prayer, "with tears and anguish, that some way would open up for me to use what talents I possessed for my fellow workers, for the poor."

When she returned to New York, she found, waiting at her door, Peter Maurin—a short, somewhat unkempt man with a thick French accent and a fire in his eyes, who began at once to preach to her the ideas, the grand vision, he had stored up during years of hard labor, study, and tramping around the country. It took a while—perhaps not at the first meeting—before she began to comprehend that this rough peasant was the answer to her prayer. He had come to bring her "a way of life and instruction."

The Catholic Worker was conceived in that meeting.

*   *   *

In later years, Dorothy would say of Peter Maurin, "If he had said, 'Go to Madison Square Garden and speak these ideas,' I would have overcome all sense of fear and would have attempted such a folly, convinced that, though it was the 'folly of the Cross' and doomed to failure, God Himself could take this failure and turn it into victory." There was certainly nothing in his appearance to inspire such confidence. The pockets of his coat were bulging with books and pamphlets. His suit looked as if he had slept in it (as indeed he had). Whether motivated by some obscure principle or simple inattention to detail, he did not bathe. (Once asked why he didn't pay more attention to his appearance, he replied, "So as not to arouse envy.") He considered himself of little importance; only his ideas mattered. For this reason, it took Dorothy a long time to extract his personal story.

Peter Maurin was born in 1877 in the ancient Languedoc region of southern France. He was one of twenty-three children, born to a peasant family who could boast of a claim to the land they farmed dating back fifteen hundred years. Educated by the Christian Brothers, Peter had breathed in the atmosphere of Catholic populism, then in ferment in France, before sailing for North America in 1909. After the failure of a homesteading project in Canada, he had crossed the border illegally into New York State, and for the next twenty years drifted through the East and Midwest, performing various kinds of hard manual labor. Believing that work should be regarded as a gift, he was happy to offer his labor in exchange for room and board. Like St. Francis, he embraced Holy Poverty as his bride, dining in skid row beaneries and sleeping wherever he could find a bed. (While working in a coal mine, he had, for a while, lived in an abandoned coke oven.) What little money he earned was either spent on books or given away to those in greater need. His mind was elsewhere. As he roamed the country, breaking rocks and mending roads, he was all the while engaged in his true work, an effort to devise a synthesis in the area of Catholic social philosophy.

The main problem with society, as Peter Maurin saw it, was that sociology, economics, and politics had all been separated from the Gospel. In the process, society had lost any sense of the ultimate, transcendent purpose of human activity. Social life had come to be organized around the drive for production and the search for profits, rather than the full development of persons. Human beings, intended by God to be co-creators by virtue of their labor, had instead become alienated and atomized, bereft of any spirit of community, and reduced generally to the status of cogs in a machine. The Church, in Peter's view, had an answer to all this, but it had failed to act on it. There was "dynamite" in the Gospels, but most members of the clergy preferred to keep it under lock and key. What was necessary was to "blow the lid" off that dynamite.

While Peter was disdainful of capitalism, he was distrustful as well of the Marxist idealization of industrialism and progress, with its faith in the laws of history and the dictatorship of the proletariat. He himself wanted to abolish the proletariat as a class, to dismantle the whole urban industrial society. What he hoped to establish in its place was a decentralized economy in which he envisaged a healthy balance between town and country, the work of the mind and of the hand, all to be fostered through the development of cottage industry, cooperatives, and communal farming. For this vision he drew inspiration from the example of the Middle Ages, when, according to his own somewhat idealized conception, learning, economic, and cultural life had been consecrated to a unified, spiritual ideal—a synthesis of what he called "Cult, Culture, and Cultivation."

There was no such thing, in Peter's philosophy, as waiting for the correct "objective circumstances." His program was a "personalist revolution," which called for "building a new world within the shell of the old." One should not await some presumably propitious moment, but instead begin at once to live by a new set of values. "The future will be different," he announced in typical style, "if we make the present different." And the revolution began with oneself. There was no need to form a committee to study the problem; the commandments of Christ were there before us, and all that remained was to give flesh to those words, to translate the Gospel into action, and attract others to the cause.

He had thought it all out and knew exactly what had to be done. He had even gone to the trouble of setting down his ideas in dozens of highly original verses, later dubbed "Easy Essays." There was only one problem: For all his enthusiasm, Peter Maurin was utterly lacking in everyday practicality, the ability to translate abstract ideas into workable actions on a scale larger than himself. He could talk for hours, seemingly without the necessity of breathing. His "essays," which sounded rather like advertising jingles composed in an abbey, were especially well adapted to street-corner declamation. The following is a typical stanza:

> The world would become better off
> if people tried to become better.
> And people would become better
> if they stopped trying to become better off.

On another occasion he proclaimed with confidence:

> They say that I am crazy
> because I refuse to be crazy
> the way everyone else is crazy.

Gladly, he recited these essays on buses, on street corners before indifferent crowds, even on the stage on amateur nights at the neighborhood cinema (he did not scorn a captive audience). He talked to anyone who would listen, and many who would have rather not. But for all this talk, he had yet to attract a single disciple to his cause. Until he met Dorothy Day.

The editor of *Commonweal* had given her name to Peter with the suggestion that he and Dorothy shared certain similar ideas. This was true in the sense that both were searching for a way to relate their faith to the urgent social issues of the day. Otherwise, it would be hard to imagine two less likely collaborators. Peter was a man of another culture, another century. His roots were in the soil, and his thoughts tethered to the pace of local, personal activity. He found his models among the Irish monks of the Middle Ages. Dorothy, on the other hand, twenty years his junior, could not have been more thoroughly American. Restless and impatient for results, she thought in terms of unions, large political movements, and the class struggle. Both would have to do some adjusting. Nevertheless, even before they had met, Peter Maurin was confident that Providence had ordained the partnership.

In his excitement at their first meeting, he nearly dispensed with introductions before launching into a discourse on his three-point program. It was relatively simple, if not simplistic: round-table discussions for "clarification of thought"; Houses of Hospitality for the practice of the Works of Mercy; and "agronomic universities," where "workers could become scholars and scholars could become workers." Sensing less than total comprehension, he expanded on these principles.

The first thing needed was to stimulate dialogue by introducing the alternative of a Catholic social philosophy. This, Peter termed "clarification of thought," for the purpose of which he envisioned forums, lectures, and round-table discussions, involving representatives of every faction and school of thought. (He was confident of the persuasive power of his own ideas in any fair debate.) Incidentally, he suggested the publication of a newspaper.

Secondly, Houses of Hospitality should be established in every parish to care for the homeless and unemployed. It was the spirit of personal responsibility, according to Peter, that held the answer to social problems. Christians ought not to think in terms of what the State or the Church should do, but of what they could do themselves. Put simply, God wished us to be our brother's keeper. The failure to realize this, he believed, was what lay behind most of what were called economic and political problems. Hunger and unemployment, properly speaking, were spiritual problems. They arose because modern society had made the bank account, rather than the Sermon on the Mount, the ultimate standard of values. The dollar was worshipped instead of Christ, and Christians were thus unable to recognize Christ in their neighbors. The antidote was to be found in the Works of Mercy: feeding the hungry, clothing the naked, sheltering the homeless—not through the impersonal agency of the State, but as Christ had commanded, "at a personal sacrifice."

The Works of Mercy were necessary, but they were not sufficient. The third part of Peter's program, the most important part, in his view, was the constructive task of effecting the transition from an "acquisitive" to a "functional" society. In a world offering the promise of wars, revolutions, and the empty struggle for economic security, Peter held that what people really desired was community, meaningful work, some sense of purpose, something to reverence and honor, some measure of control over the fundamental issues affecting their lives. The present system could not provide such things. They could only be achieved by breaking the functional units of society down to some more sensible, organic scale. As part of this task, we should move back to the land—form "agronomic universities"—and begin living by utterly different values, producing for human needs, and building in small, practical ways "the kind of society where it is easier for people to be good."

It would be some time before Dorothy fully shared Peter's ambitious vision. Had she fully understood from the beginning all it would entail, she might never have responded so enthusiastically. But one thing in particular had fired her imagination: the idea of starting a newspaper that would offer solidarity with the workers and a critique of the social system from the radical perspective of the Gospels. She had spent most of her professional life as a journalist, and already she could see how the job might be done. In fact, she was all for beginning right away. "After all, I had a typewriter, a kitchen table, plenty of paper and plenty to write about." Peter was delighted, though he had expected no less.

This first happy agreement was soon tested by the strain of differing temperaments and assumptions. While Peter labored to "indoctrinate" Dorothy in the basis of his Catholic interpretation of history, she set to work writing stories about strikes, unemployment, segregation, and breadlines. Peter was dismayed. His protégée's approach to issues seemed to smack of a "class war" attitude. The situation, he felt, did not call for more denunciation of conditions, but the annunciation of a constructive program of action. "Our job," he said, "is to make the encyclicals click." What was needed for this purpose was a serious discussion of ideas. What was needed was ... well, a paper consisting largely of his own Easy Essays. "It was amazing," Dorothy would later write, "how little we understood each other at first."

The first issue of *The Catholic Worker* was distributed at a Communist rally in Union Square, on May 1, 1933. Peter was not on hand for this adventure. Having staked out for himself the thankless task of enunciating principles, he was content to leave practical matters to his enthusiastic colleague. By the second issue, he had further emphasized his independent stance in an editorial in which he explained the removal of his name from the masthead. He was concerned, he noted pointedly, lest anyone hold him responsible for articles he had not written. Yet any reservations on Peter's part were soon overcome in light of the positive response elicited by the paper's first issues. The press run for the May issue was 2,500. Within two years the circulation had grown to 150,000. There turned out to be quite a large audience eager for a paper addressing social issues from a Catholic perspective. Seminaries and churches around the country ordered bundles. Zealous young people sold the paper on the street. And quite soon a staff of ardent volunteers began to congregate around the newspaper office, a former barbershop on the ground floor of Dorothy's Fifteenth Street apartment.

The second part of the Catholic Worker program was implemented without much forethought. Peter had written a letter to all the bishops of the country urging the establishment of Houses of Hospitality in their dioceses, citing once more the example of the Irish monks of old. The concept was self-evident to Peter, and he assumed little persuasion would be required to convince the hierarchy of its value. This proved otherwise. Instead, homeless men and women began arriving at the door, asking where to find these houses described in the paper. Dorothy's answer was to go out and rent an apartment. Soon other apartments were needed, and before long the Catholic Worker occupied its own building on Charles Street. The "breadline" began in a similarly unpremeditated fashion. There was always coffee and a pot of soup on the stove, and anyone coming to the door was welcome to share a meal. Word got around, and by 1936, a crowd of hundreds was lining up at the door each day. As Dorothy would say, it all "just happened."

Gradually, other houses began to spring up across the country—more than thirty of them in the first ten years—and the Catholic Worker was truly a movement. Though affiliated with the headquarters in New York and the principles espoused in the paper, each house was quite independent, adapting its style and organization to its own circumstances and needs. Nevertheless, a surprising degree of consistency existed (as it does still) among different Worker communities, characterized by a spirit of functional anarchy, an abhorrence of regulations, and a basic tolerance for persons of all backgrounds. In contrast to many intentional communities, with members carefully screened for personal and ideological compatibility, the Worker community consisted of whoever showed up at the door. The result was often an assemblage of characters that seemed drawn from a novel by Dostoevsky. On hand in most Catholic Worker houses was a similar cast of pilgrims, scholars, and "holy fools," the young and old, workers, loafers, and everything in between. It was a microcosm of sorts, a family, as Dorothy would say, and an example of the possibility of a diverse group of individuals residing together in relative harmony, without the need of elaborate rules. The basis for community was not an ideal to be achieved, but the recognition of a reality already accomplished in Christ— the fact that all, whether clever or dull, fit or infirm, beautiful or plain, were "members one of another."

Farming communes were eventually established. They met with varying degrees of success, only rarely living up to Peter Maurin's concept of self-sufficient agronomic universities. More often, they resembled Houses of Hospitality on the land. Still, as Peter would say, they made a point, and signified the Worker's commitment to look beyond the immediate crisis to an alternative ideal.

Dorothy, meanwhile, spent a good deal of her time traveling around the country, visiting the houses, speaking, and reporting on the dramatic labor upheavals brought on by the Depression. From the sit-down strikes of the auto workers in Detroit to the migrant workers in California, she made a point of going wherever there was trouble, wherever workers were resisting unfit conditions, to let them know there were Catholics on their side.

*   *   *

It is difficult to capture the particular excitement of those early years of the "street apostolate." It is hard, today, to imagine the heady sense of liberation then felt by many young Catholics simply at being part of a movement of *lay people,* speaking out and acting in response to the issues of the day, without recourse to clerical supervision. The Catholic Worker was offering a dramatic redefinition of the role of lay people within the Church, one which has had reverberations even to the present day. At the same time, the movement was expanding the definition of "Catholic issues" beyond the parochial concerns that were then (and, too often, still are) the prescribed reserve of Catholic action. The Christian conscience, according to Dorothy, belonged with Christ—not on the boundary, but at the center of human experience. Justice, freedom, the rights of conscience, war and peace—these were Catholic issues.

The Worker approached such concerns, furthermore, in an original manner, different from that of either the Communists or trade unionists. Peter Maurin's vision was so original, in fact, that readers from both the left and the right often found it difficult to locate the movement along the conventional political spectrum. The Catholic Workers opposed the materialism of Communism and capitalism alike; supported the right of private property in a decentralized form; opposed nationalization; supported strikes and unions, but spoke in terms of worker ownership, cooperatives, and a return to the land; endorsed the medieval ban on usury; called themselves anarchists, while claiming authority for their eclectic platform in the lives of the saints and the tradition of Irish monasticism. To many seasoned observers, the very idiosyncrasy of these positions suggested a smokescreen, designed to obscure the true intentions of its proponents.

Communists suspected a Vatican plot to coopt the sympathies of the working class. Certain Catholics, on the other hand, saw in the movement nothing more than a Red plot to infiltrate the Church, and challenged the Workers, in the words of one priest, "to come out in the open, declare yourselves Bolshevik Communists, and fight the Church like men."

The five hundred pages of the F.B.I.'s file on the Catholic Worker, recently declassified, document the government's own exasperated efforts to classify the exact brand of subversion being perpetrated by Dorothy Day and her collaborators. The file discloses the information that J. Edgar Hoover, for one, considered the movement dangerous enough to merit prosecution on the charge of sedition, and that he recommended such action to the Attorney General on three separate occasions. His counsel went unheeded, and Dorothy persisted in her suspect activities, chief of which, apparently, was her tendency to make light of the Bureau's crime-fighting efficiency. The following paragraph, in a column from 1954, served in particular to incite the Director's wrath:

Some F.B.I. man by the name of Daly came down to query me about one of our friends who is a conscientious objector. He asked me the usual questions as to how long I had known him, how he stated his position as c.o. or pacifist, whether or not he believed in defending himself. Evidently, one of my answers offended him, because he pulled back his jacket and displayed the holster of a gun under his armpit, which he patted bravely as he said, "I believe in defending myself." I could not but think, "How brave a man, defending himself with his gun against us unarmed women and children hereabouts."

Hoover exacted private satisfaction in the form of this derogatory profile added to Dorothy's already bulging file:

Dorothy Day has been described as a very erratic and irresponsible person. . . . She has engaged in activities which strongly suggest that she is consciously or unconsciously being used by communist groups. From past experience with her it is obvious she maintains a very hostile and belligerent attitude towards the Bureau and makes every effort to castigate the Bureau whenever she feels so inclined.

Such criticism, even when voiced in the open, was not seriously discouraging. A certain amount of misunderstanding was to be expected. After all, as Dorothy would quote, "The servant is not greater than his master." The young people enjoyed taking the newspaper to "the man on the street," selling it on subways and in front of churches and theaters, as well as at demonstrations and picket lines. And when they were insulted, harassed, or reviled, when papers were torn from their hands by devout patriots, they rejoiced at being "accounted worthy to suffer." But none of this early controversy prepared them for the storm that was to break over Dorothy's insistence on one simple proposition: that the violence of war could not be reconciled with the gospel of peace.

Though explicit from the beginning, the Worker's pacifist position had not excited much reaction in the early years of the movement (many people, after all, call themselves pacifists between wars). This changed abruptly in 1936, with the outbreak of the Civil War in Spain. In the eyes of most Catholics, this was a Holy War, a crusade against Atheistic Communism, and virtually every pulpit and Catholic newspaper in America was enlisted in the service of General Franco. At the same time, American liberals and radicals were just as passionately committed to the workers and peasants of the Loyalist cause. Dorothy's decision to take a neutral position in the war was a move guaranteed to provoke everyone's outrage. She was reminded by Catholics of the anticlerical atrocities being committed by certain Loyalist partisans—priests killed and churches desecrated. In Dorothy's view, the blame for such actions was shared by those Christians who had convinced the poor that the Church belonged to the rich and powerful. But those who spoke now of avenging the martyrs, who justified their own pillage and killing in the name of Christ and the cause of His Church, were guilty of the greater sacrilege. Like those who had sought to prevent the entry of Jesus into Jerusalem, or lifted their swords to save Him from arrest, they would separate Christ from His Cross, and

thus from the redemptive sacrifice He had come to offer. Jesus had answered
them in His words to Peter: "Get thee behind me, Satan. You are not
looking at things from God's point of view, but from man's" (Mark 8:33).

It was Dorothy's conviction that Jesus Christ had come to offer a radical
new definition of love as the ultimate law of our lives. "A new commandment I give you, that you love one another *as I have loved you*" (John
15:12). It was a new commandment, an utterly new dispensation, for the
love exemplified on the Cross extended beyond friends and those who were
lovable, to include the "enemy" himself. Jesus had left us a definition of
nonviolence, not only in His words, but in the manner of His life. By His
death and resurrection, He had converted the Cross, a sign of defeat, into
a symbol of life and hope. And He had come to substitute the Cross for
the sword or the bomb as an effective instrument of liberation and justice.

The audience for such a message in 1936 was limited. All across the
country, bundle orders were canceled, and the circulation of the paper fell
by 100,000. Many pleaded with Dorothy to desist from her "propaganda,"
urging her not to let her pacifism compromise her "wonderful work" with
the poor. On the subject of war and peace, it was charged, she was drifting
into the area of politics, a world of complexities and ambiguities best left
to politicians and theologians. Dorothy's response was simply to refer to
Scripture. There was nothing to add to the words of Jesus: "Love your
enemies, do good to those who persecute you" (Matthew 5:44). If we
could take liberties with Christ's relentless insistence on the way of love,
how could we claim to base clear doctrine on any other of His hard
teachings?

The Works of Mercy could not be separated from the Works of Peace.
We were told to feed the hungry, while war destroyed crops and caused
starvation. We were told to comfort the afflicted, while war brought misery
and ruin. And whatever was done "to the least of these"—whether kindness or violence—was counted as done directly to Him. These too were
His words. We were called to recognize Christ in the disguise of our
neighbors. He came disguised as a crucified Jew, and this was a scandal.
He came disguised in the body of the poor, the diseased, the unwanted,
and this was a stumbling block. It was certainly hard to see the face of
Christ in the body of a sick, unwashed, lice-ridden old woman. It was
harder still to see Him behind the face of the one called "enemy." This
was true folly in the eyes of the world. But we were not told to love up to
the point of reason, prudence, or personal safety—but to love unreason-
ably, foolishly, profligately, unto the Cross, unto death.

With World War II, Dorothy's pacifism faced its most terrible test. She understood all too clearly the meaning of Nazism. From the earliest days of Hitler's regime, she had picketed the German Embassy and warned in the paper against the sin of anti-Semitism, whether espoused in Europe or by voices closer to home. In 1939 she helped to found the Committee of Catholics to Fight Anti-Semitism, which not only lobbied for the lifting of immigration quotas for European Jews but challenged the anti-Semitism of the Catholic followers of Father Charles Coughlin. But still such facts, as she understood them, could not supersede the Gospel commandment of love. Not all her associates agreed, and her stand nearly split the movement in two. For Dorothy, it was once more an experience of the desert. She made no attempt to impede the war effort. But in the midst of a dark time, she maintained the conviction that if human beings were to survive there would have to be some few who affirmed the efficacy of a power greater than death, and held out tenaciously for the sanctity of life. In the long run, she believed, the effort to expunge the evil of Nazism by means of superior force would unleash on the world possibilities more terrible than anything known before.

By the war's end, hundreds of thousands of people had been burned alive in Hamburg, Dresden, and Tokyo—not in ovens, but in their homes and cellars. The further destruction of two cities in Japan by atomic bombs would open the window on a brave new world in which portable death camps, each with the destructive capacity of an Auschwitz, would be routinely manufactured by assembly line. It would come to pass, in the nations which "defeated" Hitler, that such interests as defense and national security would be used to justify policies threatening all life on earth.

Dorothy considered this situation in the light of the Gospel. In the face of weapons of indiscriminate destruction, the teaching of indiscriminate love had, she believed, become a practical necessity, an imperative. To live under the "protection" of such weapons without resisting, without raising an outcry, was, in her view, to participate in the ultimate blasphemy.

In the fifties, with the construction of the hydrogen bomb, atmospheric testing, civil defense drills, and the prevailing climate of fatalism and fear, the Catholic Worker's commitment to the way of peace, expressed both in words and in public witness, received an emphasis of increasing urgency. Members of the community occupied missile bases, blockaded submarines, refused to cooperate with the draft or pay federal income taxes. Many received substantial prison sentences. For her own refusal to cooperate with New York City's compulsory civil defense drills, Dorothy received several jail terms of up to thirty days.

Each act of witness was undertaken in a spirit of penance. It was never

Dorothy's desire to proclaim her own personal righteousness. On the contrary: there is, she used to say, a communion of sinners as well as of saints. Each one shares in the sin—the estrangement from God—that wars are made of. And when she fasted or went to jail, part of the gesture was an effort to take upon herself, in some small way, the guilt of Dachau, Hiroshima, and other crimes as yet uncommitted, and thus preventable. She did not expect great things to happen overnight. She knew the slow pace, one foot at a time, by which change and new life comes. It was, in the phrase she repeated often, "by little and by little" that we were saved.

To live with the poor, to forgo luxury and privilege, to feed some people, to "visit the prisoner" by going to jail—these were all small things. Dorothy's life was made up of such small things, chosen deliberately and repeated daily. It is interesting to note that her favorite saint was no great martyr or charismatic reformer, but Therese of Lisieux, a simple Carmelite nun who died within the walls of an obscure cloister in Normandy at the age of twenty-four. Dorothy devoted an entire book to Therese and her spirituality of "the little way." St. Therese indicated the path to holiness that lay within all our daily occupations. Simply, it consisted of performing, in the presence and love of God, all the little things that make up our everyday life and contact with others. From Therese, Dorothy learned that any act of love might contribute to the balance of love in the world, any suffering endured in love might ease the burden of others; such was the mysterious bond within the Body of Christ. We could only make use of the little things we possessed—the little faith, the little strength, the little courage. These were the loaves and fishes. We could only offer what we had, and pray that God would make the increase. It was all a matter of faith.

Dorothy lived to see some of that increase. Pope John XXIII's 1963 encyclical *Pacem in Terris,* followed by the Second Vatican Council, authorized a new critical evaluation by the church of the meaning of war in the modern age. In the following two decades, this developed to mean, at the least, an unequivocal rejection of nuclear war. And yet, strangely enough, it was the year following Dorothy's death that offered some of the most dramatic indications of a shift in Catholic opinion on the issues of war and peace. Among the events of 1981 were the decision announced by the Archbishop of Seattle to withhold half his federal income tax in protest against military spending; the call issued to his flock by a bishop in Texas to consider resigning from jobs in the nuclear weapons plant in their diocese; the pilgrimage to Hiroshima by Pope John Paul II, with his call for "audacious gestures" by Christians to reverse the arms race.

In the years since Vatican II, the Church as a whole has struggled to reevaluate its vocation in the modern world. Increasingly, this has been seen as a prophetic call to stand beside Christ in His victimized humanity. In Latin America and elsewhere, Christians have begun to know and share the vulnerability of the poor and powerless, and to identify with their yearning and struggle for liberation. The Church in North America has yet to shoulder that cross. And yet, as Catholics have assumed an increasingly visible presence in the disarmament and anti-war movement, some have begun to speak of the Catholic Church as an emerging "Peace Church." Such talk may be premature. But that such a suggestion is possible at all is a sign of the extraordinary distance traveled since the 1960's. In those years, many draft boards routinely denied the applications of Catholic conscientious objectors on the popularly accepted grounds that their position was contradicted by Church doctrine. If the Church in America has been able to traverse this distance, it is in large part because Dorothy Day, in her fifty years of sacrifice, prayer, and often solitary witness, labored to clear the way.

*   *   *

Dorothy defined the religious sensibility of the Catholic Worker thus: "Sacrifice, worship, a sense of reverence." It could sound simple, as indeed it was, at least in theory. The "spirituality" of Dorothy Day was based on an effort to encounter Christ in our daily lives. He was present in our everyday situations, in the choices we made, in what Caussade called "the sacrament of the present moment." He was present, too, in the people around us, especially under the aspect of their needs, the needs of those most weak and vulnerable. To find Him there we must become vulnerable too, for "we cannot even see our brother in need without first stripping ourselves." And so voluntary poverty was a part of her worship, and of the life of the Catholic Worker.

By "voluntary poverty" Dorothy did not mean an idealization of misery and squalor. She was careful to distinguish between the dignity and freedom of voluntary poverty—the freedom that comes when there is nothing one fears to lose—and the bondage of destitution. The latter was the fruit of injustice and a sign of institutionalized sin. The poverty she espoused meant reducing the area given to self-interest, learning to locate the ultimate source of security elsewhere than in material values. To become poor was to become dependent on God and available to others, and to withdraw from the spoils of exploitation, for, as the Church Fathers had frequently taught, all that we owned beyond our needs was stolen from those who were hungry. This, to a large extent, was the situation of all who enjoyed the privileged "American way of life." We were like Dives of the parable, feasting at the table while the majority, the downtrodden of the world, like Lazarus, sat at the gate with the dogs licking at their wounds. This was a matter for penance and protest.

Dorothy did not share Peter Maurin's natural sense of detachment. She had cultivated tastes; she enjoyed the opera, well-prepared food, and beautiful things. There was a fastidious side to her character, easily offended by noise and disorder. When the commotion in the women's dormitory outside her room became too much to bear, she was known to open the door and shout *"Holy Silence!"* When someone once cautioned her in a heated moment to hold her temper, she is said to have replied, "I hold more temper in one minute than you will in your entire life." Such remarks were invariably followed by remorse and prayers for a milder disposition. It required more than romantic idealism to continue, year after year, to face the same foul smells, the ugliness, the various kinds of lice, the violence that could erupt so often among the "insulted and injured." It required faith and a strong will.

A ginkgo tree grew for many years in front of the Catholic Worker house on East First Street. Dorothy drew special consolation from the presence of such living things amidst the concrete of the city. When the tree was uprooted one day by a maniacal drunk, she felt the blow in her own heart. At such times it took discipline to exercise her faith: "The mystery of the poor is this—that they are Jesus, and what you do for them you do to Him."

There was violence, sadness, and suffering among the poor. But there were also moments of grace, acts of kindness and sympathy that made her want to rejoice, moments when it became possible to see beneath the tawdry surface of life into some deeper level of reality. Dorothy's writing was filled with such moments: sitting on a bus, walking on the street, watching the line of men curling around the block as they waited for a bowl of soup, the sight of children at play, the sunlight on the water— always, there was something to recall her soul. Creation spoke to her of God.

There was a literal basis to the title of Dorothy's column, "On Pilgrimage." Since the early years of the movement, she often spent as much as half the year away from home and on her way to somewhere else. With authority, she cited St. Teresa's words, "Life is a night spent in an uncomfortable inn." Few of Dorothy's nights on the road were spent in inns, but she was well acquainted with uncomfortable buses and untrustworthy cars. As she could boast with a veteran's pride, "I have had clutch rods come out in my hands, gas pedals go down through the floor, batteries fall out into the roadside, windshield wipers fail in cloudbursts, lights go out, fan belts break, etc., etc. (Some of these things happened after inspection!)"

Not only in her familiarity with the hazards of the road did her travels resemble the missionary wanderings of the Apostle Paul. Her journeys had a pastoral, even evangelical quality, as she spread the Good News from one end of the country to the other; here giving support, there exhorting the brethren to love one another; in one place witnessing a scene of struggle, in another the foundation of a "cell of good living."

In the last two decades of her life, these travels suddenly expanded to include revolutionary Cuba, Mexico, England, Rome, Sicily, as well as points even farther from her usual circuit. In Russia, she visited the grave of John Reed, and "disrupted" a meeting of writers by expressing her admiration for Solzhenitsyn. From Tanzania, she reported on President Julius Nyerere's experiments in village socialism. In India, she visited her friend Mother Teresa of Calcutta, as well as the Gandhian centers of cottage industry. Wherever she went, she carried her diary, her breviary, and a jar of instant coffee (she could not say which was the most essential).

With the sixties, Dorothy's pilgrimage reflected the preoccupations of the time—poverty, racism, revolution, war—as well as the decade's intense spirit of competing hopes and disillusionments. She hailed the civil rights movement and the emerging spirit of militant nonviolence. And as the specter of Vietnam began to dominate the political horizon, the Worker maintained a clear and prophetic witness. In October 1965, David Miller of the Catholic Worker staff became the first to burn his draft card in public after Congress had declared this a federal offense. Others were quick to follow his example.

As members of the community began departing for prison, Dorothy prayed that their sacrifice would help bring peace. With the daring witness of the Berrigans and their associates, there began to be talk of a Catholic Left in America. But Dorothy's enthusiasm for such efforts was qualified by a fear for the direction of the anti-war movement. She perceived a growing sense of despair in the young, a frustration, an eagerness for fast "results." Many were questioning the "relevance" of such undramatic efforts as the Works of Mercy. They rejected the personalist revolution of Peter Maurin, rejecting, too, the faith that was the basis of her own radical vision. Dorothy had seen this conflict before, "the war between the young and old, between the scholar and the worker . . ."; she continued to insist that "the most effective action we can take is to try to conform our lives to the folly of the Cross." In the noise and tumult of the times, she clung to those things that were central to the daily practice of her faith: prayer, the sacraments, the Works of Mercy.

Unlike many radicals, Dorothy did not look back on the sixties with nostalgia. She remembered them as an angry and bitter time. Much more constructive work, she felt, was done in the seventies. She pointed in particular to the renewal of interest in the land, community, cooperatives—those constructive efforts to begin building the new society in the shell of the old. Their significance could not be measured by the publicity they received. She was greatly encouraged by the struggle of Cesar Chavez to create a union of farm workers by means of Gandhian nonviolence. Her last arrest, at the age of seventy-five, came in 1973 on a United Farm Workers picket line in California.

For someone who had lived an extraordinarily active life, Dorothy aged with considerable grace. She had lost a good deal of weight since her late sixties, and acquired an intense, haunting beauty. She had lost, too, her long brisk stride. Now she moved at a slower pace, resting on her walking stick, and taking in everything around her. Gradually, she was letting go.

A heart attack in 1976 put an end to the incessant traveling, and Dorothy accepted with gratitude this opportunity to decline the hundreds of invitations and requests that continued to pour in. "Tell them I'm in a state of nervous decline," she would say to those of us in charge of making her excuses. Piles of letters would appear on my desk, often with her penciled notations on the margins: "Robert, as managing editor, your task is to deal with such as this! God help you! Love, Dorothy."

At no time in her life had she tried to solidify the institutional base of the movement she had founded. The Catholic Worker, as Peter Maurin had liked to say, was not an organization but an organism. Accordingly, she made no provisions for the future; she named no "successor," established no formalized rule. Not surprisingly, speculation on the future of the movement after Dorothy's death became a standard feature of articles about the Worker. It was a topic to which Dorothy herself remained notably indifferent. Holding to her faith in personal responsibility, she believed that the "young people" should learn on their own, make their own mistakes, find their own way. In the end, it was a matter of faith. The movement would endure if that were God's will. Otherwise, it would fail. It really didn't matter.

She spent most of her time in her room at Maryhouse, a former music school on East Third Street, converted by the Catholic Worker into a shelter for homeless women. "My job now is prayer," she wrote. Still, she contributed something to the paper every month when she possibly could, even if only a few notes from her journal, "to let people know I'm still alive." She also meant to let people know, in her terse, exhausted sentences, how tired she really was. Increasingly, in her column, she spoke now in phrases and silences and those sighs, as St. Paul once wrote, "too deep for words."

Her last writing was about the beauty of nature, the loving-kindness of God, the need for more forgiveness, more mercy, more rejoicing.

*   *   *

Toward the end of her life, Dorothy began to receive the kind of attention often accorded venerable survivors. Her picture appeared in *Life* and *Newsweek,* accompanied by flattering profiles. She was cited by *Time* magazine in a cover story devoted to "Living Saints." She did not take these developments as signs that her principles had found widespread acceptance. On the contrary: "Too much praise," she observed, "makes you feel you must be doing something terribly wrong."

She did not draw her hope from the trends and fashions reported by the media. She had learned from the Gospels that the most important events occur on the margins of history, in obscure and unexpected places. Because her hope was ultimately in God alone, she could dispense with naïve optimism as to human achievement and progress. She felt the suffering and sins of the world in her own heart. But in the face of all the horrors of history, she retained her faith that God had found in this world enough good to die for. And without underestimating the reality of evil, it was our task to seek out that good, to nurture and cherish it with all our strength. Often, she quoted the confident words of Julian of Norwich, "the worst has already happened and been repaired."

"People come to join us in 'our wonderful work,'" she wrote. "It all sounds very wonderful, but life itself is a haphazard, untidy, messy affair." Indeed, people came to join the work; Dorothy saw many of them come and go. Her instructor, Peter Maurin, whom she had loved and revered, died in 1949 at the age of seventy-two. In his last five years he had been mute and feeble, disabled by a stroke that had impaired his wide mind and left him, in his own words, "unable to think." Dorothy considered the manner of his death instructive. Peter had been the poor man of his day. He had stripped himself of everything else, and finally he was stripped of the one thing he cherished. This man of vision, who had lectured university professors and debated the great intellectuals of his day, had, in the end, to be dressed and fed like a child. Yet he never complained. He accepted his condition with grace and patience. Some years before his death, he gave the community a fright by disappearing for several days. When at last he returned, confused but apparently pleased with himself, he explained that he had felt like going for a ride on a bus. After that, a note was pinned to his suit: "I am Peter Maurin, founder of the Catholic Worker movement."

Dorothy possessed what Peter Maurin had called "the art of human contacts": an ability to take people as they came, to reach out to them, to show her care, to connect in others with that, according to the Quaker phrase, which is of God. Still, she called her autobiography *The Long Loneliness*. All of us, she believed, have a yearning for love. Deep down, buried beneath the clutter of our days, there was in every person the longing for community. But there was a loneliness that persisted even in the midst of others, the essential isolation that belonged to any commitment or vocation. There was a kind of loneliness to which Christ invited His friends. Yet, of this "long loneliness," she wrote, in the words of Mary Ward, a seventeenth-century English nun, "The pain is very great, but very endurable, because He who lays on the burden also carries it."

She knew what needed to be taken seriously. But she was never too serious to forget what Ruskin called "the duty of delight." In the face of the desperate suffering in the world, she felt we had a special obligation to attend to life's joys and beauties: "We would be contributing to the misery of the world if we failed to rejoice in the sun, the moon, and the stars, in the rivers which surround this island on which we live, in the cool breezes of the bay." Frequently, in her column, she cited Dostoevsky's words: "The world will be saved by beauty."

Though resentful of the ambitious building projects of various bishops and religious orders, she never begrudged the poor their beautiful churches. Yes, certainly much of the money that went into these churches could have been spent elsewhere. But Dorothy saw in the church a place of refuge where the poor had access to beauty in their lives, as well as quiet, peace, and rest—qualities not to be undervalued in the ghetto. Tom Cornell, a former editor of the paper, has related this story:

> One day a woman came in and donated a diamond ring to the Worker. We all wondered what Dorothy would do with it. She could have one of us take it down to a diamond exchange and sell it. It would certainly fetch a month's worth of beans. That afternoon, Dorothy gave the diamond ring to an old woman who lived alone and often came to us for meals. "That ring would have paid her rent for the better part of a year," someone protested. Dorothy replied that the woman had her dignity; she could sell it if she liked and spend the

money for rent, a trip to the Bahamas, or keep the ring to admire. "Do you suppose God created diamonds only for the rich?"

There is a kind of extravagance that belongs to any proper act of charity. Tillich called it "Holy Waste," a term Dorothy would have appreciated. One thinks of Dorothy Day along with those great women of the Gospels who often seemed to know with an extra sense, lacking in the more self-conscious men, the significance of the event unfolding in their presence. There was the woman who wasted a large quantity of expensive oil anointing Christ's body beforehand for his burial. Another woman bathed His feet with her tears and dried them with her hair. It was such women as these who remained on Calvary, watching their Lord die on the Cross. And to these women was entrusted the task of rushing from the empty tomb with the incredible news that He had risen. I think of Dorothy with such women. I know there are many—myself among them—who first heard this Good News from her

The Catholic Worker is a school, she used to say. Some stayed a lifetime, but most passed on to other things, having given up some months or years of their lives to the work. We all received more than we gave. Dorothy felt the sadness of many farewells, but never turned her back on those who left. Always, she remained faithful to her friends, to her past, to all (save for her sins) that she herself had ever been.

Dorothy Day died on November 29, 1980. She was eighty-three. Her body was buried on Staten Island in a plain pinewood coffin. Her grave, on a grassy meadow overlooking the ocean, is near the place where she lived when her daughter, Tamar, was born, the place where she accepted on faith the promise that for those who give up home and family and friends for the sake of the Kingdom, all these things and more will be added unto them. And for the hundreds of members of the Catholic Worker family, young and old, who gathered in New York for her funeral, her passing was, as she had prayed, an occasion for rejoicing.

THE LONG WAY HOME

We Scarcely Know Ourselves

The following piece served as an introduction to Dorothy Day's first autobiographical work, *From Union Square to Rome* (1938).

It is difficult for me to dip back into the past, yet it is a job that must be done, and it hangs over my head like a cloud. St. Peter said that we must give a reason for the faith that is in us, and I am trying to give you those reasons. . . .

While it is often true that horror for one's sins turns one to God, what I want to bring out in this book is a succession of events that led me to His feet, glimpses of Him that I received through many years which made me feel the vital need of Him. I will try to trace for you the steps by which I came to accept the faith that I believe was always in my heart. . . .

Though I felt the strong, irresistible attraction to good, yet there was also, at times, a deliberate choosing of evil. How far I was led to choose it, it is hard to say. How far professors, companions, and reading influenced my way of life does not matter now. The fact remains that there was much of deliberate choice in it. Most of the time it was "following the devices and desires of my own heart." Sometimes it was perhaps the Baudelairean idea of choosing "the downward path which leads to salvation." Sometimes it was of choice, of free will, though perhaps at the time I would have denied free will. And so, since it was deliberate, with recognition of its seriousness, it was grievous mortal sin and may the Lord forgive me. It was the arrogance and suffering of youth. It was pathetic, little, and mean in its very excuse for itself.

Was this desire to be with the poor and the mean and abandoned not unmixed with a distorted desire to be with the dissipated? Mauriac tells of this subtle pride and hypocrisy: "There is a kind of hypocrisy which is worse than that of the Pharisees; it is to hide behind Christ's example in order to follow one's own lustful desires and to seek out the company of the dissolute."

I write these things now because sometimes when I am writing I am seized with fright at my presumption. I am afraid, too, of not telling the

3

truth or of distorting the truth. I cannot guarantee that I do not, for I am
writing of the past. But my whole perspective has changed and when I
look for causes for my conversion sometimes it is one thing and sometimes
it is another that stands out in my mind.

Much as we want to, we do not really know ourselves. Do we really
want to see ourselves as God sees us, or even as our fellow human beings
see us? Could we bear it, weak as we are? . . . We do not want to be given
that clear inward vision which discloses to us our most secret faults. In the
Psalms there is that prayer "Deliver me from my secret sins." We do not
really know how much pride and self-love we have until someone whom
we respect or love suddenly turns against us. Then some sudden affront,
some sudden offense we take, reveals to us in all its glaring distinctness
our self-love, and we are ashamed.

*   *   *

I write in the very beginning of finding the Bible and the impression it
made on me. I must have read it a good deal, for many passages remained
with me through my earlier years to return to haunt me. Do you know the
Psalms? They were what I read most when I was in jail in Occoquan. I read
with a sense of coming back to something that I had lost. There was an
echoing in my heart. And how can anyone who has known human sorrow
and human joy fail to respond to these words?

> Out of the depths I have cried to thee, O Lord:
> Lord, hear my voice. Let thy ears be attentive to the voice
>   of my supplication.
> If thou, O Lord, wilt mark iniquities:
> Lord, who shall stand it.
> For with thee there is merciful forgiveness: and by reason
>   of thy law, I have waited for thee,
> O Lord. My soul hath relied on his word: my soul hath
>   hoped in the Lord.
> From the morning watch even until night, let Israel hope
>   in the Lord.
> Because with the Lord there is mercy; and with him plentiful
>   redemption.
> And he shall redeem Israel from all his iniquities . . ."

All through those weary first days in jail when I was in solitary confinement, the only thoughts that brought comfort to my soul were those lines
in the Psalms that expressed the terror and misery of man suddenly stricken

and abandoned. Solitude and hunger and weariness of spirit—these sharpened my perceptions so that I suffered not only my own sorrow but the sorrows of those about me. I was no longer myself. I was mankind. I was no longer a young girl, part of a radical movement seeking justice for those oppressed; I was the oppressed. I was that drug addict, screaming and tossing in her cell, beating her head against the wall. I was that shoplifter who, for rebellion, was sentenced to solitary. I was that woman who had killed her children, who had murdered her lover.

The blackness of hell was all about me. The sorrows of the world encompassed me. I was like one gone down into the pit. Hope had forsaken me. . . .

And yet if it were not the Holy Spirit that comforted me, how could I have been comforted, how could I have endured, how could I have lived in hope?

The *Imitation of Christ* is a book that followed me through my days. Again and again I came across copies of it and the reading of it brought me comfort. I felt in the background of my life a waiting force that would lift me up eventually.

I later became acquainted with the poem of Francis Thompson, "The Hound of Heaven," and was moved by its power. Eugene O'Neill first recited it to me in the back room of a saloon on Sixth Avenue where the Provincetown players and playwrights used to gather after the performances.

> I fled Him, down the nights and down the days;
> I fled Him, down the arches of the years;
> I fled Him, down the labyrinthine ways
> Of my own mind; and in the mist of tears
> I hid from Him . . .

Through all my daily life, in those I came in contact with, in the things I read and heard, I felt that sense of being followed, of being desired; a sense of hope and expectation.

Through those years I read all of Dostoevsky's novels and it was, as Berdyaev says, a profound spiritual experience. The scene in *Crime and Punishment* where the young prostitute reads from the New Testament to Raskolnikov, sensing sin more profound than her own, which weighed upon him; that story "The Honest Thief"; those passages in *The Brothers Karamazov;* the sayings of Father Zossima, Mitya's conversion in jail, the very legend of the Grand Inquisitor, all this helped to lead me on. I was moved to the depths of my being by the reading of these books during my early twenties when I, too, was tasting the bitterness and the dregs of life and shuddered at its harshness and cruelty.

Do you remember that little story that Grushenka tells in *The Brothers Karamazov?* "Once upon a time there was a peasant woman, and a very wicked woman she was. And she died and did not leave a single good deed behind. The devils caught her and plunged her into a lake of fire. So her guardian angel stood and wondered what good deed of hers he could remember to tell God. 'She once pulled up an onion in her garden,' said he, 'and gave it to a beggar woman.' And God answered: 'You take that onion then, hold it out to her in the lake, and let her take hold and be pulled out. And if you pull her out of the lake, let her come to Paradise, but if the onion breaks, then the woman must stay where she is.' The angel ran to the woman and held out the onion to her. 'Come,' said he, 'catch hold, and I'll pull you out.' And he began cautiously pulling her out. He had just pulled her out when the other sinners in the lake, seeing how she was being drawn out, began catching hold of her so as to be pulled out with her. But she was a very wicked woman and she began kicking them. 'I'm to be pulled out, not you. It's my onion, not yours.' As soon as she said that, the onion broke. And the woman fell into the lake and she is burning there to this day. So the angel wept and went away."

Sometimes in thinking and wondering at God's goodness to me, I have thought that it was because I gave away an onion. Because I sincerely loved His poor, He taught me to know Him. And when I think of the little I ever did, I am filled with hope and love for all those others devoted to the cause of social justice.

"What glorious hope!" Mauriac writes. "There are all those who will discover that their neighbor is Jesus himself, although they belong to the mass of those who do not know Christ or who have forgotten Him. And nevertheless they will find themselves well loved. It is impossible for any one of those who has real charity in his heart not to serve Christ. Even some of those who think they hate Him have consecrated their lives to Him; for Jesus is disguised and masked in the midst of men, hidden among the poor, among the sick, among prisoners, among strangers. Many who serve Him officially have never known who He was, and many who do not even know His name will hear on the last day the words that open to them the gates of joy. 'Those children were I, and I those working men. I wept on the hospital bed. I was that murderer in his cell whom you consoled.'"

But always the glimpses of God came most when I was alone. Objectors cannot say that it was fear of loneliness and solitude and pain that made me turn to Him. It was in those few years when I was alone and most happy that I found Him. I found Him at last through joy and thanksgiving, not through sorrow.

Yet how can I say that either? Better let it be said that I found Him through His poor, and in a moment of joy I turned to Him. I have said, sometimes flippantly, that the mass of bourgeois smug Christians who denied Christ in His poor made me turn to Communism, and that it was the Communists and working with them that made me turn to God. . . .

A mystic may be called a man in love with God. Not one who loves God, but who is *in love with God*. And this mystical love, which is an exalted emotion, leads one to love the things of Christ. His footsteps are sacred. The steps of His passion and death are retraced down through the ages. Almost every time you step into a Church you see people making the Stations of the Cross. They meditate on the mysteries of His life, death, and resurrection, and by this they are retracing with love those early scenes and identifying themselves with the actors in those scenes.

When we suffer, we are told we suffer with Christ. We are "completing the sufferings of Christ." We suffer His loneliness and fear in the garden when His friends slept. We are bowed down with Him under the weight of not only our own sins but the sins of each other, of the whole world. We are those who are sinned against and those who are sinning. We are identified with Him, one with Him. We are members of His Mystical Body.

Often there is a mystical element in the love of a radical for his brother, for his fellow worker. It extends to the scene of his sufferings, and those spots where he has suffered and died are hallowed. The names of places like Everett, Ludlow, Bisbee, South Chicago, Imperial Valley, Elaine, Arkansas, and all those other places where workers have suffered and died for their cause have become sacred to the worker. You know this feeling, as does every other radical in the country. Through ignorance, perhaps, you do not acknowledge Christ's name. Yet I believe you are trying to love Christ in His poor, in His persecuted ones. Whenever men have laid down their lives for their fellows, they have done it in a measure for Him. This I still firmly believe, even though you and others may not realize it.

"Inasmuch as ye have done it unto one of the least of these My brethren, ye have done it unto Me." Feeling this as strongly as I did, is it any wonder that I was led finally to the feet of Christ?

I do not mean at all that I went around in a state of exaltation or that any radical does. Love is a matter of the will. . . .

What is hard to make the labor leader understand is that we must love even the employer, unjust though he may be, that we must try to overcome his resistance by nonviolent resistance, by withdrawing labor, i.e., by strikes and by boycott. These are nonviolent means, and most effective. We must try to educate him, to convert him. We must forgive him seventy times seven just as we forgive our fellow worker and keep trying to bring him to a sense of solidarity.

But how to convert an employer who has evicted all his workers because they are on strike, so that men, women, and children are forced to live in tents; who has called out armed guards as Rockefeller did in Ludlow, who has shot into those tents and fired them, so that twenty-eight women and children were burnt to death? How to forgive such a man? How to convert him? This is the question the worker asks in the bitterness of his soul. It is only through a Christ-like love that man can forgive.

Remember Vanzetti's last words before he died in the electric chair: "I wish to tell you I am an innocent man. I never committed any crime, but sometimes some sin. I wish to forgive some people for what they are now doing to me."

He said when he was sentenced: "If it had not been for these things, I might have lived out my life talking at street corners to scorning men. I might have died unmarked, unknown, a failure. Now we are not a failure. This is our career and our triumph. Never in our full life could we hope to do such work for tolerance, for justice, for man's understanding of man, as now we do by accident. Our words, our lives, our pains—nothing! The taking of our lives—lives of a good shoemaker and a poor fish peddler—all! That last moment belongs to us. That agony is our triumph."

He forgave those who had imprisoned him for years, who had hounded him to his death. He was one of those of whom Mauriac was speaking when he said, "It is impossible for any one of those who has real charity in his heart not to serve Christ. Even some of those who think they hate Him have consecrated their lives to Him."

It was from men such as these that I became convinced, little by little, of the necessity of God and of faith in my everyday life. I know now that the Catholic Church is the church of the poor, no matter what you say about the wealth of her priests and bishops. I have mentioned in these pages the few Catholics I met before my conversion, but daily I saw people coming from Mass. Never did I set foot in a Catholic church but that I saw people there at home with Him. First Fridays, novenas, and missions brought the masses thronging in and out of the Catholic churches. They were of all nationalities, of all classes, but most of all they were the poor. The very attacks made against the Church proved her Divinity to me. Nothing but a Divine institution could have survived the betrayal of Judas, the denial of Peter, the sins of many of those who professed her Faith, who were supposed to minister to her poor.

Christ is God or He is the world's greatest liar and imposter. How can you Communists who claim to revere Him as a working-class leader fail to see this? And if Christ established His Church on earth with Peter as its rock, that faulty one who denied Him three times, who fled from Him when he was in trouble, then I, too, wanted a share in that tender compassionate love that is so great. Christ can forgive all sins and yearn over us no matter how far we fall.

*　　*　　*

The experiences that I have had are more or less universal. Suffering, sadness, repentance, love, we all have known these. They are easiest to bear when one remembers their universality, when we remember that we are all members or potential members of the Mystical Body of Christ. . . .

A conversion is a lonely experience. We do not know what is going on in the depths of the heart and soul of another. We scarcely know ourselves.

From Union Square to Rome

Beginnings

"All my life I have been haunted by God," a character in one of Dostoevsky's books says. And that is the way it was with me.

*　　*　　*

It began out in California, where the family had moved from New York a year before. We were living in Berkeley in a furnished house, waiting for our furniture to come around the Horn. It was Sunday afternoon in the attic. I remember the day was very chilly, though there were roses and violets and calla lilies blooming in the garden. My sister and I had been making dolls of the calla lilies, putting rosebuds for heads at the top of the long graceful blossoms. Then we made perfume, crushing flowers into a bottle with a little water in it. Even now I can remember the peculiar, delicious, pungent smell.

And then I remember we were in the attic. I was sitting behind a table, pretending I was the teacher, reading aloud from a Bible that I had found. Slowly, as I read, a new personality impressed itself on me. I was being introduced to someone and I knew almost immediately that I was discovering God. . . .

Of course I had heard of Him previous to this. Before we moved to California, my older brothers and I had gone to school in Bath Beach, and there every morning the teacher read something from the Bible and we bowed our heads on the desk and recited the Lord's Prayer. I had forgotten that until this moment of writing. It did not impress me then, and I remember now simply raising my head after the prayer to watch my breath fade upon the varnished desk.

In the family, the name of God was never mentioned. Mother and Father never went to church, none of us children had been baptized, and to speak of the soul was to speak immodestly, uncovering what might better remain hidden.

*   *   *

We were in California until after the earthquake which shook us eastward. We were living in Oakland at the time and though I remember some years later praying fearfully during a lightning storm, I do not remember praying during that cataclysmic disturbance, the earthquake. And I remember it plainly. I was eight years old then. It was after two in the morning when it started, and it began with a fearful roaring down in the earth. It lasted for two minutes and twenty seconds, and there was plenty of time to have died of fright, yet I do not remember fear. It must have been either that I thought I was dreaming or that I was half-conscious. Pictures fell from the walls, the bed rolled from one end of the polished floor to the other. My father got my brothers out of the house and my mother was able to carry my sister—God alone knew how she did it—out of the bungalow. I think the first shock was over before they got back to me.

What I remember most plainly about the earthquake was the human warmth and kindliness of everyone afterward. For days, refugees poured out of burning San Francisco and camped in Idora Park and the racetrack in Oakland. People came in their nightclothes; there were newborn babies.

Mother had always complained before about how clannish California people were, how if you were from the East they snubbed you and were loath to make friends. But after the earthquake everyone's heart was enlarged by Christian charity. All the hard crust of worldly reserve and prudence was shed. Each person was a little child in friendliness and warmth.

Mother and all our neighbors were busy from morning to night cooking hot meals. They gave away every extra garment they possessed. They stripped themselves to the bone in giving, forgetful of the morrow. While the crisis lasted, people loved each other. They realized their own helplessness while nature "travaileth and groaneth." It was as though they were united in Christian solidarity. It makes one think of how people could, if they would, care for each other in times of stress, unjudgingly, with pity and with love.

*   *   *

It was in Chicago, where we moved to afterward, that I met my first Catholic. It was the first time we had been really poor. We lived in an apartment over a store, on Cottage Grove Avenue. There was no upstairs, no garden, no sense of space. The tenement stretched way down the block and there were back porches and paved courtyards with never a touch of green anywhere. I remember how hungry I became for green fields during the long hot summer that followed. There was a vacant lot over by the lakefront, and I used to walk down there with my sister and stand sniffing ecstatically the hot sweet smell of wild clover and listening to the sleepy sound of the crickets. But that very desire for beauty was a painful delight for me. It sharpened my senses and made me more avid in my search for it. I found it in the lake that stretched steel gray beyond the Illinois Central tracks. I found it in a glimpse of supernatural beauty in Mrs. Barrett, mother of Kathryn and six other little Barretts, who lived upstairs.

It was Mrs. Barrett who gave me my first impulse toward Catholicism. It was around ten o'clock in the morning that I went up to Kathryn's to call for her to come out and play. There was no one on the porch or in the kitchen. The breakfast dishes had all been washed. They were long railroad apartments, those flats, and thinking the children must be in the front room, I burst in and ran through the bedrooms.

In the front bedroom Mrs. Barrett was on her knees, saying her prayers. She turned to tell me that Kathryn and the children had all gone to the store and went on with her praying. And I felt a warm burst of love toward Mrs. Barrett that I have never forgotten, a feeling of gratitude and happiness that still warms my heart when I remember her. She had God, and there was beauty and joy in her life.

All through my life, what she was doing remained with me. And though I became oppressed with the problem of poverty and injustice, though I groaned at the hideous sordidness of man's lot, though there were years when I clung to the philosophy of economic determinism as an explanation of man's fate, still there were moments when, in the midst of misery and class strife, life was shot through with glory. Mrs. Barrett in her sordid little tenement flat finished her breakfast dishes at ten o'clock in the morning and got down on her knees and prayed to God.

The Harrington family also lived in that block of tenements, and there were nine children, the eldest a little girl of twelve. She was a hard-working little girl, and naturally I had the greatest admiration for her on account of the rigorous life she led. I had a longing for the rigorous life. But I had a tremendous amount of liberty compared to little Mary Harrington. It was not until after the dishes were done that she could come out to play in the evening. Often she was so tired that we just stretched out on the long back porch, open to the sky. We lay there, gazing up at the only beauty the city had to offer us, and we talked and dreamed.

I don't remember what we talked about, but I do remember one occasion when she told me of the life of some saint. I don't remember which one, nor can I remember any of the incidents of it. I can only remember the feeling of lofty enthusiasm I had, how my heart seemed almost bursting with desire to take part in such high endeavor. One verse of the Psalms often comes to my mind: "Enlarge Thou my heart, O Lord, that Thou mayest enter in." This was one of those occasions when my small heart was enlarged. I could feel it swelling with love and gratitude to such a good God for such a friendship as Mary's, for conversation such as hers, and I was filled with lofty ambitions to be a saint, a natural striving, a thrilling recognition of the possibilities of spiritual adventure.

I, too, wanted to do penance for my own sins and for the sins of the whole world, for I had a keen sense of sin, of natural imperfection and earthliness. I often felt clearly that I was being deliberately evil in my attitudes, just as I clearly recognized truth when I came across it. And the thrill of joy that stirred my heart when I came across spiritual truth and beauty never abated, never left me as I grew older.

The sad thing is that one comes across it so seldom. Natural goodness, natural beauty, brings joy and a lifting of the spirit, but it is not enough, it is not the same. The special emotions I am speaking of came only at hearing the word of God. It was as though each time I heard our Lord spoken of, a warm feeling of joy filled me. It was hearing of someone you love and who loves you.

*   *   *

It seems to me as I look back upon it that I had a childhood that was really a childhood and that I was kept in the status of a child until I was sixteen. We had a very close family life. We knew little about community life, however. There was no radio at that time, so the news of the world was not blared into the home a dozen times a day. Father was very particular, too, as to what books and magazines were brought into the home. We had Scott, Hugo, Dickens, Stevenson, Cooper, and Edgar Allan Poe. We seldom were allowed to have friends in the house because it interfered with Father's privacy.

* * *

For me, this childhood was happy in spite of moods of uncertainty and even of hopelessness and sadness. The latter mood only accentuated the joys that were truly there. Yet I knew that this happiness was a matter of temperament and disposition, too, because often on talking over past days with my sister, she could think only of her own moods of misery. From her own account, she suffered far more than I ever did. She never had religious moods, she never felt the certainty of the existence of God. She had seen far more of the tragedy of life than I, as one of her school friends had died and for a long time after she was haunted by the fear of death. . . . Much as I loved people, they did not make me suffer as they did my sister. My unhappiness always came from within myself.

* * *

A mood which came to me again and again after some happiness or triumph was one of sadness at the fleeting of human joy. One afternoon, not long after I had won a scholarship of three hundred dollars and I knew I was going away to college, I walked the streets at sunset gazing at the clouds over Lincoln Park, recognizing the world as supremely beautiful, yet oppressed somehow with a heavy and abiding sense of loneliness and sadness. . . .

When what I read made me particularly class-conscious, I used to turn from the park with all its beauty and peacefulness and walk down to North Avenue and over west through slum districts, and watch the slatternly women and the unkempt children and ponder over the poverty of the homes as contrasted with the wealth along the shore drive. I wanted even then to play my part. I wanted to write such books that thousands upon thousands of readers would be convinced of the injustice of things as they were.

* * *

I was sixteen when I graduated from high school and went to the University of Illinois. It was 1914 and that summer the war had broken out in Europe. It was talked about along Webster Avenue where we lived and it was felt by all our neighbors, many of whom were Germans, but I was not affected by it in any way. The world could be convulsed with struggle, unhappiness and misery could abound on every side, but I was supremely happy. I was leaving home for the first time. Things were happening. I was going away to school. I was grown up.

But after those first glowing weeks of happiness I suffered miserably. . . . For the first time in my life I suffered from insomnia. Everything was cold and dead to me. I wanted the warmth of my home, I wanted my own, and I felt utterly abandoned. I was so completely homesick that I could neither eat nor sleep, and I paced the brick-paved walks of that small college town with tears streaming down my face, my heart so heavy that it hung like a weight in my breast. . . .

Because I was unhappy, I felt harsh. Because I was hurt I had to turn away from home and faith and all the gentle things of life and seek the hard. In spite of my studies and my work, I had time to read, and the ugliness of life in a world which professed itself to be Christian appalled me. . . .

While I was free to go to college, I was mindful of girls working in stores and factories through their youth and afterward married to men who were slaves in those same factories.

The Marxist slogan "Workers of the world, unite, you have nothing to lose but your chains" seemed a most stirring battle cry, a clarion call that made me feel one with the masses, apart from the bourgeoisie, the smug, the satisfied.

Besides Jack London and Upton Sinclair, the Russian novelists appealed to me, too, and I read everything of Dostoevsky that I could lay my hands on. Both he and Tolstoy made me cling to a faith in God, and yet I could not endure feeling so alone in it. I felt that my faith had nothing in common with that of Christians around me.

It seems to me that I was already shedding that faith when a professor whom I much admired made a statement in class—I shall always remember it—that religion was something which had brought great comfort to people throughout the ages, so that we ought not to criticize it. I don't remember his exact words, but from the way he spoke of religion the class could infer that the strong were the ones who did not need such props. In my youthful arrogance, in my feeling that I was one of the strong, I felt then for the first time that religion was something that I must ruthlessly cut out of my life. I felt it indeed to be an opiate of the people, so I hardened my heart.

*   *   *

I was seventeen and I felt completely alone in the world, divorced from family, from all security, even from God. I felt a sense of reckless arrogance and with this recklessness, I felt a sense of danger and rejoiced in it. It was good to live dangerously. . . .

Whatever I had read as a child about the saints had thrilled me. I could see the nobility of giving one's life for the sick, the maimed, the leper. Priests and Sisters the world over could be working for the littlest ones of Christ, and my heart stirred at their work.

But there was another question in my mind. Why was so much done in remedying the evil instead of avoiding it in the first place? Disabled men, men without arms and legs, blind, consumptive, exhausted men with all the manhood drained from them by industrialism; farmers gaunt and harried with debt; mothers weighted down with children at their skirts, in their arms, in their wombs, and the children ailing, rickety, toothless—all this long procession of desperate people called to me. Where were the saints to try to change the social order, not just to minister to the slaves but to do away with slavery? . . .

Our Lord said, "Blessed are the meek," but I could not be meek at the thought of injustice. I wanted a Lord who would scourge the moneylenders out of the temple, and I wanted to help all those who raised their hand against oppression.

Religion, as it was practiced by those I encountered, had no vitality. It had nothing to do with everyday life; it was a matter of Sunday praying. Christ no longer walked the streets of this world. He was two thousand years dead, and new prophets had risen up in His place.

*   *   *

Already in this year 1915, great strides had been taken. In some places the ten-hour day and increased wages had been won. But still only about 8 percent of the workers were organized, and the great mass of workers throughout the country were ground down by poverty and insecurity. What work there was to be done!

From Union Square to Rome

Disorder

In 1922, Dorothy was living in Chicago, working on *The Liberator,* a Communist journal edited by Robert Minor. She had been passing through a period of anxious wondering about the course of her life, searching for an aim and a direction. She had found part of a solution in the spirit of youthful revolt and the promise of revolution. Though she was not yet twenty-five, her credentials as a radical were already impressive. She had worked on three left-wing journals, one of which had been suppressed by the Attorney General. She had been a member of the I.W.W. and flirted with Communism. She had been to jail with the suffragists and marched on picket lines broken up by policemen's clubs. She had been an ardent champion of justice and the cause of the poor. But for all her noble convictions, she remained an outsider. She knew she had not yet felt the full mark of injustice, nor learned with her whole being what it meant to be poor. The strange accident of a second arrest served to advance her education, leaving on her soul a lasting impression of the world's suffering and sin.

Before I left Chicago I had a strange and unforgettable experience, a shocking experience, but one which I would not have done without. I was arrested again, and this time under quite different circumstances from those in Washington some years before. Then I had been part of an organized body of women of all ages and stations in life. There had been the wife of the president of the board of trustees of Bellevue Hospital. There had been society women of Philadelphia, Baltimore, and Boston. There had been schoolteachers, writers, ardent champions of feminism, women who had worked in the cause in England as well as in the United States. There had been the solidarity of the group. Now I was to have a solitary taste of injustice, or the ugliness of men's justice, which set me more squarely on the side of the revolution.

The Industrial Workers of the World had headquarters on the West Side, on Madison Street, the Skid Row of Chicago. There were a printing press and offices and among many cheap rooming houses, also a "flophouse" where visiting Wobblies stayed. I had been there a few times.

During the year just past, I had come to know intimately a rough young woman who had been a shoplifter and a drug addict but had cured herself after many years of addiction. She had spent years in reformatories and was probably about thirty at the time. She had fallen in love with a newspaperman who had introduced her to our group, and she had been our constant companion on evening parties for some months. In a fit of depression she swallowed some bichloride-of-mercury tablets and was taken to the county hospital. Within a few days she recovered enough to sign herself out of the hospital. The tie between us was that we were in love with the same man, and when she telephoned me and asked me to come over to the Wobbly headquarters to see her and bring her something to eat and to wear, I went at once. The doctors had not been willing for her to leave the hospital, but she had insisted. When I saw how sick she still was, I decided to spend the night there in the room which the I.W.W.'s had given her. It was not a place for women, though it was clean and well cared for. They let her stay because they did not know what else to do with her. She knew some of the printers and they realized that she was sick and needed help. I do not believe they knew I was there, since I came during the evening.

It was the time of the "Palmer Red Raids," and that night detectives raided the I.W.W. hotel as a disorderly house and arrested all they found there. Many of the men, who were old radicals and had gone through persecution on the West Coast, made their escape out of fire escapes and over roofs; but Mae and I, not knowing what was happening, were awakened by a pounding on the door and the voice of the police.

Perhaps it was not a new thing to Mae, but it was an unutterably horrifying experience for me. I had opened the door in fear and trembling and had been forced to dress practically in the presence of two detectives, leering. With Mae snarling and cursing, we were then escorted down to the street corner together with several men and forced to stand there waiting for a police wagon which had been summoned. We were being arrested as inmates of a disorderly house. Fortunately I did not realize this until later, so I was able to endure the shame and humiliation of standing there at midnight on the street corner under the gaze of whatever idlers were around at that time of night. . . .

I do not like even to write about this now, but I must tell of the experience, and I am glad indeed that I had it. It was part of the experience of thousands who had worked for labor—hotel workers, miners, the textile workers—throughout the country. I had walked on picket lines in cities with restaurant workers, with garment workers; I had felt that peculiar vulnerability that the picketer feels, who is set apart by his protest from the rest of mankind. I had felt what it was to be a fool for the cause of justice, tilting at windmills like any Don Quixote.

In Washington, I had felt that suffering for all who had been in prison, but there had also been the glow at the beginning of working with others,

at being part of a noble cause. I may have lost that when I was actually
confined to a cell, but it was regained after our hunger strike; there was
never any sense of shame attached to the experience, to deepen it and
embitter it.

But this arrest in Chicago was different. I was a victim, yes, of the Red
hysteria at the time, but I was also a victim of my own imprudence, of my
own carelessness of convention. It was the I.W.W. house that was being
raided, but we as women had no right to be in that house. Our presence
there meant only one thing to the men who arrested us, and when we were
booked for the morals court, they had the law on their side, and we had
by our very presence there given that place the reputation of being a
disorderly house.

It was as ugly an experience as I ever wish to pass through, and a useful
one. I do not think that ever again, no matter of what I am accused, can I
suffer more than I did then from shame and regret, and self-contempt. Not
only because I had been caught, found out, branded, publicly humiliated,
but because of my own consciousness that I deserved it.

When Eugene Debs wrote, as he did in his innocence, that as long as
there were men in prison he was one with them, they were noble words
and went down in history. But I have always felt that he could never have
suffered, noble and gentle man that he was, that same shame and self-
contempt that I felt, and that I felt in common with the prisoners with
whom I was confined.

We were driven through the dark and silent streets of the city to the
West Chicago Avenue police station. The cell into which we were thrown
had bars in front through which we could look out into the common room
and toward the desk of the matron, whose name was Day. I gave a false
name, and always had to be spoken to twice before I recognized it. . . .

Somehow I slept soundly that first night and escaped from my misery.
Mae slept too—it was no new experience for her. She joked with the
matron and the police officers and was solicitous for me. "Keep your chin
up," she kept comforting me. "Don't take it too hard." I had thought I
was hiding my feelings, was maintaining my composure, but she saw through
me. I was twenty-two, a child to her thirty-two years.

All the next day, groups of girls were brought in, because in addition to
the Red raids there was a series of vice raids going on around Twenty-
second Street. There were three groups of five or six each who were put
in our cell, which was supposed to be for six. These girls, all under thirty
years old, I judged, carefully took off their dresses and asked for hangers

so that they would not be mussed when they had to appear in court. They went around for the rest of the day in their slips. Some of them wore only shorts and bras and cavorted gaily around the cells like a group of chorus girls. They were gay and jaunty to the authorities, jeering at them contemptuously, but they were kindly and sympathetic to me. They judged my silence to be despair, and tried to tell me that there was always a first time, not to worry, that everything passed, that life had far worse things to offer than an occasional arrest and fine. They neither realized nor would they have believed in our innocence and there was little use in talking about it. . . .

Some lost children were brought in, and the girls modified their language and put on their clothes. One little girl had been sent to the store to buy groceries and had spent the money on a red purse. She had been afraid to go home and had lost herself. A policeman brought her to the station house to wait until her relatives could be fetched. She cried at the thought of the penalty for her theft until the girls comforted her and put some money in her purse. One of them held her in her arms and sang to her and told her stories. Later in the day, when a hard-faced aunt came for the child, she told of her own two children, whom she was supporting with relatives. . . .

The next day in the city jail we were searched for drugs. We were stripped naked. We were given prison clothes and put in cells. The routine was to keep us locked in the cells, then leave us free to roam the corridors in alternate periods of several hours each. In the next cell to mine, there was a drug addict who beat her head against the bars or against the metal walls of her cell and howled like a wild animal. I have never heard such anguish, such unspeakable suffering. No woman in childbirth, no cancer patient, no one in the long year I had spent in King's County Hospital had revealed suffering like this. I pressed my hands to my ears, and covered my head with my pillow to try to muffle the sounds. It was most harrowing to think that this pain, this torture, was in a way self-inflicted, with full knowledge of the torture involved. The madness, the perverseness, of this seeking for pleasure that was bound to be accompanied by such mortal agony was hard to understand. To see human beings racked by their own will made one feel the depth of the disorder of the world.

I felt the sadness of sin, the unspeakable dreariness of sin from the first petty little self-indulgence to this colossal desire which howled through the metal walls! And yet I do not think I thought of these things as I thought of God while in the solitary confinement cell at Occoquan. I just suffered desperately and desired to be freed from my suffering, with a most urgent and selfish passion. The instinct for self-preservation made me forget everything but a frantic desire for freedom, to get away from these depths into which I had fallen.

I could get away, but what of the others? I could get away, paying no penalty, because of my friends, my background, my education, my privilege. I suffered but was not part of it. I put it from me. It was too much for me.

I think that for a long time one is stunned by such experiences. They seem to be quickly forgotten, but they leave a scar that is never healed.

The Long Loneliness

New Life

Dorothy described the event of her conversion in *From Union Square to Rome* as well as *The Long Loneliness*. The following account includes selections from both sources, as well as the story of her daughter's birth, "Having a Baby," published in the Marxist journal *The New Masses*.

I

October 1925: Every year the beaches around New York change, but so gradually, one notices the changes only year by year. The shoreline down by our little house is irregular, with many little bays and creeks wandering inland every few miles. Some years before, a pier a quarter of a mile down the beach toward the open ocean fell to ruin in a storm, with the result that the sand is washed away from our beach to be piled up on the next one. . . .

The seagulls scream over the rocks, blue and gray and dazzling white, winging their way from the wreck of the old excursion boat to the larger rocks in the water, diving with a splash into the shallow gray water for a fish. The waves, the gulls, and the cawing of the crows in the woods in back of the house are the only sounds on these fall days.

Farther up and down the beach, away from our tiny bay, the waves roll in from the ocean, crashing dull and ominous on the sands, but here by the house, except during storms, the waves are gentle and playful.

I wander every afternoon up and down the beach for miles, collecting mussels, garlanded in seaweed, torn loose from the piers—pockets full of jingle shells which look as though they are made of mother of pearl and gunmetal. When the tide goes out these little cups of shells are left along the beach, each holding a few drops of water which serve to glorify both the shape and coloring of the shell.

The little house I have furnished very simply with a driftwood stove in one corner, plenty of books, comfortable chairs and couches, and my writing table in the window where I can look out at the water all day.

*   *   *

Late this afternoon the wind dropped and I sat by the open door contemplating the sunset. The waves lapped the shore, tingling among the shells and pebbles, and there was an acrid odor of smoke in the air. Down the beach the Belgians were working, loading rock into a small cart which looked like a tumbril, drawn by a bony white horse. They stooped as though in prayer, outlined against the brilliant sky, and as I watched, the bell from the chapel over at St. Joseph's rang the Angelus. I found myself praying, praying with thanksgiving, praying with open eyes, while I watched the workers on the beach, the sunset, and listened to the sound of the waves and the scream of snowy gulls.

Later this evening the wind rose again and whistled around the house, and the noise of the sea is loud. I read now evenings until late in the night, and in my preoccupation the fire goes out, so that I have to get into bed to keep warm, clutching my books with ice-cold hands.

November. Mother sent me some of my high school books (now that I have a place of my own to keep them in) and the other day I came across these words, written on a faded slip of paper in my own writing. I do not remember writing them.

"Life would be utterly unbearable if we thought we were going nowhere, that we had nothing to look forward to. The greatest gift life can offer would be a faith in God and a hereafter. Why don't we have it? Perhaps like all gifts it must be struggled for. 'God, I believe' (or rather, 'I must believe or despair'). 'Help Thou my unbelief.' 'Take away my heart of stone and give me a heart of flesh.' "

I wrote the above lines when I felt the urgent need for faith, but there were too many people passing through my life—too many activities—too much pleasure (not happiness).

I have been passing through some years of fret and strife, beauty and ugliness, days and even weeks of sadness and despair, but seldom has there been the quiet beauty and happiness I have now. I thought all those years that I had freedom, but now I feel that I had neither real freedom nor even a sense of what freedom meant.

And now, just as in my childhood, I am enchained, tied to one spot, unable to pick up and travel from one part of the country to another, from one job to another. I am enchained because I am going to have a baby. No matter how much I may sometimes wish to flee from my quiet existence, I cannot, nor will I be able to for several years. I have to accept my quiet and stillness, and accepting it, I rejoice in it.

For a long time, I had thought I could not bear a child. A book I read years ago in school, *Silas Marner,* expressed the sorrow of a mother bereft of her child, and it expressed, too, my sorrow at my childless state. Just a few months ago I read it again, with a longing in my heart for a baby. My home, I felt, was not a home without one. The simple joys of the kitchen and garden and beach brought sadness with them because I had not the companionship of a child. No matter how much one is loved or one loves, that love is lonely without a child. It is incomplete.

And now I know that I am going to have a baby.

From Union Square to Rome

The man I loved, with whom I entered into a common-law marriage, was an anarchist, an Englishman by descent, and a biologist. His mother and father had both come from England and he and his seven sisters were born in Asheville, North Carolina. He had attended school at the University of Georgia and of Virginia, and spent most of his time during World War I hospitalized with influenza, from which he did not recover until the war was over. When I met him he was out of uniform and had begun to get back some of the seventy-five pounds he had lost during his hospital year. His friends were mostly liberals and his sympathies were decentralist and anti-industrialist, though he loved the machine and the illusion of progress. . . .

Forster's work took him into the city during the week, and I looked forward to his homecomings on Friday. Sometimes work was slack—he made gauges—and he spent all his time on the beach. We fished together, we walked every day for miles, we collected and studied together, and an entire new world opened up to me little by little. We did not talk much but "lived together" in the fullest sense of the phrase. I was an indefatigable novel reader and spent those first few winters on the beach with Tolstoy, Dostoevsky, and Dickens. I did little real studying but I began to read the Bible again and the *Imitation of Christ*. Forster read perhaps one novel a year, and his favorite authors were D. H. Lawrence and Aldous Huxley. When he came home, he would rush out to the garden with his flashlight to see how things were growing. Winter nights he had charts and studied the stars. His enthusiasms were such that I could not help but be fascinated by the new world of nature he opened up to me, and I shared in his joys. . . .

It was a peace, curiously enough, divided against itself. I was happy, but my very happiness made me know that there was a greater happiness to be obtained from life than any I had ever known. I began to think, to weigh things, and it was at this time that I began consciously to pray more.

The Long Loneliness

Still November: I am surprised that I am beginning to pray daily. I began because I had to. I just found myself praying. I can't get down on my knees, but I can pray while I am walking. If I get down on my knees I think, "Do I really believe? Whom am I praying to?" And a terrible doubt comes over me, and a sense of shame, and I wonder if I am praying because I am lonely, because I am unhappy.

Then I think suddenly, scornfully, "Here you are in a stupor of content. You are biological. Like a cow. Prayer with you is like the opiate of the people." And over and over again in my mind that phrase is repeated jeeringly, "Religion is the opiate of the people."

"But," I reason with myself, "I am praying because I am happy, not because I am unhappy. I did not turn to God in unhappiness, in grief, in despair—to get consolation, to get something from Him."

And encouraged that I am praying because I want to thank Him, I go on praying. No matter how dull the day, how long the walk seems, if I feel low at the beginning of the walk, the words I have been saying have insinuated themselves into my heart before I have done, so that on the trip back I neither pray nor think but am filled with exultation.

Along the beach I find it appropriate to say the Te Deum, which I learned in the Episcopal church. When I am working about the house, I find myself addressing the Blessed Virgin and turning toward her statue.

It is so hard to say how this delight in prayer has been growing on me.

Two years ago, I was saying as I planted seeds in the garden, "I *must* believe in these seeds, that they fall into the earth and grow into flowers and radishes and beans. It is a miracle to me because I do not understand it. The very fact that they use glib technical phrases does not make it any the less a miracle, and a miracle we all accept. Then why not accept God's miracles?"

I am going to Mass now regularly on Sunday mornings.

From Union Square to Rome

Forster, the inarticulate, became garrulous only in wrath. And his wrath, he said, was caused by my absorption in the supernatural rather than the natural, the unseen rather than the seen.

He had always rebelled against the institution of the family and the tyranny of love. It was hard for me to see at such times why we were together, since he lived with me as though he were living alone and he never allowed me to forget that this was a comradeship rather than a marriage.

He worked as little as possible, he shared in all the expenses of the house, but he never spent any money if he could help it. He hated social life and fled from it, and seemed afraid of any actual contact with the world, but he was much engrossed in its concerns. He read the *Times* faithfully, and all I knew of the political and foreign situation I knew from his reading aloud at the breakfast table. . . . I had listened to Forster's bitter comments on all man-made institutions and the blundering of our fellow creatures. He loved nature with a sensuous passion and he loved birds and beasts and children because they were not men.

The very fact that his suffering and rebellion against life as man had made it was an abstract thing and had little to do with what he had suffered personally, made me respect his ideas, as ideas honestly held, so our quarrels were not acrimonious. For instance, he loved his family tenderly, but he saw and suffered keenly at what havoc a possessive family feeling sometimes wrought. He personally had not suffered want, but economic inequality was a terrible thing to him. He personally had not been in jail, but his rage at the system which confined political agitators to jail ate into him. And yet he did nothing but enclose himself into a shell, escape out on the bay with his fishing, find comfort in digging for clams or bait, or seek refuge in tending a garden. . . .

I had known Forster a long time before we contracted our common-law relationship, and I have always felt that it was life with him that brought me natural happiness, that brought me to God.

His ardent love of creation brought me to the Creator of all things. But when I cried out to him, "How can there be no God, when there are all these beautiful things?" he turned from me uneasily and complained that I was never satisfied. We loved each other so strongly that he wanted to remain in the love of the moment; he wanted me to rest in that love. He cried out against my attitude that there would be nothing left of that love without faith. . . .

I could not see that love between man and woman was incompatible with love of God. God is the Creator, and the very fact that we were begetting a child made me have a sense that we were made in the image and likeness of God, co-creators with him. I could not protest with Sasha about "that initial agony of having to live." Because I was grateful for love, I was grateful for life, and living with Forster made me appreciate it and even reverence it still more. He had introduced me to so much that was beautiful and good that I felt I owed to him too this renewed interest in the things of the spirit.

He had all the love of the English for the outdoors in all weather. He used to insist on walks no matter how cold or rainy the day, and this dragging me away from my books, from my lethargy, into the open, into the country, made me begin to breathe. If breath is life, then I was beginning to be full of it because of him. I was filling my lungs with it, walking on the beach, resting on the pier beside him while he fished, rowing with him in the calm bay, walking through fields and woods—a new experience entirely for me, one which brought me to life and filled me with joy. . . .

It did not last all through my pregnancy, that happiness. There were conflicts because Forster did not believe in bringing children into such a world as we lived in. He still was obsessed by the war. His fear of responsibility, his dislike of having the control of others, his extreme individualism, made him feel that he of all men should not be a father.

The Long Loneliness

November Still: I am alone these days. Forster is in town all week, only coming out weekends and a few nights. I have finished the writing I was doing and feel at a loose end, thinking enviously of my friends going gaily about the city, about their work, with plenty of companionship.

The fact that I feel restless is a very good reason to stay down here and content myself with my life as a sybaritic anchorite. For how can I be a true anchorite with such luxuries as a baby to look forward to, not to speak of the morning paper, groceries delivered at the door, a beach to walk on, and the water to feast my eyes on?

*   *   *

In spite of my desire for a sociable week in town, in spite of a desire to pick up and flee from my solitude, I take pleasure in thinking of the idiocy of the pleasures I would indulge in if I were there. Teas and dinners, the conversation or lack of it, dancing in a smoky crowded room when one might be walking on the beach—the dull restless cogitations which come after dissipating one's energies—these things strike me with renewed force every time I have spent days in the city. My virtuous resolutions to indulge in such pleasures no more are succeeded by a hideous depression when neither my newfound sense of religion, my family life, my work, nor my surroundings seem sufficient to console me. I think of death and am overwhelmed by the terror and the blackness of both life and death. And I long for a church near at hand where I can go and lift up my soul.

When I am feeling these things I cannot write them, and while I am writing them I write almost self-consciously, wondering if I am not exaggerating, but the mood which possessed me yesterday was real enough and during the evening I read desperately, trying to rescue myself from the wall of silence which seemed to close me in.

But this makes me realize that often talk is an escape from doing anything. We chatter on and on to cover our feelings and to hide from ourselves and others our own futility.

Of course, conversation is often spirited and uplifts me as some books do. It helps me to glimpse the meaning in things and jolts me out of the rut in which I have been ambling along. I am spurred on to the pursuit of knowledge by a renewed love of knowledge. And yet the trouble with these conversations is that often they are not spontaneous. Some of my liberal friends, for instance, have gatherings, Sunday afternoons or Thursday nights, and the little crowd which comes feels itself a group and the conversation often seems pompous and self-congratulatory.

This exaltation of the articulate obscures the fact that there are millions of people in this world who feel and in some way carry on courageously even though they cannot talk or reason brilliantly. This very talk may obscure everything that we know nothing of now, and who knows but that silence may lead us to it.

December: It is a sunshiny, hazy day and the boats on the bay look ghost-like and unreal. The morning sun makes each blade of grass, each dry twig, stand out and the grasses in the field next to the house do not stir. There are only the starlings to break the silence and occasionally the far-off whistle of the train. Even the waves make no sound upon the beach, for there is an offshore wind.

It was pleasant rowing about in the calm bay with Forster. The oyster boats were all out, and far on the horizon, off Sandy Hook, there was a four-masted vessel. I had the curious delusion that several huge holes had been stove in her side, through which you could see the blue sky. The other vessels seemed sailing in the air, quite indifferent to the horizon on which they should properly have been resting. Forster tried to explain to me scientific facts about mirages and atmospheric conditions, and, on the other hand, I pointed out to him how our senses can lie to us.

But it is impossible to talk to him about religion or faith. A wall immediately separates us. The very love of nature and study of her secrets which is bringing me to faith, separates him from religion.

From Union Square to Rome

II

On Wednesday I received my white ticket, which entitled me to a baby at Bellevue. So far I had been using a red one, which admitted me to the clinic each week for a cursory examination. The nurse in charge seemed very reluctant about giving out the white one. She handed it to me, saying doubtfully, "You'll probably be late. They're all being late just now. And I gave them their tickets and just because they have them they run into the hospital at all times of the night and day, thinking their time is come, and find out they were wrong."

The clinic doctors acted very much disgusted, saying, "What in the world's the matter with you women? The wards are empty." And only a week before they were saying, "Stall off this baby of yours, can't you? The beds are all taken and even the corridors are crowded."

The girl who sat next to me at the clinic that day was late the week before and I was astonished and discouraged to see her still there. She was a pretty, brown-eyed girl with sweet, full lips and a patient expression. She was only about eighteen and it was her first baby. She said "ma'am," no matter what I said to her. She seemed to have no curiosity and made no attempt to talk to the women about her; just sat there with her hands folded in her lap, patient, waiting. She did not look very large, but she bore herself clumsily, childishly.

There was one Greek who was most debonair. She wore a turban and a huge, pink pearl necklace and earrings, a bright dress and flesh-colored stockings on still-slim legs. She made no attempt to huddle her coat around her as so many women do. She had to stand while waiting for the doctor, the place was so crowded, and she poised herself easily by the door, her head held high, her coat flung open, her full figure most graciously exposed. She rather flaunted herself, confident of her attractions. And because she was confident, she was most attractive.

When I got home that afternoon, thinking of her, I put on my ivory beads and powdered my nose. I could not walk lightly and freely, but it was easy to strut.

There was another woman who was late, a great, gay Irish wench who shouted raucously as she left the doctor's office, "The doctor sez they are tired of seeing me around and I don't blame them. I rushed over three times last week, thinking I was taken and I wasn't. They sez, 'The idea of your not knowing the pains when this is your third!' But I'm damned if I come in here again until they cart me in."

So, when I was philosophically preparing myself to hang around a month, waiting for my child to knock on the door, my pains started, twelve hours earlier than scheduled. I was in the bathtub reading a mystery novel by Agatha Christie when I felt the first pain and was thrilled, both by the novel and by the pain, and thought stubbornly to myself, "I must finish this book." And I did, before the next one struck fifteen minutes later.

"Carol!" I called. "The child will be born before tomorrow morning. I've had two pains."

"It's a false alarm," scoffed my cousin, but her knees began to tremble visibly because after all, according to all our figuring, I was due the next morning.

"Never mind. I'm going to the hospital to exchange my white ticket for Tamar Teresa"—for so I had euphoniously named her.

So Carol rushed out for a taxicab while I dressed myself haltingly, and a few minutes later we were crossing town in a Yellow, puffing on cigarettes and clutching each other as the taxi driver went over every bump in his anxiety for my welfare.

The driver breathed a sigh of relief as he left us at Bellevue, and so did we. We sat for half an hour or so in the receiving room, my case evidently not demanding immediate attention, and watched with interest the reception of other patients. The doctor, greeting us affably, asked which of us was the maternity case, which so complimented me and amused Carol that our giggling tided us over any impatience we felt.

There was a colored woman with a tiny baby, born that morning, brought in on a stretcher. She kept sitting up, her child clutched to her bosom, yelling that she had an earache, and the doctor kept pushing her back. Carol, who suffers from the same complaint, said that she would rather have a baby than an earache, and I agreed with her.

Then there was a genial drunk, assisted in with difficulty by a cab driver and his fare, who kept insisting that he had been kicked by a large white horse. His injuries did not seem to be serious.

My turn came next, and as I was wheeled away in a chair by a pleasant old orderly with whiskey breath, Carol's attention was attracted and diverted from my ordeal by the reception of a drowned man, or one almost drowned, from whom they were trying to elicit information about his wife, whether he was living with her, their address, religion, occupation, and birthplace— information which the man was totally unable to give.

For the next hour I received all the attention Carol would have desired for me—attentions which I did not at all welcome. The nurse who ministered to me was a large, beautiful creature with marcelled hair and broad hips, which she flaunted about the small room with much grace. She was a flippant creature and talked of Douglas Fairbanks and the film she had seen that afternoon, while she wielded a long razor with abandon. . . .

Thinking of moving pictures, why didn't the hospital provide a moving picture for women having babies? And music! Surely things should be made as interesting as possible for women who are perpetuating the race. It was comforting to think of peasant women who take lunch hours to have their children in, and then put the kids under the haystack and go on working in the fields. Hellish civilization!

I had nothing at home to put the baby in, I thought suddenly. Except a bureau drawer. Carol said she would have a clothes basket. But I adore cradles. Too bad I had been unable to find one. A long time ago I saw an adorable one on the East Side in an old secondhand shop. They wanted thirty dollars, and besides, how did I know then I was going to have a baby? Still I wanted to buy it. If Sarah Bernhardt could carry a coffin around the country with her there is no reason why I couldn't carry a cradle around with me. It was a bright pink one—not painted pink, because I examined it carefully. Some kind of pink wood.

The pain penetrating my thoughts made me sick to my stomach. Sick *at* your stomach or sick *to* your stomach? I always used to say "sick to your stomach" but William [Forster] declares it is "sick at your stomach." Both sound very funny to me. But I'd say whatever William wanted me to. What difference did it make? But I have done so many things he wanted me to, I am tired of it. Doing without milk in my coffee, for instance, because he insists that milk spoils the taste of coffee. And using the same kind of toothpaste. Funny thing, being so intimate with a man that you feel you must use the same kind of toothpaste he does. To wake up and see his head on your pillow every morning. An awful thing to get used to anything. I mustn't get used to that baby. I don't see how I can.

Lightning! It shoots through your back, down your stomach, through your legs, and out at the end of your toes. Sometimes it takes longer to get out than others. You have to push it out then. I am not afraid of lightning now, but I used to be. I used to get up in bed and pray every time there was a thunderstorm. I was afraid to get up, but prayers didn't do any good unless you said them on your knees.

Hours passed. I thought it must be about four o'clock and found that it was two. Every five minutes the pains came, and in between I slept. As each pain began I groaned and cursed, "How long will this one last?" and then when it had swept over with the beautiful rhythm of the sea, I felt with satisfaction "it could be worse," and clutched at sleep again frantically.

Every now and then my large-hipped nurse came in to see how I was getting along. She was a sociable creature, though not so to me, and brought with her a flip young doctor and three other nurses to joke and laugh about hospital affairs. They disposed themselves on the other two beds, but my nurse sat on the foot of mine, pulling the entire bed askew with her weight. This spoiled my sleeping during the five-minute intervals, and, mindful of my grievance against her and the razor, I took advantage of the beginning of the next pain to kick her soundly in the behind. She got up with a jerk and obligingly took a seat on the next bed.

And so the night wore on. When I became bored and impatient with the steady restlessness of those waves of pain, I thought of all the other and more futile kinds of pain I would rather not have. Toothaches, ear-aches, and broken arms. I had had them all. And this is a much more satisfactory and accomplishing pain, I comforted myself.

And I thought, too, how much had been written about childbirth—no novel, it seems, is complete without at least one birth scene. I counted over the ones I had read that winter—Upton Sinclair's in *The Miracle of*

Love, Tolstoy's in *Anna Karenina*, Arnim's in *The Pastor's Wife*, Galsworthy's in *Beyond*, O'Neill's in *The Last Man*, Bennett's in *The Old Wives' Tale*, and so on.

All but one of these descriptions had been written by men, and, with the antagonism natural toward men at such a time, I resented their presumption.

"What do they know about it, the idiots," I thought. And it gave me pleasure to imagine one of them in the throes of childbirth. How they would groan and holler and rebel. And wouldn't they make everybody else miserable around them. And here I was, conducting a neat and tidy job, begun in a most businesslike manner, on the minute. But when would it end?

While I dozed and wondered and struggled, the last scene of my little drama began, much to the relief of the doctors and nurses, who were becoming impatient now that it was almost time for them to go off duty. The smirk of complacence was wiped from me. Where before there had been waves, there were now tidal waves. Earthquake and fire swept my body. My spirit was a battleground on which thousands were butchered in a most horrible manner. Through the rush and roar of the cataclysm which was all about me, I heard the murmur of the doctor and the answered murmur of the nurse at my head.

In a white blaze of thankfulness I knew that ether was forthcoming. I breathed deeply for it, mouth open and gasping like that of a baby starving for its mother's breast. Never have I known such frantic imperious desire for anything. And then the mask descended on my face and I gave myself to it, hurling myself into oblivion as quickly as possible. As I fell, fell, fell, very rhythmically, to the accompaniment of tom-toms, I heard, faint about the clamor in my ears, a peculiar squawk, I smiled as I floated dreamily and luxuriously on a sea without waves. I had handed in my white ticket and the next thing I would see would be the baby they would give me in exchange. It was the first time I had thought of the child in a long, long time.

*   *   *

Tamar Teresa's nose is twisted slightly to one side. She sleeps with the placidity of a Mona Lisa, so that you cannot see the amazing blue of her eyes, which are strangely blank and occasionally, ludicrously crossed. What little hair she has is auburn and her eyebrows are golden. Her complexion is a rich tan. Her ten fingers and toes are of satisfactory length and slenderness and I reflect that she will be a dancer when she grows up, which future will relieve her of the necessity for learning reading, writing, and arithmetic.

Her long upper lip, which resembles that of an Irish policeman, may interfere with her beauty, but with such posy hands as she has already, nothing will interfere with her grace.

Just now I must say she is a lazy little hog, mouthing around my nice full breast and too lazy to tug for food. What do you want, little bird? That it should run into your mouth, I suppose. But no, you must work for your provender already.

She is only four days old but already she has the bad habit of feeling bright and desirous of play at four o'clock in the morning. Pretending that I am a bone and she is a puppy dog, she worries at me fussily, tossing her head and grunting. Of course, some mothers will tell you this is because she has air on her stomach and that I should hold her upright until a loud gulp indicates that she is ready to begin feeding again. But though I hold her up as required, I still think the child's play instinct is highly developed.

Other times she will pause a long time, her mouth relaxed, then look at me slyly, trying to tickle me with her tiny, red tongue. Occasionally she pretends to lose me and with a loud wail of protest grabs hold once more to start feeding furiously. It is fun to see her little jaw working and the hollow that appears in her baby throat as she swallows.

Sitting up in bed, I glance alternately at my beautiful flat stomach and out the window at tugboats and barges and the wide path of the early-morning sun on the East River. Whistles are blowing cheerily, and there are some men singing on the wharf below. The restless water is colored lavender and gold and the enchanting sky is a sentimental blue and pink. And gulls wheeling, warm gray and white against the magic of the water and the sky. Sparrows chirp on the windowsill, the baby sputters as she gets too big a mouthful, and pauses, then, a moment to look around her with satisfaction. Everybody is complacent, everybody is satisfied and everybody is happy.

The New Masses, June 1928

III

Our child was born in March at the end of a harsh winter. In December I had to come in from the country and take a little apartment in town. It was good to be there, close to friends, close to a church where I could stop and pray. I read the *Imitation of Christ* a great deal. I knew that I was going to have my child baptized a Catholic, cost what it may. I knew that I was not going to have her floundering through many years as I had done, doubting and hesitating, undisciplined and amoral. I felt it was the greatest thing I could do for my child. For myself, I prayed for the gift of faith. I was sure, yet not sure. I postponed the day of decision.

A woman does not want to be alone at such a time. Even the most hardened, the most irreverent, is awed by the stupendous fact of creation. Becoming a Catholic would mean facing life alone, and I clung to family life. It was hard to contemplate giving up a mate in order that my child and I could become members of the Church. Forster would have nothing to do with religion or with me if I embraced it. So I waited.

Those last months of waiting I was too happy to know the unrest of indecision. The days were slow in passing, but week by week the time came nearer. I spent some time in writing, but in general I felt inactive, incapable of going to meetings, of seeing many people, of taking up the threads of my past life.

And then the little one was born, and with her birth the spring was upon us. My joy was so great that I sat up in the bed in the hospital and wrote an article for *The New Masses* about my child, wanting to share my joy with the world. I was glad to write it for a workers' magazine because it was a joy all women know, no matter what their grief at poverty, unemployment, and class war.

*   *   *

When Tamar Teresa—for that is what I named her—was six weeks old and I was still very weak, we went down to the country. It was April and though it was still cold, it was definitely spring.

Every morning while Teresa napped on the sunny porch, well swathed in soft woolen blankets, I went down to the beach and brought up driftwood, enough to last until next morning. . . . Sometimes in the afternoon I put her in her carriage and went out along the woods, watching, almost feeling the buds bursting through their warm coats. Song sparrows, woodpeckers, hawks, crows, robins, nuthatches, and of course laughing gulls made the air gay with their clamor. Starlings chattered all day in the branches of the old pine in front of the porch. We collected azalea buds, dogwood, sassafras, and apple tree branches to decorate the room. . . .

Supper was always early and the baby comfortably tucked away before it was dark. Then, tired with all the activities that so rejoiced and filled my days, I sat in the dusk in a stupor of contentment. . . .

Yet always, those deep moments of happiness gave way to a feeling of struggle, of a long silent fight to be gone through. There had been the physical struggle, the mortal combat almost, of giving birth to a child, and now there was coming the struggle for my own soul. I knew Teresa would be baptized, and I knew the rending it would cause in human relations around me. I was to be torn and agonized again and I was all for putting off the hard day.

Then, one afternoon, as I wheeled her in her little carriage along the road which led down to St. Joseph's Home, a former estate of Charles Schwab which had been given to the Sisters of Charity, I met a Sister who was on her way to visit a neighbor of mine.

That estate had been one of my stumbling blocks. I could never pass it without thinking of Schwab's career as head of the Bethlehem Steel Corporation, of his work in breaking the Homestead strike, of how he refused to recognize unions of workers. I could not but feel that this was tainted money which the Sisters had accepted. It was money which belonged to the workers. . . .

But I was emboldened by a sense of compulsion to speak to the Sister who was hurrying by me, to ask her how to go about having a baby baptized. I had a warm feeling as I approached her, a feeling that whatever the errors of Charlie Schwab, Sister Aloysia had had no part in them, in her simplicity and poverty.

She was very matter-of-fact. She seemed to take things for granted, and was not surprised that a mother of a new baby would stop her in this casual fashion and ask her so stupendous a question. She knew of me by reputation—indeed all the neighborhood knew that we and our friends were either Communist or anarchist in sympathies. But those same dear Catholic neighbors who heard sermons excoriating "the fiendish and foul machinations of the Communists" were kindly people who came to use our telephone and bring us a pie now and then, who played with us on the beach and offered us lifts to the village in their cars. Sister Aloysia, too, had no fear, only a neighborly interest in us all.

She took me under her protection immediately. She did not make little of my difficulties, nor did she think for a minute that they were insurmountable. There was a hard row to hoe in front of us, was her attitude, but we could get through it. She would hang on to that long, formidable-looking rosary of hers, hang on to it like an anchor, and together we would ride out the gale of opposition and controversy. All we had to do was depend on prayer.

And as for practical details, we would just go ahead as though it were very simple. Did I have any Catholic relatives?

Yes, there was Cousin Grace. She was married and she and her husband could be reached, though I had not seen them or any relatives for years.

All right then, she herself, Sister Aloysia, would get in touch with the parish priest in Tottenville, a young man, very obliging. He had been coming down to offer up Mass at the Home and she could see him after breakfast the next morning.

Somehow or other, with the irregularities of her parents not being Catholic, Teresa's baptism did not take place until late June. Sister Aloysia in her anxiety that all should go well dropped in every day to see if I were persisting in my determination. She also was quite frank in her anxiety for the baby's welfare. One morning she came rushing up on the porch—"She's not dead yet?" she wanted to know, and then praised God that the baby was living and also struggling toward her baptism. Sister was sure that the powers of darkness were struggling hard for my little one—"He's greedy for souls," she said, meaning the devil, and in this case I had more confidence and hope than she because I assured her that Christ must be even more so.

But Sister Aloysia did not neglect me in her anxiety for the baby. "You must be a Catholic yourself," she kept telling me. She had no reticence. She speculated rather volubly at times on the various reasons why she thought I was holding back. She brought me pious literature to read, saccharine stories of the saints, back numbers of pious magazines.

But I was in a state of dull content—not in a state to be mentally stimulated. I was too happy with my child. What faith I had I held on to stubbornly. The need for patience emphasized in the writings of the saints consoled me on the slow road I was traveling. I would put all my affairs in the hands of God and wait.

Three times a week, Sister Aloysia came to give me a catechism lesson which I dutifully tried to learn. But she insisted that I recite word for word, with the repetition of the question that was in the book. If I had not learned my lesson, she rebuked me. "And you think you are intelligent!" she would say witheringly. "What is the definition of grace—actual grace and sanctifying grace? My fourth-grade pupils know more than you do."

I hadn't a doubt but that they did. I struggled on day by day, learning without question. I made up my mind to accept what I did not understand, trusting light to come, as it sometimes did, in a blinding flash of exultation and realization.

She used to bring me vegetables from the garden of the Home, and I used to give her fish and clams. Once I gave her stamps and a dollar to send a present to a little niece, and she was touchingly grateful. It made me suddenly realize that in spite of Charlie Schwab and his estate, the Sisters lived in complete poverty, owning nothing, holding all things in common.

She never came into the house directly, but used to peer in the window or back door with a sepulchral whisper, "Is he here?" as though it were the devil himself she was inquiring after. And if Forster was there, he used to slam out of the other door to show his displeasure, greeting her through clenched teeth. I didn't blame him, nor did I blame her. She would probably have regarded any husband so, no matter how Catholic, how exemplary. She knew little of the world of men.

Finally the great day arrived and was a thing of the past. Teresa was baptized, she had become a member of the Mystical Body of Christ. I didn't know anything of the Mystical Body, or I might have felt disturbed at being separated from her.

But I clutched her close to me and all that summer as I nursed her and bent over that tiny round face at my breast, I was filled with a deep happiness that nothing could spoil. But the obstacles to my becoming a Catholic were there, shadows in the background of my life.

I had become convinced that I would become a Catholic, and yet I felt I was betraying the class to which I belonged, the workers, the poor of the world with whom Christ spent His life. . . .

Some few times I could get up to the village to Mass on Sunday, when I could leave the baby in trusted hands. But usually the gloom that descended on the household, the scarcely voiced opposition, kept me from Mass. There were some feast days when I could slip off in the middle of the week and go to the little chapel on the Sisters' grounds. There were "visits" I could make, unknown to others. I was committed, by the advice of a priest I had consulted, to the plan of waiting, trying to hold the family together. But I felt all along that when I took the irrevocable step it would mean that Teresa and I would be alone, and I did not want to be alone. I did not want to give up human love when it was dearest and tenderest.

During the month of August many of my friends, including my sister, went to Boston to picket in protest against the execution of Sacco and Vanzetti, which was drawing near. They were all arrested again and again.

Throughout the nation and the world, the papers featured the struggle for the lives of these two men. Radicals from all over the country gathered in Boston. It was an epic struggle, a tragedy. One felt a sense of impending doom. These men were Catholics, inasmuch as they were Italians. Catholics by tradition, but they had rejected the Church.

While enjoying the fresh breeze, the feel of salt water against the flesh, the keen delight of living, the knowledge that these men were soon to pass from this physical earth, were soon to become dust, without consciousness, struck me like a physical blow. They were here now; in a few days they would be no more. They had become figures beloved by the workers. Their letters, the warm moving story of their lives, had been told. Everyone knew Dante, Sacco's young son. Everyone suffered with the young wife who clung with bitter passion to her husband. And Vanzetti, with his large view, his sense of peace at his fate, was even closer to us all.

The day they died, the papers had headlines as large as those which proclaimed the outbreak of war. All the nation mourned. All the nation, that is, that is made up of the poor, the worker, the trade unionist—those who felt most keenly the sense of solidarity—that very sense of solidarity which made me gradually understand the doctrine of the Mystical Body of Christ whereby we are the members one of another.

Forster was stricken over the tragedy. He had always been more an anarchist than anything else in his philosophy, and so was closer to these two men than to Communist friends. He did not eat for days. He sat around the house in a stupor of misery, sickened by the cruelty of life and of men. He had always taken refuge in nature as being more kindly, more beautiful and peaceful than the world of men. Now he could not even escape through nature, as he tried to escape so many problems in life.

During the time he was home he spent days and even nights out on the water fishing, so that for weeks I saw little of him. He stupefied himself in his passion for the water, sitting out on the bay in his boat. When he began to recover, he submerged himself in maritime biology, collecting, reading only scientific books, and paying no attention to what went on around him. Only the baby interested him. She was his delight. Which made it, of course, the harder to contemplate the cruel blow I was going to strike him when I became a Catholic.

From Union Square to Rome

We both suffered in body as well as in soul and mind. He would not talk about the faith and relapsed into complete silence if I tried to bring up the subject. The point of my bringing it up was that I could not become a Catholic and continue living with him, because he was averse to any ceremony before officials of either Church or State. He was an anarchist and an atheist, and he did not intend to be a liar or a hypocrite. He was a creature of utter sincerity, and however illogical and bad-tempered about it all, I loved him. It was killing me to think of leaving him.

Fall nights we read a great deal. Sometimes he went out to dig bait if there was a low tide and the moon was up. He stayed out late on the pier fishing, and came in smelling of seaweed and salt air; getting into bed, cold with the chill November, he held me close to him in silence. I loved him in every way, as a wife, as a mother even. I loved him for all he knew and pitied him for all he didn't know. I loved him for the odds and ends I had to fish out of his sweater pockets and for the sand and shells he brought in with his fishing. I loved his lean cold body as he got into bed smelling of the sea, and I loved his integrity and stubborn pride.

It ended by my being ill the next summer. I became so oppressed I could not breathe and I awoke in the night choking. I was weak and listless and one doctor told me my trouble was probably thyroid. I went to the Cornell clinic for a metabolism test and they said my condition was a nervous one. By winter the tension had become so great that an explosion occurred and we separated again. When he returned, as he always had, I would not let him in the house; my heart was breaking with my own determination to make an end, once and for all, to the torture we were undergoing.

The next day I went to Tottenville alone, leaving Tamar with my sister, and there, with Sister Aloysia as my godparent, I too was baptized conditionally, since I had already been baptized in the Episcopal Church. I made my first confession right afterward, and looked forward the next morning to receiving Communion.

I had no particular joy in partaking of these three sacraments, Baptism, Penance, and Holy Eucharist. I proceeded about my own active participation in them grimly, coldly, making acts of faith, and certainly with no consolation whatsoever. One part of my mind stood at one side and kept saying, "What are you doing? Are you sure of yourself? What kind of an affectation is this? What act is this you are going through? Are you trying to induce emotion, induce faith, partake of an opiate, the opiate of the people?" I felt like a hypocrite if I got down on my knees, and shuddered at the thought of anyone seeing me.

At my first Communion I went up to the Communion rail at the Sanctus bell instead of at the "Domine, non sum dignus," and had to kneel there all alone through the Consecration, through the Pater Noster, through the Agnus Dei—and I had thought I knew the Mass so well! But I felt it fitting that I be humiliated by this ignorance, by this precipitance.

I speak of the misery of leaving one love. But there was another love too, the life I had led in the radical movement. That very winter I was writing a series of articles, interviews with the workers, with the unemployed. I was working with the Anti-Imperialist League, a Communist affiliate, that was bringing aid and comfort to the enemy, General Sandino's forces in Nicaragua. I was just as much against capitalism and imperialism as ever, and here I was going over to the opposition, because of course the Church was lined up with property, with the wealthy, with the state, with capitalism, with all the forces of reaction. This I had been taught to think and this I still think to a great extent. . . . But I wanted to be poor, chaste, and obedient. I wanted to die in order to live, to put off the old man and put on Christ. I loved, in other words, and like all women in love, I wanted to be united in my love. Why should not Forster be jealous? Any man who did not participate in this love would, of course, realize my infidelity, my adultery. In the eyes of God, any turning toward creatures to the exclusion of Him is adultery, and so it is termed over and over again in Scripture.

I loved the Church for Christ made visible. Not for itself, because it was so often a scandal to me. Romano Guardini said that the Church is the Cross on which Christ was crucified; one could not separate Christ from His Cross, and one must live in a state of permanent dissatisfaction with the Church. . . .

Not long afterward a priest wanted me to write a story of my conversion, telling how the social teaching of the Church had led me to embrace Catholicism. But I knew nothing of the social teaching of the Church at that time. I had never heard of the encyclicals. I felt that the Church was the Church of the poor, that St. Patrick's had been built from the pennies of servant girls, that it cared for the emigrant, it established hospitals, orphanages, day nurseries, houses of the Good Shepherd, homes for the aged, but at the same time, I felt that it did not set its face against a social order which made so much charity in the present sense of the word necessary. I felt that charity was a word to choke over. Who wanted charity? And it was not just human pride, but a strong sense of man's dignity and worth and what was due to him in justice, that made me resent, rather than feel proud of, so mighty a sum total of Catholic institutions. . . .

It was an age-old battle, the war of the classes, that stirred in me when I thought of the Sacco-Vanzetti case in Boston. Where were the Catholic voices crying out for these men? How I longed to make a synthesis reconciling body and soul, this world and the next.

Where had been the priests to go out to such men as Francisco Ferrer in Spain, pursuing them as the Good Shepherd did His lost sheep, leaving

the ninety and nine of their good parishioners to seek out that which was
lost, bind up that which was bruised? No wonder there was such a strong
conflict going on in my mind and heart.

I never regretted for one minute the step which I had taken in becoming
a Catholic, but I repeat that for a year there was little joy for me as the
struggle continued.

*   *   *

A year later my Confirmation was a joyous affair. I went one Sunday
afternoon on the feast of Pentecost to the Convent of the Holy Souls on
Eighty-fifth Street near Third Avenue. There, in company with a large
group of adults, to the sweet singing of the nuns, I received the sacrament
of Confirmation. I took the name of Maria Teresa.

The Long Loneliness

Peasant of the Pavements

I

In the fall of 1932 I had been writing articles for *America* and *The Commonweal,* and the first week in December I went to Washington, D.C., to cover
the Hunger March of the Unemployed Councils and the Farmer's Convention. Both were Communist-led.

If the journalists and the police of Washington had been coached in
their parts, they could not have staged a better drama, from the Communist
standpoint, than they did in the events of that week.

Drama was what the Communist leaders of the march wanted, and
drama, even melodrama, was what they got. They weren't presenting their
petitions to Congress with any hope of immediately obtaining the cash
bonuses and unemployment relief they demanded. (Nevertheless, five years
later unemployment insurance became part of Social Security legislation.)
They were presenting pictorially the plight of the workers of America, not
only to the countless small towns and large cities through which they
passed, not only to the Congress, but through the press to the entire world.
And in addition they were demonstrating to the proletariat.

They were saying, "Come, submit yourselves to our discipline—place yourselves in our hands, you union workers, you unemployed, and we will show you how a scant 3,000 of you, unarmed, can terrorize authorities and make them submit to at least some of your demands!"

It does not matter that the victory won was only that of marching to the Capitol. To those unarmed marchers who for two days and two cold nights in December lived and slept on an asphalt highway with no water, no fires, no sanitary facilities, with the scantiest of food, surrounded by hysteria in the shape of machine guns and tear-gas bombs in the hands of a worn and fretted police force, egged on by a bunch of ghouls in the shape of newspaper men and photographers—to these marchers, the victory was a real one. They had achieved their purpose.

The papers did their best to make a riot out of it and failed. They merely presented to public view the Communist leaders who could carry through successfully a planned and disciplined demonstration. And the Washingtonians who lined the streets by the thousands to watch the procession laughed tolerantly at the songs and slogans, and said admiringly, "They sure have got gumption, standing up against the police that way."

*   *   *

I watched that ragged horde and thought to myself, "These are Christ's poor. He was one of them. He was a man like other men, and He chose His friends amongst the ordinary workers. These men feel they have been betrayed by Christianity. Men are not Christian today. If they were, this sight would not be possible. Far dearer in the sight of God perhaps are these hungry ragged ones, than all those smug, well-fed Christians who sit in their homes, cowering in fear of the Communist menace."

I felt that they were my people, that I was part of them. I had worked for them and with them in the past, and now I was a Catholic and so could not be a Communist. I could not join this united front of protest, and I wanted to.

The feast of the Immaculate Conception was the next day, and I went out to the National Shrine and assisted at Solemn High Mass there. And the prayer that I offered up was that some way would be shown me, some way would be opened up for me to work for the poor and the oppressed.

And when I returned to New York, I found Peter Maurin—Peter the French peasant, whose spirit and ideas will dominate the rest of this book as they will dominate the rest of my life.

House of Hospitality

II

When I walked into my apartment, I found waiting for me a short, stocky man in his mid-fifties, as ragged and rugged as any of the marchers I had left. I like people to look their part, and if they are workers, to look like workers, and if they are peasants to look like peasants. I like to see the shape of a man's hands, the strength of his neck and shoulders.

This man introduced himself briefly: "I am Peter Maurin." He pronounced it Maw-rin, with the accent on the first syllable, deliberately anglicizing the word. "George Shuster, editor of *The Commonweal,* told me to look you up. Also, a red-headed Irish Communist in Union Square told me to see you. He says we think alike."

How to describe Peter and the effect he had on me? Certainly I knew at once that he was French. It was difficult to become accustomed to his accent, which he kept although he had already been twenty years in America. He was intensely alive, on the alert, even when silent, engaged in reading or in thought. When he talked, the tilt of his head, his animated expression, the warm glow in his eyes, the gestures of his hands, his shoulders, his whole body, compelled your attention. I remember several things about that first meeting, characteristics of Peter that were to impress themselves more and more on me during the year that followed. He spoke in terms of ideas, rather than personalities, and he stressed the importance of theory. As people gathered around us in the movement which sprang up, this attribute stood out. While others were always analyzing, talking about one another, using one another's lives and attitudes to illustrate ideas, Peter was always impersonal, delicately scrupulous never to talk about others, never to make a derogatory remark.

"Lenin said, 'There can be no revolution without a theory of revolution,' so I am trying to give the theory of a green revolution," he said.

He delighted in the title of agitator. Though he spoke in terms of ideas, and men of ideas, he made these ideas dynamic by coloring them in his own way: "I knew a man who . . ." or "Péguy's mother mended chairs in Notre Dame Cathedral . . ."

The nearest he came to being critical with me was to tell me that my education lacked Catholic background. He began to give it to me by talking about the history of the Church, by going even further back into time and speaking of the prophets of Israel as well as the Fathers of the Church. His friends were Jews, Protestants, agnostics, as well as Catholics, and he found a common ground with all in what he termed the Thomistic Doctrine of the Common Good. He ignored differences to stress concordance. He did not use such terms as "ecumenical," though he was not afraid of the unusual word (agronomic universities were part of his program), but he thought in terms of our common humanity, of our life here today. He stressed the need of building a new society within the shell of the old— that telling phrase from the preamble to the I.W.W. constitution, "a society in which it is easier for people to be good," he added with a touching simplicity, knowing that when people are good, they are happy.

He was a man of tremendous ambition, in spite of his simplicity, or perhaps because of it. He wanted to make a new synthesis, as St. Thomas had done in the Middle Ages, and he wanted to enlist the aid of a group of people in doing this. He was no more afraid of the non-Catholic approach to problems than St. Thomas was of the Aristotelian.

With all his knowledge, he was no isolated scholar. It was the state of the world which filled him with these vast desires. Man was placed here with talents, to play his part, and on every side he saw the children of this world wiser in their generation than the children of light. They built enormous industrial plants, bridges, pipelines, skyscrapers, with imagination and vision they made their blueprints, and with reckless and daredevil financing made them actual in steel and concrete. Wheels turned and engines throbbed and the great pulse of the mechanical and physical world beat strong and steady while men's pulses sickened and grew weaker and died. Man fed himself into the machine.

Peter rejoiced to see men do great things and dream great dreams. He wanted them to stretch out their arms to their brothers, because he knew that the surest way to find God, to find the good, was through one's brothers. Peter wanted this striving to result in a better physical life in which all men would be able to fulfill themselves, develop their capacities for love and worship, expressed in all the arts. He wanted them to be able to produce what was needed in the way of homes, food, clothing, so that there was enough of these necessities for everyone. A synthesis of "cult, culture, and cultivation," he called it, as he tried to give me the long view, the vision.

It was hard for me to understand what he meant, thinking as I always had in terms of cities and the immediate need of men for their weekly paycheck. Now I can see clearly what he was talking about, but I am faced with the problem of making others see it. I can well recognize the fact that, people being as they are, Peter's program is impossible. But it would become actual, given a people changed in heart and mind, so that they would observe the new commandment of love, or desire to.

Peter made you feel a sense of his mission as soon as you met him. He did not begin by tearing down, or by painting so intense a picture of misery and injustice that you burned to change the world. Instead, he aroused in you a sense of your own capacities for work, for accomplishment. He made you feel that you and all men had great and generous hearts with which to love God. If you once recognized this fact in yourself you would expect and find it in others. "The art of human contacts," Peter called it happily. But it was seeing Christ in others, loving the Christ you saw in others. Greater than this, it was having faith in the Christ in others without being able to see Him. Blessed is he that believes without seeing.

Although Peter came to me with sheaves of writing in every pocket, which he either read aloud or pressed upon me to read and study, he had not begun to write till late in life. All his writing, even his letters to me, were in phrased sentences, broken up to look like free verse. He used this device to compel attention, to make for more reflective reading, but also because some of his writings had a swing, a rhythm like verse. He liked to consider himself a troubadour of Christ, singing solutions to the world's ills, insinuating them into men's ears with catchy phrases.

I had been coffined in a bus for eight hours; I was anxious for quiet, for a cup of coffee. I was anxious to greet my child and Tessa and John [Dorothy's brother and sister-in-law]. In fact, had it not been for Tessa, with her unfailing hospitality, her ready attention to guests, I might not have met Peter at all. For my brother was a conventional American and Peter often gave the impression of being a dangerous and unbalanced radical when he began "indoctrinating" someone who was unprepared. I speak as the conventional American myself, in spite of years in the radical movement. Peter was the most persistent soul in the world, and he was looking for apostles to share his work. When he read the articles I had written in *America, The Commonweal,* and *The Sign,* he was convinced that I was the one who was to work with him. Before he knew me well, he went about comparing me to a Catherine of Siena who would move mountains and have influence on governments, temporal and spiritual. He was a man of enthusiasm and always saw great talents in people.

When he came back the next day, for we did not share ideas at length that first night, he began at once on what he called my education. "Indoctrination" was his word. He not only wished to give me a Catholic outline of history—but he also wished to repeat over and over again his program of action: round-table discussions, houses of hospitality, and agronomic universities. We were to popularize this program for immediate needs, which in itself would be the seed for a long-range program, a green revolution, by publishing a paper for the man in the street.

Since I came from a newspaper family, with my two older brothers working on newspapers at that time, and my father still a writer though no longer an editor, I could see the need for such a paper as Peter described.

But how were we going to start it?

Peter did not pretend to be practical along these lines. "I enunciate the principles," he declared grandly.

"But where do we get the money?" I asked him, clinging to the "we," though he was making clear his role as theorist.

"In the history of the saints, capital was raised by prayer. God sends you what you need when you need it. You will be able to pay the printer. Just read the lives of the saints."

St. Francis de Sales scattered leaflets like any radical. St. John of God sold newspapers on the streets. We didn't have to do things on a big scale, Peter made it clear.

I had been reading the life of Rose Hawthorne not long before, how she started what has since become a chain of cancer hospitals in a four-room tenement apartment such as the one I was living in. Why not start a newspaper in the same way? I began to look on our kitchen as an editorial office, my brother as an assistant to write heads and to help with mechanical makeup. Tamar and I could go out to sell papers on the streets! . . .

Finding that I could have twenty-five hundred copies of an eight-page tabloid printed for twenty-five dollars by the Paulist Press, I decided to use two small checks I had just received for articles for the first printing bill, rather than for the rent or gas or electric. We would sell the paper, I decided, for a cent a copy, to make it so cheap that anyone could afford to buy.

Peter had his own ideas as to what was to be in that paper. When the first issue came out the following May Day with articles about labor, strikes, unemployment, factual accounts, columns, features, in addition to half a dozen of Peter's "Easy Essays," as John named them, he protested.

"Everybody's paper is nobody's paper," he said. And I realized that in his simplicity, in his lofty concept of his mission, he wanted nothing but his own essays to be printed, over and over, and broadcast throughout the

country. He knew that he had a message. His confidence looked like conceit
and vanity to the unknowing. He had a message, and he was filled with the
glow of it, night and day. He lived for the work he was called to do, and
the days were not long enough for research in the library, for the round-
table discussions which took place wherever he happened to be, whether
in coffee shop, on street corners, public squares, streetcar or bus.

It was amazing how little we understood each other at first. But Peter
was patient. He wanted to call the paper *The Catholic Radical,* but with
my Communist background, I insisted on calling it *The Catholic Worker.*
Peter said, "Man proposes, but woman disposes." It was always with
humor, never with bitterness or malice, that we differed.

I did not fully realize why this was until much later, when I finally could
pin him down to talking about himself. He was a Frenchman; I was an
American. He was a man twenty years older than I and infinitely wiser. He
was a man; I was a woman. We looked at things differently. He was a
peasant; I was a city product. He knew the soil; I, the city. When he spoke
of workers, he spoke of men who worked at agriculture, building, at tools
and machines which were the extension of the hand of man. When I spoke
of workers, I thought of factories, the machine, and man the proletariat
and slum dweller, and so often the unemployed. . . .

Peter saw only the land movement as the cure for unemployment and
irresponsibility, and the works of mercy as the work at hand, ignoring the
immediate needs of the workers in the unions, their conflicts and demands.
I comforted myself by saying, "Men are more single-minded. They are the
pure of heart." But I continued to think in terms of unions and strikes as
an immediate means of bettering the social order. I could not blind myself
to the conflict between us, the conflict that would continue between one
or another who came to join in the movement later. When Peter said,
"Everybody's paper is nobody's paper," when he protested the coverage of
strike news, or the introduction of the personal element into the work by
feature story, he was envisaging a sheet carrying nothing but his own
phrased writings, regrouped, rewritten principles to apply to whatever
situation came up, local, federal, or world crisis. He had lived alone for so
long, had for so long been a single apostle, that he did not realize how
grim the struggle was going to be. . . .

When I was afterward accused of class-war tactics, I retorted with St.
Augustine: "The bottle always smells of the liquor it once held." But I did
not feel the criticism just.

Peter used to say when we covered strikes and joined picket lines,

"Strikes don't strike me." Yet he took the occasion to come out on the picket line to distribute leaflets upon which some single point was made. "To change the hearts and minds of men," he said. "To give them vision—the vision of a society where it is easier for men to be good."

The Long Loneliness

III

We loved him dearly, this Peter of ours, and revered him as a saint, but we neglected him, too. He asked nothing for himself, so he got nothing.

When we all lived together under one roof in the houses of hospitality, he seldom had a room of his own. Returning from trips around the country, he never knew whether there would be a bed for him. The younger editors had their own desks and were jealous of their privacy. But Peter not only had no place to lay his head but had no place for his books and papers—aside from his capacious pockets. He had no chair, no place at table, no corner that was particularly his. He was a pilgrim and a stranger on earth, using the things of this world as though he used them not, availing himself of only what he needed and discarding all excess baggage. I think of him walking down the street slowly, leisurely, deep in thought, his hands clasped behind him. He paid no attention to traffic lights; I suppose he put his faith in his guardian angel. . . .

Someone once described me in an interview as "authoritative." Later, listening to a tape recording of a talk I had given on the plight of agricultural workers, I had to admit that I did sound didactic. Since then, I have tried to be more gentle in my approach to others, so as not to make them feel that I am resentful of their comfort when I speak of the misery of the needy and the groaning of the poor. But if I *am* didactic it is because Peter Maurin was my teacher, because he gave me principles to live by and lessons to study, and because I am so convinced of the rightness of his proposals.

"How can you be so sure?" Mike Wallace once asked me in a television interview. He spoke with wonder rather than irritation, because he felt my confidence was rooted in religion. I told him that unless I felt sure I would not speak at all. If I were ever visited by doubts—either religious ones or doubts about my vocation in this movement—I would accept it as a temptation, as a great suffering that I must share with so much of the world today.

Even then, deep within, I would be sure; even though I said to myself, "I believe because I want to believe, I hope because I want to hope, I love because I want to love." These very desires would be regarded by God as He regarded those of Daniel, who was called a man of desires, and whom He rewarded.

Loaves and Fishes

DAY AFTER DAY

The undated selections in this chapter are taken from *House of Hospitality* (Sheed and Ward, 1939), a volume which combined articles from *The Catholic Worker* with more personal reflections. The rest of the chapter consists of editorials from the early issues of the paper, and of extracts from Dorothy's original column, "Day After Day."

To Our Readers

For those who are sitting on park benches in the warm spring sunlight.

For those who are huddling in shelters trying to escape the rain.

For those who are walking the streets in the all but futile search for work.

For those who think that there is no hope for the future, no recognition of their plight—this little paper is addressed.

It is printed to call their attention to the fact that the Catholic Church has a social program—to let them know that there are men of God who are working not only for their spiritual but for their material welfare.

*   *   *

It's time there was a Catholic paper printed for the unemployed. The fundamental aim of most radical sheets is the conversion of its readers to Radicalism and Atheism.

Is it not possible to be radical and not atheist?

Is it not possible to protest, to expose, to complain, to point out abuses and demand reforms without desiring the overthrow of religion?

In an attempt to popularize and make known the encyclicals of the Popes in regard to social justice and the program put forth by the Church for the "reconstruction of the social order," this news sheet, *The Catholic Worker,* is started.

It is not as yet known whether it will be a monthly, a fortnightly, or a weekly. It all depends on the funds collected for the printing and distribution. Those who can subscribe and those who can donate are asked to do so.

This first number of *The Catholic Worker* was planned, written, and edited in the kitchen of a tenement on Fifteenth Street, on subway platforms, on the El, the ferry. There is no editorial office; no overhead in the way of telephone or electricity; no salaries paid.

The money for the printing of the first issue was raised by begging small contributions from friends. A colored priest in Newark sent us ten dollars and the prayers of his congregation. A colored Sister in New Jersey, garbed also in holy poverty, sent us a dollar. Another kindly and generous friend sent twenty-five. The rest of it the editors squeezed out of their own earnings, and at that they were using money necessary to pay milk bills, gas bills, electric light bills.

By accepting delay the utilities did not know that they were furthering the cause of social justice. They were, for the time being, unwitting cooperators.

Next month someone may donate us an office. Who knows?

It is cheering to remember that Jesus Christ wandered this earth with no place to lay His head. *The foxes have holes and the birds of the air their nests, but the Son of Man has no place to lay His head.* And when we consider our fly-by-night existence, our uncertainty, we remember (with pride at sharing the honor) that the disciples supped by the seashore and wandered through cornfields picking the ears from the stalks wherewith to make their frugal meals.

May 1933

Out of Doors

It is another hot day and people go about gleaming in the sun, walking slowly as though to move were a feat of endurance. Children sit on the front steps with nothing on but a rag to cover them. Women return from markets with laden shopping bags, fruit, salads, hot-weather vegetables, walking as though they were half asleep. Even at six-thirty, when I go out to Mass, there is a heavy haze in the air.

But the little yard back of the office is cool and fresh because Mrs. Riedel hoses it first thing in the morning and mops down the back steps. The petunias and four-o'clocks are in bloom—the gorgeous cerise color the Mexican Indians so love and which they use in their serapes and woven rugs and chairs and baskets. The fig tree has little figs on it and the wild cucumber vine in the Fourteenth Street yard across the way is spilling over the fence. There is a breeze out here and it is pleasant to have early-morning coffee and the paper outside.

It is one of the compensations of poverty to have such a garden. In the front, the street is slummish. At night, one walks warily to avoid the garbage that is hurled out of the windows in sacks. There are odors, foul odors often, out in front. I will not be so realistic as to more than hint at them. But out behind the house there is the fresh green smell of growing things.

One bathes in a white tub next to the kitchen sink, and one is thankful that it is indeed a white tub instead of two slate wash tubs with the panel between removed. It is the only white tub in the house and the snobbish landlord put it in, in consideration of the fact that the tenants who lived here before used to live in Tudor City. Poor things, to have to move from Tudor City down to East Fifteenth Street! But there are smells up there, too. We were out walking last spring and exploring down below the arrogant heights and we were delighted to be assailed by the stockyard smells of a slaughterhouse. "Delighted," I say? That is class-warrish, to be delighted at some slight sharing of the rich in the miseries of the poor. But I must admit my delight and hug it to me. I do penance through my nose continually.

House of Hospitality

For Gentle Sabotage, Style, and Economy, Dine by Candlelight

Fashion item:

"Nowadays a note of elegance is introduced by the presence of candles on the dinner table." This should be of comfort to the workingman whose electricity has been turned off for nonpayment of bills or deposit.

"Dine by candlelight" is the slogan adopted by the men who have been thrown out of work by the Brooklyn Edison Electric Co., and they are soliciting the help of other consumers and urging their ultimate advantage, by advocating this little measure of peaceful sabotage.

But, as a matter of fact, candles are expensive and it is only hostesses with ambitions toward elegance, and ladies of fading charm who wish a softer light over their dining tables and drawing rooms, who can afford candles.

It is much more practical, though it doesn't make so good a slogan, to dine by kerosene lamp. You can buy a lamp in any little hardware store, and kerosene is cheap.

If you dine by candlelight (or by kerosene) one night a week, and if a few million follow your example, the Electric Light Company suffers severely. Of course, it is a shame to inflict suffering, but then the poor consumer does a lot of suffering too when it comes to paying the bills.

May 1933

And Now a Melancholy Note

Late fall is here. A haze hangs over the city. Fogs rise from the river, and the melancholy note of the river boats is heard at night. The leaves are dropping from the fig tree in the backyard. There is the smell of chestnuts in the air, but if you buy the chestnuts, most of them are wormy. It is better to make popcorn over the fire at night. For we have fires now. The kettle sings on the range in the kitchen (the range cost eight dollars secondhand and doesn't burn much coal), and visitors to *The Catholic Worker* office are drinking much tea and coffee. The stove in the front office has burst in its exuberance and has to be mended with stove clay and a piece of tin.

And there is also the smell of grapes in the air—rich, luscious Concord grapes. If this editorial has a melancholy note, it is not because chestnuts are wormy or because the stove has cracked, but because all our Italian neighbors are too poor this year to buy grapes and make wine. Grapes that used to be one dollar a box are now one dollar fifty. And the Italian fathers who love their wine and have it in lieu of fresh vegetables and fruits all during the long winter are still out of jobs or on four-day-a-month work relief and this year there is no pleasant smell of fermenting grapes, no disorderly heaps of mash dumped in the gutters.

And Mrs. Rubino and Mr. Scaratino and Mr. Liguori will not rent a winepress together this year, and the children will not hang over them with breathless interest in the mysterious basement while they manipulate the press rented for the house.

And what is worse, Mr. Rubino will not be dropping into the office of *The Catholic Worker,* when he sees our light late at night, to console us for our long hours by the gift of a milk bottle of wine.

For the long hard winter is before us. Evictions are increasing, people come in to ask us to collect winter clothes and to help them find apartments where relief checks will be accepted.

We must work, and we must pray, and we meditate as we write this that it would be so much easier for all our Italian friends to work and pray, to have courage to fight, and also to be patient, if they could make as usual their fragrant and cheering grape wine.

November 1933

Spiritual Discourse

Teresa, aged seven, is very much around the office these first cold days. Since *The Catholic Worker* has moved to the store downstairs, there is ample room for another assistant and her little desk.

She likes even better than sitting at a desk to crawl under the furniture coverings of a set of chairs and sofa that the young woman racktender at the Paulist church sent down as a contribution to our office furniture. There, ensconced in her tent with her little friend Freddy Rubino, I heard her talking the other day.

"There now," she said, "you have committed a mortal sin, and you haven't got God in your heart anymore."

Freddy is two years younger than herself. Freddy had a few minutes before kicked his mother in the shins and called her a pig and generally scandalized the neighborhood, though everyone should have been accustomed to witnessing these scenes at least once a day.

Teresa's reproof made Freddy indignant. "He is so there," he insisted. "He's right there."

"No, there's a devil there now."

"I don't want a devil there. I want God there. He is there."

"Well, all you have to do is to say you're sorry and it will be all right."

So that was settled.

Then there was the question of mortal and venial sin. "If you just do it suddenly, then it's not a mortal sin, but if you stop to think and do it anyway, then it is. For instance, if I decide I don't want to drink any cocoa milk and don't do it."

"I wouldn't be quite so extreme and rigorous," I told her. "It has to be a serious matter, and I'm sure it's not serious if you don't drink your milk. A cow can live on grass, so I guess you can live on the amount you eat."

"What I'd like to live on are cucumbers," Teresa decided. "Or maybe popcorn with ketchup on it."

Her ideas about heaven are just as original as her ideas about food. She has it all worked out with her friends in the backyard as to just what sort of mansion she is going to have in heaven. There will be a beach there with horseshoe crabs and spider crabs and a place where she can fish. And there will be no cities but only country places and there will be no quarrels or fights. . . .

For a while the children were playing ghosts and the two younger ones, Freddy and Teresa, were going around scared. Perhaps she was reassuring herself as well as them when I heard her talking out in the kitchen while they played one rainy afternoon.

They were all having a very good time and feeling very peaceful. I didn't know it then—I was listening, charmed at the angelic dialogue—but I found out afterward that they were mixing soap powder, cocoa, and coffee together and making the most delicious little pastries which they were proceeding to cook on an electric grill. It was the peculiar smell which informed me of their doings.

The conversation proceeded thus:

"There are no ghosts. Really there aren't," said Teresa.

"But there are spirits," the little girl from upstairs said.

"God is a Spirit and that's enough," Teresa decided.

I was reminded of a story Mother Clark up at the Cenacle of St. Regis had told me of a little girl who was being instructed for her first Holy Communion. They were asking her what a spirit was and when she could not answer they started asking her questions.

"Has a spirit got eyes or hair?"

"Has a spirit arms or legs?" And so on.

She agreed that a spirit had none of these things but she finally said brightly:

"But a spirit has feathers!"

Thank God for Pope Pius X, who urged early Communion. He was the one who said that it was sufficient for a child to know the difference between her daily food and the heavenly food she would receive.

I know that if anyone started asking Teresa any questions she would not be able to answer them. She has an aversion to answering questions. My only knowledge of her spiritual processes is through her conversations, either with other children or with me. She will volunteer information, but she will not have it drawn from her by direct questioning.

There was an article in the *Journal of Religious Instruction* recently about a series of questions asked twenty-five children of Teresa's age and their answers.

I tried out the questions on Teresa and she only scratched her head and acted irritated. Her answers were barely adequate.

And yet when I hear her talk, hear her wise little comments on things I say, I feel certain as to her spiritual knowledge.

About prayer, for instance, Freddy said that he did not know how to pray. Questioned by Teresa, he said that he merely repeated prayers after his mother. All he had to do to pray was to think every now and then of God, Teresa told him. "Just remember Him," she said. "Like after I go to Communion in the morning, then lots of times during the day I suddenly remember that I've got God. That's a prayer, too."

House of Hospitality

Scavengers

A deer gets trapped on a hillside and every effort is brought to bear to rescue him from his predicament. The newspapers carry daily features.

Mrs. A., with her four children and unemployed husband living on $1.50 a week, is trapped by economic circumstances and everyone is so indifferent that it took three or four afternoons of Mike Gunn's time to see to it that the Home Relief came to the rescue. Though Mike has enough to do with his Labor Guild over in Brooklyn, he was doing his bit as part of our Fifteenth Street Neighborhood Council.

Three little pigs are crowded into a too-small cage, and the case is brought into court, the judge's findings in the case being that pigs should not be crowded the way subway riders are. And a family of eight children, mother and father, are crowded in three rooms, and the consensus of opinion is that they're lucky to have that and why don't they practice birth control anyway. . . .

A scavenger hunt is the latest game of Society. "A hilarious pastime," the *New York Times* society reporter calls it, and describes in two and one half columns the asinine procedure of several hundred society and literary figures, guests at a party at the Waldorf-Astoria, surging forth on a chase through the highways and byways of Manhattan Island. "The scavengers' hunt of last night brought an enthusiastic response even from persons whose appetites for diversion are ordinarily jaded. The hunt was a search through the city streets for a ridiculously heterogeneous list of articles."

Any morning before and after Mass and straight on through the day, there is a "scavenger hunt" going on up and down Fifteenth Street outside the windows of *The Catholic Worker* and through all the streets of the city: people going through garbage and ash cans to see what they can find in the way of a heterogeneous list of articles. The *Times* does not state what these things were but probably the list was made up of something delightfully and quaintly absurd such as old shoes, bits of string, cardboard packing boxes, wire, old furniture, clothing, and food.

If the several hundred guests at the Waldorf had to scavenge night after night and morning after morning, the hunt would not have had such an enthusiastic response.

November 1933

Bedrooms

One afternoon last month we went up to the Municipal Lodging House of the City of New York and looked at the largest bedroom in the world there. The seventeen beds in a row, the eight rows stretching way out to the very end of a pier, two-tiered beds at that, were a grim sight, the collectivization of misery.

The huge vats of stew stirred with a tremendous ladle only emphasized the ugly state which the world is in today. Every night the men stand out on Twenty-fifth Street in long lines and are hustled through, catalogued, ticketed, stamped with the seal of approval, fed in a rush, and passed on to the baths, the doctor, the beds, all with a grim efficiency which gave testimony to the length of time this need has existed for the mass care of the impoverished.

One day last summer, I saw a man sitting down by one of the piers, all alone. He sat on a log, and before him was a wooden box on which he had spread out on a paper his meager supper. He sat there and ate with some pretense of human dignity, and it was one of the saddest sights I have ever seen.

The attendant who showed us around told of how the lame, the halt, and the blind who were being housed at the "Muni" were transported in a bus to a place which the Salvation Army runs for such men where they can sit inside all day out of the wind and rain. *But what about Catholic provision for such men?* There is none. Oh, for parish Houses of Hospitality!

If the largest bedroom in the world was a sad sight the women's dormitory was even sadder. At one end of it there were beds with little cribs by the side of them for women with babies. But women know that if they are forced to accept the hospitality of the city, their older children will be taken away and only infants left to them, so not many of them go there. Our escort told us of a family which had come in the night before. The family had been evicted, and the mother was so sick she had to be carted off to the hospital, and the man, the old grandmother, and the three children had to go to the city for relief. The older children were taken to the Children's Aid and the baby left with the grandmother. And what must have been the thoughts of the mother lying in the hospital, wondering where her mother, her children, and her husband were spending the night? What but thoughts of hatred and despair that such cruelty and inhumanity can exist today.

February 1934

Another Miracle, Please, St. Joseph

Our lives are made up of little miracles day by day. That splendid globe of sun, one street wide, framed at the foot of East Fourteenth Street in early-morning mists, that greeted me on my way out to Mass was a miracle that lifted up my heart. I was reminded of a little song of Teresa's, composed and sung at the age of two.

> I'll sing a song [she warbled]
> Of sunshine on a little house
> And the sunshine is a present for the little house.

Sunshine in the middle of January is indeed a present. We get presents, lots of them, around *The Catholic Worker* office. During the holidays a turkey, a ham, baskets of groceries, five pounds of butter, plum puddings, flannel nightgowns and doll-babies, sheets, washrags, and blankets descended on us. There was even the offer of a quarter of moose from Canada, but we didn't know where we could put it, so we refused it.

We appealed in our last issue for beds, and eight beds came. Our House of Hospitality for unemployed women is furnished now, and the surplus that comes in we will give to unemployed people in the neighborhood.

During this last cold snap, one of the girls from the apartment came in to tell us that they could use four more blankets, and that very afternoon a car drove up to the office and four blankets—beautifully heavy ones— were brought in by a chauffeur.

And so it goes. Books, food (two bottles of wine and a box of cigars!— And who sent them? we wonder), clothes, and bedding.

But now our cashbox is empty. We just collected the last pennies for a ball of twine and stamps and we shall take a twenty-five-cent subscription which just came in to buy meat for a stew for supper. But the printing bill, the one hundred and sixty-five dollars of it which remains unpaid, confronts us and tries to intimidate us.

But what is one hundred and sixty-five dollars to St. Joseph, or to St. Teresa of Avila either? We refuse to be affrighted (though of course the printer may be, "oh, he of little faith!").

Don Bosco tells lots of stories about needing this or that sum to pay rent and other bills and the money arriving miraculously on time. And he too was always in need, always asking, and always receiving.

A great many of our friends urge us to put our paper on a businesslike basis. But this isn't a business, it's a movement. And we don't know anything about business around here anyway. Well-meaning friends say, "But people get tired of appeals." We don't believe it. Probably most of our friends live as we do, from day to day and from hand to mouth, and as they get, they are willing to give. So we shall continue to appeal and we know that the paper will go on.

It's a choice of technique, after all. People call up offering us the services of their organizations to raise money. They have lists, they send out telephone and mail appeals. They are businesslike and most coldly impersonal. Though they may be successful in raising funds for Jewish, Catholic, and Protestant organizations and offer us several thousand a week, minus their commission, we can't warm up to these tactics. We learn ours from the Gospels and what's good enough for St. Peter and St. Paul is good enough for us. Their technique of revolution was the technique of Christ and it's the one to go back to.

And as for getting tired of our appeals, Jesus advocated importunity thus:

> Which of you shall have a friend, and shall go to him at midnight, and shall say to him, friend, lend me three loaves, because a friend of mine is come off his journey to me, and I have not what to set before him. And if he from within should answer and say, trouble me not, the door is now shut and my children are with me in bed and I cannot rise and give thee. Yet if he shall continue knocking, I say to you though he will not rise and give him because he is his friend, yet because of his importunity he will arise and give him as many as he needeth.

So our friends may expect us to importune and to continue to ask, trusting that we shall receive.

February 1934

Thank You!

The editors wish to thank all the good friends who responded so immediately to the letter of appeal sent out a few weeks ago. God is with us, the saints protect us. Each time we have asked for aid, the money was immediately forthcoming to pay each and every bill. True, this leaves nothing for the next printing bill, which will be due as you read this paper. But God seems to intend us to depend solely on Him. We must live this lesson of dependence on Him that we preach in these pages. Economic security, something every reader and we ourselves would like to have, is not for us. We must live by faith, from day to day, knowing that we have good friends in St. Joseph, St. Teresa, St. John Bosco, who lived through these same struggles themselves.

What security did the Blessed Virgin herself have as she fled in the night with the Baby in her arms to go into a strange country? She probably wondered whether St. Joseph would be able to obtain work in a foreign land, how they would get along, and anticipated the loneliness of being without her friends, her cousin St. Elizabeth, her other kinfolk.

We accept by faith the mystery of the Trinity. We accept by faith the Holy Eucharist. When Christ says, "This is My Body," we as Catholics believe. We believe many a hard saying, so why not believe those words—

> Seek ye first the kingdom of heaven and His justice and all these things shall be added unto you. . . . Your Father knoweth that you have need of all these things. . . . What man is there among you, of whom if his son ask bread, will reach him a stone? . . . If you, then, being evil, know how to give good gifts to your children, how much more will your Father, Who is in Heaven, give good things to them that ask Him?

It is hard, we realize, to quote the Gospel to men with empty stomachs. It is hard to preach holy poverty to those who suffer perforce from poverty not only for themselves but for their loved ones. But we wish to assure our readers that most of the people who are writing for and putting out this paper have known poverty—hunger and heat and cold; some have slept in city lodging houses, in doorways, in public parks, have been in the wards of city hospitals; have walked the city with their feet upon the ground searching for work, or just walking because they had no shelter to go to. *The Catholic Worker* is edited and written by workers, for workers.

And we thank the many workers, priests, and laymen who sent in their contributions this last month to keep us going, and we pray God to bless them all.

May 1934

Why Write About Strife and Violence?

If our stories this month are ominous in tone, and if our friends would wish that we concentrated more on the joy of the love of God and less on the class strife which prevails in industry, we remind them of the purpose of this paper.

It is addressed to the workers, and what is of interest to them is the condition of labor, and the attitude of the Church in regard to it.

If we attempt with undue optimism to minimize the crisis, if we do not recognize their plight, we are forcing them to turn to sheets such as the *Daily Worker,* which does take cognizance of their condition.

Those comfortable people, too, who do not realize the unfairness of this existing order need to be told of existing conditions. They are too apt to see things from the side of the employer, since the radio, the newspapers, and public interest are usually on the side of wealth and influence. If they cooperated with the worker instead of ranging themselves on the side of the employer, justice would prevail.

We wish to arouse, too, those indifferent Catholics to the crying need of a return to the spirit of Franciscan poverty and charity.

We recall to our comfortable readers, to whom these tales of strike and riot are something outside their ken, that the Red Cross has in many cases refused to give help to starving women and children when a strike was on. That it was the Communists who collected food and clothes for the families of miners waging their industrial battles down in Kentucky, for the families of the textile strikers in North Carolina. . . .

Is it to be left to the Communists to succor the oppressed, to fight for the unemployed, to collect funds for hungry women and children? . . .To feed the hungry, clothe the naked, shelter the homeless—these Corporal Works of Mercy are too often being done by the opposition, and to what purpose? To win to the banners of Communism the workers and their children.

These workers do not realize those words of St. Paul, "If I should distribute all my goods to feed the poor, and if I should deliver my body to be burned and have not charity [the love of God], it profiteth me nothing."

Most Catholics speak of Communists with the bated breath of horror. And yet those poor unfortunate ones who have not the faith to guide them are apt to stand more chance in the eyes of God than those indifferent Catholics who sit by and do nothing for "the least of these" of whom Christ spoke.

June 1934

Small Things

Today we are not content with little achievements, with small beginnings. We should look to St. Teresa, the Little Flower, to walk her little way, her way of love. We should look to St. Teresa of Avila, who was not content to be like those people who proceeded with the pace of hens about God's business, but like those people who on their own account were greatly daring in what they wished to do for God. It is we ourselves that we have to think about, no one else. That is the way the saints worked. They paid attention to what they were doing, and if others were attracted to them by their enterprise, why, well and good. But they looked to themselves first of all.

Do what comes to hand. Whatsoever thy hand finds to do, do it with all thy might. After all, God is with us. It shows too much conceit to trust to ourselves, to be discouraged at what we ourselves can accomplish. It is lacking in faith in God to be discouraged. After all, we are going to proceed with His help. We offer Him what we are going to do. If He wishes it to prosper, it will. We must depend solely on Him. Work as though everything depended on ourselves, and pray as though everything depended on God, as St. Ignatius says. . . .

I suppose it is a grace not to be able to have time to take or derive satisfaction in the work we are doing. In what time I have my impulse is to self-criticism and examination of conscience, and I am constantly humiliated at my own imperfections and at my halting progress. Perhaps I deceive myself here, too, and excuse my lack of recollection. But I do know how small I am and how little I can do and I beg You, Lord, to help me, for I cannot help myself.

House of Hospitality

Midwinter

Bundles of clothes came in the other day, including many overcoats, and they went out as fast they came in. I'd like to have everyone see the poor, worn feet, clad in shoes that are falling apart, which find their way to our office. A man came in this rainy morning and when he took off one dilapidated rag of footwear, his sock had huge holes in the heel and was soaking wet at that. We made him put on a dry sock before trying on the pair of shoes we found for him, and he changed diffidently, there under the eye of the Blessed Virgin on the bookcase, looking down from her shrine of Christmas greens. But his poor, red feet were clean. Most of the men and women who come in from the lodging houses and from the streets manage cleanliness, with the help of the public baths. I heard of one man who washed his underwear in the public baths and sat there as long as he could in that steam-laden, enervating atmosphere until it was not quite too wet to put on again. For the rest, it could dry on his skin. Not a pleasant thought in bitter weather. Many of the men do this, he said.

Our prayer for the new year is that the members may be "mutually careful one for another."

* * *

Going on the ferry over to Staten Island to take Teresa back to St. Patrick's, where she is going to school, the gulls stood out white against the gray sky. They swept and glided, swooping down into the water now and then after a fish. Their cries and the sound of the water as the boat churned through it were the only sounds in the wintry stillness. Then there was the walk with Teresa up the country road, past a thicket of birches with the blue-green twilight sky behind them. To one side of the road was a field of yellow grass, bent by a soft wind. Alongside a path through the fields there was a little brook gurgling cheerfully beneath the ice that caked it. There are still green things showing under the stubble, bits of wild carrot, the green of vines, even some wild geranium. And as the earth lost its color and darkened, there was still the radiance of a sunset flushing the sky.

January 1935

Notes to Myself

It is just after midnight and I have been sitting in the outer office alone with two mad creatures with God in their hearts. All three of us tormented in our various ways—all three of us alone, so completely alone, too. C.'s madness consists of going in for astrology—it is his passion and it must be regarded seriously. He is a young German and very solitary and inarticulate, except on the question of astrology.

The other, Bernard Adelson, I met when I spoke at Father Rothlauf's last year. He came down the next night and has been with us ever since, off and on, one time speaking in an inspired fashion of the Mystical Body, of other Christs, of the Psalms, quoting them in Hebrew, and then going off into a perfect mania of persecution talk, holding his head and speaking of madness and death.

As I sit I am weeping. I have been torn recently by people, by things that happen. Surely we are, here in our community, made up of poor lost ones, the abandoned ones, the sick, the crazed, and the solitary human beings whom Christ so loved and in whom I see, with a terrible anguish, the body of this death. And out in the streets wandering somewhere is Mr. Minas, solitary among a multitude, surrounded by us all day long, but not one of us save in his humanity, denying, not knowing—yet clinging to some dream, some ideal of beauty which he tries to express in the poetry which no one but he can read.

*   *   *

Franciscan spirit grows hereabouts. Last night Mr. Minas, who is devoted to our black cat, was discovered washing her chest with my washrag and drying her with my towel and then anointing her with a warming unguent for a bad cough! It is good I discovered him in the act. Then big Dan, our chief-of-staff on the streets of New York (he sells the paper, either on Fourteenth Street or in front of Macy's every day), took one of my blankets to cover the old horse who helps us deliver our Manhattan bundles of papers every month. He is truly a Catholic Worker horse, Dan says, and when they go up Fifth Avenue and pass St. Patrick's Cathedral, the horse genuflects!

Dan delivers the papers all over New York every month when the new issue comes out, and then during the month he sells. He likes to get next to some Communist who is selling the *Daily Worker,* and as the latter shouts, "Read the *Daily Worker,*" Dan replies, "Read *The Catholic Worker* daily!"

Once he saw me coming and modified his shout to "*Catholic Worker,* romance on every page!"

Mary Sheehan has been a faithful saleswoman on Fourteenth Street, too. One of her sallies was reported to me recently. A Communist passing by started cursing the Cardinal. "Why, he gets drunk every Saturday night with his housekeeper!" he said, hoping to get a rise out of Mary.

"And doesn't that just show how democratic he is," she retorted.

* * *

I went to the Cenacle at three this afternoon, going up on the bus through a heavy fog. The trees on the Drive were beautiful standing out so alone, the only things of beauty in a gray, dark world. I love such days; so much is hidden, and only single things like a tree or bush stand out. These are good days to walk, not too cold, and if you go down by the docks at the foot of Twenty-third or Fourteenth or Tenth Street, the world seems to come to an end right there. There is a rare stillness only broken by the sound of the water washing against the piers. And when, as along Riverside Drive, you have trees as well as the sense of the water (if you do not have the sight of it), there is a poignant midwinter beauty, a very restful interlude in a crowded life.

* * *

Two of the girls in the House of Hospitality have been fighting constantly. Today I felt so bad about it I could have wept. I am so enraged that anyone should so consistently, month after month, act in mean, little, underhand ways that I almost wanted to beat them both. My mind was in a turmoil and yet I could not stop it. I went to church leaving word for Tina to meet me there and she came and stayed until after the rosary. Afterwards we went to the movies and saw a really delightfully funny film with Butterworth in it, and then we went home, both of us with raging headaches. It had been very hot all day. At the house it was still noisy and I wept before going to sleep, and awoke with the same feeling of oppression. To Mass and Communion, still feeling oppressed, praying with distraction. It rather amused me to place the two girls together in the hands of our Blessed Mother. But it worked!

Despite my feeling of almost hopelessness and desperation, humanly speaking, I came through the day feeling singularly calm, peaceful, and happy.

Three conclusions were the result of my praying. First: My getting into a temper helped nobody. But remaining loving toward all helped to calm them all. Hence a great responsibility rests on me. Second: It was cruel to be harsh to anyone so absolutely dependent, as they are, humanly, on my kindness. Third: It is a healthy sign that they are not crushed and humbled toward other human beings by their own miseries. I mean, going around meekly for fear of me, or being humble out of human respect.

One must be humble only from a divine motive, otherwise humility is a debasing and repulsive attitude. To be humble and meek for love of God— that is beautiful. But to be humble and meek because your bread and butter depends on it is awful. It is to lose one's sense of human dignity.

Let reform come through love of God only, and from that love of God, love of each other. . . .

The aftereffects of last night's and this morning's heavy praying have been peace and joy and strength and thanksgiving, and a great deal of humility, too, at being so weak that God had to send me consolation to prepare me for the next trial.

I should know by this time that just because I *feel* that everything is useless and going to pieces and badly done and futile, it is not really that way at all. Everything is all right. It is in the hands of God. Let us abandon everything to Divine Providence.

And I must remember, too, that often beautiful scenery or a perfect symphony leaves me cold and dreary. There is nothing the matter with either the scenery or the music—it is myself. I have endured other miseries cheerfully at times. So I must be calm, patient, enduring, and meditate on the gifts of the Holy Spirit.

I am writing this for my consolation and courage some future day when God sees fit and thinks me strong enough to bear longer-continued crosses.

It is to remind myself so that maybe I will be stronger.

House of Hospitality

Security

Christ told Peter to put aside his nets and follow him. He told the rich young man to sell what he had and give to the poor and follow Him. He said that those who lost their lives for His sake should find them. He told his followers that if anyone begged for their coats to give up their cloaks, too. He spoke of feeding the poor, sheltering the homeless, of visiting those in prison and the sick, and also of instructing the ignorant. He said: "Inasmuch as ye have done it unto one of the least of these my brethren, ye have done it unto me." He said: "Be ye therefore perfect as your heavenly Father is perfect."

But the usual comment is: "You must distinguish between counsel and precept. You forget that He said also: 'All men take not this word, but they to whom it is given.' 'He that can take it, let him take it.' "

Paul Claudel said that young people have a hunger for the heroic, and too long they have been told: "Be moderate, be prudent."

Too long have we had moderation and prudence. Today is a time of crisis and struggle. Within our generation, Russia has rejected Christianity, Germany has rejected it, Mexico fights to exterminate it, in Spain there has been a war against religion, in Italy Fascism has exalted the idea of the state and, rejecting the Kingship of Christ, has now a perverted idea of authority.

In this present situation when people are starving to death because there is an overabundance of food, when religion is being warred upon throughout the world, our Catholic young people still come from schools and colleges and talk about looking for security, a weekly wage.

They ignore the counsels of the Gospels as though they had never heard of them, and those who are troubled in conscience regarding them speak of them as being impractical.

Why they think a weekly wage is going to give them security is a mystery. Do they have security on any job nowadays? If they try to save, the bank fails; if they invest their money, the bottom of the market drops out. If they trust to worldly practicality, in other words, they are out of luck.

If they sell their labor, they are prostituting the talents God gave them. College girls who work at Macy's—is this what their expensive training was for?—boys who go into business looking for profits—is this what their Catholic principles taught them?—are hovering on the brink of a precipice. They have no security and they know it. The only security comes in the following of the precepts and counsels of the Gospels.

If each unemployed nurse went to her pastor and got a list of the sick and gave up the idea of working for wages and gave her services to the poor of the parish, is there not security in the faith that God will provide? This is but one instance of using the talents and abilities that God has given to each one of us.

What right has any one of us to security when God's poor are suffering? What right have I to sleep in a comfortable bed when so many are sleeping in the shadows of buildings here in this neighborhood of the *Catholic Worker* office? What right have we to food when many are hungry, or to liberty when the Scottsboro boys and so many labor organizers are in jail?

To those in whose minds these questions are stirring, there are those words directed:

"Today if you shall hear My voice, harden not your hearts."

July–August 1935

To Christ—To the Land!

For those who have put to us the question "What have you to offer in the way of a constructive program for a new social order?" we have replied over and over, "Peter Maurin's three-point program of *Round-table Discussions, Houses of Hospitality, Farming Communes.*" This program is so simple as to be unsatisfactory to most, who look for something to be complicated before it can be successful. Remembering the words of St. Francis that we cannot know what we have not practiced, we have tried not only to publish a paper but to put our program into practice. From the very beginning we have sought clarification of thought through *The Catholic Worker,* through round-table discussions, forums, through circulating literature. We have had a workers' school where the finest scholars of the Church have come to teach. We have had a House of Hospitality now for two years, where we gave shelter to the homeless, fed the hungry, clothed the naked, and cared for the sick. We have tried, all of us, to be workers and scholars, and to combine work and prayer according to the Benedictine ideal. We have tried to imitate St. Francis in his holy poverty. Our aim has been to combat the atheism of the day by our devotion to the liturgical movement; to combat the bourgeois spirit by the Franciscan spirit; to oppose to class-war technique the performance of the works of mercy.

We have not altogether neglected the farming commune idea, inasmuch as we had a halfway house in Staten Island where children were given vacations, weekend conferences were held and the sick cared for, and a garden cultivated.

March 1 will see the start of a serious attempt to put into practice the third point in our program. We are going to move out on a farm, within a few hours of New York, and start there a true farming commune.

We are making this move because we do not feel that we can talk in the paper about something we are not practicing. We believe that our words will have more weight, our writings will carry more conviction, if we ourselves are engaged in making a better life on the land.

This does not mean that we are going to abandon the city, which we realize is above all the home of the dispossessed, of the forgotten. We shall keep a group in New York City and the work of the apostolate of labor will go on. We shall also be sending out apostles of labor from the farm, to scenes of industrial conflict, to factories and to lodging houses, to live and work with the poor. The columns of the paper will be filled as usual with industrial news, discussion of unionism, the cooperative movement, maternity guilds, relief, public and private. But there will be more space devoted to rural life problems, and you will hear from month to month how the work of the farming commune is progressing, the difficulties, the mistakes, and the progress of the work.

Help us in this venture, which is your venture, too. And pray with us that we get out of the city by March 1.

January 1936

Grumblers

There are general grievances in the air. And generally grievances against me. For having such people around, for instance, and "What's the sense of talking about a farming commune when you haven't any farmers? It'll never come to anything. There was all that talk of a summer school and nothing was done...." Past failures are not forgotten or excused.

If you *are* discouraged, others will relapse into a state of discouragement and hopeless anger at circumstances and each other. And if you are not discouraged, everyone tries to make you so and is angry because you are not. It is hard to know what tack to take. The only thing is to be oblivious, as Peter is, and go right on....

Most of the time when people talk of efficiency and organization, they are thinking of order, outward order. What they are really criticizing is our poverty, the fact that we spend money for food instead of for paint and linoleum. We are crowded as the poor are, with people sleeping in every available corner. We have no separate room for the clothes that come in; they are packed in boxes around the dining room and hung in one hall closet and in another closet off the dining room. We are often dirty because so many thousands cross our thresholds. We are dirty ourselves sometimes because we have no hot water or bath, because we have not sufficient clothes for changes—even because we are so busy with the poor and the sick that it is hard to take time to journey to the public baths to wash.

But what am I talking about? Why am I justifying myself and my family? I am ashamed of myself for getting indignant at such criticism. It just goes to show how much pride and self-love I have. But it has been hard lately. Not only outside criticism but criticism from within, the grumbling, the complaints, the insidious discontent spread around by a few—these trials are hard to bear.

However, the thing is to bear it patiently, to take it lightly, not to let it interfere with the work. The very fact that it is hard shows how weak I am. I should be happy, however, to think that God believes me strong enough to bear these trials, otherwise I would not be having them. Father Lallemant says that we must beware when things are going too smoothly. That is the time when no progress is made.

Oh dear, I am reminded of St. Teresa, who said, "The devil sends me so offensive a bad spirit of temper that at times I think I could eat people up."

House of Hospitality

A Death in the Family

The summer was hard, but the past few months have been harder. In the summer we were dealing with healthy, normal young people. In the fall there was not only one but half a dozen sick, mentally and physically, suddenly on hand to be cared for.

And then Joe Bennett came down to die. He had worked for the last year or so in the South, and when he became critically ill, the priest with whom he was working brought him North and put him on Welfare Island. Joe got in touch with us and begged to be allowed to go down to the country.

He was fatally ill, and felt that he was not going to recover, but he fought bitterly against death. He did not want to die and he knew that only a miracle could save him. He prayed frantically, almost rebelliously, for a miracle.

"How can God be good," he moaned every time he saw me, "to let me suffer like this? He must heal me. I don't want to die."

It was heartbreaking. Mrs. J. nursed him tenderly, brought him delicacies to tempt his appetite. He read, he had a little radio by his bedside. Outside the trees were turning red and gold. There was the sound of the waves crashing on the beach in the fall storms. It was too unbearably beautiful, he cried, and he did not want to die.

We took turns going down to see him to keep him company and to try to ease the strain in the house. But it was one day when no one was there but Mrs. J. that Joe took a turn for the worse, became delirious and began beating his head up against a radiator in bitter rebellion. Mrs. J. tried to hold him. Adelson ran to a neighbor's to phone for Father McKenna, the nearest priest. He was so unmanageable that the priest advised he be taken to a little private hospital down the bay about a mile and there he died a few days later. I had been to see him the morning before as he lay there semi-conscious, no longer suffering, no longer rebellious. He had received the last rites and once when he opened his eyes clearly for a moment, he said goodbye. I kissed him as I left. The next morning he died. And for months now I have felt guilty, because I was not there with him, because he was alone in the hospital and not with his friends those last terrible moments when the soul is leaving the body. We must be alone when we die, that I know, but I do know, too, that I would like to have friends beside me to hold my hand, to make me feel the strength of their prayers, their strong happy prayers that would see where I could not see, the peace and light of the world to come. But I was not there—Joe died alone, and he was the first one to help me that May Day we started *The Catholic Worker.* There will never a day pass but that I remember him in my prayers, and I pray he remembers us now. And I ask you who read this to pray that he has found refreshment, joy, and peace.

House of Hospitality

Only the Will Remains

Low in mind all day, full of tears.

What with the Easton, New York, Boston, Ottawa, Toronto, and Missouri groups, all discouraged, all looking for organization instead of self-organization, all of them weary of the idea of freedom and personal responsibility—I feel bitterly oppressed, yet confirmed in the conviction that we have to emphasize personal responsibility at all costs. It is most certainly at the price of bitter suffering for myself. For I am just in the position of a dictator trying to legislate himself out of existence. They accept my regime which emphasizes freedom and personal responsibility, but under protest. They all complain at the idea of there being this freedom, that there is no boss.

Today I just happened to light on Dostoevsky's "Grand Inquisitor," which was most apropos. Freedom—how men hate it and chafe under it, how unhappy they are with it.

*   *   *

"Are we trying to make a farm here, or aren't we?"

A statement of that kind, an attitude of criticism of all that Peter and I stand for, has the power to down me completely, so that I feel utterly incapable of going to Boston and meeting all their trials and discourage- ments. Nothing but the grace of God can help me, but I feel utterly lacking, ineffective.

In town the usual crosses: Carney calling us all racketeers, calling the spiritual reading pious twaddle; E. with his vile accusations; the misery of M. and P.; Kate's illness; the threatened suit against us; the bills piling up—these things to be topped by such a lack of understanding of the personalist idea from those from whom you expect the most, lays me low. Since I got back from Pittsburgh, I have had this completely alone feeling. A temptation of the devil, doubtless, and to succumb to it is a lack of faith and hope. There is nothing to do but bear it, but my heart is as heavy as lead, and my mind dull and uninspired. A time when the memory and understanding fail one completely and only the will remains, so that I feel hard and rigid, and at the same time ready to sit like a soft fool and weep.

Tonight Teresa had a nosebleed, a headache and a stomachache, and although the latter probably came from eating green pears, as she confessed, still to think of the little time I have with her, being constantly on the go, having to leave her to the care of others, sending her away to school so that she can lead a regular life and not be subject to the moods and vagaries of the crowd of us! This is probably the cruelest hardship of all. She is happy, she does not feel torn constantly as I do. And then the doubt arises, probably she too feels that I am failing her, just as the crowd in Mott Street and the crowd here feel it.

"You are always away."

And then when I get to Boston—

"This is your work; why aren't you up here more often?"

Never before have I had such a complete sense of failure, of utter misery.

"O spiritual soul, when thou seest thy desire obscured, thy will arid and constrained, and thy faculties incapable of any interior act, be not grieved at this, but look upon it rather as a great good, for God is delivering thee from thyself, taking the matter out of thy hands. . . ." —St. John of the Cross.

* * *

In Boston for three days. Spoke to large group and they collected forty dollars. Nothing in the bank and two checks bouncing. Free-for-all fight on personalism and Fascism. Took boat at five for New York. Still low and dragged out. Feeling nothing accomplished. Spoke at the summer school

Thursday, ineffectively, breaking down as to voice right on the platform. Mr. Schwartz drove me down here where the atmosphere is morose and the weather does not help. Reading Caussade and New Testament and hiding my sadness from others does help.

House of Hospitality

Thanksgiving

The trees are getting bare, but still it stays warm. Coming down at night from the city, the warm, sweet smell of the good earth enwraps one like a garment. There is the smell of rotting apples; or alfalfa in the barn; burning leaves; of wood fires in the house; of pickled green tomatoes and baked beans.

Now there is a warm feeling of contentment about the farm these days— the first summer is over, many people have been cared for here, already. From day to day we did not know where the next money to pay bills was coming from, but trusting to our cooperators, our readers throughout the country, we went on with the work. Now all our bills are paid and there is a renewed feeling of courage on the part of all those who are doing the work, a sense of confidence that the work is progressing.

This month of thanksgiving will indeed be one of gratitude to God. For health, for work to do, for the opportunities He has given us of service; we are deeply grateful, and it is a feeling that makes the heart swell with joy.

During the summer when things were going especially hard in more ways than one, I grimly modified grace before meals: "We give Thee thanks, O Lord, for these Thy gifts, and for all our tribulations, from Thy bounty, through Christ our Lord, Amen." One could know of certain knowledge that tribulations were matters of thanksgiving; that we were indeed privileged to share in the sufferings of Our Lord. So in this month of thanksgiving, we can be thankful for the trials of the past, the blessings of the present, and be heartily ready at the same time to embrace with joy any troubles the future may bring us.

November 1936

The Use of Force

Christ Our Lord came and took upon Himself our humanity. He became the Son of Man. He suffered hunger and thirst and hard toil and temptation. All power was His but He wished the free love and service of men. He did not force anyone to believe. St. Paul talks of the liberty of Christ. He did not coerce anyone. He emptied Himself and became a servant. He showed the way to true leadership by coming to minister, not to be ministered unto. He set the example and we are supposed to imitate Him. We are taught that His kingdom was not of this earth. He did not need pomp and circumstance to prove Himself the Son of God.

His were hard sayings, so that even His own followers did not know what He was saying, did not understand Him. It was not until after He died on the Cross, it was not until He had suffered utter defeat, it would seem, and they thought their cause was lost entirely; it was not until they had persevered and prayed with all the fervor and desperation of their poor loving hearts, that they were enlightened by the Holy Spirit, and knew the truth with a strength that enabled them to suffer defeat and martyrdom in their turn. They knew then that not by force of arms, by the bullet or the ballot, would they conquer. They knew and were ready to suffer defeat— to show that great love which enabled them to lay down their lives for their friends.

And now the whole world is turning to "force" to conquer. Fascist and Communist alike believe that only by the shedding of blood can they achieve victory. Catholics, too, believe that suffering and the shedding of blood "must needs be," as Our Lord said to the disciples at Emmaus. But their teaching, their hard saying, is that they must be willing to shed every drop of their own blood, and not take the blood of their brothers. They are willing to die for their faith, believing that the blood of martyrs is the seed of the Church.

Our Lord said, "Destroy this temple and in three days I will raise it up." And do not His words apply not only to Him as Head of His Church but to His members? How can the Head be separated from the members? The Catholic Church cannot be destroyed in Spain or in Mexico. But we

do not believe that force of arms can save it. We believe that if Our Lord
were alive today he would say as He said to St. Peter, "Put up thy sword."

Christians, when they are seeking to defend their faith by arms, by force
and violence, are like those who said to Our Lord, "Come down from the
Cross. If you are the Son of God, save Yourself."

But Christ did not come down from the Cross. He drank to the last
drop the agony of His suffering, and was not part of the agony the hopelessness, the unbelief, of His own disciples?

Christ is being crucified today, every day. Shall we ask Him with the
unbelieving world to come down from the Cross? Or shall we joyfully, as
His brothers, "complete the sufferings of Christ"?

In their small way, the unarmed masses, those "littlest ones" of Christ,
have known what it was to lay down their lives for principle, for their
fellows. In the history of the world there have been untold numbers who
have laid down their lives for Our Lord and His Brothers. And now the
Communist is teaching that only by the use of force, only by killing our
enemies, not by loving them and giving ourselves up to death, giving
ourselves up to the Cross, will we conquer.

If 2,000 have suffered martyrdom in Spain, is that suffering atoned for
by the death of the 90,000 in the Civil War? Would not those martyrs
themselves have cried out against more shedding of blood?

Prince of Peace, Christ our King, Christ our Brother, Christ the Son of
Man, have mercy on us and give us the courage to suffer. Help us to make
ourselves "a spectacle to the world and to angels and to men." Help Your
priests and people in Spain to share in Your suffering, and in seeming
defeat, giving up their lives, without doubt there will be those like the
centurion standing at the foot of the Cross who will say, "Indeed, these
men are the sons of God."

November 1936

Mysteries

The happiest and most joyful event of the month was the birth of a calf on
the Catholic Worker farm. At three o'clock in the afternoon Victor left his
pots and pans to go up to the barn cistern for water and looked in to say
hello to the cow. She was placidly munching then. An hour later Jim and

John Filliger went in, and there was the calf. I got down to the farm three hours later and the little one was gamboling around, answering to the name of Bess, and actually cavorting with the joy of life that was in her.

The boys had fixed up the barn, new roof, new sides, whitewashed within, lots of bedding on the floor, and everything so snug and bright that it was a pleasure to contemplate the scene. It was dark and the light of the lantern cast long shadows. Never again will I meditate on the Third Joyful Mystery without thinking of that scene which brought home so closely the birth of Our Saviour amidst the kindly beasts of the field.

We were all so happy, and it was one of those moments of pure unalloyed joy so rare in this life.

Contrasted with this warm, homely scene is the one at Mott Street every morning when a hundred men or so come in to have cups of coffee. They are without coats, many of them without underwear. Their feet show bare through the cracks in their shoes. We haven't even women's sweaters to give them.

We didn't have any intention of starting a coffee line. When we didn't have clothes we invited the men to have a cup of coffee. With the cold weather the group has grown steadily larger.

There are bright aspects to the morning work. One of them is the radio hour of symphonic music over WNYC. Thanks be to God for that. Another bright spot is contemplating how men, deprived of all worldly goods, insufficiently clad and fed, maintain their courage and dignity. Of course, there are those who drink and I must confess to a lack of patience with them. But the majority of them are truly men and I respect them for their endurance and for their patience, and for the hope which they cling to in the face of tremendous odds.

December 1936

They Knew Him in the Breaking of Bread

Every morning about four hundred men come to Mott Street to be fed. The radio is cheerful, the smell of coffee is a good smell, the air of the morning is fresh and not too cold, but my heart bleeds as I pass the lines of men in front of the store which is our headquarters. The place is packed—not another man can get in—so they have to form a line. Always we have hated lines, and now the breakfast which we serve of cottage cheese and rye bread and coffee has brought about a line. It is an eyesore to the community. This little Italian village which is Mott Street and Hester Street, this little community within the great city, has been invaded by the Bowery, by the hosts of unemployed men, by no means derelicts, who are trying to keep body and soul together while they look for work. It is hard to say, matter-of-factly and cheerfully, "Good morning," as we pass on our way to Mass. It was the hardest to say "Merry Christmas" or "Happy New Year" during the holiday time, to these men with despair and patient misery written on many of their faces.

One felt more like taking their hands and saying, "Forgive us—let us forgive each other! All of us who are more comfortable, who have a place to sleep, three meals a day, work to do—we are responsible for your condition. We are guilty of each other's sins. We must bear each other's burdens. Forgive us and may God forgive us all!"

*   *   *

The work must go on. We have placed our troubles in the hands of St. Joseph. I burned a candle before his altar yesterday morning and contemplated the gallant figure of the workman saint as he stood there, his head flung back, his strong arm embracing the Child, a smile on his face as he looked down at the congregation of kneeling workers at Mass. We told him frankly:

"You must help us. The Holy Father says that the masses are lost to the Church. We must reach them, we must speak to them and bring them to the love of God. The disciples didn't know Our Lord on that weary walk to Emmaus until He sat down and ate with them. 'They knew Him in the breaking of bread.' And how many loaves of bread are we breaking with our hungry fellows these days—13,500 or so this last month. Help us to do this work, help us to know each other in the breaking of bread! In knowing each other, in knowing the least of His children, we are knowing Him.''

We were saying last night that if we could have foreseen the hordes that were to come to us the past two months, we never would have had the courage to begin. But we can only work day to day.

February 1937

Michael Martin, Porter

I find a little paragraph in my notebook, "Michael Martin, porter, idle for five years, brought in $2."

It was a thanksgiving offering, he explained, and he wanted to give it to some of our children in honor of his daughter in Ireland.

And I remembered how I spoke down in Palm Beach last month before the Four Arts Club, on the invitation of a convert. They told me, when I had finished, "You know we never pay speakers," and another woman said, with a tremor, "Miss Day, I hope you can convey to your readers and listeners that we would give our very souls to help the poor, if we saw any constructive way of doing it." And still another told me, "The workers come to my husband's mill and beg him with tears in their eyes to save them from unions. I hope you don't mind my saying so, but I think you are all wrong when it comes to unions."

They all were deeply moved, they told me, by the picture of conditions in Arkansas and the steel districts and the coal-mining districts, but: "You can't do anything with them, you know, these poor people. It seems to me the best remedy is birth control and sterilization."

We are told always to keep a just attitude toward the rich, and we try. But as I thought of our breakfast line, our crowded house with people sleeping on the floor, when I thought of cold tenement apartments around us, and the lean gaunt faces of the men who come to us for help, desperation in their eyes, it was impossible not to hate, with a hearty hatred and with a strong anger, the injustices of this world.

St. Thomas says that anger is not a sin, provided there is no undue desire for revenge. We want no revolution; we want the brotherhood of men. We want men to love one another. We want all men to have sufficient for their needs. But when we meet people who deny Christ in His poor, we feel, "Here are atheists indeed."

At the same time as I put down these melancholy thoughts, I am thinking of Michael Martin, porter, and the hosts of readers and friends of *The Catholic Worker* who have spread the work far and wide, who not only help us to keep the coffee line going, but who on their own account are performing countless works of mercy. And my heart swells with love and gratitude to the great mass of human beings who are one with their fellows, who love Our Lord and try to serve Him and show their love to His poor.

Our pastor said recently that sixty million of our one hundred and thirty million here in the United States professed no religion, and I thought with grief that it was the fault of those professing Christians who repelled the others. They turned first from Christ crucified because He was a poor worker, buffeted and spat upon and beaten. And now—strange thought— the devil has so maneuvered that the people turn from Him because those who profess Him are clothed in soft raiment and sit at well-spread tables and deny the poor.

April 1937

Letter to the Unemployed

For two and a half months I have been traveling through the country, visiting Detroit, Cleveland, Chicago, Los Angeles, San Francisco, New Orleans, and stopping off at country places in between. And everywhere I have been meeting the unemployed—around the steel mills, the employ- ment agencies, the waterfronts, around the "skid rows" and Boweries of this country, out in the rural districts where the sharecroppers and tenant farmers face lean months of hunger.

Now I am back on Mott Street, and as I get up at six-thirty there you are, a long line of hungry men extending all the way to Canal Street, waiting for the coffee and apple butter sandwiches we have to offer.

I remember how hard it was last Christmas to face you men. How could one say "Merry Christmas" to you who are gaunt and cold and ragged? Even the radio with its recipes and offerings of clothes on the installment plan, interspersed with music, did little to brighten things.

It is hard to preach the Gospel to men with empty stomachs, Abbé Lugan said. We are not a mission. We turn off the melancholy religious offerings on the radio in the morning. Religion is joy in the Holy Spirit. "Religion is a fire; it is like the coming of the Paraclete, 'a mighty wind rising'; it is a passion, the most powerful passion known to man. For religion is 'mighty to God unto the pulling down of fortifications.' Religion is a battle," writes Father Gillis.

Because it is a battle, and because you are not weaklings, we fight our own inclinations to feed only bodies to the small extent we can and let this editorial go. But it is a battle to hang on to religion when discouragement sets in. It is a battle to remember that we are made in the image and likeness of God when employers, treating you with less consideration than animals, turn you indifferently away. It is a fierce battle to maintain one's pride and dignity, to remember that we are brothers of Christ, who ennobled our human nature by sharing it.

But that very thought should give courage and should bring hope.

Christ, the Son of Man, lived among us for thirty-three years. For many of those years He lived in obscurity. When He was a baby His foster father had to flee with Him into Egypt. Joseph was a carpenter, a common laborer, and probably had no more savings than the majority of workers. When he tramped the long weary road, in the heat and dust of the deserts, he, too, and Mary and the Child were doubtless hungry. Do any of those hitchhikers, fleeing from the dust bowl into southern California across mountain and desert, remember, as they suffer, the flight into Egypt?

George Putnam, who has charge of our Los Angeles house, told me of picking up a man in the desert so starved that for the remaining days of the trip he could hold neither food nor water. Occasionally they had to stop the car and let him lie out on the ground to still the convulsive agony of his stomach. While I was in Los Angeles a young couple came to our place carrying a month-old baby and leading another eighteen months old. Some kindly worker had given them a lift on the last lap of their journey and turned his room over to them since he worked nights and could sleep days. That traveler, the father of the two little ones, was also a carpenter. Did anyone see Joseph in this unemployed man? Did they see the Holy Family, epitomized in this little group? Did they see Christ in the worker who helped them?

Christ was a worker and in the three years He roamed through Palestine

He had no place to lay His head. But He said, "Take no thought for what ye shall eat and where ye shall sleep, or what ye shall put on. Seek ye first the Kingdom of God and His righteousness and all these things shall be added unto you. . . . For your Heavenly Father knoweth that you have need of these things."

For one year now, our coffee line has been going on. Right now we are making seventy-five gallons of coffee every morning. There are too many of you for us, who wait on the line, to talk to you. We must think of the other fellow waiting out in the cold, as you remember, for you are very prompt in finishing your breakfast and making way for them. It is a grim and desperate struggle to keep the line going in more ways than one.

It is hard, I repeat, to talk to you of religion. But without faith in each other, we cannot go on. Without hope we cannot go on. Without hope we cannot live. To those who are without hope, I remind you of Christ, your brother. Religion, thought of in terms of our brotherhood through Christ, is not the opiate of the people. It is a battle "mighty to God unto the pulling down of fortifications." Do not let either capitalist or Communist kill this noble instinct in you.

December 1937

End of the Line

Last night, going downtown on the Third Avenue El, there was a shabby black-haired man with a strong impassive face sitting in the corner by the door with his eyes closed. Just before we got to each stop he called the station: "Next stop Chatham Square; change here for City Hall. This is a South Ferry train. . . . Next stop Franklin Square. . . . Next stop South Ferry. This is the end of the line . . . all out for South Ferry."

Other people sitting in the car, respectable, well-dressed people—people with jobs, people with families, people going to see their friends or coming from visits, a regular Sunday crowd—all laughed at this strange man, sitting there, his eyes closed, his face so impassive, calling the stations in a strong, loud voice.

They thought he was drunk. Maybe he was. They thought, "Just another bum going down to South Ferry to sleep at the Muni." Maybe he was.

His clothes were rags. He had no overcoat and it was fifteen above zero.

He had on two pairs of trousers; you could see one hanging below the other. He had on a ragged sweater under his too-small coat.

What was the story behind those closed eyes? What were the pictures in that tired brain, as the man called out, "South Ferry, last stop . . . the end of the line, all out for South Ferry."

He must have worked on the Elevated once. He must have had the job of opening and closing the gates, calling the stations, going to the end of the line at South Ferry and then up to the Bronx, down and up, all day long. A job that meant a paycheck, a job that was useful; he was serving others, not exploiting them, not making money off their labor.

Perhaps he thought of the home at the end of the last trip, of a warm house, a meal awaiting him, time to read the paper and listen to the radio.

Now he is one of the dispossessed. Now he possesses neither clothing, shelter, food. Now where is his family?

Nine million out of work throughout the country and plenty of good, constructive work to be done—homes to be built, schools, roads, hospitals. But we're not talking much about the unemployed now. We are talking about war and armaments.

These are the men on our breadlines. These are the men who come to us for shelter, for clothing. And while we are trying to change the social order, while we are trying to build a new civilization within the shell of the old, we must perform the Works of Mercy and take care of our brothers in need.

February 1940

A Lifetime Job

"Hell is not to love anymore," writes Georges Bernanos in *The Diary of a Country Priest*. I felt when I read this that the blackness of hell must indeed have descended on Our Lord in His agony.

The one thing that makes our work easier most certainly is the love we bear for each other and for the people for whom we work. The work becomes difficult only when there is quarreling and dissension and when one's own heart is filled with a spirit of criticism.

In the past, when I have spoken on the necessity of mutual charity, of self-criticism rather than criticism of others, the accusation has been made that I talk to the men as though they were angels, that I do not see their faults. Which is certainly not true.

The difficulty for me is not in *not* seeing the other person's faults, but in seeing and developing his virtues. A community of lay people is entirely different from a religious community like the Benedictines. We must imitate them by thinking in terms of work and prayer. But we must always remember that those who come to us are not here voluntarily, many of them, but because of economic circumstances. They have taken refuge with us. There is the choice of being on the streets, taking city care such as it is, or staying with us. Even many of the young "leaders" who give up home and position to come to help in the work are the rebel type and often undisciplined. Their great virtues often mean correspondingly great faults.

Yet those who are interested in the movement fail to see why it does not run as smoothly as a religious movement. They expect our houses and farms to be governed as a religious community is ruled, and in general they take the attitude that I am the one in authority who should rule with an iron hand, the others accepting this willingly. Truly the position of authority is the difficult one.

One of the difficulties of the work is to find those who are willing to assume authority. Leaders are hard to find. The very best in our groups, members of unions for instance, are steadfast, humble, filled with the love of God and their fellows, and their very virtues make it hard for them to assume leadership. Often, then, they leave it to the articulate ones who are often most articulate about the wrongdoings of others. They leave the foremost positions to those who like to talk rather than to do, to those who are aggressive and pugnacious and who do the movement harm rather than good. If they are not saying the wrong thing, enunciating the wrong ideas—being politicians, in other words—then they are *saying* but not *doing,* and even doing contrary to what they are saying.

It is human to dislike being found fault with. If you point out faults, rather than point out the better way of doing things, then the sting is there, and resentments and inactivity are the results. "What's the use of doing anything, it's all wrong!" Such childishness! But human beings are like that, and we must recognize their faults and try in every possible way to bring out their virtues.

On a visit to a group, there are always a half-dozen who are filled with complaints. If you try to turn their criticisms so as to change their attitude of mind, you are "refusing to listen" to them. You don't give them a chance to show you how wrong everything is. You don't know what is going on. It is in vain that you assure them you do know what is going on, just how faulty different ones have been. No, that is not enough, if you treat all with equal patience. Then you are not paying any attention to the complaints. Positive work to overcome obstacles such as people's temperaments is not enough for the fault-finders. They want recriminations and reprimands. "You are going to let him get away with that?" is the cry, when you try with courtesy and sympathy and respect to draw people together and induce cooperation.

It is very trying to receive so many complaints and not to be able to do anything about them. Those who do not complain and who try to work along the positive method are accused of being yes-men, and those who tell on each other and who always have some tale of woe are informers. So in either case there is trouble.

Oh yes, my dear comrades and fellow workers, I see only too clearly how bad things are with us all, how bad you all are, and how bad a leader I am. I see it only too often and only too clearly. It is because I see it so clearly that I must lift up my head and keep in sight the aims we must always hold before us. I must see the large and generous picture of the new social order wherein justice dwelleth. I must hold always in mind the new earth where God's Will will be done as it is in heaven. I must hold it in mind for my own courage and for yours.

The new social order as it could be and would be if all men loved God and loved their brothers because they are all sons of God! A land of peace and tranquillity and joy in work and activity. It is heaven indeed that we are contemplating. Do you expect that we are going to be able to accomplish it here? We can accomplish much, of that I am certain. We can do much to change the face of the earth, in that I have hope and faith. But these pains and sufferings are the price we have to pay. Can we change men in a night or a day? Can we give them as much as three months or even a year? A child is forming in the mother's womb for nine long months, and it seems so long. But to make a man in the time of our present disorder with all the world convulsed with hatred and strife and selfishness, that is a lifetime's work and then too often it is not accomplished.

Even the best of human love is filled with self-seeking. To work to increase our love for God and for our fellow man (and the two must go hand in hand), this is a lifetime job. We are never going to be finished.

Love and ever more love is the only solution to every problem that comes up. If we love each other enough, we will bear with each other's faults and burdens. If we love enough, we are going to light that fire in the hearts of others. And it is love that will burn out the sins and hatreds that sadden us. It is love that will make us want to do great things for each other. No sacrifice and no suffering will then seem too much.

Yes, I see only too clearly how bad people are. I wish I did not see it so. It is my own sins that give me such clarity. If I did not bear the scars of so many sins to dim my sight and dull my capacity for love and joy, then I would see Christ more clearly in you all.

I cannot worry much about your sins and miseries when I have so many of my own. I can only love you all, poor fellow travelers, fellow sufferers. I do not want to add one least straw to the burden you already carry. My prayer from day to day is that God will so enlarge my heart that I will see you all, and live with you all, in His love.

House of Hospitality

WORKS OF MERCY

Aims and Purposes

For the sake of new readers, for the sake of men on our breadlines, for the sake of the employed and unemployed, the organized and unorganized workers, and also for the sake of ourselves, we must reiterate again and again our aims and purposes.

Together with the Works of Mercy, feeding, clothing, and sheltering our brothers, we must indoctrinate. We must "give reason for the faith that is in us." Otherwise we are scattered members of the Body of Christ, we are not "all members one of another." Otherwise our religion is an opiate, for ourselves alone, for our comfort or for our individual safety or indifferent custom.

We cannot live alone. We cannot go to heaven alone. Otherwise, as Péguy said, God will say to us, "Where are the others?"

If we do not keep indoctrinating, we lose the vision. And if we lose the vision, we become merely philanthropists, doling out palliatives.

The vision is this. We are working for "a new heaven and a new *earth*, wherein justice dwelleth." We are trying to say with action, "Thy will be done on *earth* as it is in heaven." We are working for a Christian social order.

We believe in the brotherhood of man and the Fatherhood of God. This teaching, the doctrine of the Mystical Body of Christ, involves today the issue of unions (where men call each other brothers); it involves the racial question; it involves cooperatives, credit unions, crafts; it involves Houses of Hospitality and farming communes. It is with all these means that we can live as though we believed indeed that we are all members one of another, knowing that when "the health of one member suffers, the health of the whole body is lowered."

This work of ours toward a new heaven and a new earth shows a correlation between the material and the spiritual, and, of course, recognizes the primacy of the spiritual. Food for the body is not enough. There must be food for the soul. Hence the leaders of the work, and as many as we can induce to join us, must go daily to Mass, to receive food for the soul. And as our perceptions are quickened, and as we pray that our faith be increased, we will see Christ in each other, and we will not lose faith in those around us, no matter how stumbling their progress is. It is easier to have faith that God will support each House of Hospitality and farming commune and supply our needs in the way of food and money to pay bills, than it is to keep a strong, hearty, living faith in each individual around us—to see Christ in him. If we lose faith, if we stop the work of indoctrinating, we are in a way denying Christ again.

We must practice the presence of God. He said that when two or three are gathered together, there He is in the midst of them. He is with us in our kitchens, at our tables, on our breadlines, with our visitors, on our farms. When we pray for our material needs, it brings us close to His humanity. He, too, needed food and shelter, He, too, warmed His hands at a fire and lay down in a boat to sleep.

When we have spiritual reading at meals, when we have the rosary at night, when we have study groups, forums, when we go out to distribute literature at meetings, or sell it on street corners, Christ is there with us. What we do is very little. But it is like the little boy with a few loaves and fishes. Christ took that little and increased it. He will do the rest. What we do is so little we may seem to be constantly failing. But so did He fail. He met with apparent failure on the Cross. But unless the seed fall into the earth and die, there is no harvest.

And why must we see results? Our work is to sow. Another generation will be reaping the harvest.

When we write in these terms, we are writing not only for our fellow workers in thirty other houses, to other groups of Catholic Workers who are meeting for discussion, but to every reader of the paper. We hold with the motto of the National Maritime Union, that every member is an organizer. We are not speaking of mass action. We are addressing each individual reader of *The Catholic Worker*.

The work grows with each month, the circulation increases, letters come in from all over the world. It is a new way of life. But though we grow in numbers and reach far-off corners of the earth, essentially the work depends on each one of us, on our way of life, the little works we do.

"Where are the others?" God will say. Let us not deny Him in those about us. Even here, right now, we can have that new earth, wherein justice dwelleth!

February 1940

"And There Remained
Only the Very Poor"

Those were the words contained in a news account of the evacuation of
Paris. But they apply to New York in the summer. The poor cannot get
away. There is always a residue of the destitute which remains in the city
like mud in a drained pond. You see them in the parks, you see them lying
on the sidewalk in broad daylight along the Bowery, that street of forgotten
men. You see them drifting about the city, from one end to the other.

They come to us in droves: eight hundred every morning on the coffee
line; one hundred and twenty-five for lunch and again for supper. It is an
informal crowd at noon. They start gathering in the yard, men who have
passed the word along to other transients, homeless ones, that perhaps
there is food to be had. Many days the soup runs short and then there is
only coffee and cake (thanks to Macy's, which gives us their leftovers every
morning).

Many days go by with no money coming in at all. Right now our
telephone is shut off, but the man in the candy store next door calls us to
his phone for messages. Today we expect the gas and electricity to go.
What to do? We can borrow a few oil stoves and continue to cook and
feed those who come. Vegetables are contributed, soup bones, fish. But we
must buy the coffee, sugar, milk, and bread. As long as we are trusted the
bills continue to mount. Even the printer is letting us go to press with
$995 owing this summer.

And there is the children's camp on Staten Island, donated by a friend.
It holds eight children—forty can be cared for during the summer—and
they can spend their days on the beach and sleep at night to the rustle of
wind in the maples around the camp. The most beautiful sound in the
world is the sound of little waves on a hot beach. And the sweetest sight is
Viola, aged four, who lives on Grand Street in a six-flight walk-up, one of
eight children, who is playing in the sand and waves on the beach these
days. Or perhaps it is Rosemary and Barbara, Italian and Negro, with their
arms around each other's necks as they pose for a picture on the shore.

There is poverty and hunger and war in the world. And we prepare for more war. There is desperate suffering with no prospect of relief. But we would be contributing to the misery and desperation of the world if we failed to rejoice in the sun, the moon, and the stars, in the rivers which surround this island on which we live, in the cool breezes of the bay, in what food we have and in the benefactors God sends.

The heat wave which is a misery to some is to us a joy. We remember the bitter cold of the winter, and those who have to sleep under the stars nestle into the warmth of the hot pavements.

Our greatest misery is the poverty which gnaws at our vitals, an agony to the families in our midst. And the only thing we can do about it is to appeal to you, our readers, begging your help. We are stewards, and we probably manage very badly in trying to take care of all those who come, the desperate, the dispossessed. Like St. Peter, they say, "To whom else shall we go?" and they are our brothers in Christ. They are more than that; they are Christ, appealing to you.

So please help us to keep going. Help these suffering members of the sorrowing Body of Christ.

July–August 1940

Room for Christ

It is no use saying that we are born two thousand years too late to give room to Christ. Nor will those who live at the end of the world have been born too late. Christ is always with us, always asking for room in our hearts.

But now it is with the voice of our contemporaries that He speaks, with the eyes of store clerks, factory workers, and children that he gazes; with the hands of office workers, slum dwellers, and suburban housewives that He gives. It is with the feet of soldiers and tramps that He walks, and with the heart of anyone in need that He longs for shelter. And giving shelter or food to anyone who asks for it, or needs it, is giving it to Christ.

We can do now what those who knew Him in the days of His flesh did. I am sure that the shepherds did not adore and then go away to leave Mary and her Child in the stable, but somehow found them room, even though what they had to offer might have been primitive enough. All that the friends of Christ did for Him in His lifetime, we can do. Peter's mother-in-law hastened to cook a meal for Him, and if anything in the Gospels can be inferred, it surely is that she gave the very best she had, with no thought of extravagance. Matthew made a feast for Him, inviting the whole town, so that the house was in an uproar of enjoyment, and the strait-laced Pharisees—the good people—were scandalized.

The people of Samaria, despised and isolated, were overjoyed to give Him hospitality, and for days He walked and ate and slept among them. And the loveliest of all relationships in Christ's life, after His relationship with His Mother, is His friendship with Martha, Mary, and Lazarus and the continual hospitality He found with them. It is a staggering thought that there were once two sisters and a brother whom Jesus looked on almost as His family and where He found a second home, where Martha got on with her work, bustling around in her house-proud way, and Mary simply sat in silence with Him.

If we hadn't got Christ's own words for it, it would seem raving lunacy to believe that if I offer a bed and food and hospitality to some man or woman or child, I am replaying the part of Lazarus or Martha or Mary, and that my guest is Christ. There is nothing to show it, perhaps. There are no halos already glowing round their heads—at least none that human eyes can see. It is not likely that I shall be vouchsafed the vision of Elizabeth of Hungary, who put the leper in her bed and later, going to tend him, saw no longer the leper's stricken face, but the face of Christ. The part of a Peter Claver, who gave a stricken Negro his bed and slept on the floor at his side, is more likely to be ours. For Peter Claver never saw anything with his bodily eyes except the exhausted black faces of the Negroes; he had only faith in Christ's own words that these people were Christ. And when on one occasion the Negroes he had induced to help him ran from the room, panic-stricken before the disgusting sight of some sickness, he was astonished. "You mustn't go," he said, and you can still hear his surprise that anyone could forget such a truth: "You mustn't leave him—it is Christ."

Some time ago I saw the death notice of a sergeant-pilot who had been killed on active service. After the usual information, a message was added which, I imagine, is likely to be imitated. It said that anyone who had ever known the dead boy would always be sure of a welcome at his parents' home. So, even now that the war is over, the father and mother will go on taking in strangers for the simple reason that they will be reminded of their dead son by the friends he made.

That is rather like the custom that existed among the first generations of Christians, when faith was a bright fire that warmed more than those who kept it burning. In every house then, a room was kept ready for any stranger who might ask for shelter; it was even called "the stranger's room"; and this not because these people, like the parents of the dead airman, thought they could trace something of someone they loved in the stranger who used it, not because the man or woman to whom they gave shelter reminded them of Christ, but because—plain and simple and stupendous fact—he *was* Christ.

It would be foolish to pretend that it is always easy to remember this. If everyone were holy and handsome, with "alter Christus" shining in neon lighting from them, it would be easy to see Christ in everyone. If Mary had appeared in Bethlehem clothed, as St. John says, with the sun, a crown of twelve stars on her head, and the moon under her feet, then people would have fought to make room for her. But that was not God's way for her, nor is it Christ's way for Himself, now when He is disguised under every type of humanity that treads the earth.

To see how far one realizes this, it is a good thing to ask honestly what you would do, or have done, when a beggar asked at your house for food. Would you—or did you—give it on an old cracked plate, thinking that was good enough? Do you think that Martha and Mary thought that the old and chipped dish was good enough for their guest?

In Christ's human life, there were always a few who made up for the neglect of the crowd. The shepherds did it; their hurrying to the crib atoned for the people who would flee from Christ. The wise men did it; their journey across the world made up for those who refused to stir one hand's breadth from the routine of their lives to go to Christ. Even the gifts the wise men brought have in themselves an obscure recompense and atonement for what would follow later in this Child's life. For they brought gold, the king's emblem, to make up for the crown of thorns that He would wear; they offered incense, the symbol of praise, to make up for the mockery and the spitting; they gave Him myrrh, to heal and soothe, and He was wounded from head to foot and no one bathed His wounds. The women at the foot of the Cross did it too, making up for the crowd who stood by and sneered.

We can do it too, exactly as they did. We are not born too late. We do it by seeing Christ and serving Christ in friends and strangers, in everyone we come in contact with.

All this can be proved, if proof is needed, by the doctrines of the Church. We can talk about Christ's Mystical Body, about the vine and the branches, about the Communion of Saints. But Christ Himself has proved it for us, and no one has to go further than that. For He said that a glass of water given to a beggar was given to Him. He made heaven hinge on the way we act toward Him in His disguise of commonplace, frail, ordinary humanity.

Did you give Me clothes when I was hungry?

Did you give Me to drink when I was thirsty?

Did you give Me clothes when My own were all rags?

Did you come to see Me when I was sick, or in prison or in trouble?

And to those who say, aghast, that they never had a chance to do such a thing, that they lived two thousand years too late, He will say again what they had the chance of knowing all their lives, that if these things were done for the very least of His brethren they were done to Him.

For a total Christian, the goad of duty is not needed—always prodding one to perform this or that good deed. Is it not a duty to help Christ, it is a privilege. Is it likely that Martha and Mary sat back and considered that they had done all that was expected of them—is it likely that Peter's mother-in-law grudgingly served the chicken she had meant to keep till Sunday because she thought it was her "duty"? She did it gladly; she would have served ten chickens if she had had them.

If that is the way they gave hospitality to Christ, it is certain that that is the way it should still be given. Not for the sake of humanity. Not because it might be Christ who stays with us, comes to see us, takes up our time. Not because these people remind us of Christ, as those soldiers and airmen remind the parents of their son, but because they *are* Christ, asking us to find room for Him, exactly as He did at the first Christmas.

December 1945

Love Is the Measure

We confess to being fools and wish that we were more so. In the face of the approaching atom bomb test (and discussion of widespread radioactivity is giving people more and more of an excuse to get away from the philosophy of personalism and the doctrine of free will); in the face of an approaching maritime strike; in the face of bread shortages and housing shortages; in the face of the passing of the draft extension, teen-agers included, we face the situation that there is nothing we can do for people except to love them. If the maritime strike goes on there will be no shipping of food or medicine or clothes to Europe or the Far East, so there is nothing to do again but to love. We continue in our fourteenth year of feeding our brothers and sisters, clothing them and sheltering them, and the more we do it, the more we realize that the most important thing is to love. There are several families with us, destitute families, destitute to an unbelievable extent, and there, too, is nothing to do but to love. What I mean is that there is no chance of rehabilitation, no chance, so far as we see, of changing them; certainly no chance of adjusting them to this abominable world about them—and who wants them adjusted, anyway?

What we would like to do is change the world—make it a little simpler for people to feed, clothe, and shelter themselves as God intended them to do. And to a certain extent, by fighting for better conditions, by crying out unceasingly for the rights of the workers, of the poor, of the destitute—the rights of the worthy and the unworthy poor, in other words— we can to a certain extent change the world; we can work for the oasis, the little cell of joy and peace in a harried world. We can throw our pebble in the pond and be confident that its ever-widening circle will reach around the world.

We repeat, there is nothing that we can do but love, and dear God— please enlarge our hearts to love each other, to love our neighbor, to love our enemy as well as our friend.

June 1946

The Scandal of the
Works of Mercy

The Spiritual Works of Mercy are: to admonish the sinner, to instruct the ignorant, to counsel the doubtful, to comfort the sorrowful, to bear wrongs patiently, to forgive all injuries, and to pray for the living and the dead.

The Corporal Works are to feed the hungry, to give drink to the thirsty, to clothe the naked, to ransom the captive, to harbor the harborless, to visit the sick, and to bury the dead.

When Peter Maurin talked about the necessity of practicing the Works of Mercy, he meant all of them. He envisioned Houses of Hospitality in poor parishes in every city of the country, where these precepts of Our Lord could be put into effect. He pointed out that we have turned to state responsibility through home relief, social legislation, and social security, that we no longer practice personal responsibility, but are repeating the words of the first murderer, "Am I my brother's keeper?"

The Works of Mercy are a wonderful stimulus to our growth in faith as well as love. Our faith is taxed to the utmost and so grows through this strain put upon it. It is pruned again and again, and springs up bearing much fruit. For anyone starting to live literally the words of the Fathers of the Church—"The bread you retain belongs to the hungry, the dress you lock up is the property of the naked"; "What is superfluous for one's need is to be regarded as plunder if one retains it for one's self"—there is always a trial ahead. "Our faith, more precious than gold, must be tried as though by fire."

Here is a letter we received today: "I took a gentleman seemingly in need of spiritual and temporal guidance into my home on a Sunday afternoon. Let him have a nap on my bed, went through the want ads with him, made coffee and sandwiches for him, and when he left, I found my wallet had gone also."

I can only say that the saints would only bow their heads and not try to understand or judge. They received no thanks—well, then, God had to repay them. They forbore to judge, and it was as though they took off their cloak besides their coat to give away. This is expecting heroic charity, of course. But these things happen for our discouragement, for our testing. We are sowing the seed of love, and we are not living in the harvest time. We must love to the point of folly, and we are indeed fools, as Our Lord Himself was who died for such a one as this. We lay down our lives, too, when we have performed so painfully thankless an act, for our correspondent is poor in this world's goods. It is agony to go through such bitter experiences, because we all want to love, we desire with a great longing to love our fellows, and our hearts are often crushed at such rejections. But, as a Carmelite nun said to me last week, "It is the crushed heart which is the soft heart, the tender heart."

Such an experience is crueler than that of our young men in Baltimore who were arrested for running a disorderly house, i.e., our St. Anthony's House of Hospitality, and who spent a few nights in jail. Such an experience is even crueler than that which happened to one of our men here in New York who was attacked (for his pacifism) by a maniac with a knife. Actually to shed one's blood is a less bitter experience.

Well, our friend has suffered from his experience and it is part of the bitterness of the poor, who cheat each other, who exploit each other even as they are exploited, who despise each other even as they are the despised.

And is it to be expected that virtue and destitution should go together? No, as John Cogley has written, they are the destitute in every way, destitute of this world's goods, destitute of honor, of gratitude, of love; they need so much that we cannot take the Works of Mercy apart and say I will do this one or that one Work of Mercy. We find they all go together.

Some years ago there was an article in *The Commonweal* by Georges Bernanos. He ended it on a warning note for these apocalyptic times:

"Every particle of Christ's divine charity is today more precious for your security—for your security, I say—than all the atom bombs in all the stockpiles."

It is by the Works of Mercy that we shall be judged.

The Commonweal, November 4, 1949

Here and Now

Sometimes the only thing that keeps a woman going is the necessity of taking care of her young. She cannot sink into lethargy and despair because the young ones are dragging at her skirts, clamoring for something—food, clothing, shelter, occupation. She is carried outside herself. She is saved by childbearing, as it says in the Old Testament; she has a rule of life which involves others and she will be saved in spite of herself.

Yesterday afternoon I was visiting the Municipal Lodging House, where a mother of twelve was awaiting her thirteenth, and she sat there surrounded by those of her brood who were left to her. There were the four-year-old twins running around, their heads to be bound up; the eighteen-month-old girl to be rescued from the stairwell; the fourteen-year-old to send to the doctor for an examination. Though her home was, for the time, a corner in a lodging house waiting room (people are not allowed to go to their beds by charitable organizations until a proper time of the evening; it might encourage the "laziness" the poor are too prone to), still, the mother's life was filled with *activity*.

And that is the way with most of us. We fill our days with activity, and when we start to think, to see how little we can do, when we contemplate

the apparent hopelessness of the situation around us and our feeble attempts
to love people and show our love by serving them, we are overcome by the
seeming futility of it all. The mothers have the better part. They bring life
forth. They bear children, and the teeming life about them carries with it
to some extent its consolations together with its anguish. Father Damascus
Winzen said at a retreat given at Maryfarm that one tragedy of today was
a loss of the *joy of life,* joy in living, which men should have if they were
healthy and happy. Children have it. You often see it in mothers, a placidity
and serenity which is a quiet joy.

This desire to nourish, to bring forth, is strong in us women. The other
night I had a dream. I am fifty, but I thought I had a little baby and was
nursing it. And then I was amazed that I had not only the one but a little
Negro baby to foster. I felt my aging breasts to see if there was milk there
for this other one, and I had great joy that I could nurse a foster child of
those most numerous of the oppressed in our own country.

Later on, when the first sweetness of the dream had left me, I thought,
with self-probing, perhaps it was a symptom of my presumption—that I
was indeed but an empty cistern, that I needed to nourish my own spiritual
life by prayer and penance before attempting to nourish others.

But one doesn't have time to think much in this work, in this life of the
Catholic Worker.

One thing follows from another. We start to write about justice, about
changing the social order, and we are overwhelmed by those coming to
claim our pity and our sharing. We are busy from morning to night. We
have gone out in the morning to drink at the fountains at the nearest
church, and have found men sleeping in our doorways, young and old. The
breadline confronts us daily. Just now a beautiful woman came in and said
she had walked from 215th Street down to our house below First Street to
ask for clothes. Men come in every fifteen minutes looking for some
garment, some food, some conversation. It is very interesting, such a life.
It is also a great temptation.

Three men just came in, slightly tipsy, for a bite of lunch. Drink. Always
there is the problem of drink, tied up inextricably with the problem of
human misery, the suffering of body and soul. Drink will perhaps dull that
ache, that pain. Drink will perhaps give the illusion of joy of life, of
meaning to life. It will perhaps make things look "new," as St. Paul said.

I would say that the problem of drink is one thing which stops people
in their charity, in the performance of the Works of Mercy. Such human
beings, so dirty, so depraved, so animal, so lost (Christ in His degradation,
in His most hidden guise), to most people do not seem worth saving, or

worth keeping alive, or worth burying. It is poverty, destitution, in its meanest guise.

Peter Maurin used to say that people should get drunk with the Spirit, rather than with the spirits. The twelve Apostles at the third hour seemed as though drunk in their joy and exultation.

A few years ago I had to call in a woman doctor, an exile, who had been in a concentration camp in Germany for refusing to sterilize epileptic children. She was taking care of one of the women in the house. As she left she said, recognizing the apparent hopelessness of our work for the most destitute, "The only thing you can do for these sick and aged ones is to make them happy." I have often thought of that since, when people have asked us about the work, what we were trying to do; it seemed very simple to say, "We are trying to make people happy." Father Faber has three conferences in one of his published volumes on *kindness*. Kindness seems a simple enough virtue, little of the heroic about it, and rather naïve and fatuous, not very much to the point these days when righteous wrath and grim fortitude seem to be more in order. But these conferences make good spiritual reading.

We want to be happy, we want others to be happy, we want to see some of this joy of life which children have, we want to see people intoxicated with God, or just filled with the good steady joy of knowing that Christ is King and that we are His flock and He has prepared for us a kingdom, and that God loves us as a father loves his children, as a bridegroom loves his bride, and that eye hath not seen nor ear heard what God hath prepared for us!

Some distance farther north from Newburgh, where our retreat house is, there are some big dams being constructed. Our engineers are envisioning a city ever bigger, needing more and more water! One of our staff drove us there a few weeks ago and when he returned he said that it frightened him to see what man was capable of in the material order.

We have not yet begun to know what men are capable of in the spiritual order. What growth, what joy!

Father Henri de Lubac, S.J., wrote recently, "It is not the proper duty of Christianity to form leaders—that is, builders of the temporal, although a legion of Christian leaders is infinitely desirable. Christianity must generate saints—that is, witnesses to the eternal. The efficacy of the saint is not that of the leader. The saint does not have to bring about great temporal achievements; he is one who succeeds in giving us at least a glimpse of eternity despite the thick opacity of time."

We are all called to be saints, St. Paul says, and we might as well get over our bourgeois fear of the name. We might also get used to recognizing the fact that there is some of the saint in all of us. Inasmuch as we are growing, putting off the old man and putting on Christ, there is some of the saint, the holy, the divine right there.

One of the features of the retreat at Maryfarm is the renewal of the baptismal vows. Most of us do not know that we have taken vows. One of the fellows said jovially, "Let me read them over to see if I want to renew them!" We have renounced the world, the flesh, and the devil, we have already done it, there is no help for it, we are Christians, we have put on Christ, there is the seed of divine life in us. But as to whether we remain idiots, or morons, or feebleminded in this life—this does not seem to occur to most of us. We have to grow, the egg has to hatch, it has to develop wings, else it becomes a rotten egg, as C. S. Lewis says. St. Augustine says that a mother delights in nursing her child, but she does not want it to remain a child always. She wants it to grow into a man.

We are called to be saints. Sometimes we don't see them around us, sometimes their sanctity is obscured by the human, but they are there nonetheless.

And all this talk about saints, and our obligation to strive toward sanctity, is because there is a very subtle way of attacking the temporal aims of the Catholic Worker, our work in the fields of pacifism and distributism, by saying, and in so saying dismissing us as quite beyond anyone's acceptance or imitation: "Oh, they are all saints down there at Mott Street!"

All the emphasis is laid on our work for the poor, our breadline, our clothing line, our tenement-house shelter, our sharing with others, and with them the sights and sounds and smells of dirt and disease and destitution. Yet with all our sharing we hang on to too much. We have no right to talk of poverty in the face of the suffering in the world. Our farming communes are spoken of as utopian attempts to get families back on the land and to do away with the machine; we are looked upon as modern fathers of the desert who are fleeing the wrath to come. Our actions are admired and praised but only as palliatives and poultices, and our efforts to do away with the state by nonviolent resistance and achieving a distributist economy are derided and decried.

Of course we are few. But Marx and Engels and Trotsky and Stalin were few, but that did not keep them from holding *their* vision and studying and working toward it.

Our retreat house, Maryfarm, is at Newburgh, New York, and is on ninety-six acres. We are farming as much as we can to raise food for our retreatants and for the breadline on Mott Street. We have houses and barns to put up forty or fifty people who come to us for a week's retreat in silence where they can listen to conferences and pray and heed that command: "Be still and see that I am God." It is a place to develop spiritual resources, a place to think. It is a place of *action,* because we believe that spiritual action is the hardest of all—to praise and worship God, to thank Him, to petition Him for our brothers, to repent our sins and those of others. This is action, just as the taking of cities is action, as revolution is action, as the Corporal Works of Mercy are action. And just to lie in the sun and let God work on you is to be sitting in the light of the Sun of Justice, and the growth will be there, and joy will grow and spread from us to others. That is why I like to use so often that saying of St. Catherine of Siena: "All the Way to heaven is Heaven, because He said I am the Way."

The Third Hour, 1949

Inventory

This last year at St. Joseph's House of Hospitality we gave out, roughly speaking and underestimating it at that, 460,000 meals. Also 18,250 night's lodgings. This is what the world sees and if we wished to impress the world we would multiply this by eighteen years, and the figures would be truly impressive.

But suppose a mother should say, in a plea for sympathy, "I've put one thousand and ninety-five meals on the table this last year. I've washed fifty thousand plates."

It is easy to see how foolish it is to look at things in this light, in this big way. I am sure that God is not counting the meals. He is looking at Tony Aratari, Joe Monroe, Ray Taylor, turning off their alarm clocks at five every morning to go downstairs to start the coffee and cut the bread. They get no credit for being noble. They have no realization of dying to themselves, of giving up their lives. They are more often than not abused by friends and relatives for not getting jobs, using their education, "supporting themselves," instead of living on charity. "This then is perfect joy," St. Francis would say.

We all wish for recognition of one kind or another. But it is mass action people think of these days. They lose sight of the sacrament of the present moment—of the little way.

Like Lord Jim, in Conrad's story, we are all waiting for great opportunities to show heroism, letting countless opportunities go by to enlarge our hearts, increase our faith, and show our love for our fellows, and so for Him. As St. Paul says, it is by little and by little that we are saved—or that we fall. We are living in this world and must make choices now, choices which may mean the sacrifice of our lives, in the future, but for now our goods, our reputations even. Our work is called futile, our stand of little worth or significance, having no influence, winning no converts, ineffective if not a form of treason. Or it is termed defeatism, appeasement, escapism.

What a paradox it is, this natural life and this supernatural life. We must give up our lives to gain them; we must die to live; we must be pruned to bear fruit. Ah yes, when we are being called appeasers, defeatists, we are being deprived of our dearest goods—our reputation, honor, the esteem of men—and we are truly on the way to becoming the despised of the earth. We are beginning perhaps to be truly poor.

We are trying to spread the gospel of peace, to persuade others to extend the peace movement, to build up a mighty army of conscientious objectors. And in doing this we are accounted fools, and it is the folly of the Cross in the eyes of an unbelieving world.

Martyrdom is not gallantly standing before a firing squad. Usually it is the losing of a job because of not taking a loyalty oath, or buying a war bond, or paying a tax. Martyrdom is small, hidden, misunderstood. Or if it is a bloody martyrdom, it is the cry in the dark, the terror, the shame, the loneliness, nobody to hear, nobody to suffer with, let alone to save. Oh, the loneliness of all of us in these days, in all the great moments of our lives, this dying which we do, by little and by little, over a short space of time or over the years. One day is as a thousand in these crises. A week in jail is as a year.

But we repeat that we do see results from our personal experiences, and we proclaim our faith. Christ has died for us. Adam and Eve fell, and as Julian of Norwich wrote, the worst has already happened and been repaired. Christ continues to die in His martyrs all over the world, in His Mystical Body, and it is this dying, not the killing in wars, which will save the world.

Do we see results, do these methods succeed? Can we trust in them? Just as surely as we believe in "the little way" of St. Therese, we believe and know that this is the only success.

January 1951

Poverty and Precarity

It is hard to write about poverty.

We live in a slum neighborhood. It is becoming ever more crowded with Puerto Ricans, those who have the lowest wages in the city, who do the hardest work, who are small and undernourished from generations of privation and exploitation.

It is hard to write about poverty when the backyard at Chrystie Street still has the furniture piled to one side that was put out on the street in an eviction in a next-door tenement.

How can we say to these people, "Rejoice and be exceedingly glad, for great is your reward in heaven," when we are living comfortably in a warm house, sitting down to a good table, decently clothed? Maybe not so decently. I had occasion to visit the city shelter last month where homeless families are cared for. I sat there for a couple of hours, contemplating poverty and destitution—a family with two of the children asleep in the parents' arms and four others sprawling against them; another young couple, the mother pregnant. I made myself known to a young man in charge. (I did not want to appear to be spying on them when all I wanted to know was the latest on the apartment situation for homeless families.) He apologized for making me wait, explaining that he had thought I was one of the clients.

We need always to be thinking and writing about poverty, for if we are not among its victims its reality fades from us. We must talk about poverty, because people insulated by their own comfort lose sight of it. So many decent people come in to visit and tell us how their families were brought up in poverty, and how, through hard work and cooperation, they managed to educate all the children—even raise up priests and nuns to the Church. They contend that healthful habits and a stable family situation enable people to escape from the poverty class, no matter how mean the slum they may once have been forced to live in. So why can't everybody do it? No, these people don't know about the poor. Their conception of poverty is of something neat and well ordered as a nun's cell.

And maybe no one can be told; maybe they will have to experience it. Or maybe it is a grace which they must pray for. We usually get what we pray for, and maybe we are afraid to pray for it. And yet I am convinced that it is the grace we most need in this age of crisis, this time when expenditures reach into the billions to defend "our American way of life." Maybe this defense itself will bring down upon us the poverty we are afraid to pray for.

I well remember our first efforts when we started publishing our paper. We had no office, no equipment but a typewriter which was pawned the first month. We wrote the paper on park benches and the kitchen table. In an effort to achieve a little of the destitution of our neighbors, we gave away our furniture and sat on boxes. But as fast as we gave things away people brought more. We gave blankets to needy families and when we started our first House of Hospitality people gathered together what blankets we needed. We gave away food and more food came in—exotic food, some of it: a haunch of venison from the Canadian Northwest, a can of oysters from Maryland, a container of honey from Illinois. Even now it comes in, a salmon from Seattle, flown across the continent; nothing is too good for the poor.

No one working with *The Catholic Worker* gets a salary, so our readers feel called upon to give and help us keep the work going. And then we experience a poverty of another kind, a poverty of reputation. It is said often and with some scorn, "Why don't they get jobs and help the poor that way? Why are they living off others, begging?"

I can only explain to such critics that it would complicate things to give a salary to Roger for his work of fourteen hours a day in the kitchen, clothes room, and office; to pay Jane a salary for running the women's house and Beth and Annabelle for giving out clothes, for making stencils all day and helping with the sick and the poor, and then have them all turn the money right back in to support the work. Or to make it more complicated, they might all go out and get jobs, and bring the money home to pay their board and room and the salaries of others to run the house. It is simpler just to be poor. It is simpler to beg. The main thing is not to hold on to anything.

But the tragedy is that we do, we all do hold on—to our books, our tools, such as typewriters, our clothes; and instead of rejoicing when they are taken from us we lament. We protest when people take our time or privacy. We are holding on to these "goods" too.

Occasionally, as we start thinking of poverty—often after reading the life of such a saint as Benedict Joseph Labre—we dream of going out on our own, living with the destitute, sleeping on park benches or in the city shelter, living in churches, sitting before the Blessed Sacrament as we see

so many doing from the Municipal Lodging House around the corner. And
when such thoughts come on warm spring days when the children are
playing in the park, and it is good to be out on the city streets, we know
that we are only deceiving ourselves, for we are only dreaming of a form
of luxury. What we want is the warm sun, and rest, and time to think and
read, and freedom from the people who press in on us from early morning
until late at night. No, it is not simple, this business of poverty.

"Precarity," or precariousness, is an essential element in true voluntary
poverty, a saintly priest from Martinique has written us. "True poverty is
rare," he writes. "Nowadays religious communities are good, I am sure,
but they are mistaken about poverty. They accept, admit, poverty on principle, but everything must be good and strong, buildings must be fireproof.
Precarity is everywhere rejected, and precarity is an essential element of
poverty. This has been forgotten. Here in our monastery we want precarity
in everything except the church. These last days our refectory was near
collapsing. We have put several supplementary beams in place and thus it
will last maybe two or three years more. Someday it will fall on our heads
and that will be funny. Precarity enables us better to help the poor. When
a community is always building, enlarging, and embellishing, there is nothing left over for the poor. We have no right to do so as long as there are
slums and breadlines somewhere."

Over and over again in the history of the Church the saints have emphasized poverty. Every religious community, begun in poverty and incredible
hardship, but with a joyful acceptance of hardship by the rank-and-file
priests, brothers, monks, or nuns who gave their youth and energy to good
works, soon began to "thrive." Property was extended until holdings and
buildings accumulated; and although there was still individual poverty in
the community, there was corporate wealth. It is hard to remain poor.

One way to keep poor is not to accept money which is the result of
defrauding the poor. Here is a story of St. Ignatius of Sardinia, a Capuchin
recently canonized. Ignatius used to go out from his monastery with a sack
to beg from the people of the town, but he would never go to a merchant
who had built up his fortune by defrauding the poor. Franchino, the rich
man, fumed every time the saint passed his door. His concern, however,
was not the loss of the opportunity to give alms, but fear of public opinion.
He complained at the friary, whereupon the Father Guardian ordered St.
Ignatius to beg from the merchant the next time he went out.

"Very well," said Ignatius obediently. "If you wish it, Father, I will go,
but I would not have the Capuchins dine on the blood of the poor."

The merchant received Ignatius with great flattery and gave him generous alms, asking him to come again in the future. But hardly had Ignatius left the house with his sack on his shoulder when drops of blood began oozing from the sack. They trickled down on Franchino's doorstep and ran down through the street to the monastery. Everywhere Ignatius went, a trickle of blood followed him. When he arrived at the friary, he laid the sack at the Father Guardian's feet. "What is this?" gasped the Guardian. "This," St. Ignatius said, "is the blood of the poor."

This story appeared in the last column written by a great Catholic layman, a worker for social justice, F. P. Kenkel, editor of *Social Justice Review* in St. Louis (and always a friend of Peter Maurin's).

Mr. Kenkel's last comment was that the universal crisis in the world today was created by love of money. "The Far East and the Near East [and he might have said all Africa and Latin America also] together constitute a great sack from which blood is oozing. The flow will not stop as long as our interests in those people are dominated largely by financial and economic considerations."

Voluntary poverty, Peter Maurin would say, is the answer. Through voluntary poverty we will have the means to help our brothers. We cannot even see our brothers in need without first stripping ourselves. It is the only way we have of showing our love.

May 1952

Little by Little

Poverty is a strange and elusive thing. I have tried to write about it, its joys and its sorrows, for twenty years now; I could probably write about it for another twenty years without conveying what I feel about it as well as I would like. I condemn poverty and I advocate it; poverty is simple and complex at once; it is a social phenomenon and a personal matter. It is a paradox.

St. Francis was "the little poor man" and none was more joyful than he; yet Francis began with tears, with fear and trembling, hiding in a cave from his irate father. He had expropriated some of his father's goods (which he considered his rightful inheritance) in order to repair a church and rectory where he meant to live. It was only later that he came to love Lady Poverty. He took it little by little; it seemed to grow on him. Perhaps kissing the leper was the great step that freed him not only from fastidiousness and a fear of disease but from attachment to worldly goods as well.

Sometimes it takes but one step. We would like to think so. And yet the older I get, the more I see that life is made up of many steps, and they are very small affairs, not giant strides. I have "kissed a leper," not once but twice—consciously—and I cannot say I am much the better for it.

The first time was early one morning on the steps of Precious Blood Church. A woman with cancer of the face was begging (beggars are allowed only in the slums) and when I gave her money (no sacrifice on my part but merely passing on alms which someone had given me) she tried to kiss my hand. The only thing I could do was kiss her dirty old face with the gaping hole in it where an eye and a nose had been. It sounds like a heroic deed but it was not. One gets used to ugliness so quickly. What we avert our eyes from one day is easily borne the next when we have learned a little more about love. Nurses know this, and so do mothers.

Another time I was refusing a bed to a drunken prostitute with a huge, toothless, rouged mouth, a nightmare of a mouth. She had been raising a disturbance in the house. I kept remembering how St. Therese said that when you had to refuse anyone anything, you could at least do it so that the person went away a bit happier. I had to deny her a bed but when that woman asked me to kiss her, I did, and it was a loathsome thing, the way she did it. It was scarcely a mark of normal human affection.

We suffer these things and they fade from memory. But daily, hourly, to give up our own possessions and especially to subordinate our own impulses and wishes to others—these are hard, hard things; and I don't think they ever get any easier.

You can strip yourself, you can be stripped, but still you will reach out like an octopus to seek your own comfort, your untroubled time, your ease, your refreshment. It may mean books or music—the gratification of the inner senses—or it may mean food and drink, coffee and cigarettes. The one kind of giving up is not easier than the other.

How does property fit in? people ask. It was Eric Gill who said that property is "proper" to man. And St. Thomas Aquinas said that a certain amount of goods is necessary to lead a good life. Recent popes have written at length that justice, rather than charity, should be sought for the worker. Unions are still fighting for better wages and hours, and it is a futile fight with the price of living going up steadily. They are fighting for partial gains and every strike means sacrifice to make them, and still the situation in the long run is not bettered. There may be talk of better standards of living, every worker with his car and owning his own home, but still this comfort depends on a wage, a boss, a war. Our whole modern economy is based on preparations for war, and that is one of the great modern arguments for poverty. If the comfort one has gained has resulted in the deaths of thousands in Korea and other parts of the world, then that comfort will have to be atoned for. The argument now is that there is no civilian population, that all are involved in the war (misnamed "defense") effort. If you work in a textile mill making cloth or in a factory making dungarees or blankets, your work is still tied up with war. If you raise food or irrigate the land to raise food you may be feeding troops or liberating others to serve as troops. If you ride a bus you are paying taxes. Whatever you buy is taxed, so that you are, in effect, helping to support the state's preparations for war exactly to the extent of your attachment to worldly things of whatever kind.

The merchant counting his profit in pennies, the millionaire with his efficiency experts, have learned how to amass wealth. By following their example—and profiting by the war boom—there is no necessity for anyone to be poor nowadays. So they say.

But the fact remains that every House of Hospitality is full. There is a breadline outside our door, every day, twice a day, two or three hundred strong. Families write us pitifully for help. This is not poverty; this is destitution.

In front of me as I write is Fritz Eichenberg's picture of St. Vincent de Paul. He holds a chubby child in his arms and a thin pale child is clinging to him. Yes, the poor are always going to be with us—Our Lord told us that—and there will always be a need for our sharing, for stripping ourselves to help others. It will always be a lifetime job.

But I am sure that God did not intend that there be so many poor. The class structure is of *our* making and by *our* consent, not His, and we must do what we can to change it. So we are urging revolutionary change.

So many sins against the poor cry out to high heaven! One of the most deadly sins is to deprive the laborer of his hire. There is another: to instill in him paltry desires so compulsive that he is willing to sell his liberty and his honor to satisfy them. We are all guilty of concupiscence, but newspapers, radios, television, and battalions of advertising men (woe to that generation!) deliberately stimulate our desires, the satisfaction of which so often means the degradation of the family.

Because of these factors of modern life, the only way we can write about poverty is in terms of ourselves, our own personal responsibility. The message we have been given is the Cross.

We have seen the depths of the faithlessness and stubbornness of the

human soul—we are surrounded by sin and failure—and it is a mark of
our faith in Christ that we continue to hope, to write, to appeal and beg
for help for our work. And we pray also for an increase in the love of
poverty, which goes with love of our brothers and sisters.

April 1953

The Pearl of Great Price

Jacques Maritain, speaking at a Catholic Worker meeting a few years ago,
urged us to read the Gospels. Therese of Lisieux, the little saint of our day,
carried it next to her heart. Even if we read only the Gospel for Sunday,
several times, God sends us a special message for our need.

I thought of that a few Sundays ago as I read the parable about the lost
sheep. Certainly the men around the Bowery are lost sheep. They are our
brothers in Jesus; He died for each of them. What respect we should feel
for them!

When we began the Catholic Worker, we first thought of it as a headquarters for the paper, a place for round-table discussions, for learning
crafts, for studying ways of building up a new social order. But God has
made it much more than all this. He has made it a place for the poor. They
come early in the morning from their beds in cheap flophouses, from the
benches in the park across the street, from the holes and corners of the
city. They are the most destitute, the most abandoned.

It is easy for people to see Jesus in the children of the slums, and
institutions and schools are built to help them. That is a vocation in itself.
But these abandoned men are looked upon as hopeless. "No good will
come of it." We are contributing to laziness. We are feeding people who
won't work. These are the accusations made. God help us, we give them
so little: bread and coffee in the morning, soup and bread at noon. Two
scant meals.

We are a family of forty or fifty at the Catholic Worker. We keep
emphasizing that. But we are also a House of Hospitality. So many come
that it is impossible to give personal attention to each one; we can only
give what we have, in the name of Jesus. Thank God for directing our
vocation. We did not choose this work. He sent it to us. We will always,

please God, be clambering around the rocks and briars, the barrenness, the fruitlessness of city life, in search of lost sheep.

We are told to put on Christ and we think of Him in His private life, His life of work, His public life, His teaching and His suffering life. But we do not think enough of His life as a little child, as a baby. His helplessness, His powerlessness. We have to be content to be in that state too. Not to be able to do anything, to accomplish anything.

One thing children certainly accomplish, and that is that they love and wonder at the people and the universe around them. They live in the midst of squalor and confusion and see it not. They see people at the moment and love them and admire them. They forgive and they go on loving. They may look on the most vicious person, and if he is at that moment good and kind and doing something which they can be interested in or admire, there they are, pouring out their hearts to him.

Oh yes, I can write with authority. I have my own little grandchildren with me right now, and they see only the beauty and the joy of the Catholic Worker and its activities. There is no criticism in their minds and hearts of others around them.

My daughter, too, was raised among the poor and most abandoned of human beings. She was only seven when the Catholic Worker started, and now she has a daughter of seven and four others besides.

It is good to be able to write with authority about the family, about poverty in our day—the involuntary poverty which all families must endure— about insecurity and unemployment. A few years ago, visiting my daughter, I was lying awake at 2 a.m., worrying because David had just lost his job and Tamar was about to have her fifth child. The former boss, who also owned the house they lived in, had come bearing oranges for the children and to tell them to move at once. What a strange juxtaposition of gestures! And I was torn between wrath and the necessity to train oneself in loving one's enemies, hating the sin but loving the sinner.

But then I thought, "Thank God I have this suffering of joblessness and insecurity and homelessness together with others. This day, for the sake of the family, there are so many compromises. But we must learn to accept this hardest of all sufferings, the suffering of those nearest and dearest to us. Thank God for this training in suffering." Accepting this made it easier at the time to go back to sleep. Since then there has been more of the same. Thank God for everything.

The fundamental means of the Catholic Worker are voluntary poverty and manual labor, a spirit of detachment from all things, a sense of the primacy of the spiritual, which makes the rest easy. "His praise should be ever in our mouth."

The reason for our existence is to praise God, to love Him and serve Him, and we can do this only by loving our brothers. "All men are brothers." This is the great truth that makes us realize God. Great crimes, it is true, have been committed in the name of human brotherhood; that may serve to obscure the truth, but we must keep on saying it. We must keep on saying it because Love is the reason for our existence. It is what we all live for, whether we are the hanger-on in Times Square or the most pious member of a community. We are seeking what we think to be the good for us. If we don't know any better, often it is because radio, news-papers, press and pulpit have neglected so to inform us. We love what is presented to us to love, and God is not much presented. It is as hard to see Jesus in the respectable Christian today as in the man on the Bowery. And so "the masses have been lost to the Church."

We who live in this country cannot be as poor as those who go out to other countries. This is so rich a country that luxury has developed at the expense of necessities, and even the destitute partake of the luxury. We are the rich country of the world, like Dives at the feast. We must try hard, we must study to be poor like Lazarus at the gate, who was taken into Abraham's bosom. The Gospel doesn't tell us anything about Lazarus' virtues. He just sat there and let the dogs lick his sores. He would be classed by any social worker of today as a mental case. But again, poverty, and in this case destitution, like hospitality, is so esteemed by God, it is something to be sought after, worked for, the pearl of great price.

July–August 1953

The Insulted and the Injured

Last week, stopping to browse as I passed a secondhand bookstore on Fourth Avenue, I came across a battered old copy of Dostoevsky's *The Insulted and Injured,* a story which I had not read for many years. It was only twenty-five cents. I got it, and started reading it that very evening.

It is the story of a young author—it might be Dostoevsky himself—of the success of his first book, and of how he read it aloud to his foster father. The father said, "It's simply a little story, but it wrings your heart. What's happening all around you grows easier to understand and to remember, and you learn that the most downtrodden, humblest man is a man, too, and a brother." I thought as I read those words, "That is why *I* write."

And that is why I set down the story I am going to tell now, the story of Felicia.

* * *

She came into St. Joseph's House one afternoon to see if we had any extra clothes. She needed a coat for herself and some things for her children. We had known her for several years. Felicia is twenty-two, a tall Puerto Rican colored girl; she would be very pretty if it were not for two front teeth missing. Her husband is also twenty-two. She had to grow up in a hurry, for she had her first baby, out of wedlock, when she was fourteen. At the hospital she lied about her age, and when she came out, friends took her in with her baby. For the first two years she was able to keep him; then she lost her job and had to board him out. It was not until after she was married and had two more children that she was able to get him back.

By the time we met her, she'd been through a lot. Not long after she had the second baby, her husband lost a couple of fingers in the machine shop where he was working, and his mother agreed to take him in and the baby, too. But not Felicia. The woman had never wanted the marriage, and her house was already filled with eight people. Eight in four rooms. Felicia slept in the hall. That was when we first knew her. She was pregnant again, so she came to Peter Maurin Farm for a while. Then her husband got better and found another job, and they took a two-room apartment on Eldridge Street. It was hideous, scabrous. The plaster was falling off the walls; the toilets, located in the halls, were continually out of order, and the stairs smelled of rats and cats. The apartment she has now, she has told us, is much better. Her oldest child is seven. The others are one and a half and two and a half, and both are walking. You can see Felicia has some sense of dignity, now that she is a householder, with a place of her own.

* * *

She talked on and on the other afternoon, and finally stayed for supper. We had meatballs and spaghetti; afterward she got sick and could scarcely walk home. "Food doesn't seem to do me any good," she said. "I feel so heavy after eating I can't walk."

"But your husband's been looking after the children all afternoon," I protested. "You'd better be getting home."

It turned out that, on the contrary, the seven-year-old was the baby-sitter. "And her gas and electricity are turned off," somebody exclaimed. "There's an oil stove in the house—that's all the heat they have."

Aghast, we packed her off home, sending someone with her to carry her package of clothes. I had asked whether there was anything else she needed. She did not mention food or money or more clothes, but she looked wistfully at the radio which was playing in the room. She told me diffidently that if ever an extra one came in she'd love to have it. "You gotta stay in the house so much with the kids," she exclaimed. "I'd like to help my husband. He gets only thirty-five a week as a messenger, and I wish I could work. But there are no nurseries to take the babies—at least not until they are three years old. Tony's all right—he goes to school."

Later in the week, someone gave us a radio, and one cold sunny morning we brought it over to her. She and the children were keeping warm in the janitor's flat. The janitress didn't mind two extra kids; she had twelve of her own, eight of them still living at home. Since a lot of those were in school, it wasn't too crowded with a half-dozen kids running through the kitchen and living room. Every now and then one of them would fall asleep on the floor or bed—there were beds all over the place—and the others would play around them. Maybe they didn't make much noise because they didn't eat too much. But the poor are like that. Always room, always enough for one more—everyone just takes a little less.

The children stayed downstairs while we went up to her apartment, taking the radio. We had forgotten that Felicia had no electricity, but here again we saw the generosity of the janitress. Her husband had put an extension wire up the air shaft from his own apartment to Felicia's kitchen; with a double socket we were able to connect the set and see that it played.

We sat down to talk a little, and in the quiet of her bare little apartment she told me the history of her furniture.

"How I got this place," she began, "it was this way. You know people don't like to rent to Puerto Ricans. So we have to hunt and hunt to find a place to live. This house has Italians and Jews, and we're the first Puerto Ricans. The place is all run-down—as you can see—and nobody cares about anything as long as the rent is paid. Each apartment brings in twenty-eight dollars a month. There are four on a floor and seven floors to the house, walk-up. I'm lucky I'm on the third floor with the kids. Well, there was a woman living in the building, and when I was over at Eldridge Street in that two-room place she told me about this place. We were desperate.

The water was frozen, the toilet was stopped up, so we had to move. She said, 'There's an empty place in the house where I live, where some friends of mine moved out. It has my furniture in it. If you buy the furniture you can get the apartment. Twenty-three dollars a week.'

"My husband was getting thirty-five a week, and here we were going to have to pay twenty-three. Well, we have to move, that's all. So we signed a paper—that was last June—and moved in. From June to December 17 we paid her twenty-three dollars a week. And she paid the rent."

Felicia got up from the chair by the kitchen table (that table and four chairs were the only furniture in the room), and fetched a box from the kitchen shelf, full of papers and odds and ends. She began sorting through them. "These are my receipts for the statue of the Blessed Mother—you pay every week until you pay thirteen dollars and thirty four cents and it takes twenty-five weeks. A store down on Chambers Street. And here are the receipts for the rent."

We began to look at them together. This, I thought, is how the poor exploit the poor. One set of immigrants exploiting the newest set of immigrants!

"I got sick in December," Felicia went on. She was coughing as she spoke. "Manuel had to stay home from work to take care of me and the children, so he didn't get any pay. She changed it then, this woman. She said I could pay her ten dollars a week for the furniture and then pay my own rent to the landlord when he came around. Now that is the way we do it. And here are those receipts." She tumbled more pieces of paper out on the table. They were all dated seven days apart; each testified to the fact that Felicia was paying ten dollars a week on the scrubby set of furnishings I saw around me.

In the front room there were a dresser and two overstuffed chairs and a davenport bed that another tenant had given her. There was a crib they had bought at a secondhand store; an icebox, the old-fashioned kind into which you put a cake of ice, when you have the money to buy it; and a combination coal-and-gas stove. However, the gas was turned off, the coal stove was full of holes, and the pipe to the chimney in back had fallen away.

I didn't look in the two bedrooms, but there was space for little more than the beds. They were in the rear, off the kitchen, and got air and a little light from an airshaft. Windows looked out on other windows; only by peering out and looking far up to the sky, four stories above, could one tell whether it was raining or the sun was shining. The rear room could be closed off from the other three and a door led into the hall, so, since there were toilets in the hall, one could rent such a room to another tenant. My first home in Manhattan, when I worked on the East Side for the New York *Call,* had been just such a rear room. But there it was warm; I had a white-covered featherbed and there was always the good smell of cooking in the house. Here there was no fire to cook by.

I sat there with Felicia at her kitchen table and pondered the slips before me. For seven months she had put out $92 a month for rent and payment on the furniture. Since then she had paid $40 a month to the avaricious widow and $28 to the landlord, $68 in all, instead of $92—a generous reduction indeed!

"But this is terrible," I told her, frowning over the arithmetic.

"The furniture was pretty good when we moved in," Felicia explained, trying to account for the way she had been exploited and taken in. "It looked wonderful. You can't imagine how good it looked after Eldridge Street."

Well, perhaps it did. Having lived in Italian slums for many years, I knew how the housewives scrubbed and cleaned, and how they made everything shine with elbow grease and detergents. But Felicia had neither elbow grease nor money for soaps and cleansers. She probably wasn't very efficient about keeping a place up. After all, she was still young, and she had not had much experience, either.

"How much longer are you supposed to keep on paying?" I asked her, thinking of the papers she said she and her husband had signed. Probably it was all quite legal.

"We'll be finished a year from this June."

I gasped. Over a thousand dollars paid for junk; and nothing would be left of it by the time it was paid for. Enough money for a down payment, almost, on a house in the country.

While we were looking over the receipts, the gas and electric bill fell out. It was for $38.64. And how would that ever be paid? I thought of a remark which Louis Murphy, head of the Detroit House of Hospitality, was very fond of making. "It's expensive to be poor."

For some time as we talked I had been looking at an object hanging on the wall by the useless stove. Suddenly I saw what it was: a nylon shopping bag, the kind that bears heavy loads of groceries for shopping mothers without ripping at the seams or giving way in the handles. Oh, the irony of that shopping bag—and no money with which to go shopping, and no stove to cook on, either. No wonder she was sick, little Felicia, after eating meatballs and spaghetti on an empty stomach. She might well have felt heavy.

Never mind, Felicia, I thought to myself as I went home. Spring is here, and you won't have to heat that apartment, or live with the smell of oil stoves. Soon a hot sun will be pouring into the dank canyons of the New York streets; the park benches will be crowded; and the children after the long winter can drink in the bright sunlight and fresh air.

Walking across the park, I saw the sycamore trees turning golden green and the buds bursting. Green veils the bushes around the housing projects people can't afford to live in. Even the grass is brightening and starting up from the brown city soil. The earth is alive, the trees are alive again. Oh, mysterious life and beauty of a tree!

Out in the woods of Staten Island (still a nickel on the ferry) there are birches, and beeches with their round gray bolls, the willows yellow-twigged, the pines bright green, the maples rosy even on a gray day. There is green moss in the swamps, and the spring peepers have started their haunting call. Skunk cabbages in all their glory of striped green and maroon have started up from the marshes and line the little brook at the foot of Peter Maurin Farm. Oh love, oh joy, oh spring, stirring in the heart. Things can't be so bad, if the sun shines. Oh, if you, Felicia, could be there. The ground is soft now, there is good dirt for the children to dig in, and plenty of room for them to leap like the young goats on the farm next door. But in the country there are no houses for you, nor jobs for your husband. In the city there are houses—shelter, such as they are—and there is human warmth, but the pavements are as hard as the greed of men, and there is no clean dirt for children, only men's filth. The country now is oh, joyfulness, and the city where Felicia lives is woe, woe and want. Never mind, Felicia, God is not mocked. He is our Father, and all men are brothers, so lift up your heart. It will not always be this way.

Loaves and Fishes

FRIENDS AND FAMILY

Peter Maurin

A POOR MAN

"Precious in the sight of the Lord is the death of his saints," and the details of such a death are precious.

Plato said, "Other people are not likely to be aware that those who pursue philosophy aright study nothing but dying and being dead. But if this be true, it would be absurd to be eager for nothing but this all their lives, and then be troubled when that came for which they had all along been eagerly practicing."

And St. Paul said, "We will not have you ignorant, brethren, concerning them that are asleep, that you be not sorrowful, even as others who have no hope."

So it is with a spirit of joy that I write this month, because Peter is no longer suffering, no longer groaning within himself and saying with St. Paul, "Who will deliver me from the body of this death?"

No, we are sure that he welcomed Sister Death with joy, and that underneath him he felt the Everlasting Arms.

I am writing this in New York, up in my room on the third floor, and all winter, he waited up here for the weather to clear so that he could go to the country. He had to lie in bed much of the time, and the plaster is all picked off the wall by the side of his bed. He must have been very weary of lying in bed, he who had traveled north and south, east and west in this vast country. Everybody was always so reassuring, exclaiming how well he looked, how bright he was, but we who had known him these past seventeen years felt only the tragedy of the death in life he was living. Truly he practiced for death a very long time.

Peter was the poor man of his day. He was another St. Francis of modern times. He was used to poverty as a peasant is used to rough living, poor food, hard bed or no bed at all, dirt, fatigue, and hard and unrespected work. He was a man with a mission, a vision, an apostolate, but he had put off from himself honors, prestige, recognition. He was truly humble of heart, and loving. Never a word of detraction passed his lips, and as St. James said, the man who governs his tongue is a perfect man. He was impersonal in his love in that he loved all, saw all others around him as God saw them. In other words, he saw Christ in them.

He never spoke idle words, though he was a great teacher who talked for hours on end, till late in the night and early morning. He roamed the streets and the countryside and talked to all who would listen. But when his great brain failed, he became silent. If he had been a babbler, he would have been a babbler to the end. But when he could no longer think, as he himself expressed it, he remained silent.

For the last five years of his life he was this way, suffering, silent, dragging himself around, watched by us all for fear he would get lost, as he did once for three days; he was shouted at loudly by visitors as though he were deaf, talked to with condescension as one talks to a child for whom language must be simplified even to the point of absurdity. That was one of the hardest things we had to bear, we who loved him and worked with him for so long—to see others treat him as though he were simpleminded.

The fact was, he had been stripped of all. He had stripped himself throughout life; he had put off the old man, to put on the new. He had done all that he could to denude himself of *the world,* and I mean the world in the evil sense, not in the sense that "God looked at it and found it good." He loved people, he saw in them what God meant them to be. He saw the world as God meant it to be, and he loved it.

He had stripped himself, but there remained work for God to do. We are to be pruned as the vine is pruned so that it can bear fruit, and this we cannot do ourselves. God did it for him. He took from him his mind, the one thing he had left, the one thing perhaps he took delight in. He could no longer think. He could no longer discuss with others, give others, in a brilliant overflow of talk, his keen analysis of what was going on in the world; he could no longer make what he called his synthesis of *cult, culture, and cultivation.*

He was sick for five years. It was as though he had had a stroke in his sleep. He dragged one leg after him, his face was slightly distorted, he repeated, "I can no longer think." When he tried to, his face would have a strained, suffering expression.

He had always been a meager eater, getting along on two meals a day, never eating between meals. He used to say when he was offered anything, "I don't need it." But toward the close of his life, he was inclined to stuff down his food hastily like a child, and he had to be cautioned to eat slowly. Perhaps this was a hangover from the hunger of a childhood in that large family where there was never too much to eat. There were twenty-three children in all, over the years.

Other habits clung to him. When I'd go in to see if he was warm enough, I'd find him lying in bed with his pants folded neatly and under his head, and his coat wrapped around his feet, a habit I suppose he got from living in flophouses where clothes are often stolen. And once I found him sleeping in the dead of winter with only a spread over him, in a stony-cold room. Someone had taken his blankets.

One thing we can be happy about is that he felt he had finished his work before his mind failed. He used to say, "I have written all I have to say; I have done all I can; let the younger men take over." So he suffered, but not with the feeling that there was much still that he could do.

Recently we tried to record Peter's voice on a wire recorder, and we had him read aloud all his essays on Houses of Hospitality. His voice strangely enough was louder and clearer than it had been for a long time. We spent quite a few days over this, Dave Mason and I, because Peter tired easily. Then, after we had triumphantly made a fifteen-minute spool, someone else tried to work the machine and erased it all.

For the past two months I had been at the farm, and while returning from the funeral of Larry Heaney, I received a telephone call telling me of Peter's death. Just before I had left, I had told him of Larry's sudden death, and he said yes, to my question as to whether he remembered Larry. He had loved him very much, had sent him his quotations listed as *cult, culture, and cultivation* over the years, and rejoiced in his total acceptance of his teaching. When I said to him, "Now you will have someone waiting for you in heaven," his face lit up in a radiant smile. He had not smiled for months; there had only been a look of endurance, even of pain on his face.

That was our goodbye. Over the telephone in Avon, Ohio, at Our Lady of the Wayside Farm, I heard the news.

It was midnight and I had already fallen asleep. Dorothy and Bill Gauchat were still awake. When I hung up the receiver Bill suggested we say Vespers of the Office of the Dead for Peter, so we knelt there in that farm living room and prayed those beautiful psalms that are like balm to the sore heart. No matter how much you expect a death, no matter how much you may regard it as a happy release, there is a gigantic sense of loss. With our love of life, we have not yet gotten to that point where we can say with the desert father, St. Anthony, "The spaces of this life, set over against eternity, are brief and poor."

John Filliger had shaved him Saturday, and Michael Kovalak had dressed and cared for him on Sunday, conducting him to the chapel for Mass that morning, taking him to and from his room to rest. He had looked in again at Peter at nine Sunday night and found him sleeping rather restlessly. At eleven that night, Hans said, Peter began coughing, and it went on for some minutes. Then he tried to rise, and fell over on his pillow, breathing heavily. Hans put on the light and called Father Faley, our resident priest. Michael, Eileen, and others came too, and there were prayers for the dying around the bedside. He died immediately, there was no struggle, no pain. . . .

Peter was buried in St. John's Cemetery, Queens, in a donated grave. He was another St. John, a voice crying in the wilderness, and a voice, too, saying, "My little children, love one another." As the body was carried out of the church those great and triumphant words rang out, the *In Paradisum*.

> May the angels lead thee into paradise; may the martyrs receive thee at thy coming, and lead thee into the holy city of Jerusalem. May the choir of angels receive thee, and mayest thou have eternal rest with Lazarus, who once was poor.

"We need to make the kind of society," Peter had said, "where it is easier for people to be good." And because his love of God made him love his neighbor, lay down his life indeed for his brother, he wanted to cry out against the evils of the day—the state, war, usury, the degradation of man, the loss of a philosophy of work. He sang the delights of poverty (he was not talking of destitution) as a means to making a step to the land, of getting back to the dear natural things of earth and sky, of home and children. He cried out against the machine because, as Pius XI had said, "raw materials went into the factory and came out ennobled and man went in and came out degraded"; and because it deprived a man of what was as important as bread—his work, his work with his hands, his ability to use all of himself, which made him a whole man and a holy man.

Yes, he talked of these material things. He knew we needed a good social order where we could grow up to our full stature as men and women. And he also knew that it took men and women to make such a social order. He tried to form them, he tried to educate them, and God gave him poor weak materials to work with. He was as poor in the human material he had around him as he was in material goods. We are the offscourings of all, as St. Paul said, and yet we know we have achieved great things in these brief years, and not ours is the glory. God has chosen the weak things to confound the strong, the fools of this earth to confound the wise.

Peter had been insulted and misunderstood in his life as well as loved.

He had been taken for a plumber and left to sit in the basement when he had been invited for dinner and an evening of conversation. He had been thrown out of a Knights of Columbus meeting. One pastor who invited him to speak demanded his money back which he had sent Peter for carfare to his upstate parish because, he said, we had sent him a Bowery bum, and not the speaker he expected. "This then is perfect joy," Peter could say, quoting the words of St. Francis to Friar Leo.

He was a man of sincerity and peace, and yet one letter came to us recently, accusing him of having a holier-than-thou attitude. Yes, Peter pointed out that it was a precept that we should love God with our whole heart and soul and mind and strength, and not just a counsel, and he taught us all what it meant to be children of God, and restored to us our sense of responsibility in a chaotic world. Yes, he was "holier than thou," holier than anyone we ever knew.

"Don't forget," Mary Frecon, head of the Harrisburg house said before she left, "don't forget to tell of the roots of the little tree that they cut through in digging his grave. I kept looking at those roots and thinking how wonderful it is that Peter is going to nourish that tree—that thing of beauty." The undertaker had tried to sell us artificial grass to cover up "the unsightly grave," as he called it, but we loved the sight of that earth that was to cover Peter. He had come from the earth, as we all had, and to the earth he was returning.

Around the grave we all said the Rosary and after the Benedictus we left.

June 1949

Mr. O'Connell

A FRIEND OF THE FAMILY

Somewhere in the Psalms it says that we can look forward to threescore years and ten, if we are strong, but any more years are toil and trouble. Undoubtedly they are, but I suppose most people want to hang on to this life, life they know, as long as possible. Not that anyone will ever be ready for death in the sense that they feel prepared to face God and the judgment. Old Maurice O'Connell, who lived with us from 1936 to 1947 at Mary-

farm, Easton, Pennsylvania, lived to be eighty-four. After the Catholic
Worker moved to Newburgh, Maurice remained behind. When the priest
from St. Bernard's Church came to anoint him a few weeks before his
death, he announced jauntily that he would drop in to see him next time
he was in Easton. His appearance there was not so casual. Yesterday,
February 26, a Requiem Mass was sung at ten o'clock and the body of Mr.
O'Connell was laid in a grave in St. Bernard's Cemetery, behind St. Joseph's
Church, up on the Palisade over the Lehigh River. It was a clear, spring-
like day, though the ground was hard under foot.

I thought, as the coffin was being lowered into the grave, a cheap gray
coffin of proper shape but God knows what materials, the handles decora-
tive rather than functional, that Mr. O'Connell had made a coffin for me
back in 1940 or so, but that he had not made himself one. I should have
brought him mine and let Hans Tunnesen make me another. The coffin he
made for me is of proper size and varnished with the bright yellow varnish
that he had used on the altar, the sacristy closet, and the benches which
he had made for our chapel at Easton, Pennsylvania, when Father Palmer
and Father Woods first came to vacation with us back in 1937.

Mr. O'Connell put in a lot of work on that chapel. The altar, vestment
closet, and benches are all now in use at Maryfarm, Newburgh, and will
be for many a year to come.

In addition to my coffin, which my daughter now uses to store blankets
and other bedding, and the chapel furnishings, Mr. O'Connell took an old
tool shed and made himself a comfortable little house in which he lived for
all the last years of his life, until this last year, when he went to the Smiths'
and Christophers' and boarded there. He had an old-age pension and
preserved a strong feeling of independence. He enjoyed being with the
children. He helped John Filliger remodel his chicken house and he
constructed the Montague and Buley houses, all of them long rectangular
affairs that could be divided into three or four rooms, small and narrow
like the emergency barracks veterans are forced to live in now, utilitarian,
with tarpaper-covered roofs and sides, neither beautiful nor imaginative.

We had to remind ourselves very often of how much Mr. O'Connell had
done for us in the years that we lived at Easton, because he possessed a
violent temper. He was, in fact, something of a terror. He had come from
Ireland so many years before that he remembered, he said, when Canal
Street was not a street but a canal. He was one of twenty-one children,
and his father was an athlete and a carpenter. Maurice pictured him as a
jaunty lad with his children, excelling in feats of strength and looked upon
with admiring indulgence by his wife, who, according to Maurice, nursed

all her children herself, baked all her bread, spun and wove, did all her housekeeping, and never failed in anything. It was, indeed, a picture of the valiant woman that Maurice used to draw for us when any of the women were not able to nurse their children (not to speak of other failures).

He was an old soldier and had worn many a uniform, in South Africa, in India, and in this country. He had no truck with pacifists. And as for community!

According to St. Benedict, there should be a benevolent old man at the gate to receive the visitors, welcome them as other Christs, exemplify hospitality.

Maurice's little cabin was on the road at the very entrance of the farm, and he never missed a visitor. If they were shabby, he shouted at them; if well dressed, he was more suave. He had many a tale to tell of his fellows in the community. He was not a subtle man. His thought was simple, not involved. "Thieves, drunkards, and loafers, the lot of them," he would characterize those who make up what was intended to be a farming commune. And if anyone living on the farm had any skill, it was: "What jail did ye learn that in?" One man who became a Catholic after living with us for a year was greeted with taunts and jeers each time he passed the cabin door. "Turncoat! Ye'd change yer faith for a bowl of soup!"

He was ready with his fists too, and his age of course protected him. Once when he was infuriated by a woman guest who was trying to argue him into a more cooperative frame of mind, he beat his fist into a tree and broke all his knuckles. A violent and enraged man, if anyone differed with him, was Mr. O'Connell.

By the ninth year of Mr. O'Connell's stay with us, he had all the tools of the farm locked up in his cabin and would guard them with a shotgun. That first winter, when Peter and Father Roy and the men had a dormitory in the barn, Mr. O'Connell became ill and was persuaded to be nursed in the dormitory. He was kept warm and comfortable, meals were brought to him on a tray, and he soon recovered his vigor. He decided to stay for the cold months and ensconced himself by the side of the huge potbellied stove. One end of the barn was the sanctuary, and was separated with curtains from the center where the stove, benches, chairs, and bookshelves were. Peter and Mr. O'Connell sat for hours in silence, the latter with his pipe and a book, Peter motionless, his chin sunk in a great sweater that all but engulfed him. Mr. O'Connell was a great reader of history, but it was hard to understand him when he was trying to make a dissertation, especially when his teeth were out, as they usually were.

It was a difficult few months, especially in the morning. We sang the

Mass every day, thanks to Father Roy, and Mr. O'Connell did not enjoy this at seven in the morning. He had been used to sleeping until ten or eleven. On occasion his very audible grumbling was supplemented by a banging on the floor of the dormitory with his shoe. Taken to task for this, he would snarl, "I was just emptying the sand out of my shoe." It was a winter when we had to dig ourselves out to the outhouses.

When Lent came, we were reading Newman's sermons during meals, and whether it was because Maurice did not like Newman as an Englishman, or a convert (he decidedly did not like converts), or whether it was because he thought the reading was directed at him, he used to stomp angrily away from the table and refuse to eat. Stanley had always gotten along well with him (he had never worked with him), but Stanley had a habit when he was reading pointed chapters from the *Imitation,* or Newman, of saying, "This is meant for Dorothy," or "This is meant for Hans." Mr. O'Connell decided the reading was meant for him, and would put up with it no longer. He moved back to his cabin, and his meals were brought to him on a tray. When spring came, he came up to the kitchen and fetched them himself.

The cooking was good that winter. Either Hans or Duncan managed the kitchen, and "we never had it so good." Especially since Father Roy used to go down to the A&P on a Saturday night and beg their leftovers. They were very generous, especially with cold-storage fish or turkeys that would not last, even in the icebox, until Monday. Part of our Sunday preparation was cleaning fish and fowl and seeing what we could do to preserve them. I shudder now when I think of the innards, so soft that all parts seemed to merge into one. However, we had good cooks. And most of the time we had simple foods that did not need to be disguised.

It was about that time, spring and summer, when many retreatants came, that Mr. O'Connell took to telling them all that we never gave him anything to eat, never anything to wear. The fact was that we respected his distaste for complicated dishes, and he had a regular order in at the grocer's for eggs, cheese, milk, bread and margarine, and canned soups. Not to speak of the supplies on our kitchen shelves, which Maurice (or anyone else) felt free to come and help himself to. Our cooks had good training in "if anyone asks for your coat, let him have your cloak too. To him that asks give and do not turn him away, and do not ask for a return of what is borrowed."

All our friends coming for retreats came with generous hearts, of course, anxious to give to the poor, to feed the hungry and clothe the naked. Maurice had many an alms given him, and many were the packages of clothes that were addressed to him. It is wonderful that people have so charitable a spirit, I often thought, but what must they think of us, accused so constantly of this neglect? Surely they were not thinking the best of us! That is to put it positively. To put it crudely, everyone seemed quite ready to think the worst of us. Or maybe they just said, "They are injudicious in that they take on more than they can handle." One can always escape from being uncharitable by being injudicious. It is a nicer word.

I find little paragraphs in my notebook from that time. "What to do about M.'s having six pairs of shoes, a dozen suits of underwear when others go without, Peter for instance. Is it right to let him get away with taking all the tools and probably selling them for drink? Where does the folly of the Cross begin or end? I know that love is a matter of the *will,* but what about common sense? Father Roy is all for non-sense."

And Father Roy was right, of course. "A community of Christians is known by the love they have for one another. 'See how they love one another.'"

"Nobody can say that about us," I would groan.

"If you wish to grow in love, in supernatural love, then all natural love must be pruned, as the vine is pruned. It may not look as though love were there, but have faith."

We were being pruned, all right. Not only through Mr O'Connell but on all sides. Putting it on the most natural plane, I used to think, "How sure people are of us that we believe in what we say, that all men are brothers, that we are a family, that we believe in love, not in use of force, that we would never put them out no matter how hard we are tried. If they act 'naturally' with no servility, even to an extreme of showing bitterness and hatred, then one can only count that as a great victory. We believe in a *voluntary* cooperation. Our faith in these ideas must be tried as though by fire."

And then I would look upon Maurice with gratitude and with pity, that God should choose him to teach us such lessons. It was even as though he were a scapegoat, bearing the sins of ingratitude, hatred, venom, suspicion for all the rest of us, all of it gathered together in one hardy old man.

And, on the other hand, to go with these subtleties, what about this business of letting the other fellow get away with it? Isn't there something awfully smug about such piety—building up your own sanctification at the expense of the increased guilt of someone else? This turning of the other cheek, this inviting someone else to be a potential murderer, or thief, in order that we might grow in grace—how obnoxious! In that case I'd rather be the striker than the meek one struck. One would all but rather be a sinner than a saint at the expense of the sinner. In other words, we must be saved together.

And so I firmly believe, I have faith, that Maurice O'Connell, in addition to being a kind of friend who built the furniture of our chapel and some barracks for our families, who sat and fed the birds and talked ever kindly to the children on the sunny steps before his little house, was an instrument chosen by God to make us grow in wisdom and faith and love.

God rewarded him at the end. He received consciously the great Sacrament of the Church, Extreme Unction, he was surrounded by little children to the end, and even at his grave he had the prayers of kind friends; he had all any pope or king could receive at the hands of the Church, a Christian burial in consecrated ground. May he rest in peace.

March 1952

Father Roy

COSTLY LOVE

There have been so many priests who took time out of their vacations to visit us, and who have come to give us days of recollection and weeks of retreat, that it would be hard to list them all. But Father Pacifique Roy, a Josephite, is one who stands out. When he walked into our back kitchen on the second floor of the Mott Street tenement, he said he felt immediately at home. He was accustomed to living with the poor in the South, among whom he had done much of his work.

All that first morning, Father Roy talked. Work was put aside as people gathered around to listen to him. The cooking had to go on, and the serving; visitors came and went, but we continued to listen. Father Roy, we soon realized, had the same direct approach to the problems of the day that we had. Wherever he was, he set out at once to better conditions, giving what he had in money and skill and spiritual help. St. Ignatius said, "Love is an exchange of gifts." To Father Roy the spiritual and the material gifts were inseparable. He went on to talk not about the social order but about love and holiness, without which man cannot see God. That day found him giving, and us receiving, a little "retreat." It was the retreat of

Father Lacouture, his fellow French Canadian, which had once inspired him as now he inspired us, so that we began "to see all things new."

Although he was stationed in Baltimore, he thought nothing of running up to New York on his day off. Many a day of recollection he gave us when we, in turn, went to Baltimore to visit him. He was a great believer in fasting on bread and water during these days, although the "water" at breakfast could consist of black coffee, which helped keep us awake during the conference. At the close of day, he would feast many of us down in the basement of the rectory, where the janitor, Mr. Green, used to cook up a good meal. One time we had roast groundhog!

In 1945, Father Roy got permission to come to stay with us at Maryfarm. There the first thing he did was to put in electricity, wiring the place with his own hands. Then he set himself and all other hands to digging ditches to bring water from the spring on the hill down to the barn (in which the kitchen was downstairs and the chapel, library, and dormitories were upstairs).

Father Roy slept in the men's upper dormitory with Peter Maurin, Duncan Chisholm, Hans Tunnesen, Joe Cotter, old Mr. O'Connell, and I don't know how many others. They all loved him, with one exception. Mr. O'Connell, who was our collective trial, didn't love anyone. To put it charitably, he was perhaps going through "the dark night." All natural love seemed to be drained from him, as were piety and patience. One morning when we were singing Mass in the chapel, Mr. O'Connell began banging on the floor with his shoe, roaring for us to "cut out that noise!"

We had just started to sing the Mass and those first months must have been hard on Father Roy. He used to look wryly at the servers who sat on either side of him singing the Gloria out of tune. To Father Roy, Mass was truly the work of the day, and he spared no effort to make our worship as beautiful as possible. During even the coldest weather, when the water froze in the cruet and his hands became numb, he said Mass slowly, reverently, with a mind intent on the greatness, the awfulness of the Sacrifice.

To a priest who was complaining of his powerlessness to cope with the darkness of the times, Father Roy said courageously (it is hard to correct a fellow priest in so personal a matter) that if only he would stop gargling the words of the Mass in his throat in a parody of oral prayer, he would at least be making a beginning.

To us he said repeatedly that when we had participated in this great work of the day we had done the most we could possibly do. One member of our community took this too much to heart. On days when Father Roy was away and we had no priest, this fellow worker used to tramp down and up the long hills to St. Joseph's Church, two miles away. Afterward, he would lie at his ease while the others—including his wife—chopped wood, carried water (the house was not piped), and did the work that meant food and shelter for him as well as for the community. He had done his work for the day, he said, carrying the spiritual burden for us all.

But Father Roy's Mass, once offered, did not prevent him from being a most diligent worker. He had what Peter Maurin called "a philosophy of labor." He took great joy in it, counting any day lost that did not see some heavy manual work performed. He felt he could not eat his bread without having shed some sweat. And if visitors and errands and other duties deterred him during the day, he would start in after supper, putting up shelves, hammering, sawing, finishing off some piece of work, going on until midnight.

Father Roy was a good-looking man—tall, lean, with warm and yet piercing eyes; slow, sure, meditative in his movements. He had good hands, well used to toil. I remember when I once cut my hand slicing bread, he laughed and said, "Rejoice in the Lord always!" Later he cut his own hand on the circular saw and had to drive himself, streaming with blood, to the hospital four miles away. I asked him when I returned from the city whether he had rejoiced. "I danced with joy," he said, "especially when they were sewing me up."

He liked to sing French folk songs. Once, with French discretion, he apologized for his "frivolity," justifying his singing by saying, "One must reach people in many ways, you know." But he was more severe in some things than we were. He didn't like a radio in the house, and certainly he would never have allowed television. Both let in too much of the world. He loved parties, however, and we celebrated many feast days.

He also enjoyed going down to the chain stores on Saturday night to collect the leftovers which the countermen gave us free. When he had to pay for food, he'd buy pigs' feet or such cheap delicacies, although Eileen McCarthy, a teacher who visited us one winter, used to beg him for "a little of the pig higher up." She meant a ham, of course, but Father countered her Irish wit with some of his own; he brought her some pigs' tails.

Besides shopping he dug, he built, he all but started a lumber mill. One day, during his hour's meditation, as he sat with his eyes glued to the floor before him, it occurred to him that the boards of the barn floor, originally laid to accommodate farm trucks and tractors, were unnecessarily thick for a chapel and library. At the conclusion of this hour, he started tearing them up, leaving great chasms looking down to the depths of the former cow stalls below; it did not matter that a retreat was scheduled to start the following Friday night. There were still gaps in the floor when the retreatants began to arrive. They were put to work nailing down the boards which had come back from the mill on the hill, sawed from the four-inch-thick flooring he had taken up. He doubled his supply of lumber by the move.

Hans Tunnesen kept up with him in much of the work, although Hans was cooking and baking at the same time. Hans complained, however, that everything Father Roy built was geared to tall men—the sink was too high, the shelves too high, the tables and benches too high; even the toilet seats in the new outhouse which Father Roy built were too high! But his manifold accomplishments simply go to show how all-encompassing was his fatherly concern for us, how all-embracing his love.

Our life was indeed beautiful, with work, with song, with worship, with feastings and fastings. He was strict about the latter, however, and at times we sat down to the table with no more than cornmeal mush or oatmeal for supper. He ate it with us, he shared all our hardships, he rejoiced and sorrowed with us. He heard our confessions and he gave us the bread of life.

He also gave us conference after conference, and he gave the same conferences over and over again with the same enthusiasm. We didn't mind when he would insist that Father Onesimus Lacouture was the greatest preacher since St. Paul. We were used to enthusiasms that tended to exaggeration and hyperbole. We knew what he meant. He convinced us that God loved us and had so loved us that He gave His own Son, Who by His life and death sent forth a stream of grace that made us His brothers in grace, closer than blood brothers to Him and to each other. He made us know what love meant, and what the inevitable suffering of love meant. He taught us that when there were hatred and rivalries among us, and bitterness and resentments, we were undergoing purifications, prunings, in order to bear a greater fruit of love. He made us feel the power of love, he made us keep our faith in the power of love.

Above all things in the natural order, he loved his active life of work. He had a passion for work—you could see it—just as Peter Maurin had a passion for thinking, for indoctrination. Both men were great teachers, who taught by their single-mindedness and the example of their own lives. And both had to pay the price.

One morning, not long after his return from extensive traveling and preaching in the South (it showed the greatness and wisdom of his superior that Father Roy was given such complete liberty), he got up to say Mass in our barn chapel. We were horrified to find him suddenly communicating right after the Sanctus bell, before he had consecrated the Host. By the vagueness of his words and gestures, we saw that something had happened. He might have had a slight stroke in his sleep which impaired his memory; it might have been a blood clot on the brain; none of us knew enough about these things. It was hard to get him to a doctor. What he wanted, he said, reverting to his childhood, was to go home. He wanted to go back to Montreal, where, in the bosom of his family, he could be diagnosed and treated. "Maybe I need to have the rest of my teeth pulled out," he said naïvely. (His nephew was a dentist and could do it.)

So one of the young men went with him by plane to his sister's home in Montreal. There was a long silence. The next thing we heard, he was in a hospital, the Hôtel-Dieu, in the ward for mental patients. What had happened was that he had wandered away in northern Quebec and got lost. He was found in a tiny village, living with a priest and serving as an altar boy. The priest did not know Father Roy was a priest, too, dressed as he was in a suit over a pair of pajamas, but took him to be some poor man. (Mauriac said that Christ was a man so much like other men that it took the kiss of Judas to single him out.)

I went to see him in the mental hospital, where, as is customary here in the States also, people who have lost their memories are confined. He remembered me, but not the others at the farm. He cried a little when he showed me the bruises on his face where one of the other patients, another priest, had struck him. He told me how an attendant, while changing his bed, had called him a dirty pig. He wept like a child and then suddenly smiled and said, "Rejoice!" I was crying too, and in our shared tears I felt free to ask him something I would never have said otherwise, feeling that it would be an unwarranted and most indelicate prying. "Are you . . . have you offered yourself," I asked, "as a victim?"

It was then that he said to me, "We are always saying to God things we don't really mean, and He takes us at our word. He really loves us and believes us."

Father Roy didn't have to stay in the hospital very long. He went home again to his dearly loved sister, who with her husband carefully watched over him. (His order always paid all his expenses.) Then an opportunity came for him to live in a retreat house for old and ill priests at Trois-Rivières, Quebec, where, with the help and guidance of a brother priest, he was enabled to offer up once more the Holy Sacrifice of the Mass.

He had this joy for only two months, and then he became ill with what they took to be a slight case of grippe. Within less than a fortnight he died. He was fully conscious when he received the last rites of the Church; and he died, his sister wrote me, rejoicing.

Loaves and Fishes

Ammon Hennacy

PROPHET WITHOUT HONOR

It is easier to write about those who are dead than those who are alive. I have never tired of writing about Peter Maurin and Father Pacifique Roy, and shall probably write more about them before I die. They are unique and I can never do them justice. Other people will write about them too, and will in a way do a better job, but I must write as I have seen them, so there will always be a great deal of "I" in such writing.

And now I want to write about Ammon, knowing that he will not object. He is considered self-centered and egotistical and vain by many, and so he is in a way, enough so that he will rather appreciate my writing about him than not. There is an old American saying, "Every knock a boost," and certainly Ammon would rather people talk of him adversely than not talk of him at all. Hatred or love, but never indifference.

Ammon wants to be paid attention to, because he has a message, because he is a prophet. His sense of mission leads him constantly to talk about what he is doing. Yet this is combined with a kind of humility, as though to say, "If I can do it, you can too. See what one small man of reasonable strength and intelligence can do. I did this, I did that, this is the way I meet a crisis, and if we all did it together we would ride out the gale and come through safely."

Undoubtedly he is right, irritatingly right. So he has become a prophet without honor in his own country. And it must be admitted that he is often hard to take. Someone said last year that a little of Ammon goes a long way. No one else I know, however, seems capable of the sustained effort, the perseverance so needed at this time of crisis. Most of us are inclined to shrug and say with St. Teresa of Avila, "All times are dangerous times," and then settle down to our daily affairs, trusting God to take care of everything. So long as we say a few prayers each day, get to Mass, and go on living our comfortable lives, we feel secure because we have "the faith." To Ammon, this whole lifetime is a time of crisis. "And none recognizes that there is a crisis," he says sadly.

As I write now about Ammon, it is two days before he begins his yearly fast—that is, his yearly *long* fast. (Every Friday he fasts for the sake of health and discipline.) His long fast begins on the Feast of the Transfiguration, August 6, which is also the anniversary of the first dropping of the atom bomb on Hiroshima. There had been obliteration bombings before—entire cities had been set aflame—but this work of one bomb surpassed them all in horror. Since then, Ammon has fasted a day for each year since the bomb was dropped. This year his fast will last eleven days. During this period he will picket the income tax office, giving out literature and carrying a sign as a protest against the payment of income tax, 80 percent of which is for war purposes. "If we pay taxes," he says simply, "we pay for the bomb."

He has presented us all with a problem. What kind of work can we do for which we need not pay federal income tax? Even if we do not pay it directly, there is a withholding from pay, and the hidden federal taxes on tobacco, liquor, the theater.

Ammon solved the problem for himself by working by the day, at hard labor, in the Southwest. He irrigated, picked cotton, worked in the fields all around Phoenix, Arizona, and took home his daily pay. He lived like the early fathers of the desert on vegetables and bread and sent his money to his two daughters so they could finish their education at Northwestern University. When he had fulfilled this obligation, he came to New York and joined our staff. Here he works for board and room, as the rest of us do, and so does not have to pay federal income tax here, either.

The men in the kitchen all like Ammon—for one reason, because he has been in prison, because he feels that all men who have been in prison are most especially his comrades. Many a man who has worked with us, dishwashing, waiting on tables, and cooking, has seen the inside of our jails. It is easy enough to go to jail if you are poor. You can be sentenced for vagrancy, for sleeping on a park bench or in the subway, for begging, for selling neckties without a license, even for walking through the park after midnight. Ammon served his sentence, his long sentence as a conscientious objector during the First World War, when he spent nine months in solitary confinement, and another year besides.

Ammon is a vegetarian, but he doesn't "make a religion of it." He sees to it that he gets enough to eat: fruit in the morning, soup at noon, and a goodly meal of cheese, eggs, vegetables, and salads at night. Betweentimes he doesn't scorn a wedge of pie, hot chocolate or tea, either. But he does without coffee, as one other of the unnecessary things of life. Put him out on the desert and he would find some way of living, even if it meant chopping mesquite and selling the wood from door to door in the nearest town. He has subsisted on the gleanings from the immense vegetable fields of the Southwest. Working in date orchards, he has lived on dates.

We like to call Ammon our American peasant, just as Peter Maurin was our French peasant. He was born in southern Ohio (pronounced "O-hi-a") near the Pennsylvania and West Virginia borders. His grandfather was a farmer, and he worked on the farm as a young boy. He lived in a tiny mining town and once drove Mother Jones in a horse and buggy to a meeting of miners in Cannelton, West Virginia, only a few miles away. It was one of his earliest encounters with a radical. Despite a Baptist background, Ammon very early became an atheist and socialist. Eugene Debs and Mother Jones were his heroes, and he believed in trade unions and political action. It was while he was in Atlanta Penitentiary, in solitary confinement with only a Bible to read, that he became a religious pacifist. Reading all of Tolstoy later confirmed him in his pacifism and anarchism. From then on, guided by the Sermon on the Mount, he wanted to lead a life of poverty, loving-kindness, and peacefulness.

Besides being a "peasant" and so possessed of great endurance and vitality, Ammon is also a great salesman. In my bitter moments I have called him a Babbitt. He enjoys getting out on the street to sell, whether it be the paper, his book, or his ideas. This is his way of meeting the crisis.

I speak of "bitter moments," and I mean that it is irksome to live with someone who is always right, who points out that he knows how to work, that he knows how to eat, to fast, to sleep, to meet each and every problem of the day. He would like to have followers, disciples, but Americans do not make good followers—they each want to go their own way. But living in community is saving Ammon. He is learning not to give the ready answer to every problem, not to be surprised at criticism, at the nagging that goes with community life. He is learning to recognize that all men have their various talents, physical, mental, and spiritual. That the vocation of one is not the vocation of all.

His too-hasty judgments of others and his inability to see that he himself is ever wrong—these are his most obvious faults. (We all have them, but we hide them more.) His faults seem to be faults of speech rather than action. "Do what he does and pay no attention to what he says," I often feel like declaring when he is guilty of some evident heresy or lack of charity. With most of us, it is just the opposite—we are so much better in our speech than in our actions. But in all that he does Ammon is charity itself. When an extra bed has been needed, he has given up his own over and over again.

It is Ammon who will meet visitors at the railroad station and stay up nights to entertain them. He is always faithful in getting the mail and answering the telephone. He likes to have every moment accounted for, and spends from eleven to three each day on the street—on Wall Street, at Forty-third and Lexington, at Fordham University (where he loves meeting priests and nuns), at Union Square, or in front of Cooper Union or the New School.

How many thousands has he contacted personally, face to face, with his good news of the Kingdom of God, where the lion may lie down with the lamb, where no man calls his cloak his own, where there is a companion for every weary mile. Ammon believes and acts on the belief that here and now is the time to begin.

It would take too long to explain his "anarchism," which is an individual brand. What he is really fighting is the modern state and war, which is "the health of the state." But he loosely bandies about the words "government" and "law" as though he would throw them all out the window. Peter Maurin used to do very much the same sort of thing. "It makes to think," he used to say. "It is good to shock people into thinking."

Yet if all men were like Ammon, caring for others, washing the feet of others, taking the least place, there would be no need for courts, judges, or police. How strange it is that all the anarchists I have met have been the most disciplined of men, lawful and orderly, while those who insist that discipline and order must prevail are those who out of plain contrariness would refuse to obey and are most unable to regulate themselves. But perhaps these are generalizations.

The fact remains that Ammon is a prophet, and will walk the streets fasting and calling on man to awaken to the crisis of the time and the part he could play in averting it.

On the night before his fast he will gird himself for the ordeal, taking fruit juices and going to bed early. On Monday he will be up for seven o'clock Mass. He will go down by bus to Battery Park, where he will begin to pace the street, carrying a poster and giving out literature. With a few moments of rest every hour, he will picket this way, eight hours a day, each day except Saturday and Sunday (when the offices are closed and no one is there to see him). And as the week goes on, his voice will get weaker;

when he comes home he will lie on one of the long low tables in the back office for a bit of rest, until he can regain enough strength to climb the four flights to his bed.

There are some ways in which we can cooperate with him. We can take turns picketing with him, walking up and down, giving out papers, listening to the scoffs and jeers of some of the men and women who go by, and even perhaps shield him from possible attack (as we have had to do on several occasions).

Why picket as well as fast? some will ask. In a way it is easier to move than to sit still. It is easier to keep moving slowly, up and down the streets on a warm summer day, watching the boats go down the bay, talking to passersby, even if only exchanging a word. One year Ammon announced that he was fasting until the crisis was over, but I talked him out of that, since we are perpetually in crisis. There is always one more crisis, but who knows which will be the one to precipitate war?

But Ammon Hennacy is never a victim of that dread disease of the day, *futility*. He is vital and alive, he reverences life and is grateful to God for the gift of life. He has his sense of mission and is convinced as an anarchist that what is going to happen depends on each one of us and the part we play. And his part is that of a John the Baptist, a voice in the wilderness: "Make straight the way of the Lord."

The Third Hour, 1956

II

One of the great things that Ammon did for the Catholic Worker was to increase our ecumenical spirit. In those days there was not much talk of ecumenism in the Holy Roman Catholic Church. There were complaints among our staff that they never knew whether I was quoting the Douay version of the Scriptures or the King James version. When we started to publish Ammon Hennacy's articles, "Life at Hard Labor," and he made slighting remarks about Holy Mother Church, there were adverse comments among the staff and even more severe criticisms from some of our readers. It was in vain that we pointed him out as the most ascetic, the most hard-working, the most devoted to the poor and the oppressed of any we had met, and that his life and his articles put us on the spot. He was an inspiration and a reproach.

Even before he came to New York to join us, he introduced us to the Molokans, the Doukhobors, the Hutterites, and many another sect which had come to this country to escape war and conscription in their own countries. He was interested, in fact, in all religious points of view if they resulted in a real effort to conform one's life to one's profession of faith. He still spoke contemptuously of Jesus-shouters and religious demagogues who blessed the state and war, and he stated unequivocally that he did not like St. Paul, that St. Paul had betrayed Christ when he said, "Servants, obey your masters."

"Obedience," of course, was a bad word, as was "authority." In vain I pointed out that he accepted the authority of those who were authorities and knew what they were doing, and how to do it.

On his coming to New York in the late forties, he attended a retreat at Maryfarm at Newburgh on the Hudson. During the Mass each morning, he knelt on the hard floor next to a man by the name of Kenneth Little, who died some years ago. Kenneth kept pointing out to him all the words in the Mass that had to do with peace.

"Mercifully give *peace* in our days . . . The *peace* of the Lord be always with you . . . Lamb of God who takes away the sins of the world, grant us *peace* . . . Lord Jesus Christ, who said to your apostles: *Peace* I leave with you, my *peace* I give to you . . . be pleased to grant to your Church *peace* and unity according to your will."

Poor Kenneth, he did so want to assure Ammon that the Church indeed did desire peace. But I am afraid that neither Ammon nor I could forget how the scrap metal was heaped in the churchyards during the Second World War and blessed by the priests, and war stamps sold to the children, and bombs named after the Blessed Mother, and so on.

Ammon knew much labor history, but very little about Church history. He could get no encouragement from the fact that in ages past there had been far greater scandals of wealth and warfare than even today. Or were there? One priest said of Ammon's anti-clericalism that perhaps he saw the sins of the Church as a human institution far more clearly than we did. Another priest said of Ammon that he had received so great a light during that first jail sentence of his in Atlanta Penitentiary that it had blinded him. He had read through the Bible nine times and all but memorized the Sermon on the Mount. By the time he came out, he had become a Bible Christian, in the sense not of a sect, but of one who accepted the *Word*.

For a time, Ammon was a Catholic. It was before the aggiornamento, and though he had been christened a Baptist, a valid baptism, he was conditionally baptized again by Father Marion Casey in Minnesota. His instruction had been slight, in spite of the retreats and conferences which we were in the habit of having at the Newburgh farm. He assented to what he agreed with, had no mind for philosophy or theology, and he no longer read the Scriptures. "I read them nine times in jail," he said on a number of occasions. And once, flippantly, "If I had only had a telephone book I would have read that nine times." Just as he said later on, "If Dorothy had been a Methodist, I would have become a Methodist." These were wounding words. I could never understand them.

He was with us—how many years? Long enough to make an impression on that great pagan city of New York. Peter Maurin quoted Cardinal Newman—"If you wish to reach the man in the street, go to the man in the street." Ammon went directly to people and persevered in friendship with them, though he soon realized that they were not going to go very far in building up a new society. In spite of his critical attitude, he had a great warmth and loved to be with people and made them feel his closeness to them. I would not say he ever despaired or felt hopeless. He could not have gone on if he did. Part of his love for people came from his great inner loneliness—there were so few to work for the nonviolent revolution, so few ready to sacrifice all for it.

Of course, Ammon was basically a romantic Irishman, and never lost that sense of drama, that love of life, tragic though its outcome so often was. He literally would have liked to give his life for the obliteration of wars and all injustice from the face of the earth. He would have welcomed being shot as Joe Hill was, that labor martyr for whom he named his House of Hospitality in Salt Lake City. But Ammon's death was a triumph just the same. His first heart attack came to him on the picket line on his way to the Federal Court Building in Salt Lake City. He died suddenly a week later, when his friends thought that he was on the way to recovery.

He died protesting the execution of two of the least of God's children, who had been justly sentenced, as the Mormons thought (believing as they do in the shedding of blood to atone for the shedding of blood).

I have said that Ammon was a romantic, and once he said to me, "I don't remember the time that I wasn't in love with some woman." Believing as I do that being "in love" is a reflection of the love God has for each and every one of us, I am glad that this kind of love illumined the last seven years of Ammon's life.

He had long ceased attending Mass, though on his travels, as his wife states, he went to Mass with her and even received Communion. But "in peace was his bitterness most bitter." He rejected the "institutional church" even while he received the Sacrament. The monks at the Holy Trinity Monastery with whom he was friends never questioned him, nor would I. Who can understand another, who can read another's heart?

I do not think that Ammon expected to die. All felt he was on the way to recovery, so there was no question of his preparing for death in the way of confession or asking for the last rites, or the Sacrament of the Sick, as it is now called. In fact, I am not sure if Ammon knew what the Sacraments were, or what they were all about, that they were channels of grace. If they had been explained, I am sure he would have considered that grace had already been poured out upon him abundantly in the sufferings he had endured in jail. God's ways are not our ways.

One of Ammon's favorite quotations from Scripture was: "Let him who is without sin cast the first stone." But I must admit that Ammon was a great one to judge when it came to priests and bishops and his words were coarse on many an occasion, so that it was hurtful to me to hear him, loving the church as I do. But there's that love-hate business in all of us, and Ammon wanted so much to see priests and bishops and popes stand out strong and courageous against the sins and the horrors and the cruelty of the powers of this world. But we cannot judge him, knowing so well his own strong and courageous will to fight the corruption of the world around him.

February 1970

Elizabeth Gurley Flynn

RED ROSES FOR HER

Elizabeth Gurley Flynn, Secretary of the Communist Party of the United States, died in Moscow on September 5, 1964, at the age of seventy-two. Dorothy, invited to speak at the memorial meeting held for her in Community Church, New York City, was unable to attend. Instead she sent the following message to be read aloud.

I dreamed of Gurley Flynn last night, and woke up thinking of how, on Christmas Eve in 1957, Ammon Hennacy and I had gone to her apartment just off Second Avenue, which she shared with her sister. Not long before, she had been released from the Women's Federal Reformatory, at Alderson, West Virginia. Ammon and I had just come from the Women's House of Detention, over in Greenwich Village, outside of which we had been singing Christmas carols with a group of about fifty young people. It was a custom we had started the year before, after the first of four brief sentences a number of us served for breaking the State Civil Defense Law by refusing to take shelter during the air-raid drills.

I had served a sentence of thirty days. But Gurley Flynn had spent twenty-eight months in a jail (I hate to call them "reformatories") far away from home and friends. Her sister had faithfully visited her each month. Ammon had brought a red rose for each of them, but it was really to Elizabeth Gurley Flynn that he was paying tribute. First of all, because she had valiantly endured jail many times; she had laid down her life for her brothers in this way. Certainly, going to jail is dying to oneself and living according to the great commandment of Jesus, who went beyond the Old Testament when He said: "A new commandment I give you." (Not only loving your neighbor as yourself, but loving him enough to lay down your life for him.)

In my dream I was there again with Ammon and Gurley Flynn, experiencing again her warmth, her equanimity, her humor, and above all, the *purpose* of her life—her aim to help bring about the kind of society where each would work according to his ability and receive according to his needs, truly one of the noblest possible aims in life.

I had first met her when I was eighteen and she was lecturing at some workers' hall in Brooklyn. I was a reporter on the New York *Call,* which boasted a staff of socialist, anarchist, and Wobbly reporters, in addition to trade-unionists who divided their allegiance between the American Federation of Labor and the Amalgamated Clothing Workers, who had stayed outside the Federation. She was a member of the I.W.W. (Industrial Workers of the World), that truly indigenous form of unionism and radicalism. There had been no revolution in Russia as yet, and the I.W.W. was fought as bitterly as the Communists are today. In fact, it seems to me that anything that threatens money or property, anything that aims at a more equitable distribution of this world's goods, has always been called communism. I like the word myself; it makes me think of the communism of the religious orders. In fact, the success and prosperity of religious orders shows how beneficial communism could be if it were practiced for all, rather than for only those professed religious who give up family, marriage, and personal belongings to devote themselves to the problems of poverty. But, as the Ecumenical Council has stressed, this is the age of the laity, and the laity comprises all those who are not monks, priests, or nuns, but just ordinary brothers and sisters, in the widest sense of the word. Gurley Flynn was of the laity, and she was also my sister in this deep sense of the word. She always did what the laity is nowadays urged to do. She felt a responsibility to do all in her power in defense of the poor, to protect them against injustice and destitution.

On that night I first met her, she was speaking in behalf of the Mesabi iron miners of Minnesota, who were on strike at the time, and her words moved the large audience to tears. She charmed us out of our meager money; people emptied their pockets when the collection was taken for the strikers. I forsook all prudence and emptied my purse, not even leaving myself carfare to get back to the office. (My salary at the time was not more than ten dollars a week.) In this way she aided countless workers—miners throughout the Far West, workers in wheat, lumber, textiles, all have benefited from her early work. If there had not been an I.W.W., there would have been no C.I.O.

You must forgive me if my emphasis is religious. Whenever Jesus spoke about the attitude man ought to have toward his brother, He always emphasized the problems of wealth and poverty. He told the story of the rich man who burned in hell while the poor man who had sat at his gate, sick and unemployed, was taken up into Abraham's bosom. (How loving a phrase that is!) He told the story of how the men who came to work at the end of the day got paid as much as those who had worked since early morning. How different from the attitude of the associated farmers of California, who consider themselves Christians! And when people asked Jesus, "When did we see You hungry or homeless, or in jail or sick, and did not visit You?" He answered them: "In so far as you did not do it to the least of these My brothers, you did not do it to Me."

The great English writer George Orwell once said that one of the greatest tragedies of our age has been the loss of a sense of personal immortality. It may sound exaggerated to say that Gurley Flynn's *name* will be immortal in the labor and radical movements, but it brings out the point I wish to make. Orwell spoke of *personal* immortality, and that is the kind people who have religious faith believe in, because it is clearly taught in the New Testament. "If we did not believe this, how vain our faith would be," St. Paul wrote. It is the core of our faith.

I don't think anyone really wants to die. Unless, of course, he is in such pain that he seeks death as a relief. But not a person as vital as Gurley Flynn, who enjoyed life so much, found so much to do, lived so keen an intellectual life (not in a philosophical sense, but rather in a "sociological" sense), who loved so ardently—no, I do not think that she wished to die, to go into oblivion, personally, she herself.

She has long been in my prayers, and I really believe that one's prayer is always answered. "Ask, and you shall receive," Jesus said. And He also said that God wills that *all* men be saved. I was once told by a good priest, and have often read it since, that there is no *time* with God. That is a difficult concept, philosophically and theologically. But it means that in this particular case all the prayers I have said, and will say in the future, will have meant that Gurley Flynn held out her arms to God (and the word God itself means Good, Truth, Love, all that is most beautiful) at the moment of her death, and was received by Him. And she will be judged by the love that is in her heart.

November 1964

Mike Gold

FAREWELL, OLD COMRADE

Mike Gold, author of *Jews Without Money,* and one of the leading Communist journalists in America, died on May 14, 1965. He was Dorothy's oldest friend.

I last saw Mike Gold two years ago when I visited Oakland, where he was living with Elizabeth, his wife. She and I had gathered shells and rocks together on the beaches of Staten Island ten years ago, just as Mike and I had explored those beaches forty years before. It was the year the old *Masses* was suppressed, and during the last months of its existence there was a general feeling of irresponsibility, stemming from our incapacity to do anything in the face of the war into which we had just been dragged, after a presidential election won with the slogan "He kept us out of the war." We were marking time.

When I first met Mike, I had been working on the socialist New York *Call.* When it came to all the conflicts after the Russian Revolution, we were young enough not to pay much attention to the old guard, rejoicing instead in a victorious revolt of the proletariat and the peasants of Russia. We all went to meetings, to picnics, to dances at Webster Hall, stayed up all night and walked the streets, sat on the piers and sang. Great things were happening in the world, along with the senseless capitalistic war, which to us represented the suffering and death that must come before the victorious resurrection. I thought in those terms then. "Unless the seed fall into the ground and die it remaineth alone. But if it die it bears much fruit." The suffering and the death that accompanied war and revolution seemed to make the keenness of our joy the more poignant. The revolution was world-shaking, it liberated the people, the ancient lowly, the burden bearers, the poor, the destitute, and opened up to them a new life. We longed ourselves to be able to take part in that suffering.

We were far away from it all, of course. We were young, we had found ourselves, in that we had a cause, and we served it in our writing. It was through his writing that I came to know Mike. In the summer of 1917, I had been left alone in the office of *The Masses* as an editor's assistant while Floyd Dell was on vacation and Max Eastman away on a money-raising and speaking expedition. I opened the office and answered the mail and sent back the work of some eminent poets with rejection slips and one written word, "Sorry." In my haste to get through with office duty and go out into the streets, to meetings and to the beaches, the work of *The Masses* did not seem of vital importance.

I walked the streets of the East Side, which I had come to love, down on Cherry Street, on East Broadway, on Madison Street. I knew the Jews and their life there; I bathed with the women in those little bathhouses (there were no baths or hot water in the tenements). I visited Mike's home on Chrystie Street, down the street from the present location of the Catholic Worker. His mother, a stern and beautiful woman who wore the wig and observed the dietary laws, offered me food, even though I was a shiksa, but she did not speak to me.

My suffering at that time was brief, but Mike's was profound. I went to jail in Washington, upholding the rights of political prisoners. An anarchist then as I am now, I have never used the vote that the women won by their demonstrations before the White House. But Mike was suffering the threat of the draft, which then, as now, hung over all young men. It was a physical as well as a mental and spiritual anguish, and it undermined his health. Finally Max Eastman helped him get away to Mexico, where the "draft dodgers," as they are always contemptuously termed, were taking refuge.

In those days, conscientious objectors had no rights. There was no alternative service. There were no discussions as to whether you were opposed to all wars or only the present one, whether your conviction was a religious one or not. Mike was certainly not opposed to war as such. He thought that the revolution had to be a violent one; although the workers did not want violence or advocate it, it would be forced upon them, and they would be exercising their right to defend themselves and their dear ones. His faith in the class struggle and violent revolution never wavered over the years.

Some years after the war I saw Mike in Chicago, where I worked briefly for Bob Minor on *The Liberator*. Then I returned to New York and, thanks to the sale of my first novel to Hollywood, I was able to buy a beach bungalow on a section of Staten Island that is almost as undeveloped today as it was then. I was living a married life, spending a good deal of time reading and going through a painful and tortured, yet joyful process of conversion to a public acknowledgment of faith. It was painful because I had to give up a common-law husband with whom I was very much in love and with whom I still feel a most loving friendship. I write of these personal matters because Mike was very much around at that time; two of his brothers had bought a beach bungalow three doors down the road from mine, and we all swam and dug clams and fished together and spent long hours on the beach. One of his brothers was married and had two little children who played with my two-year-old daughter. Mike, who loved kids and did not yet have any of his own, came down often to be with us all.

Never for a moment did Mike try to argue me out of the step I was about to take. My small daughter was already baptized and I tried to get to Mass every Sunday in the little village church, although I was not yet a baptized Catholic. Mike was editor of the *New Masses* at the time, and I wrote a few things for him. He seemed to understand my misery and to sense that there had to be a price to pay, sometimes a heartbreaking price, in following one's vocation. Neither revolutions nor faith is won without keen suffering. For me Christ was not to be bought for thirty pieces of silver but with my heart's blood. We buy not cheap in this market. Because I was so unhappy I clung to my old friends. I did not know a single Catholic and I suppose I considered Mike my oldest friend.

Mike was indirectly involved with the beginning of the Catholic Worker. In 1932 I was doing some free-lance writing and Mike's brother George was one of the leaders of the hunger march that was to converge on Washington in December. George and Mike used to drop in to see me where I was living with my brother and his wife on the East Side, and I became so enthusiastic about the march that I went down to cover it for *America*. It was the march and the devout prayers I said at the shrine of the Immaculate Conception at Catholic University that brought the French peasant and teacher Peter Maurin to my doorstep to start me editing *The Catholic Worker*.

One day in the fifties, after Peter was dead, Mike, his wife Elizabeth, and their two sons Carl and Nicholas visited us on our farm on Staten

Island. They had brought me a gift, an old print with a painted representation of a pilgrimage to the shrine of St. Anne of Brittany. They had brought it from France, carefully rolled in a newspaper. We framed it and hung it in the dining room of the farm. St. Anne is the patron saint of grandmothers, since she was the mother of the Blessed Virgin and the grandmother of Jesus of Nazareth. We still talked of how man's freedom could be protected, how man's basic needs could be provided for through collectives, or cooperatives, or farming communes, as Peter Maurin always called them. But we always came back to the problem of the use of force in bringing about the common good.

I remember the one time Mike had turned bitter against me and *The Catholic Worker*. "The brotherly love *The Catholic Worker* preaches would be more understandable if it were not that they were pro-Franco during the Spanish Civil War," he wrote in his column in the *Daily Worker*. We were not, of course, pro-Franco, but pacifists, followers of Gandhi in our struggle to build a spirit of nonviolence. But in those days we got it from both sides; it was a holy war to most Catholics, just as world revolution is holy war to Communists. I call attention to these fundamental differences about religion and the attitude toward force to show how there can be strong personal friendship between a Catholic and a Communist and constant seeking of concordances and agreements.

It was indeed more than a personal friendship; it was a friendship between families. Mike was best man at my sister's wedding forty years ago and last week, when her son wrote to her of Mike's death, he recalled his gentle and loving spirit. He indeed had a gentle and loving spirit, but some of his writing was strong stuff, because of the bitterness that the sight of poverty and human distress always inspired in him.

June 1967

Hugh Madden

DEATH OF A PILGRIM

Hugh Madden is dead, struck down by a car as he was cycling his way to the shrine of Our Lady of Guadalupe in Mexico City. He had started out early to be there on her feast day, December 12, and he had gotten as far as Glade Springs, Virginia, when he was killed. We had his body brought back to Tivoli, where the Catholic Worker farm has a cemetery plot, and his funeral was last Friday, a Requiem Mass at which Monsignor Kane delivered a eulogy. He was buried with all his fellow workers at the farm standing by.

Even before his death, Hugh had become a legendary figure on East and West Coast in Catholic Worker circles.

The first time I met him was when Ammon Hennacy was picketing the tax offices. He was conducting his usual fast on one of the anniversaries of the dropping of the atom bomb on Hiroshima and Hugh had come East from California to join him in his picketing. He showed up on the line dressed in rags, literally, a peculiarly patched-together costume with a poncho which, in some way, was like a priest's chasuble. His old sweat-stained felt hat was studded with medals and buttons. If the weather was hot he wore old army pants cut off at the knee, and being hipless, he often had to hitch them up in the interests of modesty. Often his shirt did not meet the trousers in the rear, an added coolness but an added distraction to the beholder. His legs were thin and bare, and his feet were sandaled. He was in a way like a St. Benedict Joseph Labre in appearance, except that he kept himself clean. In all, he was a spare, gaunt figure of a man, with a little goatee on an otherwise clean-shaven face; it brought out his resemblance to pictures of Uncle Sam—and so the men at the farm immediately dubbed him.

One might be astounded at the picture of Hugh at first, but somehow the aspect of a man doing penance shone through. On the picket line that first day he got down on his knees at the stroke of noon and there on that populous street, jostled by the crowd on their way to lunch, he bowed to the ground and prayed the Angelus; and since he had no bells to ring and there were no bells from neighborhood church to call to prayer, he pounded with his bare knuckles on the harsh pavement, to accent the three versicles and the three Hail Marys. "The angel of the Lord appeared unto Mary; she conceived by the Holy Spirit. Behold the handmaid of the Lord: be it done unto me according to Thy word. The word was made flesh and dwelt among us."

He lived with us for a time at Spring Street. After praying on his knees before a statue of the Blessed Mother, he would spread out a mat on the floor and sleep. He came to the farm at Staten Island and visited the beach houses. At the farm we had a ship's bell and he rang it each morning at six, again for the Angelus, again at noon and suppertime. One time there was a sick priest with us, who slept late after sleepless nights, but that did not deter Hugh. He was stern with himself and though he said little he presented his stern visage to us.

For a time he ran a House of Hospitality on the West Coast. The house in Oakland was efficiently run, even harshly run, and when many of the group protested his rule, Hugh came back East to us.

By this time I had heard a little more of the legend. He had been a seaman most of his life, and one story had it that he was washed ashore after being long adrift at sea (the ship had been torpedoed). He had then spent six years at Gethsemane as a Trappist brother. He left there to work on a ranch he owned in California where the church was thirty miles away. The story is that he milked the cows Saturday night, set out for Mass, arriving in the morning, and after attending Mass and receiving Holy Communion, walked the thirty miles back again. This was repeated winter and summer every Sunday.

He lived with us at the Catholic Worker farm these last years, between pilgrimages. In the summer he cycled to Canada to visit the shrines of Our Lady and of Ste. Anne de Beaupré. He had a ten-speed bicycle and it had carried him from Oakland to the East Coast as well as to the Quebec shrine and the one in Mexico. These wanderings of his reminded me of those of the Russian pilgrims who traveled vast distances, from Archangel to Irkutsk.

At the farm there was no telling where he slept. There is a tunnel, a mysterious affair extending from the old de Peyster mansion in two directions, out front toward the high bank above the railroad tracks, and from the basement of the house under the driveway to the ravine. Hugh slept in this damp tunnel for a time until it crippled him, and then one day I caught him digging a cave into the patch of sunny hillside and bade him stop. It was liable to fall in on him, I said, and I deemed this childish nonsense.

He looked at me with a stubborn glint in his eye. Then he pointed to the chapel in the old schoolhouse and said, "I'm going to pray about this, and if the Holy Spirit as well as you tells me to stop I will, but if He doesn't I'll hit the road."

Finally he settled in a cabin which had been put up in the woods at the end of the property. It was well built but terribly cluttered.

Hugh had a small check from the government which he used to ask Walter Kerell to hold for him until he set out, and when he died he had ten dollars in cash and something over a hundred in traveler's checks on his person. He earned his way with us by most conscientiously doing all the pot washing. He also baked the most peculiar concoctions of bread, mixing every kind of flour and cereal we had in the house. I liked his cornmeal loaf best myself.

I cannot close without speaking of Hugh's behavior in church, which I am afraid was a grave distraction to our Tivoli population at first. Hugh liked to kneel in the aisle when he attended Mass. Someone had explained to him that it was forbidden by canon law to take up money at the door for the pews, so he refused to use them. He always approached the altar rail on his knees and received Communion kneeling.

When Monsignor Kane preached the funeral sermon, he said he only spoke at this requiem, which was contrary to his custom, because he felt he owed so much to Hugh. The latter had stimulated his devotion to the Blessed Sacrament and to our Blessed Mother.

He said nothing in his sermon about Hugh's penitential practices, but later in the day he asked me if Hugh's pliers or his monkey wrench had been put in the coffin with him. He knelt on these, Monsignor Kane explained, adding hastily, "He didn't tell me, I caught him at it one day."

Hugh had told me once that he did penance. I had asked him why he had stayed so long in Mexico City, and he said he had been in the hospital with an infection. "A little too much penance," he added grimly, and from the way he put his hand against his side, I took it to mean he had been using an instrument of penance such as I had heard or read of. Sure enough, when his "effects," as they are termed, came back with his "remains," and Ron and I went over his clothes to see what could be given away on the Bowery, we found there a circlet, a belt, twisted at the end to form a hook and eye. It was, very simply, a piece of barbed wire.

Why penance? For the napalm, the bombings in Vietnam perhaps. Because we are all guilty. God help us.

September 1967

GIFTS OF THE SPIRIT

A Baby Is Born

It is January 9, 1941, and the New York *Times* this morning is filled with news of total war and total defense. Every day four-column headlines of the costs of war: "1942 Budget $17,485,528,049. Funds for British to Be Sought Later."

Wonder what that $49 tacked on at the end of the $17,485,528,000 is for? Fifty dollars, we know, will pay for a baby, if you are poor, at any hospital in the city. A flat rate of fifty dollars, ward care, the ministrations of any doctor that happens to be on hand, and ten days' hospitalization.

At Bellevue Hospital, if you are poor, if you are a resident of the great City of New York, it doesn't cost a cent.

William, our new baby down here at Mott Street, is hereby headlined on our front page, as the biggest news of the month, the gayest news, the most beautiful news, the most tragic news, and indeed more worthy of a place in a headline than the seventeen billion, four hundred and eighty-five million, five hundred and twenty-eight thousand, and forty-nine dollars headlined in the New York *Times* this morning. William himself is worth more than that sum, more indeed than all the money in the world. He is indeed but dust, the Lord knoweth it, but he is also little less than the angels. He is a creature of body and soul, a son of God and (by his baptism down at Transfiguration Church last Sunday at 2 p.m.) a temple of the Holy Ghost. For his sake our Lord God came down from heaven, was begotten by the Holy Ghost, born of the Virgin Mary, was made man, lived with us for thirty-three years, and suffered and laid down His life. For William's sake as well as for the sake of each one of us.

And this tiny creature, who little realizes his dignity as a member of the Mystical Body of Christ, lies upstairs from me now as I write, swaddled in a blanket and reposing in a laundry basket. He is rosy and calm and satisfied, a look of infinite peace and complacency upon that tiny countenance. He little knows what is in the world, what horrors beset us on every side.

We had awaited his arrival, the week before Christmas, breathlessly. Every night before we went to bed we asked the young mother, "How do you feel?" and asked each other (us women on the two top floors of St.

Joseph's House on Mott Street), "Is there taxi money?" in case it would be too late to call an ambulance.

And then, one morning at five, I heard rapid footsteps in the room above, the voice of the ambulance intern in the hall, "I'll be waiting downstairs." And I realized that the great moment had arrived.

It was still dark out, but it was indubitably morning. Lights were on in the kitchens of surrounding tenements. Fish peddlers, taxi drivers, truck-men, longshoremen, were up and on their way to work. The business of life was beginning. And I thought, "How cheerful to begin to have a baby at this time of the morning!" Not at 2 a.m., for instance, a dreary time of low vitality, when people sink beneath their woes and courage flags. Five o'clock is a cheerful hour.

Down in our little backyard (where we had the Christmas tree this year), down in that cavernous pit with tenements looming five and seven stories up around, we could hear them dragging out the ash cans, bringing in the coffee cans for the line.

Peter Clark and his crew were on hand, cutting pumpernickel (none of this already sliced, pasty, puffy white bread for us), getting out the cups, preparing the coffee for our eight hundred or so breakfast guests.

Out in front the line was forming already and two or three fires in the gutters brought out in sharp relief the haggard faces of the men, the tragedy of their rags. The bright flames, the blue-black sky, the gray buildings all about, everything sharp and clear, and this morning a white ambulance drawn up in front of the door.

This is not the story of the tragedy of the mother. We are not going into details about that. But I could not help thinking that while I was glad the morning was beginning, it was a miserable shame that the departure of the young woman for her ordeal should be witnessed by a long, silent waiting line of men. They surveyed her, a slight figure, bundled on the cruelly cold morning (and pain and fear make the blood run cold), come running down from the dark, silent house to get into the ambulance.

Not one man, not a dear husband, not a protector on whom she could lean for comfort and strength. There was no Joseph on this winter morn-ing. But there were hundreds of men, silent, waiting and wondering perhaps, as they watched the ambulance, whether it was life or death that had called it out.

"This is worse than war," one woman friend said a few days before, contemplating the situation. And we agreed, wondering if anything indeed could be more desperate and sad than a woman left to have her child alone.

There you have the tragedy of the refugee, there you have the misery of homelessness, the uncertainty as to food and clothing and shelter (and this woman had known hunger). And there, too, you have the pain and agony of the flesh. No soldier with his guts spilled out on the battlefield, lying for hours impaled upon barbed wire, suffers physically more than a woman in childbirth. Physically, I say, because does not the soldier in his horror and pain wonder what has brought him to this pass—what is being accomplished by the gigantic agony of war? With the woman the suffering brings forth life. In war, death. And despite shame and fear and uncertainty, as in this case, still there cannot but be joy over a child born into the world.

So it is with joy that we announce the newcomer to our House of Hospitality on Mott Street, knowing that our readers who have suffered with us in the past will be glad to rejoice with us now.

For us most truly this has been a season of happiness. "For unto us a son is born, unto us a child is given." Christ Himself came so truly to us this Christmas Day in this baby boy, just as in the persons of the hungry men. "For inasmuch as ye have done it unto one of the least of these My brethren, ye have done it unto me."

January 1941

About Mary

This morning, after Communion, I thought of writing about Mary, and since the thought came to me at *that* time, I took it as an order. I always say to the Blessed Mother after Communion—"Here He is in my heart; I believe, help thou mine unbelief; Adore Him, thank Him and love Him for me. He is your Son; His honor is in your hands. Do not let me dishonor Him."

And since, too, at that moment came this thought, those glimpses of all she has meant to me—all the little contacts with her that brought me to Him—I felt I must write.

One of the reasons I do not write more is that there is always housework, cleaning, scrubbing, sewing, washing (right now it is cleaning fish), etc., to do. Just as she had to do these things, and probably never neglected them. But then, too, I can see her sitting seemingly idle beside a well on just such a day as this, just thanking Him, with each happy breath.

*   *   *

Down in New Orleans twenty years ago I was working for the *Item,* an afternoon paper, and the job was not a very satisfactory one. Women writers, "girl reporters," had to write feature stuff. I started in writing a column about homely things—the same kind of a column I write now in *The Catholic Worker.* But they soon gave me assignments, some good, some bad. I had to interview Jack Dempsey, and such like, visiting celebrities. Once I had to cover the political situation and write a series of interviews with the retiring governor and the newly elected governor of the state. I had to work in a dance hall for a week as a taxi dancer and write a series of articles, in one of which I insulted, so they said, the United States Navy. Representatives of the sailors of a battleship in port at the time came to the newspaper office to rebuke me. It was a change from the work I had been doing in Chicago in the radical movement. But I didn't like it much.

Across the street from where I lived, I think it was on St. Peter Street, there was the side entrance to the Cathedral. Every night I used to go in there for Benediction. Perhaps I was influenced by reading the novels of Huysmans that I had borrowed from Sam Putnam's library in Chicago. My roommate was Mary Gordon (when I last heard of her, she was working for the League for Spanish Democracy in Chicago, a Communist affiliate), and that Christmas she gave me a rosary. So in this case I was led to the Church through two Communists. I did not know how to say the rosary, but I got a little prayer book at a Catholic bookstore which I often visited, and I learned how. Once in a while I said it. I remember expressing the desire to talk to a priest—to the girl who ran the bookshop—but nothing came of it.

*   *   *

My first statue of the Blessed Mother. Peggy Baird was my cellmate in jail in Washington. When we were in the Occoquan workhouse we had adjoining cells. In the Washington city jail I had the upper berth on one of the upper tiers, and Peggy had the lower. I read the Bible and she wrote a book of poetry—"Poems to My Lovers," she called it. I also read letters from the boys I was going with at the time, one of them, my most regular correspondent, a United States sailor. It was during the last war. Some years afterward Peggy gave me a little statue of the Blessed Mother which had been brought from Czechoslovakia. It was made of wax, and very delicate, and there was a golden watchspring-like halo around its head, and golden curly hair and a bright blue robe. How I loved that statue! Down in

Staten Island in my little shore cottage I kept it on a shelf by the door with a vigil light burning in front of it.

Peggy also was a member of the Communist Party at different times, but being an undisciplined creature and an artist, I don't think she was a paid-up member for long.

* * *

One summer right after I became a Catholic, I was taking care of a number of little boys from a school "for individual development." Together with Freda, my next-door neighbor, whose friend it was who ran the school, we took the responsibility for about a dozen boys between eight and twelve. Quite a few of them were children of Communist parents, and several of them have grown up now to be members of the Young Communist League. I used to read them the *Little Flowers of St. Francis,* which they enjoyed immensely, and they used to command each other "in the name of holy obedience" to perform this or that act of mischief. They also used to ask me to burn candles for them before the little blue statue of the Blessed Mother. Do any of them remember her now?

* * *

When my daughter was born almost eighteen years ago, I turned her over to the Blessed Mother. "What kind of a mother am I going to be?" I kept thinking to myself. "What kind of a Catholic home is she going to have, with only me?" And with the Catholic Worker movement starting six years later the home problem was even more acute.

There was a solution, of course, to such a difficulty. "You," I told the Blessed Mother, "will have to be her mother. Under the best of circumstances I'm a failure as a homemaker. I'm untidy, inconsistent, undisciplined, temperamental, and I have to pray every day for final perseverance."

It is only these last few years that it has occurred to me why my daughter has never called me "Mother." From the time she first spoke, it was "Dorothy." I'd think: "Of course, with no other children around calling me 'Mother' it is natural for her to call me by my first name." I'd correct her, but it did no good. Later on I'd ask her, "How will anyone know I'm your mother if you do not call me 'Mother'? They'll think I adopted you. They'll think I'm your aunt or something." "I don't care," she would say firmly, "I just can't call you 'Mother.'" And for a child really extremely obedient, it was hard to understand such stubbornness.

Once, in the little post office on Staten Island—she was four then—the postmistress said, "I'd like to hear a child of mine call me by my first name! I'd give it to her!"

When she was in convent school her brief letters began "*Dear Mother,*" but it was under compulsion. The Sisters would not let her write unless she so began. But away from school, the letters continue, "Dear Dorothy."

And then a few years ago, it came like a flash of light. "The Blessed Virgin Mary is Mother of my child. No harm can ever come to her with such a Mother."

The Commonweal, November 5, 1943

Servant of Peace

In April 1963, Dorothy joined a group of fifty women on a pilgrimage to Rome. Their intention was to express their gratitude to Pope John XXIII for his work for peace, and to urge him to an even more radical condemnation of the instruments of modern war. The women left Rome exhilarated by the knowledge that their message had reached the Pontiff. In less than a month, however, came the news that Pope John was dead.

Monday, June 3, I landed from the *Vulcania,* an Italian Line ship at Forty-fifth Street in New York, at eight o'clock in the morning. Pope John was still alive. (On board ship we had been getting only the most meager reports as to the Pope's health. Each morning at Mass the chaplain had asked our prayers for the Holy Father, and each afternoon at Benediction we had repeated those prayers.)

At three o'clock that afternoon we were still sitting at our lunch with people coming and going in the little apartment on Kenmare Street when someone came in with news of the Pope's death. It had been a long agony, and daily I had prayed the Eastern Rite prayer for "a death without pain" for this most beloved Father to all the world. But I am afraid he left us with the suffering which is an inevitable part of love, and he left us with fear, too, if the reports of his last words are correct, fear that his children, as he called all of us in the world, were not listening to his cries for *pacem in terris.* He was offering his sufferings, he had said before his death, for the continuing Council in September, and for peace in the world. But he had said, almost cheerfully, that his bags were packed, that he was ready to go, and that after all death was the beginning of a new life. "Life is changed, not taken away," as the Preface in the Mass for the dead has it. And just as Thercse of Lisieux said that she would spend her heaven doing good upon earth, so in his love, John XXIII will be watching over us.

It was on the day before I sailed for New York, May 22, Wednesday, that I had the tremendous privilege of being present at his last public appearance. He stood in his window looking out over the crowd in front of St. Peter's. An audience had been scheduled as usual for that Wednesday at ten-thirty, and the great Basilica was crowded to the doors when the announcement was made that the Pope had been too ill the night before to make an appearance that day but that he would come to the window and bless the crowd, as he was accustomed to do each Sunday noon.

I had had an appointment that morning for ten-thirty at the office of Cardinal Bea, to see his secretary, Father Stransky, the Paulist, about a meeting I was to have with the Cardinal that night, and was leaving the bus at the colonnade to the left of St. Peter's. I noticed that the people leaving the bus were hastening to the square. Word gets around Rome quickly and when I inquired I was told that the Holy Father would be at the window in a moment. I hastened to a good position in the square and was there in time to see the curtains stir and the Pope appear. I had not realized how tremendous that square was until I saw how tiny the Pope's figure seemed, up at that window of the apartment under the roof. Those rooms used to be servants' quarters and had been occupied by the popes since Pius X.

The voice of the Holy Father came through a loudspeaker, of course, and seemed strong. He said the Angelus (which we say before meals at the Peter Maurin Farm), then the prayers to the guardian angels, and ended with a requiem prayer for the dead.

It was the last time the public saw his face. (Many of the crowd had opera glasses, so one can use that expression.) Questioning those at the little convent where I had been staying in Rome the last week, I learned the subject of the Pope's last talk, at his last Wednesday audience. He had urged all to read and study his last encyclicals, the call to the Council, *Mater et Magistra* and *Pacem in Terris*. He had said all he had to say; this was the message he left to the world:

> There is an immense task incumbent on all men of good will, namely the task of restoring the relations of the human family in truth, in justice, in love and in freedom; the relations between communities; between political communities themselves; between individuals, families, intermediate associations and political communities on the one hand and the world community on the other.

This is a most exalted task, for it is the task of bringing about true peace in the order established by God.

Admittedly, those who are endeavoring to restore the relations of social life according to the criteria mentioned above, are not many; to them We express Our paternal appreciation and We earnestly invite them to persevere in this work with greater zeal. And We are comforted by the hope that their number will increase especially among those who believe. For it is an imperative of duty, it is a requirement of Love.

Yes, we will meditate on his words to us all, because he said he was addressing *all men of good will,* and we will know, too, as we have known in the past, how difficult it is to apply these words to individual situations. We need all the gifts of the Holy Spirit for our work; we need all the help of our guardian angels; and to make our non-Catholic and non-believing readers know what these words mean, we are printing, together with this usual column of pilgrimage, definitions of the gifts of the Holy Spirit, as well as what the guardian angels mean to us who believe. And not to know these things, for those of us who do believe, means not to know the treasure we have, the resources we have to draw upon.

To report further about the trip to Rome: It came about because a group of women, mostly of other faiths, and including those who did not believe, had called for this attempt to reach the Holy Father with a plea for a condemnation of nuclear war and a development of the ideas of nonviolent resistance. This very attempt brought out clearly how difficult are these attempts at unity and coexistence.

It is no easier to receive a hearing with the Princes of the Church than it is to receive one from the princes of this world. There is protocol; there are hierarchies and blocs of one kind or another; there is diplomacy in what we generally consider to be the realm of the spirit.

The day of the audience arrived and the big buses came to the door, and it did not seem that we were being treated as of any more importance than the busloads of schoolchildren who were coming from all over Europe during their Easter holiday to see Rome and attend the large general audience which took place each Wednesday at St. Peter's.

We waited, as everyone else waited, outside in the square, two of our members in wheelchairs. We passed through the gates showing our unprivileged tickets, and back past the Bureau of Excavations and through one of the side doors and around into a section already packed with people.

It was long to wait. Probably people were standing two hours, and it was not until twelve-twenty that finally there was a surge in that vast mob and a sudden silence followed by almost a roar of greeting. With the Pope borne aloft on his chair (and how could any have seen him if he were not conducted in this way), the procession proceeded around the columns, and then the Pope, blessing all, was conducted up to his throne, where he sat while a list of all the groups of pilgrims was read aloud. As the names of the villages of Italy, and the schools of the Continent, and of England and the United States were read out, applause came from various parts of this vast group. And our pilgrimage was not mentioned!

But then the Pope began to speak and the words that fell from his lips seemed to be directed to us, to our group, speaking as he did about the "Pilgrims for Peace" who came to him, and his gratitude for their encouragement. The young woman who had helped us find our places was translating his words as fast as he spoke them and writing them down while two of us read over her shoulder. She kept beaming at us, and all those around us, seeing our buttons, large almost as saucers, bright blue and bearing the legend "Mothers for Peace" in Italian; she also smiled and, indicating the Holy Father and us in turn, seemed to be letting us know that he was speaking to us especially.

It seemed too good to be true, and if all those around us had not kept assuring us he was speaking to us, I would have considered it but a coincidence. Our messages had reached him, we felt, impossible though it had seemed they would.

June 1963

A Brief Flame

On November 6, 1965, Dorothy stood with several young men on a platform in Union Square to lend her support as they burned their draft cards. As the cards were actually burned, a group of counter-demonstrators across the street sent up a mocking cry: "Burn yourselves, not your cards!" Watching the scene was Roger LaPorte, a gentle young man who had spent time in seminary and with the Trappists, searching for a vocation. He had recently moved to New York in order to study to become a teacher and had become involved with the Catholic Worker, helping part-time on the soup line. Three days later, without informing anyone of his plans, he sat in the middle of First Avenue across from the United Nations, doused his clothes with gasoline, and struck a flame. "I am a Catholic Worker," he said to the ambulance attendants. "I'm against war. All wars." He remained alive for thirty-three hours in Bellevue Hospital.

A Carmelite priest was called to the Emergency Ward of Bellevue Hospital last month where Roger LaPorte lay dying of the burns which covered his body. According to the priest, Roger, having made his confession, made an act of contrition in a loud, clear voice. We must believe that he knew and realized, with the clarity of one who lay dying, that he was wrong in taking his own life, in trying to immolate himself to give his life for the cause of peace. He had said he wanted to "end the war in Vietnam."

It has always been the teaching of the Catholic Church that suicide is a sin, but that mercy and loving-kindness dictated another judgment; that anyone who took his life was temporarily unbalanced, not in full possession of his faculties, even to be judged temporarily insane, and so absolved of guilt.

Many years ago, when the eighteen-year-old son of a friend of ours committed suicide, a priest told me: "There is no time with God, and all the prayers you will say in the future for this unhappy boy will have meant that God gave him the choice at the moment of death, to choose light instead of darkness, good instead of evil, indeed the Supreme Good." I had been a Catholic only a year, and I had the names in my prayer book of ten people I knew who had taken their own lives. As I look back, I recall how many of my own dear dead never had in this life a living faith.

But the case of Roger LaPorte was different, and must be spoken of in a far deeper context. It is not only that many youths and students throughout the country are deeply sensitive to the sufferings of the world. They have a keen sense that they must be responsible and make a profession of their faith that things do not have to go on as they always have—that men are capable of laying down their lives for others, taking a stand, even when the all-encroaching State and indeed all the world are against them.

In Ignazio Silone's novel *Bread and Wine*, the revolutionary in hiding risks capture by going out and chalking slogans on the walls of the village where he has taken refuge, and when he is scoffed at for the seeming futility of this gesture, he answers:

"The Land of Propaganda is built on unanimity. If one man says 'No,' the spell is broken and public order is endangered."

Throughout our country the protests against the war in Vietnam have grown and young men have been imprisoned, some of them for years. (One was recently sentenced to five years for refusal to cooperate with the draft.) Stories keep coming out in the press of planes spraying napalm, gasoline jelly, over the "enemy," over villages of men, women, and children. In forty-eight hours last week, there were six massive air strikes. There were more killed on both sides last week than at any time since the war began.

The Wall Street Journal for November 3 had a front-page headline:
"Vietnam Spurs Planning for Big Rise in Outlays for Military Hardware. Spending on Tanks, Copters, Other Gear May Double . . .

" 'Now that we are finally committed to an active combat role in Vietnam the whole amosphere has changed within the Pentagon and elsewhere in Government,' says one Defense official. *Extra Zip for Economy* . . . Both the Army's spending plans and those of the other services promise added zip for the nation's peppy economy . . . added billions will be funneled into pocketbooks in many parts of the land." The story goes on with "shopping lists" and paragraph after paragraph listing the expenditures to be made for this "five-year package," as it is blithely called. There is something satanic about this kind of writing.

One day at our Catholic Worker farm, John Filliger, talking of drying up the cow a few months before she was about to calve, said, "The only way to do it with a good cow like this is to milk her out on the ground. She gets so mad at the waste of her milk that she dries right up." That may be an old wives' tale—or an old farmer's tale, in this case—but there is a lesson in it: if we waste what we have, the source of supply will dry up. Any long-range view of the colossal waste of the resources of the earth and human life points to an exhaustion of our economy, not to speak of man himself.

On the other hand, witness Roger LaPorte. He embraced voluntary poverty and came to help the Catholic Worker because he did not wish to profit in this booming economy of which *The Wall Street Journal* speaks so gloatingly.

Roger LaPorte was giving himself to the poor and the destitute, serving tables, serving the sick, as St. Ignatius of Loyola did when he laid down his arms and gave up worldly combat.

And now he is dead—dead by his own hand, everyone will say, a suicide. But there is a tradition in the Church of what are called "victim souls." I myself have known several of them, and would not speak of them now if it were not for the fact that I want to try to understand what Roger must have been thinking of when he set fire to himself in front of the United Nations early Tuesday morning. There have been the self-immolations of the Buddhist monks in Vietnam. A woman in Detroit and a Quaker in Washington have done the same—all trying to show their willingness to give their lives for others, to endure the sufferings that we as a nation are inflicting upon a small country and its people, to lay down their own lives rather than take the lives of others. It is the teaching of the Church that only in the Cross is there redemption.

In *Man's Fate*, André Malraux said that once a man had taken the life of another, all was changed for him, that he had crossed a certain point and would never really recover from the effects, no matter how hidden.

Last week, on the occasion of a college talk, I was the guest of a priest who had been a chaplain in the Army. He told me that he would use any weapon if he were about to be attacked, gun or bayonet. But he added that he had encountered many soldiers who refused to use their arms, who would accept death, rather than inflict it. Such an action might come under the heading of suicide, being a direct refusal to save one's life.

In this month's *Theology Digest*, Father Karl Rahner, S.J., has an article called "Good Intention." Roger "intended" to lay down his life for his brother in Vietnam. The article is about purifying one's intention and how complex and elusive a thing an intention is and how often other motives of which we are unaware are at work. There will undoubtedly be much discussion and condemnation of this sad and terrible act, but all of us around the Catholic Worker know that Roger's intent was to love God and to love his brother.

May perpetual light shine upon him and may he rest in peace.

November 1965

Holy Obedience

When I became a Catholic, it never occurred to me to question how much freedom I had or how much authority the Church had to limit that freedom. . . . I had reached the point where I wanted to obey. I was like the child in the *New Yorker* cartoon (I was nearly thirty years old) who said, "Do I have to do what I want to do today?" I was tired of following the devices and desires of my own heart, of doing what I wanted to do, what my desires told me I wanted to do, which always seemed to lead me astray. . . . Obedient to my conscience, I became a Catholic, was conditionally baptized and said, "I do believe," to the great and solemn and beautiful truths proposed to me.

For the next five years no great problems came up of obedience. The Church held up a tremendous ideal for the follower of Christ, and no matter how many times one failed, fell flat on one's face, one might say, the Church, Holy Mother Church, was there with her sacraments of Penance and Holy Eucharist to reassure and forgive and sustain and nourish one.

In 1933 I met Peter Maurin, a French peasant who proposed to me the idea of starting a paper which had the purpose of bringing the social teachings of the Church to the man on the street.

I had been writing articles for *America*, the Jesuit weekly, for *The Sign*, the Passionist monthly, and I had been going for spiritual direction to Father Joseph McSorley, formerly superior of the Paulist congregation in New York. I asked each of these men for advice as to whether it was necessary to ask permission before starting a venture of this kind, and both editors, Father Wilfrid Parsons and Father Harold Purcell, as well as Father McSorley, told me in no uncertain terms: No, it was not necessary to ask for permission. The thing to do was to go ahead on one's own, and if the work were of God it would continue.

I could well understand this. If Peter and I started something on our own, we alone would be responsible for its mistakes. If it were begun with the permission of the hierarchy, then they might be held responsible. I was not thinking in terms of financial responsibility. I was thinking of the positions we would take in regard to civil rights and social justice. Without knowing St. Augustine too well (I had only read his *Confessions*), his dictum "Love God and do as you will" had a familiar ring. The words breathed freedom, the freedom found even in obedience to a temporary injustice, even in such a temporary injustice as stopping us once we had begun. I have never felt so sure of myself that I did not feel the necessity of being backed up by great minds, searching the Scriptures and the writings of the saints for my authorities.

Bishop O'Hara of Kansas City was a good friend and visited us in the earliest days of our work. He kept up his friendship with us, helping us when we sent out an appeal and writing us when there were things in the paper with which he disagreed. But he said to Peter on one memorable visit, "Peter, you lead the way, and we [the bishops] will follow."

Peter knew what he meant. He meant that it was up to the laity to be in the vanguard, to live in the midst of the battle, to live in the world which God so loved that He sent His only begotten Son to us to show us how to live and to die, to meet the last great enemy, Death. We were to explore the paths of what was possible, to find concordances with our opponents, to seek for the common good, to try to work with all men of goodwill, and to trust all men, too, and to believe in that goodwill, and to forgive our own failures and those of others seventy times seventy times. *We* could venture where priest and prelate could not or ought not, in political and economic fields. We could make mistakes without too great harm; we could retrace our steps, start over again in this attempt to build a new society within the shell of the old, as Peter and the old radicals used to say.

I speak of these incidents to show the tremendous freedom there is in the Church, a freedom most cradle Catholics do not seem to know they possess. They do know that a man is free to be a Democrat or a Republican, but they do not know that he is also free to be a philosophical anarchist by conviction. They do believe in free enterprise, but they do not know that cooperative ownership and communal ownership can live side by side with private ownership of property.

Obedience is a matter of love, which makes it voluntary, not compelled by fear or force. Pope John's motto was *Obedience and Peace*. Yet he was the pope who flouted conventions which had hardened into laws as to what a pope could or could not do, and the Pharisees were scandalized and the people delighted.

All his life long he had done his work, which sometimes meant silence, solitude, and inactivity, as in his years in Bulgaria and Turkey. But now that he was pope and his decisions concerned the whole world, he ceased to obey men. Father Ernesto Balducci, in his book *John: The Transitional Pope*, calls him a man of vast and vital ideas and says that his temperament led him "to escape whenever possible from behind the velvet curtains of ecclesiastical offices into the roads and squares where living men and women move." He had accepted the frustrations of his life and his plans because "obedience is not only a moral virtue but a specific principle of faith, and as such, has reasons that reason cannot understand."

Pope John compared his own life during those years of frustration to the waiting of Simeon in the Temple, who seemed to be "wasting the years, pouring out his life as a total loss. And his life was not lost at all. The time he spent in waiting prepared him to present Christ to the world. And now I tell you that my own poor life continues to be poured out as you know; with my usual hair shirt which is so dear to me, on my back." This he wrote in a letter to a friend some years before his election to the papacy.

Immediately following his election as pope he went to visit the prison in Rome—"You could not come to see me, so I came to see you," he told the prisoners. Every day of his long priestly life he had prayed at the third hour of the Office, "Let our love be set aflame by the fire of Your love and its heat in turn enkindle love in our neighbors." God had so answered his prayer that his own love kindled a fire which is sweeping over the world, and the whole Church is enkindled.

This may sound like an extravagant way of speaking when we know full well the turmoil, the controversy, the impatience in the Church today which has led so many to leave convents and monasteries and even the priesthood, that high estate. Men and women have begun to exercise their freedom and are examining their own obedience, as to whether it was a matter of fear or of habit. To examine, too, the kind of training they had received from the earliest years in the home and in the school.

Someone said that Pope John had opened a window and let in great blasts of fresh air. With all his emphasis on obedience, I do not think he has been understood. What the American people—and I speak only of them, not knowing the condition of the Church in other countries—now feel free to do is to criticize, speak their minds. They have always been accused of a lack of diplomacy, or at least of bad manners, and they have felt it a virtue in themselves, the virtue of honesty, truthfulness. Freedom has meant searching and questioning. What do we really believe? It is as though man were realizing for the first time what is involved in this profession of Christianity. It is as though we were going through the Creed slowly, and saying to ourselves, "Do I believe this, and this, and this?"

Faith is required when we speak of obedience. Faith in a God who created us, a God who is Father, Son, and Holy Spirit. Faith in a God to Whom we owe obedience for the very reason that we have been endowed with freedom to obey or disobey. Love, Beauty, Truth, all the attributes of God which we see reflected about us in creatures, in the very works of man himself whether it is bridges or symphonies wrought by his hands, fill our hearts with such wonder and gratitude that we cannot help but obey and worship.

Lord, I believe, help Thou my unbelief. My faith may be the size of a mustard seed but even so, even aside from its potential, it brings with it a beginning of love, an inkling of love, so intense that human love with all its heights and depths pales in comparison.

Even seeing through a glass darkly makes one want to obey, to do all the Beloved wishes, to follow Him to Siberia, to antarctic wastes, to the desert, to prison, to give up one's life for one's brothers since He said, "Inasmuch as ye have done it unto one of the least of these My brethren, ye have done it unto Me."

But how much easier it is to obey the least ones than the great ones of the earth, whether they are princes of the Church or the State.

Philosophical anarchism, decentralism, requires that we follow the Gospel precept to be obedient to every living thing: "Be subject therefore to every human creature for God's sake." It means washing the feet of others, as Jesus did at the Last Supper. "You call me Master and Lord," He said, "and rightly so, for that is what I am. Then if I, your Lord, have washed your feet, you also ought to wash one another's feet. I have set you an example; you are to do as I have done for you." To serve others, not to seek power over them. Not to dominate, not to judge others.

Simone Weil has a great deal to say about obedience. "The idea of the despised and humiliated hero which was so common among the Greeks and is the actual theme of the Gospels," she writes, "is almost outside our Western tradition which has remained on the Roman road of militarism, centralization, bureaucracy and totalitarianism.

"Every new development for the last three centuries has brought men closer to the state of affairs in which absolutely nothing would be recognized in the whole world as possessing a claim to obedience except the authority of the State."

How strong and positive a virtue is this obedience to God and to one's conscience! St. Peter said, speaking for himself and the Apostles: "We must obey God rather than men."

Certainly the staff of editors and all the volunteers who are so at home with us that they call themselves Catholic Workers must have tried the patient endurance of the chancery office in New York, not only because of our frequent sojourns in jail and because of the controversial nature of the issues taken up in the paper and by our actions, but also because of the false ideas put forward by many of our friends as being our positions.

One time I made the statement, whether in writing or in a speech I do not remember, that I was so grateful for the freedom we had in the Church that I was quite ready to obey with cheerfulness if Cardinal Spellman ever told us to lay down our pens and stop publication. Perhaps I had no right to speak for more rebellious souls than mine. Or for those whose consciences dictated continuance in a struggle, even with the highest authority, the Church itself. Perhaps I have sounded too possessive about *The Catholic Worker* itself and had no right to speak for the publication, but only for myself. I do know that Peter Maurin would have agreed with me. Most cradle Catholics have gone through, or need to go through, a second conversion which binds them with a more profound, a more mature love and obedience to the Church.

I do know that my nature is such that gratitude alone, gratitude for the faith, that most splendid gift, a gift not earned by me, a gratuitous gift, is enough to bind me in holy obedience to Holy Mother Church and her commands. . . . My gratitude for this sureness in my heart is such that I can only say, I believe, help Thou my unbelief. I believe and I obey.

Ave Maria

"What Do the Simple Folk Do?"

This talk was a contribution to a symposium on "Transcendence," sponsored by the Church Society for College Work in 1968. It was first published in the C.S.C.W. *Journal,* and later, in its present form, in *The Catholic Worker.*

You will recognize the words of one of the songs of the Broadway musical *Camelot,* which kept much of the beauty of the Arthurian legend (whereas the movie loses completely the charm of love, natural and supernatural). I use this title because I find too often the ideas of transcendence expressed on a cosmic scale rather than a human one, and in language which would need to be translated, or perhaps illuminated, just as ancient psalm books were illuminated by the monks throughout the Middle Ages and the earlier days of the Faith.

When my mother lay on her deathbed, she said to me one day, "Do not pray that I live longer. I have been through two world wars, the San Francisco earthquake, and the Florida hurricane, and I have had enough!" She had had two sons involved in the First World War and one in the Second, so she had known much human fear and misery. And in her life she had seen, too, in the words of St. Paul, "All nature itself which travaileth and groaneth even unto now."

And yet, at the same time, on the very day she died, she sat up in bed and, sipping a cup of tea, remarked on how comforting it was. She had taken up a little bouquet of violets, her favorite flower, and, holding it up to her face, smiled with happiness. Life was sweet, even in her last illness.

The Poor People's March on Washington speaks to the world today of the "misery of the needy and the groaning of the poor," and we are living now in the midst of such tragedies that the mind is appalled; assassinations of national leaders; fear of "the fire next time," foretold at the time of the Flood; remembrance of the horrors we have already lived through in this short lifetime—the massacre of the Armenians in the First World War; the ghastly and obscene holocaust of the Jews, God's chosen people (and God does not change), during the Second World War; and, more recently and almost unnoticed in the press, the massacre of 800,000 suspected Communists in Indonesia. And today, the slaughter which is going on in Vietnam.

God made men and women to be happy. When I visited Cuba in 1962, that was the appealing slogan which I read on the billboards: "Children are born to be happy." Yet, how can we be happy today? How can we transcend this misery of ours? How can we believe in a Transcendent God when the Immanent God seems so powerless within time, when demonic forces seem to be let loose? Certainly our God is a hidden God.

*   *   *

I would say that there are evidences of transcendence in the striving for community among the poor and the destitute among whom we live in city and country.

Men and women have persisted in their hope for happiness. They have hoped against hope though all the evidence seemed to point to the fact that human nature could not be changed. Always they have tried to recover the lost Eden, and the history of our own country shows attempts to found communities where people could live together in that happiness which God seemed to have planned for us. Charles Dickens writes about one such community on the Mississippi in *Martin Chuzzlewit,* and Dostoevsky refers to a community in Illinois where two of the characters in *The Possessed* had gone to look for earthly happiness. Most of these references to community poke fun at the attempt, and Edmund Wilson's history of community in *To the Finland Station* is certainly not sympathetic. Martin Buber, in his *Paths in Utopia,* was the only modern writer who held out hope for a modern voluntary community as a place where men and women could live in love and in the happiness which God intended for them.

St. Teresa said that you can only show your love for God by your love for your neighbor, for your brother and sister. François Mauriac, the novelist, and Jacques Maritain, the philosopher, said that when you were working for truth and justice you were working for Christ, even though you denied Him.

But how to love? That is the question.

All men are brothers, yes, but how to love your brother or sister when they are sunk in ugliness, foulness, and degradation, so that all the senses arc affronted? How to love when the adversary shows a face to you of implacable hatred, or just cold loathing?

The very fact that we put ourselves in these situations, I think, attests to our desire to love God and our neighbor. Like Daniel, we are men of desires. And Daniel was rewarded by God because he was a man of desires. Searching for transcendence in community has resulted in the Catholic Worker Houses of Hospitality and our so-called farming communes. Actually, Peter Maurin, the founder of the Catholic Worker and a French peasant, liked to call them agronomic universities, and there have been many attempts throughout the country to get these small centers under way, most of them resulting in failure as far as one could judge. But no one who ever lived in one of them ever forgets this "golden period" of his or her life. It has always required an overwhelming act of faith. I believe because I wish to believe, "help Thou my unbelief." I love because I want to love, the deepest desire of my heart is for love, for union, for communion, for community.

How to keep such desires, such dreams?

Certainly, like Elias, who, after making valiant attempts to do what he considered the will of God, fled in fear, all courage drained from him, and lay down under a juniper tree and cried to God to make an end of his misery and despair.

The grace of hope, this consciousness that there is in every person *that which is of God,* comes and goes in a rhythm like that of the sea. The Spirit blows where it listeth, and we travel through deserts and much darkness and doubt. We can only make that act of faith, "Lord, I believe, because I want to believe." We must remember that faith, like love, is an act of the will, an act of preference. God speaks, He answers these cries in the darkness as He always did. He is incarnate today in the poor, in the bread we break together. We know Him and each other in the breaking of bread.

* * *

Once I lived on Ludlow Street on the Lower East Side, where my back windows looked out on a yard with an ailanthus tree. Out in front were always trucks from the South piled high with crates of young cucumbers ready for pickling. The house was filled with Puerto Ricans, and the families in the front apartments kept spotlessly clean homes. I could see into their kitchens because they had screen doors on the hall to maintain a crosscurrent of air. What used to be four-room apartments, unheated, now had turned into two-room apartments at three or four times the rent. These people worked hard, earned a living for their families, or rather,

scarcely a living wage, because those who worked in hospitals had to have
their earnings supplemented by Welfare.

The transcendence in their lives was found in the Bibles they carried out
at night on their way to meetings in the little storefront churches which
abound everywhere in the slums, in Harlem, East and West, and in the
Lower East Side, in Brooklyn and the Bronx.

In the word of God they found the nourishment their souls needed.
They found the Word made flesh.

Closest to me are those fellow workers, those companions of ours (the
very word "companions" means those who break bread together) who
come to sit down at the Catholic Worker table. There is a little Polish man,
who cannot speak English, who rents a pushcart each day and walks the
streets, collecting cartons and paper boxes, which he folds carefully and
piles up until he has a veritable mountain before him and it is a wonder he
can see to get through traffic. He earns enough money for his rent but eats
with us, always with a little Gospel pamphlet before him. When there is a
place next to him and I take it, he urges me to hasten with my meal so
that I can read a psalm in English to him and he repeats the words with
me.

He reminds me of a soldier I met in Cuba, who sat next to me in the
station wagon which took a group of us on a tour through a big school for
children in Oriente Province. I was not too interested in the pig farm
which we were being shown, and stayed in the car to rest, and he remained
with me. Like all Cubans, he carried a book on Marxism-Leninism, and
when I asked to see it and tried to read the Spanish, he shared it with me,
and we read together, much as I read with the Polish pushcart man.

Both these men have encountered experiences which transcended their
ordinary lives and lifted them into another realm, where all things were
possible, whether it was building a successful socialist country, ninety miles
from a Goliath of a capitalist land, or a present heaven in the midst of a
city slum within a capitalist society.

On at least four occasions, I have seen men reading the Gospel on the
soup line, which started by itself at our door many years ago. The house
was not big enough to hold the waiting men, so they formed a line and
waited, in snow and rain, winter and summer. When I saw them reading
in this way, I could only accept this as another incident of transcendence,
and it was their destitution which they had transcended. They were poor
men, not destitute men, when they were able to read in this way.

"Take and read," St. Augustine heard a voice, and it led to his conver-

sion. His heaven was to understand, to know. Who has not been moved to
tears by the scene between Raskolnikov and Sonya, the murderer and the
prostitute, when she read to him from the Scriptures. There was the sense
of the transcendent there, in this scene of squalor and despair.

*   *   *

The transcendental is thought of often as manifesting itself in signs and
wonders, prophecies and voices from the dead. There is evidence of it in
the miracles which take place around us, miracles which are more common
than we suppose, and which the Catholic Church is very hesitant to
confirm without long investigation. There may well be more of them than
we know, since most of us, if a miracle were performed for us in the way
of healing, would prefer not to submit to long investigation. Most of us
would be reluctant to report, or even perhaps to believe in, the miraculous.

Catholics do not generally ask for miracles. They leave the extraordinary
in the hands of God. They are quite conscious that before prayer of petition
there must be offered prayer of adoration and thanksgiving as their bounden
duty to a Creator and to themselves. Spiritual graces, yes, they ask for
these, but when it comes to asking for relief from pain and suffering, it is
almost as though they thought, "Why should I refuse what is the common
lot of humanity? Why should I ask to be spared when I see the suffering of
the family next door?" Suffering borne with courage means to the devout
mind a participation in the sufferings of Christ and, if bravely endured, can
lighten the sufferings of others. It is not a cult of suffering. It is an
acceptance of the human condition.

There is an old expression used in the Church: the *victim soul*. We used
to laugh at this expression, especially since the old German priest who
visited us from his monastery in Minnesota spoke to us of those whom he
called "wictim souls." But we have not continued to laugh. I have known
personally at least three priests who offered themselves, literally offered
their lives, for the souls in their charge. One was a young priest in a rural
parish where there had been a number of suicides of children. His heart
was torn by the sufferings of these little ones, and torn, too, by what he
considered an intimation of the hardened state of the souls of the materialistic, middle-class adults whom he served. He was stricken, not long
after, with a tumor of the brain and died some months later. Another
priest, whom we knew very well, and who stayed with us a year on one of
our farms, was suddenly stricken with a loss of memory. He lost his mind,
as the saying is. I was one of the few people he recognized, and when I

visited him once at the hospital and found his face bruised from the attack of one of the other patients, I wept with him at what had happened and asked him, "Father, did you ever offer yourself as a victim soul?" Suddenly, he looked at me and smiled. "We say so much to God which we do not mean," he said, "but He takes us at our word."

It would take too long to tell of other incidents where people have asked God to let them bear some of the sufferings of others to give them relief, scarcely realizing that with this request they are almost showing a lack of faith, because God has also given grace and courage to endure. I realize I am using religious terminology (one might say religious jargon) which is unfamiliar and even slightly ridiculous to many. But I cannot use the word "transcendence" and "immanence" without relating them to God, the living God, the personal God in whom I believe.

There are evidences of martyrdoms, too, in our time. Perhaps not so much in the present, since facts are not yet known, but I can think of a number of martyrdoms which took place less than a hundred years ago. There are the martyrs of Uganda in Africa, and that of Théophane Venard in Vietnam, in what was then Indochina. In each case it was a martyrdom anticipated and endured with joy and patience and, at the end, without pain. Indeed the martyrs of Uganda, a dozen in one case (in 1885), went to their martyrdom by fire singing psalms. They could have escaped by fleeing, but they did not.

"When the martyr suffers and dies, it is so truly Christ Who suffers and dies, that the suffering is transcended, and the risen Christ is revealed in the martyr's very death," writes Father Louis Bouyer in *Liturgical Piety*. He points out that the most remarkable fact about the death of early martyrs like St. Polycarp, St. Ignatius of Antioch, St. Perpetua, and St. Blandina is that the martyrs did not seem to suffer.

"The importance of the liturgical celebration itself implies a correlative importance in what we do, after the liturgical celebration, in daily living." Certainly we can say that the worship offered by a Martin Luther King resulted in his great mission and in the courage with which he expected his own martyrdom.

These people worked on the plane of this world, but it was the spirit that animated the weak flesh. Henri de Lubac, S.J., whose *Drama of Atheist Humanism* was published in 1950, wrote: "So long as we talk and argue and busy ourselves on the plane of this world, evil seems the stronger, it alone seems real. The thing is to enter upon another plane, to find that fourth dimension which represents the Kingdom of the Spirit. Then Freedom is Queen, then God triumphs, and man with Him."

*   *   *

Is suffering and death, and the strength to bear them, all there is in this struggle? This search for God would be a pretty grim affair if this were all, and transcendence too high a goal for simple folk.

Let us remember *other* elements, too.

"What is it that I love when I love my God?" St. Augustine cried out in his *Confessions.* "It is a certain light that I love and melody and fragrance and embrace that I love when I love my God—a light, melody, fragrance, food, embrace of the God-within, where for my soul, that shines which space does not contain; that sounds which time does not sweep away; that is fragrant which the breeze does not dispel; and that tastes sweet which, fed upon, is not diminished, and that clings close which no satiety disparts— this is what I love when I love my God."

And Catherine of Siena assures us that "all the way to heaven is heaven, because He said, I am the Way."

May 1978

Penance

Penance seems to be ruled out today. One hears the Mass described as Sacrament, not as Sacrifice. But how are we to keep our courage unless the Cross, that mighty failure, is kept in view? Is the follower greater than his master? What attracts one in a Che Guevara and a Ho Chi Minh is the hardship and the suffering they endured in living their lives of faith and hope. It is not the violence, the killing of one's enemies. A man is a man, and to hear him crying out in pain and anguish, whether he is friend or enemy, is to have one's heart torn in unutterable sorrow. The impulse to stand out against the state and go to jail rather than serve is an instinct for penance, to take on some of the suffering of the world, to share in it.

Father Anthony Mullaney, O.S.B., who is one of the Milwaukee 14 priests and laymen who burned draft records with napalm—"burning property, not people"—told me, when I met him in Boston the other day, that over a hundred of the students at St. Anselm's in Manchester, New Hampshire, signed a petition to the court, which they are going to send when the Milwaukee 14 are sentenced, offering to divide up the months or years the fourteen have to serve, and take on the sentences for them. What is this but an offer to do penance, another example of trying to follow in the steps of Christ, who took on Himself our sins and in so doing overcame both sin and death?

This is, in effect, what Chuck Matthei, Chicago draft refuser, is doing, in not cooperating with the prison authorities when they seized him most brutally and literally dragged him, handcuffed, to the West Street federal prison in New York, where he is now fasting from food, and sometimes water, too.

Just to read about these things or hear of them is not enough. One must meet Chuck and see the brightness of his face, feel his gentle, joyous, and truly loving spirit, to get a glimpse of an understanding of what he is doing.

The thing is to recognize that not all are called, not all have the vocation, to demonstrate in this way, to fast, to endure the pain and long-drawn-out nerve-racking suffering of prison life. We do what we can, and the whole field of all the Works of Mercy is open to us. There is a saying, "Do what you are doing." If you are a student, study, prepare, in order to give to others, and keep alive in yourself the vision of a new social order. All work, whether building, increasing food production, running credit unions, working in factories which produce for true human needs, working the smallest of industries, the handicrafts—all these things can come under the heading of the Works of Mercy, which are the opposite of the works of war.

It is a penance to work, to give oneself to others, to endure the pinpricks of community living. One would certainly say on many occasions: Give me a good thorough, frank, outgoing war, rather than the sneak attacks, stabs in the back, sparring, detracting, defaming, hand-to-hand jockeying for position that goes on in offices and "good works" of all kinds, another and miserably petty kind of war. St. Paul said that he "died daily." This too is penance, to be taken cheerfully, joyfully, with the hope that our own faith and joy in believing will strengthen Chuck and all the others in jail.

So let us rejoice in our own petty sufferings and thank God we have a little penance to offer, in this holy season. "An injury to one is an injury to all," the Industrial Workers of the World proclaimed. So an act of love, a voluntary taking on oneself of some of the pain of the world, increases the courage and love and hope of all.

February 1969

Adventures in Prayer

Rabbi Abraham Heschel said at the Liturgical Conference in Milwaukee that what we needed, what the world needed, was prayer.

And now I pick up Thomas Merton's last book, *Contemplative Prayer,* which I am starting to read, and the foreword by our good Quaker friend Douglas Steere brought back to my memory a strange incident in my life. He quotes William Blake: "We are put on earth for a little space that we may learn to bear the beams of love." And he goes on to say that to escape these beams, to protect ourselves from these beams, even devout men hasten to devise protective clothing. We do not want to be irradiated by love.

Suddenly I remembered coming home from a meeting in Brooklyn many years ago, sitting in an uncomfortable bus seat facing a few poor people. One of them, a downcast, ragged man, suddenly epitomized for me the desolation, the hopelessness of the destitute, and I began to weep. I had been struck by one of those "beams of love," wounded by it in a most particular way. It was my own condition that I was weeping about—my own hardness of heart, my own sinfulness. I recognized this as a moment of truth, an experience of what the *New Catechism* calls our "tremendous, universal, inevitable and yet inexcusable incapacity to love." I had not read that line when I had that experience, but that is what I felt. I think that ever since then I have prayed sincerely those scriptural verses, "Take away my heart of stone and give me a heart of flesh." I had been using this prayer as one of the three acts of faith, hope, and charity. "I believe, help Thou my unbelief." "In Thee have I hoped, let me never be confounded." "Take away my heart of stone and give me a heart of flesh," so that I may learn how to truly love my brother because in him, in his meanest guise, I am encountering Christ.

Perhaps I knew in that moment in the bus in Brooklyn what St. Augustine meant when he cried out, "May I know myself so that I may know Thee." Because I felt so strongly my nothingness, my powerlessness to do anything about this horrifying recognition of my own hardness of heart, it drove me to the recognition that in God alone was my strength. Without

Him I could do nothing. Yet I could do all things in Him Who strengthened me. So there was happiness there, too. The tears were of joy as well as grief.

While I am thinking of this I remember things that Ammon Hennacy told me, about two moments in his life. Two moments of truth, I would call them, relating them to my own experience, finding them similar in a way.

I am very critical of Ammon, especially when he speaks of religion and sees only the contemptible in churchmen, and judges them so severely and at the same time exalts his own integrity. St. Paul says that we would not see our brother's faults so clearly if they were not a reflection of our own. He is the mirror into which we gaze, and when we sadly see that which leaves so much to be desired of a man, a son of God, we do not realize that it is ourselves we are seeing, and go away forgetting what kind of a person we are ourselves.

The two incidents Ammon spoke of were these. First, on an occasion when he had not as yet accepted Catholicism. He was selling *The Catholic Worker* outside of a church in Phoenix, Arizona. He was friendly with the priest of that church, though that jovial young Father used to tell Ammon that he would willingly mount a machine gun in the steeple of his church to defend it against any enemy who sought to burn it. At the same time he was glad, he said, to see Ammon selling a paper which was avowedly pacifist and anarchist and he would always defend his right to do so. Ammon had never set foot inside that church. He was in contact with the congregation only as it came to the Sunday Masses.

One day he ventured inside. I have seen this reluctance in many a non-Catholic to walk into a church, though they would not feel at all self-conscious in entering any of the Protestant churches which are open for "rest, meditation, and prayer."

He knelt as he saw others doing, and suddenly, he said, he felt *something*. He felt, too, a warmth toward these kneeling, ordinary people whom he was apt to despise as conservative and with no knowledge, he thought, of the meaning of the Sermon on the Mount. He felt that they too had *something*.

The second moment he spoke of was when he was on Riker's Island, in prison for five days. One of the domineering clergy who he felt were typical of the Church of Rome, of which he was now a member, had had him arrested for selling *The Catholic Worker* on the street corner nearest to his church. Ammon went there regularly to catch the noonday weekday crowd going and coming from Mass. This was at Forty-third Street and Lexington Avenue.

The policeman on the beat had reluctantly done the old pastor's bidding, and had arrested Ammon on his refusal to go away. In court Ammon refused to pay a fine, and went triumphantly away to his five-day sentence in the city prison.

A *New York Times* reporter, hearing of this from the American Civil Liberties Union lawyer who appealed the case, wrote a short feature article defending Ammon, and later the appeal brought about a reversal of the sentence. The lawyer had urged Ammon to pay the fine, but Ammon preferred jail, even though the court could not give him back his five days. They could have returned the fine.

It was in jail that Ammon had again one of those experiences that I speak of. All around him were the poor—the same poor he saw daily coming to the Catholic Worker for soup, coffee, and bread. He told me later that the sight of them somehow moved him to go to confession, a sacrament that he had never understood or felt necessary from the time of his reception into the Catholic Church. I can only think that these were moments when he knew God because he suddenly knew himself, knew and accepted the fact of his humanity, his share in universal guilt.

These to me are incidents in the realm of the supernatural—these sudden overwhelming insights, or recognition of Love and the abyss of nothingness, of emptiness into which we would sink if we were not upheld by Christ's loving hand.

I have thought many times since that I would hesitate to ask God to "let me know myself," remembering the unbearable pain, as well as the joy of that experience. What if the joy did not come?

But more and more I see that prayer is the answer, it is the clasp of the hand, the joy and keen delight in the consciousness of that Other. Indeed, it is like falling in love.

*   *   *

Surrounded by the slums as we are, I have long been impressed by the sight of the storefront churches where the poor come to worship and praise God and petition Him for their needs. There was one tenement I lived in on Ludlow Street. My neighbors were good and happy housekeepers, gentle with their children, hard-working, very often both mother and father going off to one of the loft factories in the neighborhood and leaving the grandmother to take care of the children. The women in the front apartment used to go out each night with Bibles under their arms to one of these little churches, and I thought, "These are termed the poor, but they are rich compared to so many of our readers. They have the Gospel. They pray."

*   *   *

I heard a strange story a year ago about seizures in a youth house of detention, where young prisoners were held without bail for months before trial. It was spoken of by the social worker who told me of this as a series of hysterical outbursts which ended in girls one by one falling to the floor in what seemed to be epileptic fits. This spread throughout the prison. It was not a story which appeared in the papers, and I heard nothing but these bare facts. Recently numbers of men in a western prison crippled themselves as a protest against rules and regulations, cutting tendons in their legs. What unbearable suffering there is in the world today, all around us, in mental hospitals, in prisons as well as in war, and we know little more about them than the Germans claimed to know of the atrocities committed during the Holocaust in Europe. When we do know, what can we do? We cry out helplessly, to lighten the burden of suffering in the world. We have the teaching of Jesus on the works of mercy listed in the twenty-fifth chapter of St. Matthew, of course.

I have been overcome with grief at times, and felt my heart like a stone in my breast, it was so heavy, and always I have heard, too, that voice, "Pray."

What can we do? We can pray. We can pray without ceasing, as St. Paul said. We can say with the Apostles, "Lord, teach me to pray." We can say with St. Paul, "Lord, what wilt Thou have me to do?" Will our Father give us a stone when we ask for bread?

We remember Jesus' words, "I tell you solemnly once again, if two of you on earth agree to ask anything at all, it will be granted to you by My Father in heaven. For where two or three meet in My Name, I shall be there with them." (Matthew 18)

There is another bit of Scripture which stands out in my mind these days. It is this: "Where sin abounds, there did grace more abound." Resting in this promise, I am content.

The Third Hour, 1970

THERESE

For years, Dorothy spoke of a desire to write a life of her favorite saint, Therese of Lisieux. Throughout the fifties, one finds references in her columns to progress on the work. In an article written in 1952, she notes her concern that the "social implications" of the saint's teachings have yet to be studied. "The significance of our smallest acts! The significance of the little things we leave undone! The protests we do not make, the stands we do not take, we who are living in the world."

Dorothy's book, *Therese*, was finally published by Fides Publishers of Notre Dame in 1960. The following chapter consists of short fragments from the book, selected to give the flavor of Dorothy's personal meditations on the life of Therese. As a life of "the Little Flower," her book is perhaps unexceptional. But as a discourse on the "spiritual implications" of her own social activism, it is a moving document of great interest.

The first time I heard the name of St. Therese of the Child Jesus and of the Holy Face (to give her her whole title), also known as Therese of Lisieux, the Little Flower, was when I lay in the maternity ward of Bellevue Hospital in New York. Bellevue is the largest hospital in the world, and doctors from all over the world come there. If you are poor you can have free hospital care. At that time, if you could pay anything there was a flat rate for having a baby—thirty dollars for a ten days' stay, in a long ward with about sixty beds. I was so fortunate as to have a bed next to the window looking out over the East River, so that I could see the sun rise in the morning and light up the turgid water and make gay the little tugs and the long tankers that went by the window. When there was fog it seemed as though the world ended outside my window, and the sound of fog horns haunted the day and the night.

As a matter of fact, my world did end at the window those ten days that I was in the hospital, because I was supremely happy. If I had written the greatest book, composed the greatest symphony, painted the most beautiful painting, or carved the most exquisite figure, I could not have felt more the exalted creator than I did when they placed my child in my arms. To think that this thing of beauty, sighing gently in my arms, reaching her little mouth for my breast, clutching at me with her tiny beautiful hands, had come from my flesh, was my own child! Such a great feeling of happiness and joy filled me that I was hungry for Someone to thank, to love, even to worship, for so great a good that had been bestowed upon

me. That tiny child was not enough to contain my love, nor could the
father, though my heart was warm with love for both.

We were radicals and had no particular religious affiliations. If I was
drawn to any "organized church," it was to the Catholic. I knew of such
saints as St. Francis of Assisi and St. Augustine, and William James, in his
Varieties of Religious Experience, had introduced me to St. Teresa of Avila,
that well-traveled yet cloistered contemplative, with her vigorous writing
and her sense of humor.

"What are you going to name your baby?" the girl in the next bed to
mine asked me.

"Teresa," I told her. "Tamar Teresa. I have a dear friend whose husband
is a Zionist, and she has a little girl named Tamar. It means little palm tree,
in Hebrew."

"And Teresa is after the Little Flower?"

I had never heard of the Little Flower and she had never heard of Teresa
of Avila. She was a Catholic, and although she didn't read much, she knew
the outlines of the life of St. Therese of Lisieux. In her pocketbook, where
she kept her powder and lipstick, tissues and rosary beads, money to buy
candy and the *Daily News* when the boy made his rounds, she also had a
medal of the Little Flower. "Here, I will give it to you for your baby," she
said. "Pin it on her."

I was some years from being a Catholic and I shied away from this
manifestation of superstition and charm-wearing. I wanted no such talis-
man. Besides, the baby might swallow it. The pin might come unloosed
and pierce that tender flesh.

"But if you love someone, you want something around you to remind
you of them," the girl protested. So I took the medal, and after hearing of
St. Therese as the young novice mistress of a far-off convent of Lisieux in
Normandy, who had died the year I was born, and whose sisters were still
alive, I decided that although I would name my child after the older saint,
the new one would be my own Teresa's novice mistress, to train her in the
spiritual life. I knew that I wanted to have the child baptized a Catholic
and I wanted both saints to be taking care of her. One was not enough.

*   *   *

The next time I heard of St. Therese of Lisieux was in 1928, a year after
I had been baptized a Catholic. I was thirty years old. I had read the New
Testament, the *Imitation of Christ,* St. Augustine, and had dipped into the
writings of some of the saints William James had introduced me to. I had
a daily missal, too, which presented a little biography of the saint of the

day, commemorated in the Mass. I still knew nothing of modern saints. Perhaps, I thought, the days of saints had passed.

At that time I did not understand that we are all "called to be saints," as St. Paul puts it. Most people nowadays, if they were asked, would say diffidently that they do not profess to be saints, indeed they do not want to be saints. And yet the saint is the holy man, the "whole man," the integrated man. We all wish to be that, but in these days of stress and strain we are not developing our spiritual capacities as we should and most of us will admit that. We want to grow in love but we do not know how. Love is a science, a knowledge, and we lack it.

My confessor at the time was Father Zachary, an Augustinian Father of the Assumption, stationed at the Church of Our Lady of Guadalupe on West Fourteenth Street. He was preparing me for Confirmation, giving me a weekly evening of instruction.

One day Father Zachary said to me, "Here is a book that will do you good." He had already given me Challoner's *Meditations* and the St. Andrew Missal. The book he now handed me was *The Little White Flower: The Story of a Soul,* an unbound book which had a tan cover with a not too attractive picture of a young nun with a sweet insipid face, holding a crucifix and a huge bouquet of roses. I was by now familiar with the statues of this little Sister which were to be seen in every church. They always called her little, although it is said she was very tall, and completely emaciated when the last photographs of her were taken. She had a proud face, however, and her habit and cloak concealed how thin she was. She was very young and her writing seemed to me like that of a schoolgirl. I wasn't looking for anything so simple and felt slightly aggrieved at Father Zachary. Men, even priests, were very insulting to women, I thought, handing out what they felt suited their intelligence—in other words, pious pap.

I dutifully read *The Story of a Soul* and am ashamed to confess that I found it colorless, monotonous, too small in fact for my notice. What kind of a saint was this who felt that she had to practice heroic charity in eating what was put in front of her, in taking medicine, enduring cold and heat, restraint, enduring the society of mediocre souls, in following the strict regime of the convent of Carmelite nuns which she had joined at the age of fifteen? A splash of dirty water from the careless washing of a nun next to her in the laundry was mentioned as a "mortification," when the very root of the word meant death. And I was reading in my Daily Missal of saints stretched on the rack, burnt by flames, starving themselves in the desert, and so on.

Joan of Arc leading an army fitted more into my concept of a saint, familiar as I was with the history of labor with its martyrs in the service of their brothers. "Love of brothers is to lay down one's life on the barricades, in revolt against the hunger and injustice in the world," I told Father Zachary, trying to convert him to my point of view. Living as we were in a time of world revolution, when, as I felt, the people of the world were rising to make a better world for themselves, I wondered what this new saint had to offer.

As a matter of fact, I was working at the time for the Anti-Imperialist League, a Communist Party affiliate with offices on Union Square. I had been given the job by a young Jewish intellectual whom I had known when he went to Columbia University and took part in the anti-conscription campaign of the First World War, who went to Russia to attend the Third International, was active in the Party for some years, and was dismissed in one of the frequent Party purges some years later. My companions were two women, both of them former Catholics, who looked on me indulgently and felt that my "faith" was a neurotic aspect of my character and something quite divorced from my daily life.

The work that we were engaged in was to publicize and raise funds for General Sandino, who was resisting American aggression in Nicaragua. Our marines were hunting him in the mountains, and the work of our committee was to raise funds and medical supplies. I did the publicity.

I was so new a Catholic that I was still working for this committee for some months after my Baptism, and I talked to Father Zachary about the work. "I am in agreement with it," I told him. "We should not be sending our marines to Nicaragua. I am in agreement with many of the social aims of Communism. 'From each according to his ability and to each according to his need.'"

Father Zachary could only quote Lenin to me, saying, "Atheism is basic to Marxism." He was the gentlest of confessors with me, who, at that time, was a female counterpart of Graham Greene's Quiet American, wanting to do good by violence.

But I did not feel he understood me when he gave me the life of St. Therese to read. What did she have to do with this world conflict, in which I in my way was involved?

I obtained other work which took me out of the Party work. I was engrossed with my child, and with earning a living. I saw more and more the basic oppositions between Catholicism and Marxism. But it took me a longer time to realize the unique position of Therese of Lisieux in the Church today.

*   *   *

Therese remembers a dream she had at the age of three which, she said, left a very deep impression. She was walking alone in the garden and suddenly she saw "two horrible little devils near the arbor, dancing on a barrel of lime with amazing agility in spite of having heavy irons on their feet." They looked at her with flaming eyes and then, as if overcome by fear, threw themselves in the twinkling of an eye to the bottom of the barrel. They escaped in some mysterious way, and ran off to hide in the linen room, which opened onto the garden. "When I saw how cowardly they were I put my fears aside and went over to the window to see what they were up to. There the little wretches were, running around and around the table, and not knowing how to escape my gaze. From time to time they came nearer, still very agitated, to peep through the window; then when they saw that I was still there, they began racing about again in abject misery."

She does not give much importance to this dream but she says she felt that God made use of it to show her that anyone in a state of grace had no need to fear.

She was beginning, even at that very early age, to see what the spiritual life meant, the series and successions of definite choices, the preference which means the life of love, the ordering of every little thing in life as though we were "practicing the presence of God." "What would He have me to do?" "Speak Lord, for Thy servant heareth." Samuel, St. Paul, all the saints had that attitude, that attraction to the good, that sense of the importance of the present moment.

*   *   *

Those were sunny years of childhood with delightful memories. Her father used to take the children to the pavilion where he kept his fishing tackle and books; he took them for walks on Sunday and then her mother was with them. She remembers the wheat fields studded with poppies and cornflowers and daisies. She loved, she said—she who was to wall herself in at the age of fifteen in a severely cloistered order—she loved "far distances, wide spaces and trees." Her whole soul was steeped in beauty and love, and her own happy nature made life all the more delightful. For four and a half years, the whole world was sunny for her.

And then came her mother's illness and death.

*   *   *

Now Therese's natural gaiety left her, and the second part of her life—the saddest she calls it—was to begin. This lasted from the time she was four and a half until she was fourteen. She was no longer lively and open, but diffident and oversensitive, crying if anyone looked at her. She could not bear to be anywhere but in the intimacy of her own family, where she could be herself. Her father and her two oldest sisters overwhelmed her with loving-kindness.

She would not have lived, she wrote, if she had not had this warmth and kindness.

*   *   *

The very fact that children come face to face with death and suffering early, makes for that paradox, "rejoicing in tribulation," that the New Testament speaks of. Therese suffered, hovered on the verge of tears, could not bear to go abroad, was hypersensitive. The light of life seemed to have gone out with her mother, and yet she spoke of delightful times in their new home, of visiting their cousins and going on holidays.

"I die, yet behold I live," St. Paul says. One has to experience this to write about it. In cold words, it is hard to convey this sense of tears and joy, soft rain and sunshine.

Every afternoon Mr. Martin took his youngest daughter for a walk, to pay a visit to the Blessed Sacrament in each of the churches in the town. When she was five she visited Carmel for the first time and heard her father tell how the holy nuns spent their time in prayer behind the grille, and never went out for walks, never set foot outside their walls.

*   *   *

Therese learned much at an early age and this child knew what evil was. She herself spoke of the goodness of the Father who had removed all obstacles from the path of His child, knowing her capacity for sin, her danger of falling. She well knew her weakness, she well knew the world. She recognized and said over and over again that it was because of her parents, her sisters, her home life, the training she had received, and finally her life in the convent that she had been saved from falling into the most appalling depths of sin.

But she also suffered intensely from scruples and for so long that it was a neurosis, like the need to be forever washing one's hands. She was tempted to vanity and wept, and then wept because she had wept. Vanity may seem to be only a slight sin, but to what depths vanity has led many a woman, perhaps only a woman can know. The vanity of Eve, that desire to exercise power, to seduce, to drag down!

Just as this child longed for the martyrdom of a Joan of Arc, an Ignatius of Antioch, as an atonement, as a way of showing her love, so also she recognized the capacity to sin which she possessed. Her love, she felt, should be greater than that of a Magdalene, because she had been prevented from sin by a loving Father who knew her weakness, knew to what depths she could have fallen. She gave up, too, her desire for great and noble deeds.

In other words, she expected nothing of herself, she was "the little grain of sand," trampled underfoot, forgotten, and God would do it all in making her a saint, because He wanted it. He wanted just such a saint as she was to become, because she was ordinary, just like many another girl, a child of comfortably situated, hard-working parents. She was one of "the people." When she spoke of herself as a "little flower," a comparison her father had made, it was of a common, ordinary, and fragile little flower of the spring, common as grass, that she was thinking.

*　　*　　*

As I understand her, St. Therese is teaching the necessity of loving God first, and then "all these things shall be added unto you." All these happy loves of earth, family, friends, husband, children. "Seek ye first the kingdom of God, *and all these things shall be added unto you.*" This is blind faith, a naked faith in love. A little child is told these things early, and with his trusting heart and open mind he accepts these truths though he has not experienced them.

Therese takes no credit to herself. It is all God's doing. "Behold the handmaid of the Lord, be it done unto me according to Thy word." Knowing that it is all God's work in her soul, she can say with the Psalmist—"Enlarge my heart that Thou mayest enter it." "Make me *desire* to walk in the way of Thy commandments." The emphasis is on God, and His grace. She, of course, responds to this grace, and grace, which is defined as "participation in the divine life," grows in her, so she can say, "Now not I, but Christ in me." It made her infinitely daring in her desire to be a saint. "God would not give us these desires if He did not want us to satisfy them," she writes.

Many of the Little Flower's admirers have been frightened by the austerity of such teaching. What—have no human affection whatever? Not love friends and relatives? The bleakness of such an outlook is indeed frightening. But it is part of the tremendous affirmation of faith in love on the part of Therese. She was ready to stake her life on this renunciation of love. We must be ready to give up everything. We must have already given it up, before God can give it back, transfigured, supernaturalized. "He who does not hate father, mother, sister, brother, for My Name's sake, is not worthy to be My disciple."

He is indeed a jealous lover. He wants all.

*   *   *

In Therese's world, she was faced with only three choices. She could look forward to marriage, or to living at home as a single woman and caring for her father, or to entering the convent. The atmosphere of this home was one of such liberty that the girls were always free to decide what they wanted, what they themselves thought was God's will for them.

On the feast of Pentecost, Therese told her father of her desires. She did it in fear and trembling, at the close of the day, after they had come home from Vespers. Her father was sitting in the garden; it was sunset at the end of a most beautiful day. She had prayed to the Holy Spirit and to the Apostles to help her to speak, to ask her father's permission. After all, she was only fourteen.

The very words she uses in her autobiography show how important she considered her vocation, how out of the ordinary, not in the least like that of others. She felt herself to be, she wrote, "a child destined by God to be, by means of prayer and sacrifice, an apostle of apostles." Already once before, when out walking with her father, she had pointed to the large T made by the configuration of the stars and said childishly, "Look, my name is written in heaven." She felt her vocation to be a saint—and a special kind of saint for our times.

When she told her father, he wept at first. He tried to tell her she was too young to leave him, to take such a step into a harsh and rigorous life. But they continued to talk as they walked up and down the garden path, and her heart grew light with joy when she realized that he had consented. After they had walked for some time together, he stooped down to a little rock garden and picked a small white flower, which came out by the roots. Then he spoke to her of her sheltered life, and how God had chosen her, a little flower, preserving her in her fragility and obscurity. From then on she thought of herself as "a little white flower"—the name she first gave to her book. She took the flower and pressed it in her prayer book and since the roots had come up with the stem, she thought of herself as being transplanted to Carmel. Later, when the stem broke, she took it as a sign that she was going to die young, as she did.

*   *   *

Therese's life of work and study continued and she felt herself growing in the love of God. It is here that she speaks of experiencing "transports of love." Over and over again in books on St. Therese, it is emphasized that her way is a most ordinary way, a way open to all. She herself says that it was her destiny to show the world of today that holiness is accessible to all, that all are called, and that it is a "little way," a simple way for all to follow. And never once does she say that these transports, these joys are not for all. As well as the Cross, there are the joys of the spiritual life.

*   *   *

There is no question but that the Carmelite cloister was a fervent one. The life was hard. Therese said that when her dream of gaining admittance was at last realized, "peace flooded my soul, a deep, sweet, inexpressible peace, an inward peace which has been my lot these eight and a half years. It has never left me, not even when trials were at their height. Everything here delighted me, our little cell most of all; it was as though I had been transported to my faraway desert."

She kept saying to herself that at last she was where she wanted to be. "I am here forever now." It had been so hard those last months; there had been the long period of waiting and then the last days of farewell to the family, the last Holy Communion together, the last breakfast in that much-loved dining room, the parting with father and uncle and aunt, cousins and sisters. They went with her to Carmel and after Mass said goodbye to her at the door. She felt at that moment as though her heart would burst and that she would die. It was a truly terrible moment, a fearful moment, but she was always sure of just what she wanted. Her will was set on God. God alone!

"Illusions!" she was to write later. "Thanks to God's mercy I had none at all; the religious life was just what I had expected."

*   *   *

Looking forward to her clothing, when—dressed as a bride in white satin and a magnificent and priceless veil of Alençon lace such as her mother had spent her life in making—she would be presented by her father to her Lord, she found herself in a state of dryness.

She confessed to being in trouble with one of the Sisters and on the verge of tears. "Jesus riddles me with pinpricks," she complains. Recognizing her nothingness, she had referred to herself as a little ball which

the child Jesus played with or tossed aside. "The poor *little ball* can take
no more; all over it are tiny holes which cause it more suffering than if it
had but one great gash. Nothing from Jesus. Dryness! . . . Sleep! . . . But
at least there is silence! Silence does good to the soul. But creatures!
creatures! . . ."

She said she shuddered at the thought of them. She had to keep reminding herself that it was Jesus who pierced her with these small wounds and
then she could feel suffering to be sweet. "Suffering is only sweetness, His
hand is *so sweet!* . . . But creatures! . . . Those who surround me are good,
of course, but there is a touch of something in them that repels me! I can't
explain it to you. All the same I am VERY *happy,* happy at suffering what
Jesus wants me to suffer. If He does not Himself pierce His *little ball,* it is
He who guides the hand that pierces it."

She goes on to write that He sleeps, that He puts Himself to no trouble
about her. "He shows me that I am not a stranger by treating me like this.
I assure you He simply doesn't bother to make conversation with me."

Her desire to love was boundless. She wished to be indifferent to all the
things of this world. What mattered all created beauties?

"Possessing them I should be utterly unhappy, my heart would be so
empty. It's incredible how big a thing my heart seems when I consider the
world's treasures . . . since all of them massed together would not content
it . . . but how small a thing it seems when I consider Jesus! . . . I want to
love Him so! . . . To love Him more than He has ever been loved!—My sole
desire is to do the will of Jesus always."

*   *   *

One of the reasons for stressing this struggle to attain to true love is St.
Therese's statement that her mission was to make Love loved and to show
that she was not dealing in abstractions. She never wrote anything that she
had not experienced.

The first part of Therese's life was spent in illustrating to the world the
tender love of a child for its father, the dependence, the trust of a creature
for the Creator.

In the convent of Carmel she became the Spouse of Christ, and she did
not hesitate to say that "He had kissed her with the kiss of His mouth."

*   *   *

Sometimes it seems to me that nuns know more of sin in man than of
the Christ in him, but it was not so with Therese. She knew the dangers
of the world and she knew what was in man, but always her faith in her

supernatural weapons was so great that she saw him as saved. Hers was not the vision of "sinners falling into hell like snow flakes," but of men at death seizing hold of a crucified Christ and embracing Him. Love was the measure by which she wished to be judged, and she sang of a merciful Father, of a Father who loved His children to folly. But she knew, too, that to love is to suffer, and just as a mother brings forth her children with anguish, she offered herself to the suffering that would result from her desire for souls. Who can doubt that God made "her, the barren woman, to dwell in her house, the joyful mother of children."

* * *

Always she was praying that she would see things as they were, that she would live in reality, not in dreams.

Certainly she had little time to dream. According to the Benedictine Rule, the *Opus Dei*—the work of God which must come before all other work—is that of offering up the Holy Sacrifice of the Mass and reciting the Divine Office. So the prime work of the Carmelite is to acquire a love for and a knowledge of God as well as to praise Him. This Rule obliges her to recite the Breviary. The Carmelite also fits reading and meditation into her schedule.

Six or seven hours of prayer, a life of hard work in silence the rest of the time, two brief periods of recreation when there was permission to talk, sew, paint, or take up the "busy work" all women delight in. In addition to the works of the community, whether it was laundry, kitchen, dining room, sacristy, much of the work was done alone. When it came to the sewing, the fine embroidery done by the community, the tradition was to work in one's cell.

Therese's habit was of coarse serge, her stockings of rough muslin, and on her feet she wore rope sandals. Her bed was made of three planks, covered by a thin pad and one woolen blanket. There was scarcity of food, inadequate bedding, no heat in the convent except for one small stove in one room. Prayer and penance! These are indeed spiritual works, spiritual weapons to save souls, penance for luxury when the destitute suffer, a work to increase the sum total of love and peace in the world.

* * *

By the time she was twenty, Therese had gone through many intense experiences, losing father and mother, feeling an orphan, but emphasizing for that reason her dependence on God as a Father. Over and over again through her writings "God appears to her understanding," writes Father

Liagre, "and above all to her heart (for she lived much more by her heart than her understanding) as a Father, as her Father, as the most affectionate and tender of fathers; in a word, as fatherly love, and that at its very highest perfection."

Her familiarity with God the Father, God the Son, and God the Holy Spirit might be called her recognition of the immanence of God, and this very familiarity which leads her to liken herself to a little plaything, a ball, a little grain of dust to be trampled underfoot, points to God's transcendence, to the infinite distance between God and creatures. On the one hand He is closer than the air we breathe, and on the other hand we are the grain of sand on the seashore, lost in the nothingness before the All-Powerful.

*   *   *

It was in the spring of 1896, in April, that she received the first warning of the sickness that caused her death. Therese tells the story of the beginning of her illness, how on going to her cell one night in the bitter cold, and undressing in the dark, she suffered a hemorrhage from the lungs which soaked her handkerchief with blood. She did not even light her lamp, but lay down on her hard pallet to take the few hours of sleep allowed Good Friday night. She says she was overwhelmed with joy at the thought that she was going to go soon to God. She did not lie awake, since it was already midnight, but she woke with a sense of expectation, as though she had something good and exciting to look forward to, and going to the window, saw that her handkerchief was all stained with blood.

*   *   *

She knew with a certainty beyond doubt that she was teaching the way of the early Christians, the way Jesus Himself spoke of when He said, "I am the Way, the Truth and the Life."

She knew with a certainty that is heaven itself, or a foretaste of heaven, that she had been taught the secret, the "science of love." She died saying, "Love alone matters." She died saying that she did not regret having given herself up to love.

Her secret is generally called the Little Way, and is so known by the Catholic world. She called it little because it partakes of the simplicity of a child, a very little child, in its attitude of abandonment, of acceptance.

We know of course that not all children, not even infants, are so gifted. But generally speaking, the little child is dependent and trustful, ready to accept everything from the hand of its parent, with no knowledge of prideful independence. Therese is content to be considered always the little child, the little grain of sand, the creature who can give nothing to its Creator but the willing acceptance of this status, taking from the hand of its Creator all that comes in daily life.

* * *

To the community she gave every appearance of serenity and peace, and yet "in peace is my bitterness most bitter," she quotes. On another occasion she says, "Let us suffer, if need be, with bitterness." She, the realist, well knew that suffering of body and soul is not lofty and exalted, but mean and cruel, a reflection of the blackness of hell. It was not suffering for itself that she embraced. It was a means to an end; the very means used by Jesus Himself.

In order to hide this suffering from others, she wrote poems about the joys of faith, hope, and charity, and yet in the night of sense and soul that she was passing through, she felt none of these joys. She wanted her suffering to be hidden even from God, if that were possible, in order to atone for lack of faith in the world. She asked consolation from no one, not even from God. She had wanted martyrdom, and this heavy weight of despair is martyrdom.

She says that she wants to offer this blackness for all those in the world today who do not believe, who "have lost the precious treasures of faith and hope and with them all joy that is pure and true." She says she has no sense of joy whatever, and yet she can still say, "Thou hast given me, O Lord, a delight in Thy doings." Since it is suffering of a most cruel kind that she is laboring under, a blackness of the mind and soul, she "wills" a delight in this suffering. If suffering is a part of love, suffering then will become her delight.

* * *

During this period of spiritual and physical suffering, Therese was able to go on with all the exercises of the religious life, even the hardest manual labor. She went on washing windows, washing clothes, and the work was laborious indeed. Sometimes she could scarcely walk up the stairs she was so exhausted, but went from step to step, breathing heavily, scarcely able to lift one foot after the other. Sometimes it took her an hour to undress, the effort was so great.

She never complained, she went on with the work of the day in chapel and out of it, and said nothing. The Rule calls for complete silence except

during the two hours of recreation, one after the noonday meal, and the
other after the evening collation. At these times she was merry, there was
always a smile to disguise the deadly fatigue, and no mention was made of
the fact that she was dying by inches.

*   *   *

Before the end, she became skin and bones. Father Petitot said that she
became so thin that her bones protruded through her skin. Tuberculosis of
the intestines set in and gangrene, and when she was raised up in bed to
get her breath, she gasped that it was as though she were sitting on spikes.

The flies tormented her very much during the last hot summer. It must
have been no little part of the suffering of Christ on the Cross, nailed and
enduring the crawling of flies on His eyes, His wounds, His flesh. "They
are my only enemies," Therese said when she was tormented by them.
"God commanded us to forgive our enemies, and I am glad I have some
occasion to do so. That is why I spare them."

*   *   *

When her sister Celine sat reading her a conference on eternal beatitude,
suddenly Therese interrupted her—"It is not that which attracts me. It is
love! To love and be loved!, and to return to earth to make Love to be
loved!"

It was on July 17 that she said, "I feel that my mission is about to begin;
my mission of making souls love the good God as I love Him, to teach my
little way to souls. If my desires receive fulfillment, I shall spend my heaven
on earth even until the end of time. Yes, I will spend my heaven doing
good upon earth."

"It is the way of spiritual childhood," she said in response to a question
about her "little way." "It is the path of total abandonment and confidence.
I would show them the little method I have found so perfectly successful
and tell them there is but one thing to do on earth; to cast before Jesus
the flowers of little sacrifices. That is what I have done and that is why I
shall be so well received."

There has been so much discussion of the diminutive "little" which
Therese used constantly that it is good to remember her words of explanation of August 6. "To be little . . . is . . . not to attribute to ourselves the
virtues we practice, nor to believe ourselves capable of practicing virtue at
all. It is rather to recognize the fact that God puts treasures of virtue into
the hands of his little children to make use of them in time of need, but
they remain always treasures of the good God. Finally, to be little means

that we must never be discouraged over our faults, for children often fall but they are too small to harm themselves very much."

* * *

"Oh, Mother, is it not yet the agony, am I not going to die?" Therese is said to have cried out. "It might be some hours yet," Mother Marie de Gonzague, who had sat by many a deathbed in her community, assured her.

"Ah well! So be it! So be it! Oh, I do not wish to suffer less. Oh I love Him. My God, I love You!"

These were her last words. The Sisters were summoned quickly back into the infirmary to kneel about the bedside and to witness the last moments of this girl who wished to die of love. According to her sister Pauline, her face at that moment suddenly lost all look of suffering and there was a sudden blooming, a sudden joy transforming her.

* * *

Therese Martin died on September 30, 1897. Only seventeen years later, when those who had been born in the same year with her were just forty-one years of age, the fame of her sanctity had so spread among the people that her cause was introduced at Rome. She was beatified on April 29, 1923, and canonized on May 17, 1925, an unusually rapid process for the Church in modern times.

So many books have been written about St. Therese, books of all kinds, too, so why, I ask myself again, have I written one more? There are popular lives, lives written for children, travelogue lives following her footsteps, lives for the extrovert, the introvert, the contemplative, the activist, the scholar, and the theologian.

Yet it was the "worker," the common man, who first spread her fame by word of mouth. It was the masses who first proclaimed her a saint. It was the "people."

What was there about her to make such an appeal? Perhaps because she was so much like the rest of us in her ordinariness. In her lifetime there are no miracles recounted; she was just good, good as the bread which the Normans bake in huge loaves. Good as the pale cider which takes the place of the wine of the rest of France, since Normandy is an apple country. "Small beer," one might say. She compares to the great saints as cider compares with wine, others might complain. But it is the world itself which has canonized her, it is the common people who have taken her to their hearts. And now the theologians are writing endlessly to explain how big she was, and not little, how mature and strong she was, not childlike and

dependent. They are tired of hearing people couple her name with that of
Teresa of Avila, whom they call the "Great Teresa" as distinguished from
the "Little Therese."

What did she do? She practiced the presence of God and she did all
things—all the little things that make up our daily life and contact with
others—for His honor and glory. She did not need much time to expound
what she herself called her "little way." She wrote her story, and God did
the rest. God and the people. God chose for the people to clamor for her
canonization.

What stands out in her life? Her holiness, of course, and the holiness of
her entire family. That is not an ordinary thing in this day of post-war
materialism, delinquency, and all those other words which indicate how
dissatisfied the West is with its economy of abundance while the East sits
like Lazarus at the gate of Dives.

With governments becoming stronger and more centralized, the common
man feels his ineffectiveness. When the whole world seems given over to
preparedness for war and the show of force, the message of Therese is
quite a different one.

She speaks to our condition. Is the atom a little thing? And yet what
havoc it has wrought. Is her little way a small contribution to the life of
the spirit? It has all the power of the spirit of Christianity behind it. It is
an explosive force that can transform our lives and the life of the world,
once put into effect. In the homily he gave after the Gospel at the Mass of
her canonization, Pope Pius XI said: "If the way of spiritual childhood
became general, who does not see how easily would be realized the refor-
mation of human society . . ."

The seeds of this teaching are being spread, being broadcast, to be
watered by our blood perhaps, but with a promise of a harvest. God will
give the increase. At a time when there are such grave fears because of the
radioactive particles that are sprinkled over the world by the hydrogen
bomb tests, and the question is asked, what effect they are going to have
on the physical life of the universe, one can state that this saint, of this
day, is releasing a force, a spiritual force upon the world, to counteract
that fear and that disaster. We know that one impulse of grace is of
infinitely more power than a cobalt bomb. Therese has said, "All is grace."

She declared, "I will spend my heaven doing good upon earth." "I will
raise up a mighty host of little saints." "My mission is to make God loved,
to make Love loved."

And one can only remember the story of Abraham and how he asked,
"Wilt Thou destroy the just with the wicked? If there be fifty just men in

the city, shall they perish withal? And wilt Thou not spare that place for the sake of the fifty just, if they be therein? Far be it from Thee to do this thing, and to slay the just with the wicked, and for the just to be in like case as the wicked. This is not beseeming Thee: Thou, who judgest all the earth, wilt not make this judgment."

The mystery of suffering has a different aspect under the New Covenant, since Christ died on the Cross and took on Himself men's sins. Now St. Paul teaches that we can fill up the sufferings of Christ, that we must share in the sufferings of the world to lessen them, to show our love for our brothers. But God does not change, so we can trust with Abraham that for even ten just men, He will not destroy the city. We can look with faith and hope to that *mighty army of little ones* that St. Therese has promised us and which is present now among us.

ON PILGRIMAGE
(1948)

Nineteen hundred forty-eight was a quiet year, as the country rested between wars. At the Catholic Worker, life was filled with the everyday domestic chores, the small joys and sorrows that are always with us. It was a restful and reflective period for Dorothy, as well. The Catholic Worker Retreats were in full swing. Their message, though austere, provided Dorothy with consolation and yearning: we must sow natural love to reap supernatural; we must "put off the old man, and put on Christ."

The Catholic Worker itself published a volume of Dorothy's columns and journal reflections for the year in *On Pilgrimage*, from which the following selections have been condensed.

As the year began, Dorothy was enjoying a visit to the farm in Stotler's Crossroad, West Virginia, where her daughter, Tamar, and son-in-law, David Hennessy, were expecting their third child.

January

January 17, 1948, West Virginia, 5°: When you are in the country, the temperature is important. To write, I lie in bed with a hot-water bottle at my feet, a loose old coat covering me. A bathrobe would not be enough. The hot-water bottle is a pint-size whiskey bottle.

This is a good house, a good farm, in spite of the fields being far from the house beyond the woods. Spring, summer, and fall are so beautiful in the country, but the winters are hard.

Yesterday the snow fell all day and the children ran out getting pans of it to eat. My son-in-law David calls it the poor man's manure, as it is filled with chemicals that enrich the soil. It tastes sooty, just as it does in the city. The wheat, barley, and rye in the bottomlands, green and frozen, were soon blanketed. The hills, ridges, and paths were outlined and all was black and white, blue and gray with a hint of lavender behind the trees. We are indeed in the depths of winter.

Our days are spent in cooking, dishwashing, clothes washing, drawing water, keeping two fires going, feeding babies, consoling babies, picking up after babies. The bending and lifting alone should take the place of exercise. But tomorrow we are going to pretend our long porch is the deck of a ship and we are going to take a brisk walk up and down and around, just to get out of the house and enlarge our vision a bit. It always fascinated me, how the Brontë sisters paced the floor of their living room in front of the fire. It must have been a very large room. My friend Tina has a habit of pacing the floor, and in small quarters it can be nerve-racking for non-pacers.

January 19: The moon is increasing to full and it is now the coldest time of the month. Tamar is uneasy about her time. She is expecting the baby in a week. We do hope and pray she is not taken in the dead of night when it is coldest, and hard to get the car started. And so hard for her, too, to go out into the night and the cold. I do wish she could have it at home.

We are so far from church, and the snow kept us from getting to Mass Sunday, so we read the Epistle and Gospel for the day and have been doing it daily since. Sunday's Epistle was about the marriage feast of Cana. When my friends are in sorrow and trouble, or even when they are just without spirit, I like to pray, "Jesus, they have no wine," or "Mary, they have no wine." It is a good prayer for many sad hearts today.

Not much time for prayer these busy days. Only the short ones. And not much time to think of self either; or comfort—physical, spiritual, or mental. So that is good, too. "Self" is the great enemy. "Deny yourself, take up your cross and follow me."

Of course, in a way, taking care of your own, children and grandchildren, is taking care of your self. On the other hand, there is the sacrament of duty, as Father McSorley calls it. There is great joy in being on the job, doing good works, performing the Works of Mercy. But when you get right down to it, a work which is started personally often ends up by being paperwork—writing letters, seeing visitors, speaking about the work while others do it. One can become a veritable Mrs. Jellyby, looking after the world and neglecting one's own who are struggling with poverty and hard work and leading, as such families with small children do these days, ascetic lives. There are vigils, involuntary ones, fasting, due to nausea of pregnancy, for instance. But St. Angela of Foligno says that penances voluntarily undertaken are not half so meritorious as those imposed on us by the circumstances of our lives and cheerfully borne.

The Christian life is certainly a paradox. The teaching of St. John of the Cross is of the necessity for detachment from creatures; of the need of traveling light through the dark night.

Most of us have not the courage to set out on this path wholeheartedly, so God arranges it for us.

January 20: How to lift the heart to God, our first beginning and last end, except to say with the soldier about to go into battle—"Lord, I'll have no time to think of Thee but do Thou think of me." Of course, there is grace at meals, a hasty grace, what with Sue trying to climb out of her high chair onto the table. Becky used to fold her hands and look holy at the age of eighteen months but now she does nothing. If you invite her participation, she says, "I won't." If you catch Sue in a quiet, unhungry mood, she will be docile and fold her hands. But rarely. She is usually hungry and when she starts to eat she starts to hum, which is thanks too.

But there is that lull in the morning before the mailman comes when I can take out the missal and read the Epistle and Gospel for the day and the Collect, which is always pertinent.

What do I talk to myself about? When I am truly alone, with no babies around, as when I am alone in church, I pray. I say the rosary, I read my Psalms. And there is time. At home, kneeling by my bed—or, in the bitter cold, lying in bed—my prayers are brief, half conscious, and the planning, the considering, the figuring of ways of "making ends meet" goes on. Until I catch myself and turn to God again.

"All these things shall be added unto you." "He knoweth that ye have need of these things." St. Teresa of Avila says we should not trouble Our Lord with such petty trifles. We should ask great things of Him.

So I pray for Russia, for our own country, for our fellow men, our fellow workers, for the sick, the starving, the dying, the dead.

January 23: There is so much fear and distraction these days over the state of the world—there is sadness in the Pope's Christmas message, in articles, in letters, in all endeavors. And yet surely, all times, as St. Teresa said, "are dangerous times."

It is one of the strange paradoxes of the Christian life that we can say with St. Paul, "As dying, yet behold we live." We can suffer with others, we can see plainly the frightful chaos, the unbelievable misery of cold and hunger and bitter misery, yet all the time there is the knowledge that "the sufferings of this time are not to be compared to the joy that is to come."

Often we comfort ourselves only with words, but if we pray enough, the conviction will come, too, that Christ is our King—not Stalin, Bevin, or Truman. That He has all things in His hands, that "all things work together for good to those that love Him."

Oh, but the misery of those who do not, of those who because of suffering turn from Him and curse God and die!

It is hard to think of these things. It is not to be understood, we cannot expect to understand. We must just live by faith, and the faith that God is good must be tried as though by fire. "I believe, Lord, help Thou my unbelief."

February

February 4, Feast of St. Agatha: One cannot help thinking that the men have an easier time of it. It is wonderful to work outside on such a day as this with the snow falling lightly all around, chopping wood, dragging in fodder, working with the animals. Women are held pretty constantly to the house. Tomorrow I shall take to reading and pacing the porch, one of my favorite occupations. I've been reading the Psalms for Matins and Vespers and by taking a stroll midmorning or afternoon I can get in the Little Hours.

I was reading in *David Copperfield* how Betsey Trotwood paced the floor for two hours while she unraveled problems, and at eighty could still do a five-mile stretch!

February 6, Feast of St. Dorothy: St. Dorothy is the patroness of gardeners and when I think of a garden I think of a garden enclosed, as the Blessed Mother is described. A wall is a lovely thing—with fruit trees and hollyhocks and tall things growing against it. A garden not too small to have a grape arbor at one end where there can be tables and chairs and benches for outdoor meals. Such a garden is for women and children, so that there can be no straying of little feet.

St. Dorothy, pray we may one day have such a garden, that we may settle long enough in one place to put down roots—if not our own, since we are pilgrims, at least a tree's, a vine's.

Still no baby!

March

March 8: The baby has arrived! Eric Dominic Hennessy was born on February 20 and christened on March 7, which happens to fall this year on Laetare Sunday, "rejoicing" Sunday, a fine day for a baptism. Mother, father, and grandmother are all content!

The ceremony of baptism is certainly impressive, with the priest beginning, "What dost thou ask of the Church of God?" and the sponsor answering for the child, "Faith . . ."

"Meditations for women," these notes should be called, jumping as I do from the profane to the sacred over and over. But then, living in the country, with little children, with growing things, one has the sacramental view of life. All things are His and all are holy.

I used to wish I could get away from my habit of constant, undisciplined reading, but in a family one is certainly cured of it. If you stop to read a paper, pick up a book, the children are into the tubs or the sewing machine drawers. Everything is interrupted, even prayers, since by nightfall one is too tired to pray with understanding. So I try to practice the presence of God after the manner of Blessed Lawrence, and pray without ceasing, as St. Paul advised. He might even have had women in mind. But he himself was active enough, weaving goat's hair into tents and sailcloth to earn a living, and preaching nights and Sundays. So I am trying to learn to recall my soul like the straying creature it is as it wanders off over and over again during the day, and lift my heart to the Blessed Mother and His saints, since my occupations are the lowly and humble ones, as were theirs.

March 10: St. Teresa says, "No one need be afraid of our committing excesses here, by any chance—for as soon as we do any penances our confessors begin to fear that we shall kill ourselves with them . . ."

Every time I am making what I consider a thorough confession—that is, telling tendencies that I wish I could overcome, like eating between meals, indulging in the nibbling that women do around a kitchen, and mention it in confession as a venial sin not only in regard to myself but my neighbor who is starving all over the world, the confessor makes no attempt to understand, but speaks of scruples. One confessor said, "I order you to eat between meals!"

These are tendencies to gluttony, and gluttony is one of the seven deadly sins. So little is expected of us lay people that, as Father Joseph, our dear Benedictine friend, once said, "the moral theology we are taught is to get us into heaven with scorched behinds."

What kind of an unwilling, ungenerous love of God is this? We do little enough, and when we try to do a little more, we are lectured on Jansenism! I don't even know what it is. I only know that I am self-indulgent.

March 11: David and Tamar are getting enough eggs now to sell some, and since eggs are good for forty-eight cents a dozen at the crossroads store a mile away, that means that four dozen eggs will buy a few staples.

Spring is coming, though it is still only twenty above zero when we get up in the morning. The frogs are croaking and green things are pushing up on the hillsides and the fields. The sun is warm in the middle of the day, but oh dear, how sharp the wind is, so that the children come wailing in off the porch after too short a respite for those of us working in the house. Right now they are in again. I write at the kitchen table, and Becky is going around singing, "The baby is all baptized," putting it to various tunes.

One can get by if one's wants are modest. One can withdraw from the factory, refuse to make munitions, airplanes, atom bombs. In sections like this, rent is ten dollars a month, sometimes even five, and there are empty houses. But city people are afraid—afraid of the country, afraid of the dark, afraid to be alone, afraid of the silence. They confess to it. And I remember myself, once, as a little girl, wandering out along the beach down at Fort Hamilton, sitting at the edge of a swamp and listening to the cicadas on a hot summer day, and suddenly being overcome by fear. Even as a little child of six I often awoke in the dark and felt the blackness and terror of non-being. I don't know whether I knew anything of death, but these were two terrors I experienced as a child, a terror of silence and loneliness, and a sense of Presence, awful and mysterious.

March 28: Tamar has had her baby and spring is here. Much as I would love to, I have no excuse to stay. It has been two and a half months since I left New York. So now tomorrow I start off again—"on pilgrimage," for we have here no abiding city. Much as we may want to strike our roots in, we are doomed to disappointment and unhappiness unless we preserve our detachment. It is the paradox of the Christian life, to hate father and mother, sister and brother and children on the one hand, if they stand between us and God, and, on the other hand, to follow the teaching of St. Paul, "If any man have not care of his own, and especially those of his own house, he hath denied the faith and is worse than an infidel"; not to be solicitous for the things of the world, and yet to do everything with love, for the love of God. Moreover, much as I appreciate St. Peter's mother-in-law and how "she rose and ministered to them," and much as I love St. Paul's talk of grandmothers, I know that mother-in-law and grandmother should not be too much in evidence or trying to live the lives of the younger people. If we are there to serve, it is one thing. But usually we are not nearly so much needed as we think we are. There are such things as guardian angels, and our dear Lord watches over all.

April

Whenever I groan within myself and think how hard it is to keep writing about love in these times of tension and strife which may, at any moment, become for us all a time of terror, I think to myself: What else is the world interested in? What else do we all want, each one of us, except to love and be loved, in our families, in our work, in all our relationships? God is Love. Love casts out fear. Even the most ardent revolutionist, seeking to change the world, to overturn the tables of the money changers, is trying to make a world where it is easier for people to love, to stand in that relationship to each other. We want with all our hearts to love, to be loved. And not just in the family, but to look upon all as our mothers, sisters, brothers, children. It is when we love the most intensely and most humanly that we can recognize how tepid is our love for others. The keenness and intensity of love brings with it suffering, of course, but joy too because it is a foretaste of heaven. I often think in relation to my love for little Becky, Susie, and now Eric: "That is the way I must love every child and want to serve, cherish, and protect them."

When you love people, you see all the good in them, all the Christ in them. God sees Christ, His Son, in us. And so we should see Christ in others, *and nothing else,* and love them. There can never be enough of it.

There can never be enough thinking about it. St. John of the Cross said that where there was no love, put love and you would draw love out. The principle certainly works. I've seen my friend Sister Peter Claver with that warm friendliness of hers which is partly natural, but is intensified and made enduring by grace, come into a place which is cold with tension and conflict, and warm the house with her love.

And this is not easy. Everyone will try to kill that love in you, even your nearest and dearest; at least, they will try to prune it. "Don't you know this, that, and the other thing about this person? He or she did this. If you don't want to hear it, you must hear. It is for your good to hear it. It is my duty to tell you, and it is your duty to take recognition of it. You must stop loving, modify your loving, show your disapproval. You cannot possibly love—if you pretend you do, you are a hypocrite and the truth is not in you. You are contributing to the delinquency of that person by your sentimental blindness. It is such people as you who add to the sum total of confusion and wickedness and soft appeasement and compromise and the policy of expediency in this world. You are to blame for Communism, for industrial capitalism, and finally for hell on earth!"

The antagonism often rises to a crescendo of vituperation, an intensification of opposition on all sides. You are quite borne down by it. And the only Christian answer is *love,* to the very end, to the laying down of your life.

To see only the good, the Christ, in others! Perhaps if we thought of how Karl Marx was called "Papa Marx" by all the children on the street, if we knew and remembered how he told fairy stories to his children, how he suffered hunger and poverty and pain, how he sat by the body of his dead child and had no money for coffin or funeral, perhaps such thoughts as these would make us love him and his followers. *Dear God, for the memory of that dead child, or that faithful wife, grant his stormy spirit "a place of refreshment, light, and peace."*

And then there was Lenin. He hungered and thirsted and at times he had no fixed abode. Mme. Krupskaya, his widow, said that he loved to go into the peace of the pine woods and hunt mushrooms. He lived one time in the slums of Paris and ate horsemeat. He started schools for the poor and workers. "He went about doing good." Is this blasphemy? How many people are dying and going to God their Father and saying sadly, "We have not so much as heard that there is a Holy Spirit." And how will they hear if none preaches to them? And what kind of shepherds have many of them had? Ezekiel said in his day, "Woe to the shepherds that feed themselves and not their sheep!"

And if there have been preachers, has there been love? If people will not listen, one can still love, one can still find Christ in them to love, and love is stronger than death. Dear God, may Lenin too find a place of refreshment, light, and peace. Or don't we believe in retroactive prayers? There is no time with God.

*   *   *

It is always a terrible thing to come back to Mott Street. To come back in a driving rain to men crouched on the stairs, huddled in doorways, without overcoats because they sold them, perhaps the week before when it was warm, to satisfy hunger or thirst, who knows. Those without love would say, "It serves them right, drinking up their clothes."

God help us if we got just what we deserved!

May

Naturally speaking, people are filled with repulsion at the idea of holiness. We have so many sad examples of Pecksniffs in our midst. But we are filled with encouragement these days to find that it is not only the Catholic Worker but writers like Ignazio Silone, Aldous Huxley, and Arthur Koestler who are crying aloud for a synthesis—the saint-revolutionist who would impel others to holiness by his example. And, recognizing the difficulty of the aim, Silone has drawn pictures of touching fellowship with the lowly, the revolutionist living in voluntary poverty, in hunger and cold, in the stable, and depending on "personalist action" to move the world. *Bread and Wine* and *The Seed Beneath the Snow* are filled with this message.

After the last war, everyone was talking about the lost generation. After this war, thank God, they are talking more about saints. A few years ago there was a book review by W. H. Auden in *The New York Times* about Greek and Christian tragedy and *Moby Dick* as an allegorical novel. In that review it was pointed out that unlike Greek tragedy, where one's fate is written and it is only left to the hero to play the heroic part, the Christian has a *choice* and each and every Christian is forced to make that choice. According to Auden:

> . . . there is the possibility of each becoming exceptional and good; this ultimate possibility for hero and chorus alike is stated in Father Mapple's sermon, and it

is to become a saint, i.e., the individual through his own free will surrenders his will to the will of God. In this surrender he does not become the ventriloquist's doll, for the God who acts through him can only do so by his consent; there always remain two wills, and the saint therefore never ceases to be tempted to obey his own desires.

The saint does not ask to become one; he is called to become one and assents to the call. The outward sign that Ahab is so called is the suffering which is suddenly intruded into his life. He is called to give up hunting whales—"the normal, cannibalistic life of this world."

Archbishop Robichaud, in his book *Holiness for All,* emphasizes the fact that the choice is not between good and evil for Christians—that it is not in this way that one proves one's love. The very fact of baptism, of becoming children of God, presupposes development as children of God. C. S. Lewis points out that the child in the mother's womb would perhaps refuse to be born if given the choice, but it does not have that choice. It has to be born. The egg has to develop into the chicken with wings. Otherwise it becomes a rotten egg. It is not between good and evil that the choice lies, but between good and better. In other words, we must give up over and over again even the good things of this world, to choose God. Mortal sin is a turning from God and a turning to created things—created things that are good.

It is so tremendous an idea that it is hard for people to see its implications. Our whole literature, our culture, is built on ethics, the choice between good and evil. The drama of the ages is on this theme. We are still living in the Old Testament, with commandments as to the natural law. We have not yet begun to live as good Jews, let alone as good Christians. We do not tithe ourselves, there is no year of jubilee, we do not keep the Sabbath, we have lost the concept of hospitality. It is dog eat dog. We are all hunting whales. We devour each other in love and in hate; we are cannibals.

In all secular literature it has been so difficult to portray the good man, the saint, that Don Quixote is made a fool and Prince Myshkin an epileptic, in order to arouse the sympathy of the reader, appalled by unrelieved goodness. There are, of course, the lives of the saints, but they are too often written as though they were not in this world. We have seldom been given the saints as they really were, as they affected the lives of their times—unless it is in their own writings. But instead of that strong meat we are too generally given the pap of hagiography.

Too little has been stressed the idea that *all* are called. Too little attention has been placed on the idea of mass conversions. We have sinned against the virtue of hope. There have been in these days mass conversions to Nazism, Fascism, and Communism. Where are our saints to call the masses to God? Personalists first, we must put the question to ourselves. Communitarians, we will find Christ in our brothers and sisters.

June

This morning as I went to Mass, my eyes stung from the fumes of the cars on Canal Street. I crossed a vacant lot, a parking lot filled with cinders and broken glass, and longed for an ailanthus tree to break the monotony of the prison-gray walls and ground all about. Last night we all went to a meeting on Distributism, and the talk was so good and stimulating that in spite of the noise, the fumes, the apathy which the city brings, I was impelled this morning to write.

We could list perhaps fifty among our friends (and if we went through the files of our readers we could find many more) who have gone to the land. They have got the right philosophy. The growth of these toeholds on the land is an encouraging sign.

On the other hand, there are such stories as the one in the last issue of *Commonweal* about the DiGiorgio strike in the long Central Valley of California, of 58,000 acres owned by one family, of 2,000 employees, of horrible living conditions, poor wages, forced idleness, "times of repose" between crops when machines are cared for but not men, women, and children.

Assembly-line production in the factory and mass production on the land are part of a social order accepted by the great mass of our Catholics. Even when they admit it is bad, they say, "What can we do?" And the result is palliatives, taking care of the wrecks of the social order, rather than changing it so that there would not be quite so many broken homes, orphaned children, delinquents, industrial accidents, so much destitution in general.

Palliatives, when what we need is a revolution. Each one of us can help start it. It is no use saying we are bored with the word. Let us not be escapists but admit that it is upon us. We are going to have it imposed upon us, or we are going to make our own.

If we don't do something about it, people may well say, "Why bring children into the world, the world being what it is?" We bring them into it and start giving them a vision of an integrated life so that they too can start fighting.

This fighting for a cause is part of the zest of life.

But how can one have a zest for life under such conditions as those we live in on Mott Street? How can that laundry worker down the street, working in his steamy hell of a basement all day, wake each morning to a zest for life?

To live in Newburgh, on our farm, to be arranging retreats, to be making bread and butter, taking care of and feeding children there, washing and carding wool, gathering herbs and salad greens and flowers—all these things are so good and beautiful that one does not want to take time to write except that one has to share them and the knowledge of how to start to achieve them.

The whole purpose of the retreat movement is to teach people to "meditate in their hearts," to start to think of these things, to make a beginning, to go out and start to love God in all the little things of every day, to so make one's life and one's children's life a sample of heaven, a beginning of heaven. The retreats are to build up a desire, a knowledge of what to desire.

Yes, we must write of these things, of the love of God and the love of His creatures, man and beast, plant and stone.

The Catholic Worker farm at Newburgh has ninety-six acres. We are raising hay, corn, vegetables, pigs, chickens, a cow. There are peas, broccoli, Swiss chard, and lettuce. It is getting easier to feed the forty or so retreatants who come every few weeks to the farm, as well as the twenty who are there all summer.

I tell these things to make the mouth water. In the fall we are going to put in a field of wheat, and next summer, God willing, we will have our own flour for the good whole-wheat loaves that come out of the oven every day.

We are not expecting utopia here on this earth. But God meant things to be much easier than we have made them. We are eminently practical, realistic.

July–August

Maryfarm, Notes from a retreat: One time I was traveling, far from home and lonely, and I awoke in the night almost on the verge of weeping with a sense of futility, of being unloved and unwanted. And suddenly the thought came to me of my importance as a daughter of God, daughter of a King, and I felt a sureness of God's love and at the same time a conviction that one of the greatest injustices (if one can put it that way) which one can do to God is to distrust His love, not realize His love. God so loved me that He gave His only begotten Son. "If a mother will forget her children, never will I forget thee." Such tenderness. And with such complete ingratitude we forget the Father and His love!

This morning between conferences I wept, partly for joy and partly for the misery of life; partly at being so overwhelmed with demands made upon me and partly with fatigue and nerves. It is always a few days before I really settle down in peace and quiet to a retreat. The first day is a delight, but the second is hard. By the third I am well into it and beginning to feel firm and sure of the way I shall go in the coming year.

My troubles are still with me for the first few days. This morning, for instance, one of the "friends of the family" came in, stood up in back for a while, sat down, got up again, sat down again. Again at rosary the chapel was crowded, so he had to kneel in the conference room. He chose a huge overstuffed chair to kneel before, and, bending over it, buried his face in the depths of the upholstery. It was a heavy August day. These little things would not bother me except that from that same person as well as from a number of others there is a long history of such behavior, appealing for attention, coming to bang on my door at midnight, asking to be allowed to go to the farm, demanding it, claiming that I, by the very things I write, must care for them, support them all. And the burden gets too heavy; there are too many of them; my love is too small; I even feel with terror, "I have no love in my heart, I have nothing to give them." And yet I have to pretend that I have.

But strange and wonderful, the make-believe becomes true. If you will to love someone, you soon do. You will to love this cranky old man and someday you do. It depends on how hard you try.

But how hard it is, sometimes, to love! How often it seems you turn the other cheek, you give your cloak and your trousers and your shoes, and then when you are left naked, you are beaten and reviled besides. There are two women at this moment, as there have been many more through the years, who accept for months our ministrations, our help and loving-kindness, only to turn and rend us. Lies, scandal, accusations roll from their lips in a torrent and a flood of poison.

Failures. It is these things that overwhelm one. Physical sickness like epilepsy, senility, insanity, drug cases, alcoholics; and just the plain, ordinary poor who can't get along, can't find a place to live, who need clothes, shelter, food, jobs, care, and most of all love, these are our daily encounters.

So it is wonderful that this retreat comes in the middle of summer, when one can stop and think in one's heart about these things. I have made this retreat eight times, and always there is something new, always there is something to learn about how to progress in the love of God and one's neighbor.

I am speaking of heavenly things, but heaven and earth are linked together as truly as body and soul. We begin to live again each morning, we rise from the dead, the sun rises, spring comes around, and then resurrection. And the great study of how truly to become the children of God, to be made like God, to participate in the life of God, this is the study of the retreat. It is a painful study. It is breathing rarefied air; one must get used to this air of the mountains, so clear, cold, sharp, and fresh. It is like wine, and we have prayed to Mary and said, "We have no wine," and she has given us wine, the body and blood of her Son, the life of her Son, the love of her Son.

My whole life, so far, my whole experience has been that our failure has been not to love enough. This conviction brought me to a rejection of the radical movement after my early membership in the Socialist Party, the Industrial Workers of the World, and the Communist affiliates I worked with. "Youth demands the heroic," as Claudel said, so the work of these militant groups had appealed to me. One could not read such books as Sinclair's *Jungle* and not want to join with someone to do something about it. And who else was doing anything? Employers, landlords, political bosses, all professed Christians, were corrupt and rotten to the core, I felt. What was there to love in them? Certainly, it seemed madness to think of reforming them, converting them. Such an Augean stable was beyond cleaning up; it needed flushing out. So I reasoned. Certainly, youth is always looking for a "strong conflict."

It was not that I was ever disillusioned. My conviction that there was work to be done never wavered. Things did not need to be as bad as they were. There was a possibility of change.

Certainly, too, there was always an inward conviction that we were but dust. Alone by ourselves we could do nothing. Probably all my early religiousness as a child was still with me, and that included a conviction of sin, of the depravity that was in us all.

I wanted to believe that man could right wrongs, could tilt the lance, could love and espouse the cause of his brother because "an injury to one was an injury to all." I never liked the appeal to enlightened self-interest. I wanted to love my fellows, the poor. I could not be happy unless I shared their poverty, lived as they did, suffered as they did.

Well, now at fifty, I cannot say that I have been disillusioned. But neither can I say that I yet share the poverty and suffering of the poor. No matter how much I may live in a slum, I can never be poor as the mother of three, six, ten children is poor (or rich either). I can never give up enough, I have always to struggle against self. I am not disillusioned with myself either. I know my talents and abilities as well as failures. But I have done woefully little. I am fifty, and more than half of my adult life is passed. Who knows how much time is left after fifty. Newman says the tragedy is never to have begun.

September

September 10, West Virginia: I arrived at Dave and Tamar's between heavy thunder showers that settled down to an all-night and all-day downpour. Coming after a month of drought, it is too late to do the garden any good. It is all burned up now and there is nothing left to can. The early crops were good, however. David is working in the tomato cannery a mile down the road, and his wage is sixty cents an hour.

Toward late afternoon the weather cleared and we got a few lines of wash out and a few more tubfuls put to soak. Tamar got some weaving done—she is making rag rugs to sell—and baked a cake, besides driving to and from the cannery twice for practice in driving. She has no license yet.

It is a full day, with animals to feed and re-tether, and three babies and a seven-room house to look after. Nothing ever gets done thoroughly, but that's the way things have to be with children. A mother has to keep her mind on a number of things at once, on the cake in the oven, on Becky, Susie, and Eric, planning and replanning what she wants to do, and what she has to do, and what she *can* do. There is not much time wasted. Now it is eight-thirty and Tamar is reading *Kristin Lavransdatter,* and David, *Blackfriar's,* and I am adding these few pages to my notebook.

So many pages are given over to ideas, theorizing, figuring things out, setting things down—for my own benefit as well as my readers'—that it is good to write about just facts, the account of a day.

I must say I feel good, physically and mentally refreshed to have had this day with babies after weeks of seeing and talking to people in the office, in the House of Hospitality, at the retreat house; writing, answering letters, going to meetings. This is living, not just talking about it.

September 19, St. Januarius: I think of the tremendous noise in New York at this time of year, what with fiestas, marching bands, and processions. People drag out chairs and tables and live on the sidewalks night and day.

And down here in West Virginia, only a few hours out of Washington, D.C., and one mile from Stottler's Crossroad, there is silence. That is, comparative silence. Crickets outside make the night alive, and Susie upstairs has kept up a conversation and a singing with herself for an hour and a half. She is tireless.

Becky, who is three, goes to bed quietly, insists upon having her covers arranged tidily, composes herself, turns her face to the wall, and that is all from her for the night. Susie, on the other hand, just two, acts as though wound up. Constant motion, constant noise. She wanders in and out of bed, makes a wreck of her covers, drags everything out of bureau drawers, dresses and undresses herself, until finally in the midst of reading or conversation downstairs, we realize that there is *silence.* The great silence has then descended on the house. Susie has run down.

Eric, seven months old, presents no problem as yet. He is suckled, he sleeps. He awakes, eats applesauce or cereal, plays, laughs, practices crawling, and again is suckled and sleeps.

Today *Commonweal* came with a chapter from Thomas Merton's book about his entrance into the Trappist monastery in Kentucky. He mentions the need we have in our religious life for a formal observance of prayer, the need for ritual.

And I remember reading in Father Faber's *At the Foot of the Cross* how our Blessed Mother in Egypt, a pagan land, must have surrounded herself with articles and customs which reminded her of her country and her people and their faith.

David has a crucifix in every room, even on the porch, and it brings me a great sense of comfort when I see it, black against the whitewashed wall. The children love their morning prayers and even when I am rocking them and singing "All ye works of the Lord" they fold their tiny hands reverently. When the Church is not near at hand, one is forced to see that there is religion in the home.

We are all sitting around the Aladdin lamp, which gives just as good a light as electricity, and Tamar is reading a geological survey of Morgan County, and David is reading a book on rural sociology, describing the dismal condition of the farmer.

Tamar gets very impatient sometimes at the lack of such facilities as running water, but there is a possibility of getting a well drilled outside the back door. Until then, she must leave it to David to cart pails of water from the spring five hundred feet away. Sometimes they arrive with little fish swimming in them. Today, during a thunder shower, while the children danced in the downpour, we filled pails and tubs and a hogshead with water, which will simplify the washing problem Monday.

Tomorrow I must leave, after this brief week's visit, and it is so beautiful, so peaceful here, far from noise and traffic and the world, that I hate to go. But it is only a day away from New York and we will visit again soon. It is so good to have such beginnings as this to come to, for "refreshment, light, and peace."

As Eric Gill says in one of his letters to Graham Carey,

> I am sure that all attempts to create cells of the good life in the form of small communities are not only much to be encouraged, but are the only hope. . . .
> It is to me perfectly clear that communities of layfolk religiously cutting themselves off from the money economy are an absolute necessity if Christianity is not to go down, either into the dust or the catacombs. . . . There are lots of little attempts going on in England today in spite of everything. But of course they are pretty hard up against it, and they get jolly little encouragement from the ordinary population, and still less from the Catholic.

There are lots of little attempts in the United States too, but in all I have visited, there is still a hankering for the "fleshpots," and strangely enough, the pots are in this case modern plumbing. The men, as much as the women, insist on having it, and it is ridiculous to think that so many are deterred from achieving freedom because of this.

Father Gindler, who is a parish priest in the coal regions, once said to me, "Do you always have to mention outhouses?"

I feel like the Meagles family in *Little Dorrit* who are always talking about how *practical* they are. A place with an outhouse costs between $1,200 and $2,500. A place with plumbing begins at $8,000. What a difference to pay!

It is ten o'clock and time for sleep. David is closing all the downstairs windows to keep out the morning damp. The house is heavenly quiet.

October

Käthe Kollwitz, who died recently, spent her life drawing pictures of the poor. She felt it was her job to arouse the consciences of those who looked at her pictures, and since she was the wife of a doctor and saw a great deal of human suffering, she had many a model for her work. I was reminded so much of her work this month when I visited Mary Frecon in Harrisburg at her Martin de Porres House of Hospitality.

It has been about ten years now, maybe more, that Mary has worked there in Harrisburg combating the indifference of the whites to the tragedy of the blacks.

I arrived in Harrisburg one Sunday evening last month before the weather turned cold, and it was a good time to be there, because the night was alive with dark faces and bodies, sitting on the steps of the ramshackle houses, nursing their babies, watching their children, listening to the music, the rhythm of tambourines, the clapping of hands, the singing from the Tabernacles, churches of the Lord, the Pentecostal churches on every corner.

All through the warm night there was the smell of rats, the smell of dead things, the smell of rotting garbage. If you have ever been in a town where there are stockyards, fertilizer factories, paper mills, you know the peculiar odors of our industrial system. They are not sweet.

And there was Mary Frecon, nursing a diabetic woman, swollen, heavy with water, holding her up at night so she can breathe, bringing the priest to her, looking after her materially and spiritually. And Susie, burned out of her apartment by a jealous rival, her shoulders infected, cut by glass from broken windows when she tried to escape the fire, nursed back to health of body and soul. Katie, dying of cancer, tuberculosis, and syphilis, her body now dung indeed, but once a thing of beauty, strung taut with life and pleasure, and now overwhelmed with torrents of pain. Lucille Pearl, dying in an alley, flies and worms feasting on the open sores of her flesh. These women, dying and yet alive today in heaven, literally dragged into the wedding feast, dying happy and sure, and already before their deaths given a foretaste of the life to come.

How to draw a picture of the strength of love! It seems at times that we need a blind faith to believe in it at all. There is so much failure all about us. It is so hard to reconcile oneself to such suffering, such long-enduring suffering of body and soul, that the only thing one can do is to stand by and save the dying ones who have given up hope of reaching out for beauty, joy, ease, and pleasure in this life. For all their reaching, they got little of it. To see these things in the light of faith, God's mercy, God's justice! His devouring love! I read one story of the death of the Little Flower, and her death was just as harrowing in its suffering as that of Mary's Katie. Her flesh was a mass of sores, her bones protruded through her skin, she was a living skeleton, a victim of love. We have not such compassion, nor ever will have. What we do is so little.

The stink of the world's injustice and the world's indifference is all around us. . . .

Compassion—it is a word meaning to suffer with. If we all carry a little of the burden, it will be lightened. If we share in the suffering of the world, then some will not have to endure so heavy an affliction. It evens out. What you do here in New York, in Harrisburg, helps those in China, India, South Africa, Europe, Russia, as well as in the oasis where you are. You may think you are alone. But we are members one of another. We are children of God together.

November

There is a character in *The Plague,* the novel by Albert Camus, who says that he is tired of hearing about men dying for an idea. He would like to hear about a man dying for love for a change. He goes on to say that men have forgotten how to love, that all they seem to be thinking of these days is learning how to kill. Man, he says, seems to have lost the capacity for love.

What is God but Love? What is a religion without love? We read of the saints dying for love and we wonder what it means. There was a silly verse I used to hear long ago, "Men have died and worms have eaten them, but not for love." And nowadays in this time of war and preparations for war, we would tend to agree. But still there are the saints. Yes, they have died for love of God. But Camus' character would say, "I mean for love of man." Our Lord did that, but most people no longer believe in Him. So one can talk and write of Love. People want to believe in that even when they are all but convinced that it is an illusion. (It would be better still to love, rather than to write about it. It would be more convincing.)

In the Old and New Testaments there are various ways in which the relationship between God and man is mentioned. There is the shepherd and his sheep—"The Lord is my shepherd." There is the servant and the master, the son and the father. And there is the bride and the bridegroom. "Behold, the bridegroom cometh." The Song of Songs, the Canticle of Canticles is all about love. "Let Him kiss me with the kisses of His mouth."

It is hard to believe in this love. In a book of Hugh of St. Victor which I read once on the way from St. Paul to Chicago, there is a conversation between the soul and God about this love. The soul is petulant and wants to know what kind of a love it is which loves everyone indiscriminately, the thief and the Samaritan, the wife and the mother and the harlot? The soul complains that it wishes a *particular* love, a love for itself alone. And God replies fondly that, after all, since no two people are alike in this world, He has indeed a particular fondness for each one of us, an exclusive love to satisfy each one alone.

It is hard to believe in this love, it is so tremendous. If we do once catch a glimpse of it we are afraid. Once we recognize that we are children of God, that the seed of divine life has been planted in us at baptism, we are overcome by that obligation placed upon us of growing in the love of God. And what we do not do voluntarily, He will do for us.

Father Roy, our dear Josephite friend who worked with us at Easton and who has been these past two years in a hospital in Montreal, learning what it is to be loved, used to tell a story of a leper he met at a hospital up on the Gaspé Peninsula. The leper complained to him, how could he believe in the love of God?

Father Roy proceeded to tell his favorite story. First of all there is dirt, the humus from which all things spring, and the flower says to the dirt, "How would you like to grow and wave in the breeze and praise God?" And the dirt says, "Yes," and that necessitates its losing its own self as dirt and becoming something else. Then the chicken comes along and says to the flower, "How would you like to be a chicken and walk around as I do, and praise God?" and the flower assures the chicken that it would like it indeed. But then it has to cease to be a flower. And the man comes to the chicken and says to it, "How would you like to be a man and praise God?" and of course the chicken would like this too, but it has to undergo a painful death to be assimilated to the man, in order to praise God.

When Father Roy told this story he said with awe, "And the leper looked at me, and a light dawned in his eyes, and he clasped my hands and gasped, 'Father!' And then we both cried together."

Father Roy is a childlike man, and the Russian leper up in the Canadian peninsula was a simple sufferer, and he saw the point that Father Roy was trying to make and he began to believe in this love, and to see some reason for his sufferings. He began to comprehend the heights and the depths and the strange mystery of this love. But it still takes the eyes of faith to see it.

The love of God and man becomes the love of equals as the love of the bride and the bridegroom is the love of equals, and not the love of the sheep for the shepherd, or the servant for the master, or the child for the parent. We may stand at times in the relationship of servant, and at other times in that of child, as far as our feelings go and in our present state. But the relationship we hope to attain is that of the love of the Canticle of Canticles. If we cannot deny the *self* in us, kill the self love, as He has commanded, and put on the Christ life, then God will do it for us. We must become like Him. Love must go through these purgations.

And where are the teachers to teach of this love, the stages of this love, the purgations, the sufferings entailed by this love, the stages through which natural love must pass to reach the supernatural?

We have repeated so many times that those who have two cloaks should follow the early Fathers who said, "The coat that hangs in your closet belongs to the poor." And those who have a ten-room house can well share it with those who have none. How many large houses could be made into several apartments to take in others? Much hospitality could be given to relieve the grave suffering today. But people are afraid. They do not know where it all will end. They have all gone far enough in generosity to know that an ordeal is ahead, that the person taken in will most likely turn into "the friend of the family." No use starting something that you cannot finish, they say. Once bitten is twice shy. We have all had our experiences of ingratitude, of nursing a viper in our bosom, as the saying goes. So we forget about the necessity of pruning, in the natural order, to attain much fruit. We don't want to pay the cost of love. We do not want to exercise our capacity to love.

There are many stories one could tell about Catholic Worker life, but it is always better to wait until years have passed so that they become more impersonal, less apt to be identified with this one or that.

There is a story, however, about a reader of the paper, and this happened long enough ago so that we can tell it. Our friend adopted a young girl and educated her, and the young girl proved to be a great joy and comfort. Now she has entered a contemplative order to spend her life in prayer and work. The same reader then took in another young woman, who brought home a fatherless baby, and when that was forgiven her, went out and brought in still another, and there was apt to be a third. Our friend wrote and begged us for advice and help as to what to do. Was she contributing to the delinquency of this girl by forgiving seventy times seven, and was she perhaps going to have seventy times seven children to take care of?

It is good to think of the prophet Hosea, whom I have mentioned before in writing on love. He was commanded by God to take a harlot to wife, and she had many children by other men. He was a dignified, respected teacher of his people, and he was shamed and humiliated by the wife of his bosom. Yet he was to go down in history as the type of the love of God for His adulterous people.

Love must be tried and tested and proved. It must be tried as though by fire. And fire burns.

We may be living in a desert when it comes to such perceptions now, and that desert may stretch out before us for years. But a thousand years are as one day in the sight of God, and soon we will know as we are known. Until then we will have glimpses of brotherhood in play, in suffering, in serving, and we will begin to train for that community, that communion that Father Perrin talked so much of in his story of the worker priests in Germany.

This last month, there was an article by John Cogley in *America* about his experiences in the Chicago House of Hospitality. He writes of it as in the dim and distant past, and tells of the "mushroom growth" of such houses back in the thirties. In the present there are a few still struggling along, he writes, and a few farms existing in dire poverty.

Yes, the problems have become intensified, a great many have left the running. Where there were thirty-two Houses of Hospitality and farms, there are now eleven. But in those eleven we are still trying to work out a theory of love, a study of the problem of love so that the revolution of love, instead of that of hate, may come about and we will have a new heaven and a new earth wherein justice dwelleth.

December

The love of the humanity of Our Lord is the love of our brother. I have meditated on this fact during the past month. The only way we have to show our love for God is by the love we have for our brother. And as Father Hugo likes to say, "You love God as much as the one you love the least."

Love of brother means voluntary poverty, stripping one's self, putting off the old man, denying one's self. It also means non-participation in those comforts and luxuries which have been manufactured by the exploitation of others. While our brothers suffer, we must suffer with them. While our brothers suffer from lack of necessities, we will refuse to enjoy comforts. These resolutions, no matter how hard they are to live up to, no matter how often we fail and have to begin over again, are part of the vision and the long-range view which Peter Maurin has been trying to give us these past years.

And we must keep this vision in mind, recognize the truth of it, the necessity for it, even though we do not, cannot, live up to it. Like perfection. We are ordered to be perfect as our heavenly Father is perfect, and we aim at it, in our intention, though in our execution we may fall short of the mark over and over. As St. Paul says, it is by little and by little that we proceed.

If our jobs do not contribute to the common good, we pray God for the grace to give them up. Have they to do with shelter, food, clothing? Have they to do with the Works of Mercy? Everyone should be able to place his job in the category of the Works of Mercy.

This would exclude jobs in advertising, which only increases people's useless desires, and in insurance companies and banks, which are known to exploit the poor of this country and of others. Whatever has contributed to the misery and degradation of the poor may be considered a bad job, and not to be worked at.

If we examined our consciences in this way we would soon be driven into manual labor, into humble work, and so would become more like Our Lord and our Blessed Mother.

Poverty means non-participation. It means what Peter calls regional living. This means fasting from tea, coffee, cocoa, grapefruit, pineapple, etc., from things not grown in the region in which one lives. One day last winter we bought broccoli which had the label on it of a corporation farm in Arizona or Texas, where we had seen men, women, and children working at two o'clock in the morning with miner's lamps on their foreheads in order to avoid the terrible heat of the day. These were homeless migrants, of which there are some million in the United States. For these there is "no room at the inn."

We ought not to eat food produced under such conditions. We ought not to smoke, not only because it is a useless habit, but also because tobacco impoverishes the soil and pauperizes the farmer, and means women and children working in the fields.

Poverty means having a bare minimum in the way of clothes, and seeing to it that these are made under decent working conditions, proper wages and hours, etc. The union label tries to guarantee this.

As for the dislocation in employment, if everyone started to give up their jobs? Well, decentralized living would take care of such a situation. And when we look at the dirty streets and lots in our slums, the unpainted buildings, the necessity of a nationwide housing project, the tearing down that needs to be done, then we can see that there is plenty of employment for all in the line of providing food, clothing, and shelter for our own country and for the world.

Poverty means not riding on rubber while horrible working conditions prevail in the rubber industry. Poverty means not riding on rails while bad conditions exist in the coal mines and steel mills. Poverty means not accepting that courteous bribe from the railroads, the clergy rate. Railroads have been built on robbery and exploitation. There once were stagecoaches, of course, and we are only about a century past them. But pilgrims used to walk, and so did the saints. They walked from one end of Europe and Russia to the other.

Of course, we are not all given the grace to do such things. But it is good to call to mind the *vision*. It is true, indeed, that until we begin to develop a few apostles along these lines we will have no mass conversions, no social justice, no peace. We need saints. God, give us saints!

How far we all are from it! We do not even see our infirmities. Common sense tells us, "Why live in a slum? It is actually cheaper to live in a model housing project, have heat and hot water, a mauve or pink bath and toilet, etc. We can manage better; we can have more time to pray, meditate, study. We would have more money to give to the poor." Yes, this is true,

according to the candlelight of common sense—but not according to the
flaming heat of the sun of justice. Yes, we will have more time, with modern
conveniences, but we will not have more love. "The natural man does not
perceive the things of the spirit." We need to be fools for Christ. What if
we do have to buy coal by the bucket instead of by the ton? Let us squander
money, be as lavish as God is with His graces, as He is with His fruits of
the earth.

Let us rejoice in poverty, because Christ was poor. Let us love to live
with the poor, because they are specially loved by Christ. Even the lowest,
most depraved, we must see Christ in them, and love them to folly. When
we suffer from dirt, lack of privacy, heat and cold, coarse food, let us
rejoice.

When we are weary of manual labor and think, "What foolishness to
shovel out ashes, build fires, when we can have steam heat! Why sew when
it can be better done on a machine? Why laboriously bake bread when we
can buy so cheaply?" Such thoughts have deprived us of good manual labor,
in our city slums, and have substituted shoddy store-bought goods, clothes,
and bread.

Poverty and manual labor, they go together. They are weapons of the
spirit, and very practical ones, too. What would one think of a woman
who refused to wash her clothes because she had no washing machine, or
clean her house because she had no vacuum, or sew because she had no
machine? In spite of the usefulness of the machine, and we are not denying
it, there is still much to be done by hand. So much, one might say, that it
is useless to multiply our tasks, go in for work for work's sake.

But we must believe in it for Christ's sake. We must believe in poverty
and manual labor, for love of Christ and for love of the poor. It is not true
love if we do not know them, and we can only know them by living with
them, and if we love with knowledge we will love with faith, hope, and
charity.

On the one hand, there is the sadness of the world—and on the other
hand, when I went to church today and the place was flooded with sunshine
and it was a clear, cold day outside, suddenly my heart was so flooded with
joy and thankfulness and so overwhelmed at the beauty and the glory and
the majesty of our God that I could only think of St. Dionysius, "Concerning the Godhead":

"It is the Cause and Origin and Being and Life of all creation. And It is
to them that fall away from It, a Voice that doth recall them and a Power
by which they rise; and to them that have stumbled into a corruption of
the Divine Image within them, It is a Power of Renewal and Reform; and

a Sacred Grounding to them that feel the shock of unholy assault, and a Security to them which stand; and upward Guidance to them that are being drawn unto It, and a Principle of Illumination to them that are being enlightened; a Principle of Perfection to them that are being perfected; a Principle of Deity to them that are being deified; and of Simplicity to them that are being brought into simplicity; and of Unity to them that are being brought into unity."

The immanence of God in all things! In Him "we live and move and have our being." "He is not far from every one of us." (Acts 17:28)

"Hear, O Israel: the Lord our God is one Lord. Thou shalt love the Lord thy God with thy whole heart, and with thy whole soul and with thy whole strength.

"And these words which I command thee this day, shall be in thy heart. And thou shalt tell them to thy children. And thou shalt meditate upon them sitting in thy house and walking on thy journey, sleeping and rising. And thou shalt bind them as a sign on thy hand; and they shall be and move between thy eyes. And thou shalt write them in the entry and on the doors of thy house." (Deuteronomy 6:4–9)

*   *   *

To love with understanding, and without understanding. To love blindly, and to folly. To see only what is lovable. To think only of these things. To see the best in everyone around, their virtues, rather than their faults. To see Christ in them!

IN FIELDS AND FACTORIES

Labor

The Catholic Worker, as the name implied, was directed to the worker, but we used the word in its broadest sense, meaning those who worked with hand or brain, those who did physical, mental, or spiritual work. But we thought primarily of the poor, the dispossessed, the exploited.

Every one of us who was attracted to the poor had a sense of guilt, of responsibility, a feeling that in some way we were living on the labor of others. The fact that we were born in a certain environment, were enabled to go to school, were endowed with the ability to compete with others and hold our own, that we had few physical disabilities—all these things marked us as the privileged in a way. We felt a respect for the poor and destitute as those nearest to God, as those chosen by Christ for His compassion. Christ lived among men. The great mystery of the Incarnation, which meant that God became man that man might become God, was a joy that made us want to kiss the earth in worship, because His feet once trod that same earth. It was a mystery that we as Catholics accepted, but there were also the facts of Christ's life, that He was born in a stable, that He did not come to be a temporal King, that He worked with His hands, spent the first years of His life in exile, and the rest of His early manhood in a crude carpenter shop in Nazareth. He fulfilled His religious duties in the synagogue and the temple. He trod the roads in His public life and the first men He called were fishermen, small owners of boats and nets. He was familiar with the migrant worker and the proletariat, and some of His parables dealt with them. He spoke of the living wage, not equal pay for equal work, in the parable of those who came at the first and the eleventh hour.

He died between two thieves because He would not be made an earthly King. He lived in an occupied country for thirty years without starting an underground movement or trying to get out from under a foreign power. His teaching transcended all the wisdom of the Scribes and Pharisees, and taught us the most effective means of living in this world while preparing for the next. And He directed His sublime words to the poorest of the poor, to the people who thronged the towns and followed after John the

Baptist, who hung around, sick and poverty-stricken, the doors of rich men.

He had set us an example and the poor and destitute were the ones we wished to reach. The poor were the ones who had the jobs of a sort, organized or unorganized, and those who were unemployed or on work-relief projects. The destitute were the men and women who came to us in the breadlines, and we could do little with them but give what we had of food and clothing. Sin, sickness, and death accounted for much of human misery. But aside from this, we did not feel that Christ meant we should remain silent in the face of injustice and accept it, even though He said, "The poor ye shall always have with you."

In the first issue of the paper we dealt with Negro labor on the levees in the South, exploited as cheap labor by the War Department. We wrote of women and children in industry and the spread of unemployment. The second issue carried a story of a farmers' strike in the Midwest and the condition of restaurant workers in cities. In the third issue there were stories of textile strikes and child labor in that industry; the next month coal and milk strikes. In the sixth issue of the paper we were already combating anti-Semitism. From then on, although we wanted to make our small eight-page tabloid a local paper, that is, covering the American scene, we could not ignore the issues abroad. They had their repercussions at home. We could not write about these issues without being drawn out on the streets on picket lines, and we found ourselves in 1935 with the Communists picketing the German consulate at the Battery.

It was not the first time we seemed to be collaborators. During the Ohrbach Department Store strike the year before, I ran into old friends from the Communist group, but I felt then, and do now, that the fact that Communists made issue of Negro exploitation and labor trouble was no reason why we should stay out of the situation. "The truth is the truth," writes St. Thomas, "and proceeds from the Holy Ghost, no matter from whose lips it comes."

There was mass picketing every Saturday afternoon during the Ohrbach strike, and every Saturday the police drove up with patrol wagons and loaded the pickets into them with their banners and took them to jail. When we entered the dispute with our slogans drawn from the writings of the popes regarding the condition of labor, the police around Union Square were taken aback and did not know what to do. It was as though they were arresting the Holy Father himself, one of them said, were they to load our pickets and their signs into their patrol wagons. The police contented themselves with giving us all injunctions. One seminarian who stood on the sidelines and cheered was given an injunction too, which he cherished as a souvenir.

*   *   *

The most spectacular help we gave in a strike was during the formation of the National Maritime Union. In May 1936, the men appealed to us for help in housing and feeding some of the strikers, who came off the ships with Joe Curran in a spontaneous strike against not only the shipowners but also the old union leaders.

We had then just moved St. Joseph's House to 115 Mott Street and felt that we had plenty of room. Everyone camped out for a time while seamen occupied the rooms, which they made into dormitories. There were about fifty of them altogether during the course of the next month or so, and a number of them became friends of the work. . . .

That first strike was called off, but in the fall, after the men built up their organization, the strike call went out again. For the duration of the strike we rented a store on Tenth Avenue and used it as a reading room and soup kitchen where no soup was served, but coffee and peanut butter and apple butter sandwiches. The men came in from picket lines and helped themselves to what they needed. They read, they talked, and they had time to think. Charlie O'Rourke, John Cort, Bill Callahan, and a number of seamen kept the place open all day and most of the night. There was never any disorder; there were no maneuverings, no caucuses, no seeking of influence or power; it was simply a gesture of help, the disinterested help of brothers. . . . Our headquarters were a tribute to the seaman's dignity as a man free to form association with his fellows, to have some share in the management of the enterprise in which he was engaged. . . .

Many times we have been asked why we spoke of *Catholic* workers, and so named the paper. Of course, it was not only because we who were in charge of the work, who edited the paper, were all Catholics, but also because we wished to influence Catholics. They were our own, and we reacted sharply to the accusation that when it came to private morality, the Catholics shone, but when it came to social and political morality, they were often conscienceless. Also Catholics were the poor, and most of them had little ambition or hope of bettering their condition to the extent of achieving ownership of home or business, or further education for their children. They accepted things as they were with humility and looked for a better life to come. They thought, in other words, that God meant it to be so.

*   *   *

One winter I had a speaking engagement in Kansas and my expenses were paid, which fact enabled me to go to Memphis and Arkansas to visit the Tenant Farmers' Union, which was then and is still headed by a Christian Socialist Group. The headquarters were a few rooms in Memphis, where the organizers often slept on the floor because there was no money for rent other than that of the offices. Those days I spent with them I lived on sandwiches and coffee because there was no money to spend on regular meals either. We needed to save money for gas to take us around to the centers where dispossessed sharecroppers and tenant farmers were also camping out, homeless, in railroad stations, schools, and churches. They were being evicted wholesale because of the purchase of huge tracts of land by northern insurance agencies. The picture has been shown in *Tobacco Road, In Dubious Battle,* and *Grapes of Wrath*—pictures of such desolation and poverty and in the latter case of such courage that my heart was lifted again to hope and love and admiration that human beings could endure so much and yet have courage to go on and keep their vision of a more human life.

During that trip I saw men, women, and children herded into little churches and wayside stations, camped out in tents, their household goods heaped about them, not one settlement but many—farmers with no land to farm, housewives with no homes. They tried with desperate hope to hold on to a pig or some chickens, bags of seed, some little beginnings of a new hold on life. It was a bitter winter, and frame houses there are not built to withstand the cold as they are in the North. The people just endure it because the winter is short—accept it as part of the suffering of life.

I saw children ill, one old man dead in bed and not yet buried, mothers weeping with hunger and cold. I saw bullet holes in the frame churches, and their benches and pulpits smashed up and windows broken. Men had been kidnapped and beaten; men had been shot and wounded. The month after I left, one of the organizers was killed by a member of a masked band of vigilantes who were fighting the Tenant Farmers' Union.

There was so little one could do—empty one's pockets, give what one had, live on sandwiches with the organizers, and write, write to arouse the public conscience. . . .

I spoke to meetings of the unemployed in California, to migrant workers, tenant farmers, steelworkers, stockyard workers, auto workers. The factory workers were the aristocrats of labor, yet what a struggle they had! . . . Paul St. Marie, president of the first Ford local, took me around to the auto plants and showed me what the assembly line meant. I met the men who were beaten to a pulp when they tried to distribute literature at plant gates, and I saw the unemployed who had fire hoses turned on them during an icy winter when they hung around the gates of the Ford plant looking for work. . . .

Going around and seeing such sights is not enough. To help the organizers, to give what you have for relief, to pledge yourself to voluntary poverty for life so that you can share with your brothers is not enough. One must live with them, share with them their suffering too. Give up one's privacy, and mental and spiritual comforts as well as physical. . . .

Yes, we have lived with the poor, with the workers, and we know them not just from the streets, or in mass meetings, but from years of living in the slums, in tenements, in our hospices in Washington, Baltimore, Philadelphia, Harrisburg, Pittsburgh, New York, Rochester, Boston, Worcester, Buffalo, Troy, Detroit, Cleveland, Toledo, Akron, St. Louis, Chicago, Milwaukee, Minneapolis, Seattle, San Francisco, Los Angeles, Oakland, even down in Houma, Louisiana, where Father Jerome Drolet worked with Negroes and whites, with shrimp shellers, fishermen, longshoremen, and seamen.

Just as the church has gone out through its missionaries into the most obscure towns and villages, we have gone, too. Sometimes our contacts have been through the Church, and sometimes through readers of our paper, through union organizers or those who needed to be organized.

We have lived with the unemployed, the sick, the unemployables. The contrast between the worker who is organized and has his union, the fellowship of his own trade to give him strength, and those who have no organization and come in to us on a breadline, is pitiable.

They are stripped then, not only of all earthly goods, but of spiritual goods, their sense of human dignity. When they are forced into line at municipal lodging houses, in clinics, in our Houses of Hospitality, they are then the truly destitute. Over and over again in our work, many young men and women who come as volunteers have not been able to endure it and have gone away. To think that we are forced by our own lack of room, our lack of funds, to perpetuate this shame, is heartbreaking.

"Is this what you meant by Houses of Hospitality?" I asked Peter.

"At least it will arouse the conscience," he said.

Many left the work because they could see no use in this gesture of feeding the poor, and because of their own shame. But enduring this shame is part of our penance.

"All men are brothers." How often we hear this refrain, the rallying call that strikes a response in every human heart. These are the words of Christ, "Call no man master, for ye are all brothers." It is a revolutionary call which has even been put to music. The last movement of Beethoven's Ninth Symphony has that great refrain—"All men are brothers." Going to the people is the purest and best act in Christian tradition and revolutionary tradition and is the beginning of world brotherhood.

Never to be severed from the people, to set out always from the point of view of serving the people, not serving the interests of a small group or oneself. "To believe in the infinite creative power of the people," Mao Tsetung, the Secretary of the Communist Party in China, wrote with religious fervor. And he said again in 1943, "The maxim 'three common men will make a genius' tells us that there is great creative power among the people and that there are thousands and thousands of geniuses among them. There are geniuses in every village, every city." It is almost another way of saying that we must and will find Christ in each and every man, when we look on them as brothers.

*   *   *

As Peter pointed out, ours was a long-range program, looking for ownership by the workers of the means of production, the abolition of the assembly line, decentralized factories, the restoration of crafts and ownership of property. This meant, of course, an accent on the agrarian and rural aspects of our economy and a changing of emphasis from the city to the land. . . .

We published many heavy articles on capital and labor, on strikes and labor conditions, on the assembly lines and all the other evils of industrialism. But it was a whole picture we were presenting of man and his destiny and so we emphasized less, as the years went by, the organized-labor aspect of the paper.

It has been said that it was *The Catholic Worker* and its stories of poverty and exploitation that aroused the priests to start labor schools, go out on picket lines, take sides in strikes with the worker, and that brought about an emphasis on the need to study sociology in the seminaries.

And many a priest who afterward became famous for his interest in labor felt that we had in a way deserted the field, had left the cause of the union man. Bishops and priests appearing on the platforms of the A.F. of L. and C.I.O. conventions felt that we had departed from our original intention and undertaken work in the philosophical and theological fields that might better have been left to the clergy. The discussion of the morality of modern war, for instance, and application of moral principle in specific conflicts. Labor leaders themselves felt that in our judgment of war, we judged them also for working in the gigantic armaments race, as indeed we did. Ours is indeed an unpopular front.

When we began our work, there were thirteen million unemployed. The greatest problem of the day was the problem of work and the machine.

The state entered in to solve these problems by dole and work relief, by setting up so many bureaus that we were swamped with initials. N.I.R.A. gave place to N.R.A., and as N.R.A. was declared unconstitutional another organization, another administration was set up. The problem of the modern state loomed up as never before in American life. The Communists, stealing our American thunder, clamored on the one hand for relief and on the other set up Jeffersonian schools of democracy.

Peter also quoted Jefferson—"He governs best who governs least." One of his criticisms of labor was that it was aiding in the creation of the Welfare State, the Servile State, instead of aiming for the ownership of the means of production and acceptance of the responsibility that it entailed.

The Long Loneliness

Our Stand on Strikes

Let us be honest, let us say that fundamentally, the stand we are taking is not on the ground of wages and hours and conditions of labor, but on the fundamental truth that men should be treated not as chattels, but as human beings, as "temples of the Holy Ghost." When Christ took on our human nature, when He became man, He dignified and ennobled human nature. He said, "The Kingdom of Heaven is within you." When men are striking, they are following an impulse, often blind, often uninformed, but a good impulse—one could even say an inspiration of the Holy Spirit. They are trying to uphold their right to be treated not as slaves, but as men. They are fighting for a share in the management, for their right to be considered partners in the enterprise in which they are engaged. They are fighting against the idea of their labor as a commodity, to be bought and sold.

Let us concede that the conditions at the RCA Victor plant down in Camden, where a strike involving 13,000 men started last month, are not bad conditions, and that wages and hours are not bad. There is probably a company union which is supposed to take care of such conditions and complaints, but it perpetuates the enslavement of the worker.

Let us concede that the conditions of the seamen are not so atrocious as the *Daily Worker* contends. Let us get down to the fundamental point that the seamen are striking for: the right to be considered partners, sharers in responsibility, the right to be treated as men and not as chattels.

Is it not a cause worth fighting for? Is it not a cause which demands all the courage and all the integrity of the men involved? *Let us be frank and make this our issue.*

Let us be honest and confess that it is the social order which we wish to change. The workers are never going to be satisfied, no matter how much pay they get, no matter what their hours are. And it is to reconstruct the social order that we are throwing ourselves in with the workers, whether in factories or shipyards or on the sea.

The popes have hit the nail on the head. "No man may outrage with impunity that human dignity which God Himself treats with reverence. . . . Religion teaches the rich man and the employer that their work people are not their slaves; that they must respect in every man his dignity as a man and as a Christian; that labor is an honorable employment: and that it is shameful and inhuman to treat men like chattels to make money by, or to look upon them merely as so much muscle or physical power."

These are fundamental principles which the A.F. of L. has neglected to bring out. They have based their appeal on enlightened self-interest, a phrase reeking with selfishness and containing a warning and a threat. A warning to the workers of the world that they are working for themselves alone, and not as "members one of another." One can see how it has worked out in this country. What percentage of the workers are organized? Only a fraction. And how has the highly organized workman cared for his poorer brother? There has grown up an aristocracy of labor so that it is an irksome fact that bricklayers receive more than farmers in the necessary goods of this world—in goods which we should strive for in order that we may have those God-given means to develop to the full and achieve the Kingdom of Heaven.

We are not losing sight of the fact that our end is spiritual. We are not losing sight of the fact that these better conditions of labor are means to an end. But the labor movement has lost sight of this fact. The leaders have forgotten such a thing as a philosophy of labor. They have not given to the worker the philosophy of labor, and they have betrayed him.

And the inarticulate rank and file throughout the world are rising up in rebellion, and are being labeled Communists for so doing, for refusing to accept the authority of such leaders, which they very rightly do not consider just authority. They intuitively know better than their leaders what they are looking for. But they have allowed themselves to be misled and deceived.

We have so positive a program that we need all our energy, we have to bend all our forces, material and spiritual, to this end, to promulgate it. Let us uphold our positive program of changing the social order.

But let us, too, examine the Communist means to the end which they claim they are working for, a true brotherhood of man. We do not talk about a classless society, because we acknowledge functional classes as opposed to acquisitive classes.

We agree with this end, but we do not agree on the means to attain it.

The Communists say: "All men are our brothers except the capitalists, so we will kill them off." They do not actually believe in the dignity of man as a human being, because they try to set off one or another class of men and say, "They are not our brothers and never will be. So let us liquidate them." And then to point their argument they say with scorn, "Do you ever think to convert J. P. Morgan, or Rockefeller, or Charlie Schwab?"

They are protesting against man's brutality to man, and at the same time they perpetuate it. It is like having one more war to end all wars. We disagree with this technique of class war, without which the Communist says the brotherhood of man can never be achieved.

"Nothing will be achieved until the worker rises up in arms and forcibly takes the position that is his," the Communist says. "Your movement, which trusts to peaceful means, radical though it may seem, is doomed to failure."

We admit that we may seem to fail, but we recall to our readers the ostensible failure of Christ when He died on the Cross, forsaken by all His followers. Out of this failure a new world sprang up. We recall to our readers the folly of the Cross St. Paul talks about.

When we participate in strikes, when we go out on picket lines and distribute leaflets, when we speak at strike meetings, we are there because we are reaching the workers when they are massed together for action. We are taking advantage of a situation. We may not agree that to strike was the wise thing to do in that particular case. We believe that the work of or-ganization must be thorough before any strike action occurs, unless indeed the strike is a spontaneous one which is the outcome of unbearable conditions.

We oppose all use of violence as un-Christian. We do not believe in persuading scabs with clubs. They are workers, too, and the reason they are scabs is because the work of organization has been neglected.

We oppose the misuse of private property while we uphold the right of private property. The Holy Father says that "as many as possible of the workers should become owners," and how else in many cases except by developing the cooperative ideal?

While we are upholding cooperatives as a part of the Christian social order, we are upholding at the same time unions, as organizations of workers wherein they can be indoctrinated and taught to rebuild the social order. While we stress the back-to-the-land movement so that the worker may be "deproletarianized," we are not going to leave the city to the Communists.

Month by month, in every struggle, in every strike, on every picket line, we shall do our best to join with the worker in his struggle for recognition. We reiterate the slogan of the old I.W.W.'s: "An injury to one is an injury to all." St. Paul says, "When the health of one member of the Mystical Body suffers, the health of the whole body is lowered."

We are all members, one of another, in the Mystical Body of Christ, so let us work together for Christian solidarity.

July 1936

Memorial Day in Chicago

On Memorial Day, May 30, 1937, police opened fire on a parade of striking steel workers and their families at the gate of the Republic Steel Company, in South Chicago. Fifty people were shot, of whom ten later died; one hundred others were beaten with clubs.

Have you ever heard a man scream as he was beaten over the head by two or three policemen with clubs and cudgels? Have you ever heard the sickening sounds of blows and seen people with their arms upraised, trying to protect their faces, stumbling blindly to get away, falling and rising again to be beaten down? Did you ever see a man shot in the back, being dragged to his feet by policemen who tried to force him to stand, while his poor body crumpled, paralyzed by a bullet in the spine?

We are sickened by stories of brutality in Germany and Russia and Italy. A priest from Germany told me of one man who came to him whose back was ridged "like a washboard," by the horrible beatings he had received at the hands of the German police in concentration camps. I shudder with horror at the thought of the tortures inflicted on Catholics, Protestants, Jews, and Communists in Germany today.

And here in America, last month, there was a public exhibition of such brutality that the motion-picture film, taken by a Paramount photographer in a sound truck, was suppressed by the company for fear that it would cause riots and mass hysteria, it was so unutterably horrible.

I am trying to paint a picture of it for our readers because so many did not read the story of the Memorial Day "riot" in Chicago in front of the Republic Steel Mills.

Try to imagine this mass of people—men, women, and children—picketing, as they have a right to do, coming up to the police line and being suddenly shot into, not by one hysterical policeman, but by many. Ten were killed and one hundred were taken to the hospital wounded. Tear gas and clubs supplied by the Republic Steel Company were used.

I am trying to picture this scene to our readers because I have witnessed these things firsthand, and I know the horror of them. I was on a picket line when the "radical" squad shot into the line and pursued the fleeing picketers down the streets, knocking them down and kicking and beating them. I, too, have fled down streets to escape the brutality and vicious hatred of the "law" for those whom they consider "radical." And by the police anyone who protests injustice, who participates in labor struggles, is considered a radical.

Two years ago I wrote an account in *The Catholic Worker* of two plainclothesmen beating up a demonstrator. I told of the screams and the crumpling body of the man as two men who had dragged him into a hallway beat him up against the wall, aiming well-directed blows at his face, smashing it to a pulp.

We protested this to the Police Commissioner, and our protest was respected and acted upon.

We are repeating the protest against the Chicago massacre because the only way to stop such brutality is to arouse a storm of protest against it.

On whom shall the blame be laid for such a horrible spectacle of violence? Of course, the police and the press in many cases lay the blame on the strikers. But I have lived with these people, I have eaten with them and talked to them day after day. Many of them have never been in a strike before, many of them were marching in the picket line, as in a supplicatory procession, for the first time in their lives. They even brought children on that line in Chicago.

Shall we blame only the police? Or shall we blame just Tom Girdler of the Republic Steel Company? God knows how he can sleep comfortably in his bed at night with the cries of those strikers, of their wives and children, in his ears. He may not hear them now in the heat of battle, but he will hear them, as there is a just God.

Or shall we blame the press, the pulpit, and all those agencies who form public opinion, who have neglected to raise up their voices in protest at injustice and so have permitted it? In some cases the press have even instigated it so that it would come to pass. Inflammatory, hysterical head-lines about mobs, about expected riots, do much to arouse the temper of the police to prepare them for just what occurred. The calm, seemingly reasonable stories of such papers as the *Herald Tribune* and the *Times,* emphasizing the violence and the expectation of violence, do much to prepare the public to accept such violence when it comes to pass.

In that case we all are guilty inasmuch as we have not "gone to the workingman" as the Holy Father pleads and repeats. Inasmuch as we have not inclined our hearts to him, and sought to incline his to us, so that we could work together for peace instead of war, inasmuch as we have not protested such murder as was committed in Chicago—then we are guilty.

One more sin, suffering Christ, worker Yourself, for You to bear. In the garden of Gethsemane, You bore the sins of all the world—You took them on Yourself, the sins of those police, the sins of the Girdlers and the Schwabs, of the Graces of this world. In committing them, whether igno-rantly or of their own free will, they piled them on Your shoulders, bowed to the ground with the weight of the guilt of the world, which You assumed because You loved each of us so much. You took them on Yourself, and You died to save us all. Your Precious Blood was shed even for that policeman whose cudgel smashed again and again the skull of that poor striker, whose brains lay splattered on the undertaker's slab.

And the sufferings of those strikers' wives and children are completing Your suffering today.

Have pity on us all, Jesus of Gethsemane—on Tom Girdler, those police, the souls of the strikers, as well as on all of us who have not worked enough for "a new heaven and a new earth wherein justice dwelleth."

July 1937

The Disgraceful Plight
of Migrant Workers

An auto camp outside Bakersfield. The hot weather has begun and a haze of heat hangs over the valley, so that you can barely see the mountains. I have just come down through the San Joaquin Valley, and now forests of oil wells loom on the horizon. It has been ninety-five in the shade for the past three days and already, early in the morning, there is promise of another broiling day.

For the last week I have been covering the government migrant camps from Yuba City, north of San Francisco, down the valley. There are thirteen of these camps, housing 3,000 families. If you count five to an average family, that takes care of 15,000 people. But the estimate is that there are 300,000 migrant workers in the state. The season of peak labor, when 250,000 are used, lasts only five months, and the rest of the time only 50,000 are needed.

Mrs. Robert McWilliams is assistant chairman of the State Central Committee of the Democratic Party and for years she has been interested in the condition of the migrant. Last week we drove to Salinas, about a hundred miles down the valley from San Francisco, and as we drove she told me about the Salinas lettuce strike. The workers had a good union, A.F. of L., good wages and conditions. But the growers, packers, and shippers were determined to break the union by not renewing the contract when it expired. A strike followed, scabs were imported, sheds were built for them inside "riot fences." The frames are still there; I saw them this afternoon, a threat and a warning to the workers.

It was a bloody strike; there were citizen's committees, vigilantes, everyone was deputized. They organized the shopkeepers not to sell to the thousands of workers living around the town.

Mrs. McWilliams told of treating the eyes of the workers with a paregoric solution to ease the pain of the tear-gas attacks. Nauseating gas resulted in diarrhea and vomiting. The boys at the manual training high school were given the job of weighting ax handles with iron to be used as weapons against the strikers.

It was a time of terror for three weeks; then an agreement was signed which left out of account the 6,000 Filipino workers. Another strike occurred and then the union was broken completely.

*   *   *

A trailer camp outside Marysville. Down in the hollow, back of the road, there are forty families encamped. On either side of the highway, nestled under the levee of the Feather River, there are more families. Many of the camps are surrounded by water and mud. The stars are reflected in the pools of water in the fields and the orchards. Last week there was a flood up here so bad that most of the roads were under water.

It is so sad to see this constant coming and going, hundreds of thousands of people on the move from place to place. In the Northwest there was the tragedy of greed in the overcut, ruined land. Here the tragedy is of a landless people, homeless, meagerly fed, housed like animals rather than like creatures made in the image and likeness of God. Those in power have waxed fat and have forgotten the things of the spirit. Those in misery have forgotten that they are temples of the Holy Spirit. And how could they remember?

More than ever I am convinced that the solution lies only in the Gospel and in such a leader as St. Francis. Peter Maurin has been talking these past two years of recruiting troubadours of Christ. More and more I am convinced that besides the purely material efforts of building up hospices and farming communes, we need these fellow travelers with the poor and dispossessed to share with them their poverty and insecurity and to bring them the reminder of the love of God.

It is the hardest work anyone could do, in the face of that saying, "Religon is the opiate of the people." It is a sad saying that has made cowards of many who are afraid to speak of God to those with empty stomachs. But they are not just mouths to be fed, bodies to be housed. They are creatures of body and soul. The Communist goes among them, lives with them in his zeal for "leaders who themselves are workers," in his zeal to build up a people who will fight oppression.

Where are our Catholic college youth who will make a vocation of their unemployment, and use it as an opportunity to tramp about the country like St. Francis and bring the Gospel to these forgotten ones?

May 1940

Blood on Our Coal

A long time ago I read a Russian story about a mother and daughter who earned their living by sewing. They sat by a window and rested their eyes by lifting them from their work now and then to survey the scene outside. Then someone came and built a house right next to their window which rose like a massive wall and shut out the light and sun and air. They worked in sorrow for many years. Then the wall was demolished, and when it was gone, they grieved for it. They had come to enjoy being shut in by the tenement next door! I remember how extraordinary this gloomy story seemed to me.

Once a migrant worker said to me fervently, "There's nothing I like better than getting out in that hot field and chopping cotton." He meant it, too, with the hot sun on his back and the vast field all around, and silent men, women, and children working down the long rows around him—a long, endless, stupefying work that identifies the man with the field he works in.

Down in Derry, Pennsylvania, in the soft-coal regions, almost worked out now, a miner told me after we had talked together for several days, "Miners don't want to do anything else. They don't want to be farmers. Many of them that leave their work and try something else go back to it again." And I suppose it is true.

The entire industrial world has so little to offer, what with its cannibalism, its competition, that the men go back to their black holes and their nine hours a day underground, six days a week, and begin to take pride in its hazards, its own unique misery.

"It's black down there," he said. "No light but what you carry on your hat." How can men love darkness rather than light? How can men choose such an occupation except that they have been forced to it?

It is not so many hundred years ago that the only way they could get miners was to make bondsmen of them. Technically they were not slaves, but they were bonded over to the owners of the mines—men, women, and children—and if they tried to escape they were beaten back to work.

How much do we meditate on coal and its uses? There is a limited amount of it in the earth; many of the mines in Pennsylvania are worked out now, leaving ghost towns. The forests, too, are cut down so fast we will have neither wood nor coal, looking at things from the long view. Yet it is not with any knowledge of organic farming, the necessity for tree planting, the use of other forms of energy, that miners revolt against this form of labor. They revolt because it is inhuman, it demands too much of a man. If they do not leave it for other work it is because that other work, whether it is farming for profit or working in factories, is also inhuman and "takes it all out of a man."

People want to know what this present coal strike is about. It is about shorter hours, for one thing—instead of the fifty-four-hour weeks the men work now. And it is about the welfare fund. Up to this time there have been no pensions, no recreation, no education, no adequate medical services. The need for such a fund is evidenced by these figures: Every year some 1,500 miners are killed; some 60,000 to 70,000 are injured, many of them so badly they are thrown on the scrap heap.

When we can read figures like these, when we read of the inhuman suffering of the workers, when we remember the blood that is on our coal, we know what the Holy Father means when he says that the world has lost a sense of sin. Not personal sin, but *social sin*. When priests do not cry out for the workers, try to share with the workers their poverty, then surely this is what the Holy Father means when he speaks of the devitalization of the Church. They are dead branches indeed.

"All the way to heaven is heaven, because Christ said, 'I am the Way.'" And work should be part of heaven, not part of hell. In the black underground caverns where the miners lose all light of day—month after month, from early fall till late spring—there is a glimpse of "everlasting night where no order is and everlasting horror dwelleth." We want to change man's work; we want to make people question their work; is it on the way to heaven or hell?

Man gains his bread by his work. It is his bread and wine. It is his life. We cannot emphasize the importance of it enough. We must emphasize the holiness of *work,* and we must emphasize the sacramental quality of *property,* too. That means the property of the poor. They have very little of it. We know that it is dangerous, it corrupts, it is almost a testing ground in this life of attachment and detachment. We must love it as a sample of God's providence and goodness and we must be ready to give it up.

The Holy Father says we must deproletarize the workers. That is, we must get them out of the wage-slave class and into the owner class. One very good reason is that a man loves what is his, and has a sense of responsibility for it, almost a sacramental sense in regard to his house, his land, and his work on them.

When we talk about property, we do not think of stocks and bonds, shares in coal mines, the property of the gentlemen hunters in their red coats and silk top hats whom we saw prancing by on Thanksgiving morning. They have no respect for property. For example, it turns out that the farmers around Pennsylvania only own their ground plow-deep. They do not know this until they begin to object to the mining operations which undermine their homes and cause them to settle in the cave-ins so prevalent throughout the state. When the operators finish taking out all the coal in a given place they start to retreat, taking out pillars of wood and pillars of coal. The roof falls in and the ground above settles. This goes on all through that region, and the farmer who objects is told he can pay for all the coal which the miners would have been able to mine from his acres.

There is no respect for property here. So why do we talk of fighting Communism on the grounds that it does away with private property? We have done that very well ourselves in this country. Or because Communism denies the existence of God? We do not see Christ in our brothers in the mines, in our brother John L. Lewis. We deny Christ here. And what about that other argument about the use of force? We live in an age of war, and the turning of the wheels of industry, the very working of the mines depends on our wars.

We heard Louis Budenz speak at the Harrisburg forum as we passed through on our way to the mining sections, and one of his messages to Catholics was this warning: that the Communists would try to foment anticlericalism and divide the people from the hierarchy.

There is really no need of their doing it. It is already an accomplished fact. Pope Pius XI himself said, "The workers of the world are lost to the Church."

Our good readers absolve us from any charges of anticlericalism as they read these rather severe articles on the Church and work. They know that the wish of our heart is to bring closer together the priest and the people. There is a great division between the two, and one of the very reasons for the Catholic Worker's existence is to bridge this gap.

December 1946

Of Justice and Breadlines

Why do we give so much attention in *The Catholic Worker* to such matters as the condition of workers, unions, boycotts? This month I have had several letters, written undoubtedly by sincere and pious people who want to think only of contributing to breadlines and the immediate needs of the poor. "Please spend this money for bread," they will write, "not on propaganda."

Let me say here that the sight of a line of men, waiting for food, ragged, dirty, obviously "sleeping out" in empty buildings, is something that I never will get used to. It is a deep hurt and suffering that this is often all we have to give. Our houses will not hold any more men and women, nor do we have workers to care for them. Nor are there enough alternatives or services to take care of them. They are the wounded in the class struggle, men who have built the railroads, worked in mines, on ships, and in steel mills. They are men from prison, from mental hospitals. And women, too. They are simply the unemployed.

We will never stop having "lines" at Catholic Worker houses. As long as men keep coming to the door, we will keep on preparing each day the food they need. There were six hundred on Thanksgiving day in Los Angeles. I helped serve there.

Even now as I write I can see the Berlin-like wall, the high riot fencing topped with rolls of barbed wire, which separates the barrios of Tijuana from the lush fields of southern California. As far as the eye can see there are those shacks made of cartons and old bits of tarpaper and carpeting, wall to wall, the wall of one a wall for the next, acres and acres of destitution. Most horrible of all, there is caught in that barbed wire topping the high fences, bits of clothing, a sleeve of a coat, a sock, a ragged shirt, caught there and torn from the scratched and bleeding body of some desperate person trying to get over the fence.

There are so many empty buildings belonging to the Church, so many Sisters and Brothers who want to serve the poor, surely there should be more guest houses, hostels, than there are.

But I repeat: Breadlines are not enough, hospices are not enough. I know we will always have men on the road. But we need communities of work, land for the landless, true farming communes, cooperatives and credit unions. There is much that is wild, prophetic, and holy about our work—it is that which attracts the young who come to help us. But the heart hungers for that new social order wherein justice dwelleth.

January 1972

A Brief Sojourn in Jail

Though the Catholic Worker had originally been conceived, at least in part, as a voice for the workers, Dorothy had gradually become disillusioned with the limited vision of the trade union movement. Too often, she felt, the unions settled for improvements in wages and hours, rather than working to build a new social order. After World War II, the paper devoted relatively little space to labor news. The major exception to this was Dorothy's consistent support, over fifteen years, for the United Farm Workers' Union, led by Cesar Chavez. The U.F.W., she believed, was a social and religious movement, building community, fighting for justice and the dignity of the most victimized of all workers, while educating the public as to the power and meaning of nonviolent action.

In a tribute written after Dorothy's death, Chavez referred to the experience recounted in this article:

> It makes us very proud that Dorothy's last trip to jail took place in Fresno, California, with the farm workers. The summer of 1973 was probably the most painful period we have gone through—the union's future existence was being decided in the strike and later in the boycott. Thousands of farm workers went to jail that summer rather than obey unconstitutional injunctions against picketing, hundreds were injured, dozens were shot and two were killed. And Dorothy came to be with us in Fresno, along with nearly a hundred priests and nuns and lay people. The picture that was taken of her that day, sitting amongst the strikers and the police, is a classic portrayal of her internal peace and strength in the midst of turmoil and conflict. Dorothy Day has gone to be with God. We in the farm workers' movement give thanks for her life and for the gifts she has given us. We know she is at peace and we know we shall never forget her.

July 30. We left Kennedy Airport at noon for San Francisco, Eileen Egan and I. She was attending, as I, too, was supposed to, the 50th Anniversary of the War Resisters League. Joan Baez had invited me to be at her Institute for the Study of Nonviolence for the week with some members of Cesar Chavez's United Farm Workers' Union. When we arrived, the plans had changed because of the mass arrests of farm workers for defying an injunction against mass picketing in Kern County. There was now a strike in the vineyards, as well as the lettuce fields, because the growers would not renew their contracts with the farm workers and were instead making new contracts with the Teamsters.

The strike was widespread and mass arrests were continuing. My path was clear: the U.F.W. has everything that belongs to a new social order. Since I had come to picket where an injunction was prohibiting picketing, it appeared that I would spend my weeks in California in jail, not at conferences.

July 31. A very hot drive down the valley to Delano, arriving as the strike meeting ended. Today many Jesuits were arrested. Also Sisters who had been attending a conference in San Francisco. Mass in the evening at Bakersfield ended a tremendous demonstration, flag-carrying Mexicans, singing, chanting, marching. When the Mass began there were so many people that it was impossible to kneel, but there was utter silence.

August 1. Up at 2 a.m., picketed all day, covering many vineyards. Impressive lines of police, all armed—clubs and guns. We talked to them, pleaded with them to lay down their weapons. One was black. His mouth twitched as he indicated that, no, he did not enjoy being there. Two other police came and walked away with him. I told the other police I would come back the next day and read the Sermon on the Mount to them. I was glad I had my folding chair-cane so I could rest occasionally during picketing, and sit there before the police to talk to them. I had seen a man that morning sitting at the entrance to workers' shacks with a rifle across his knees.

August 2. Slept at Sanger with nurses from one of the farm workers' clinics. Up at 4 a.m., was at the park before dawn. Cesar came and spoke to us about the injunction and arrests (wonder when he sleeps?) and we set out in cars to picket the area where big and small growers had united to get the injunction. Three white police buses arrived some time later and we were warned that we were to disperse. When we refused we were ushered into the buses and brought to this "industrial farm" (which they do not like us to call a jail or prison, though we are under lock and key and our barracks surrounded by barbed wire). Here we are, ninety-nine women and fifty men, including thirty Sisters and two priests.

August 3. Maria Hernandez got ill in the night. Taken to Fresno Hospital, cardiograph taken, and she was put in the Fresno jail. (She was returned to us still ill August 7. She worries about her children.) Another Mexican mother in our barracks has ten children and there certainly was a crowd visiting her. Such happy, beautiful families—it reminded me of the tribute paid to the early Christians when they were imprisoned and the hordes of their fellow Christians visited them, and made a great impression on their guards.

I must copy down the charges made against me (we were listed in groups of ten): "The said defendants, on or about August 2, were persons remaining present at the place of a riot, rout and unlawful assembly, who did willfully and unlawfully fail, refuse and neglect after the same had been lawfully warned to disperse."

Some of the other women listed in the criminal complaint in my group of ten were Demetria Landavazo de Leon, Maria de Jesus Ochoa, Efigenia Garcia de Rojas, Esperanza Alanis de Perales. How I wish I could list them all.

During crucial meetings between Cesar Chavez and the Teamsters the Sisters all signed up for a night of prayer, taking two-hour shifts all through the night, while the Mexican woman all knelt along the tables in the center and prayed the rosary together. Barracks A, B, and D were alive with prayer.

Tonight a young Mexican legal assistant of the union was brutally and contemptuously ordered out when he attempted to talk to us. There were only three incidents I could have complained of: another case of rudeness, and the attempt to search the bodies of the prisoners for food smuggled in.

Today I had interesting conversations with Jo von Gottfried, a teacher of rhetoric in Berkeley, a great lover of St. Thomas and St. Augustine. I tried to understand what "rhetoric" really means and she explained, but I cannot remember now.

August 8. Today Joan Baez, her mother, and Daniel Ellsberg visited us. Joan sang to us and the other prisoners in the yard. There was a most poignant prison song. It tore at your heart. She was singing when other prisoners were being brought to the dining room and she turned her back to us and sang to all of them directly, as they stopped their line to listen.

Daniel Ellsberg said Cesar Chavez, the thought of him, had given him courage during his two-year ordeal in the courts.

August 9. I'm all mixed up in my dates. Dr. Evan Thomas came today, ninety-one and tall, lean, strong-looking. God bless him. And Father Don Hessler, whom we've known since he was a seminarian at Maryknoll. He suffered years of imprisonment under the Japanese in World War II.

August 11. Good talks with Sister Felicia and Sister Timothy of Barracks B, who are good spokeswomen for our group. Two writers from *Newsweek* called. They were interested in "the religious slant" of the strike.

August 12. Union lawyers visiting us say we'll be free tomorrow. A peaceful Sunday. Mass in the evening. Today the Mexican girls were singing and clapping and teaching the Sisters some Mexican dancing. They reminded me of St. Teresa of Avila playing her castanets at recreation.

August 13. We packed our bags last night and a first busload, including me, left our farm labor camp this morning, reached the jail, and were turned back! We then spent hours in the "rec" hall, where a team of "public defenders," whom we were supposed to have seen Sunday, sat around (perhaps I saw *one* working), while Sister Felicia interviewed all the women in our barracks for the rest of the day and filled out the forms which the judge required.

In the evening we were all finally loaded in vans and brought to Fresno, where, with a great crowd in the park in front of the courthouse, we celebrated Mass.

*   *   *

There is still no contract signed by grape growers with the union. Instead, there have been two deaths, that of Naji Daifullah, an Arab striker from Yemen, and Juan de la Cruz of Delano. We attended the funeral service of Naji at Forty Acres. A mile-long parade of marchers walked the four miles in a broiling sun from Delano with black flags, black armbands, and ribbons, and stood through the long service while psalms from the Office of the Dead were heard clearly over loudspeakers and the words from the Book of Wisdom: "In the sight of the unwise they seemed to die but they are at peace." There were Moslem chants as well. Five hundred Arabs recently came here from Yemen—to this land of opportunity—and one has met with death, his skull fractured by a deputy wielding a heavy flashlight.

Juan de la Cruz was shot in the chest. His funeral Mass was offered by Bishop Arzube of Los Angeles. Two men have shed their blood. Cesar Chavez has requested a three-day fast and a renewed zeal in boycotting lettuce and grapes. There is no money left in the treasury of the union, especially after death benefits have been paid to the families of the dead strikers. One of the Mexican girls in jail told me proudly that their $3.50 dues paid benefits for lives born and lives lost. And there were all the clinics operating at Calexico, Delano, Sanger, and other places. The Farm Workers' Union is a community to be proud of, and would that all our unions might become a "community of communities."

I must mention a prayer I wrote in the front of my New Testament, and hope our readers, while they read, say this for the strikers:

Dear Pope John—please, yourself a *campesino,* watch over the United Farm Workers. Raise up more and more leader-servants throughout the country to stand with Cesar Chavez in this nonviolent struggle with Mammon, in all the rural districts of North and South, in the cotton fields, beet fields, potato fields, in our orchards and vineyards, our orange groves—wherever men, women, and children work on the land. Help make a new order wherein justice flourishes, and, as Peter Maurin, himself a peasant, said so simply, "where it is easier to be good."

September 1973

POLITICS AND PRINCIPLES

Our Country Passes from Undeclared to Declared War; We Continue Our Christian Pacifist Stand

*In Addition to the Weapons of Starvation of Its Enemy,
Our Country Is Now Using the Weapons of Army, Navy, and Air Force—
In a Month of Great Feasts, a Time of Joy in Christian Life, the World
Plunges Itself Still Deeper into the Horror of War*

Dear Fellow Workers in Christ:

Lord God, merciful God, our Father, shall we keep silent, or shall we speak? And if we speak, what shall we say?

I am sitting here in the church on Mott Street writing this in Your presence. Out on the streets it is quiet, but You are there, too, in the Chinese, in the Italians, these neighbors we love. We love them because they are our brothers, as Christ is our Brother, and God our Father.

But we have forgotten so much. We have all forgotten. And how can we know unless You tell us? " 'For whoever calls upon the name of the Lord shall be saved.' How then are they to call upon Him in whom they have not believed? But how are they to believe Him whom they have not heard? And how are they to hear, if no one preaches? And how are men to preach unless they be sent? As it is written, 'How beautiful are the feet of those who preach the gospel of peace.' " (Romans X)

Seventy-five thousand copies of *The Catholic Worker* go out every month. What shall we print? We can still print what the Holy Father is saying, when he speaks of total war, of mitigating the horrors of war, when he speaks of cities of refuge; of feeding Europe....

We will print the words of Christ, who is with us always, even to the end of the world. "Love your enemies, do good to those who hate you, and pray for those who persecute and calumniate you, so that you may be children of your Father in heaven, who makes His sun to rise on the good and the evil, and sends rain on the just and the unjust."

We are at war, a declared war, with Japan, Germany, and Italy. But still we can repeat Christ's words, each day, holding them close in our hearts, each month printing them in the paper. In times past Europe has been a battlefield. But let us remember St. Francis, who spoke of peace, and we will remind our readers of him, too, so they will not forget.

In *The Catholic Worker* we will quote our Pope, our saints, our priests. We will go on printing the articles of Father Hugo, who reminds us today that we are all "called to be saints," that we are other Christs, reminding us of the priesthood of the laity.

We are still pacifists. Our manifesto is the Sermon on the Mount, which means that we will try to be peacemakers. Speaking for many of our conscientious objectors, we will not participate in armed warfare or in making munitions, or by buying government bonds to prosecute the war, or in urging others to these efforts.

But neither will we be carping in our criticism. We love our country and we love our President. We have been the only country in the world where men and women of all nations have taken refuge from oppression. We recognize that while in the order of intention we have tried to stand for peace, for love of our brothers and sisters, in the order of execution we have failed as Americans in living up to our principles.

We will try daily, hourly, to pray for an end to the war, such an end, to quote Father Orchard (October 28, *The Commonweal*), "as would manifest to all the world, that it was brought about by divine action, rather than by military might or diplomatic negotiation, which men and nations would then only attribute to their power or sagacity."

Let us add that unless we continue this prayer with almsgiving, in giving to the least of God's children; and fasting in order that we may help feed the hungry; and penance in recognition of our share in the guilt, our prayer may become empty words.

Our Works of Mercy may take us into the midst of war. As editor of *The Catholic Worker,* I would urge our friends and associates to care for the sick and the wounded, to the growing of food for the hungry, to the continuance of all our Works of Mercy in our houses and on our farms. We understand, of course, that there is and that there will be great differences of opinion even among our own groups as to how much collaboration we can have with the government in times like these. There are differences more profound and there will be many continuing to work with us from necessity, or from choice, who do not agree with us as to our position on war, conscientious objection, etc. But we beg that there will be mutual charity and forbearance among us all.

Because of our refusal to assist in the prosecution of war and our insistence that our collaboration be one for peace, we may find ourselves in difficulties. But we trust in the generosity and understanding of our government and our friends, to permit us to continue to use our paper to "preach Christ crucified."

And may the Blessed Mary, Mother of beautiful love, and of fear, and of knowledge, and of holy hope, pray for us.

January 1942

II

Father Stratmen writes: "We think with Cardinal Faulhaber that Catholic moral theology must in fact begin to speak a new language, and that what the last two Popes have already pronounced in the way of general sentences of condemnation on modern war should be translated into a systematic terminology of the schools. The simple preacher and pastor can, however, already begin by making his own, words of the reigning Holy Father [Pius XI], 'murder,' 'suicide,' 'monstrous crime.' "

"But we are at war," people say. "This is no time to talk of peace. It is demoralizing to the armed forces to protest, not to cheer them on in their fight for Christianity, for democracy, for civilization. Now that it is under way, it is too late to do anything about it." One reader writes to protest against our "frail" voices "blatantly" crying out against war. (The word "blatant" comes from "bleat," and we are indeed poor sheep crying out to the Good Shepherd to save us from these horrors.) Another Catholic newspaper says it sympathizes with our sentimentality. This is a charge always leveled against pacifists. We are supposed to be afraid of the suffering, of the hardships of war.

But let those who talk of softness, of sentimentality, come to live with us in cold, unheated houses in the slums. Let them come to live with the criminal, the unbalanced, the drunken, the degraded, the perverted. (It is not decent poor, it is not the decent sinner who was the recipient of Christ's love.) Let them live with rats, with vermin, bedbugs, roaches, lice (I could describe the several kinds of body lice).

Let their flesh be mortified by cold, by dirt, by vermin; let their eyes be mortified by the sight of bodily excretions, diseased limbs, eyes, noses, mouths.

Let their noses be mortified by the smells of sewage, decay, and rotten flesh. Yes, and the smell of the sweat, blood, and tears spoken of so blithely by Mr. Churchill, and so widely and bravely quoted by comfortable people.

Let their ears be mortified by harsh and screaming voices, by the constant coming and going of people living herded together with no privacy.

Let their taste be mortified by the constant eating of insufficient food cooked in huge quantities for hundreds of people, the coarser foods, so that there will be enough to go around; and the smell of such cooking is often foul.

Then when they have lived with these comrades, with these sights and sounds, let our critics talk of sentimentality. As we have often quoted Dostoevsky's Father Zossima, "Love in practice is a harsh and dreadful thing compared to love in dreams."

Our Catholic Worker groups are perhaps too hardened to the sufferings in the class war, living as they do in refugee camps, the refugees being, as they are, victims of the class war we live in always. We have lived in the midst of this war now these many years. It is a war not recognized by the majority of our comfortable people. They are pacifists themselves when it comes to the class war. They even pretend it is not there.

Many friends have counseled us to treat this world war in the same way. "Don't write about it. Don't mention it. Don't jeopardize the great work you are doing among the poor, among the workers. Just write about constructive things like Houses of Hospitality and Farming Communes." "Keep silence with a bleeding heart," one reader, a man, pro-war, and therefore not a sentimentalist, writes us.

But we cannot keep silent. We have not kept silence in the face of the monstrous injustice of the class war, or the race war that goes on side by side with this world war (which the Communists used to call the imperialist war).

Read the letters in this issue of the paper, the letter from the machine-shop worker as to the deadening, degrading hours of labor. Remember the unarmed steel strikers, the coal miners, shot down on picket lines. Read the letter from our correspondent in Seattle who tells of the treatment accorded agricultural workers in the Northwest. Are these workers supposed to revolt? These are Pearl Harbor incidents! Are they supposed to turn to arms in the class conflict to defend their lives, their homes, their wives and children?

Last month a Negro in Missouri was shot and dragged by a mob through the streets behind a car. His wounded body was then soaked in kerosene. The mob of white Americans then set fire to it, and when the poor anguished victim had died, the body was left lying in the street until a city garbage cart trucked it away. Are the Negroes supposed to "Remember Pearl Harbor" and take to arms to avenge this cruel wrong? No, the Negroes, the workers in general, are supposed to be "pacifist" in the face of this aggression.

Perhaps we are called sentimental because we speak of love. We say we love our President, our country. We say that we love our enemies, too.

"Greater love hath no man than this," Christ said, "that he should lay down his life for his friend."

"Love is the measure by which we shall be judged," St. John of the Cross said.

"Love is the fulfilling of the law," St. John, the beloved disciple, said.

Read the last discourse of Jesus to his disciples. Read the letters of St. John in the New Testament. And how can we express this love—by bombers, by blockades?

Here is a clipping from the *Herald Tribune,* a statement of a soldier describing the use of the bayonet against the Japanese:

"He [his father] should have been with us and seen how good it was. We got into them good and proper, and I can't say I remember much about it, except that it made me feel pretty good. I reckon that was the way with the rest of the company, by the way my pals were yelling all the time."

Is this a Christian speaking?

Love is not the starving of whole populations. Love is not the bombardment of open cities. Love is not killing, it is the laying down of one's life for one's friends.

Hear Father Zossima, in *The Brothers Karamazov:*

"Love one another, Fathers," he says, speaking to his monks. "Love God's people. Because we have come here and shut ourselves within these walls, we are no holier than those that are outside, but on the contrary, from the very fact of coming here, each of us has confessed to himself that he is worse than others, than all men on earth. . . . And the longer the monk lives in his seclusion, the more keenly he must recognize that. Else he would have no reason to come here.

"When he realizes that he is not only worse than others, but that he is responsible to all men for all and everything, for all human sins, national and individual, only then the aim of our seclusion is attained. For know, dear ones, that every one of us is undoubtedly responsible for all men and everything on earth, not merely through the general sinfulness of creation, but each one personally for all mankind and every individual man. For monks are not a special sort of man, but only what all men ought to be. Only through that knowledge, our heart grows soft with infinite, universal, inexhaustible love. Then every one of you will have the power to win over the whole world by love and to wash away the sins of the world with your tears. . . . Each of you keep watch over your heart and confess your sins to yourself unceasingly. . . . Hate not the atheists, the teachers of evil, the materialists, and I mean not only the good ones—for there are many good ones among them, especially in our day—hate not even the wicked ones. Remember them in your prayers thus: Save, O Lord, all those who have none to pray for them; save too all those who will not pray. And add, it is not in pride that I make this prayer, O Lord, for I am lower than all men. . . ."

I quote this because that accusation "holier than thou" is also made against us. And we must all admit our guilt, our participation in the social order which has resulted in this monstrous crime of war.

We used to have a poor, demented friend who came into the office to see us very often, beating his breast, quoting the Penitential Psalms in Hebrew, and saying that everything was his fault. Through all he had done and left undone, he had brought about the war, the revolution.

That should be our cry, with every mouthful we eat—"We are starving Europe!" When we look to our comfort in a warm bed, a warm home, we must cry, "My brother, my mother, my child is dying of cold."

"I am lower than all men, because I do not love enough. O God, take away my heart of stone and give me a heart of flesh."

February 1942

III

Mr. Truman was jubilant. President Truman. True man; what a strange name, come to think of it. We refer to Jesus Christ as true God and true Man. Truman is a true man of his time in that he was jubilant. He was not a son of God, brother of Christ, brother of the Japanese, jubilating as he did. He went from table to table on the cruiser which was bringing him home from the Big Three conference, telling the great news; "jubilant" the newspapers said. *Jubilate Deo.* We have killed 318,000 Japanese.

That is, we hope we have killed them, the Associated Press, on page one, column one, of the *Herald Tribune* says. The effect is hoped for, not known. It is to be hoped they are vaporized, our Japanese brothers, scattered, men, women, and babies, to the four winds, over the seven seas. Perhaps we will breathe their dust into our nostrils, feel them in the fog of New York in our faces, feel them in the rain on the hills of Easton.

Jubilate Deo. President Truman was jubilant. We have created. We have created destruction. We have created a new element, called Pluto. Nature had nothing to do with it.

"A cavern below Columbia was the bomb's cradle," born not that men might live, but that men might be killed. Brought into being in a cavern, and then tried in a desert place, in the midst of tempest and lightning, tried out, and then again on the eve of the Feast of the Transfiguration of Our Lord Jesus Christ, on a far-off island in the Eastern Hemisphere, tried out again, this "new weapon which conceivably might wipe out mankind, and perhaps the planet itself."

"Dropped on a town, one bomb would be equivalent to a severe earthquake and would utterly destroy the place. A scientific brain trust has solved the problem of how to confine and release almost unlimited energy. It is impossible yet to measure its effects."

"We have spent two billion on the greatest scientific gamble in history and won," said President Truman jubilantly.

("UNRRA meets today facing a crisis on funds. It is close to scraping the bottom of its financial barrel, will open its third council session tomorrow, hoping to get enough new funds to carry it through the winter.")

(Germany Is Told of Hard Winter by Eisenhower.)

(Pall of Apathy Shrouds Bitter, Hungry Vienna.)

The papers list the scientists (the murderers) who are credited with perfecting this new weapon. One outstanding authority, "who earlier had developed a powerful electrical bombardment machine called the cyclotron, was Professor E. O. Lawrence, a Nobel Prize winner of the University of California. In the heat of the race to unlock the atom, he built the world's most powerful atom smashing gun, a machine whose electrical projectiles carried charges equivalent to 25,000,000 volts. But such machines were found in the end to be unnecessary. The atom of Uranium-235 was smashed with surprising ease. Science discovered that not sledgehammer blows, but subtle taps from slow-traveling neutrons managed more on a tuning technique were all that were needed to disintegrate the Uranium-235 atom."

(Remember the tales we used to hear, that one note of a violin, if that note could be discovered, could collapse the Empire State Building. Remember, too, that God's voice was heard not in the great and strong wind, not in the earthquake, not in the fire, but "in the whistling of a gentle air.")

Scientists, army officers, great universities (Notre Dame included), and captains of industry—all are given credit lines in the press for their work of preparing the bomb—and other bombs, the President assures us, are in production now.

Great Britain controls the supply of uranium ore in Canada and Rhodesia. We are making the bombs. This new great force will be used for good, the scientists assured us. And then they wiped out a city of 318,000. This was good. The President was jubilant.

Today's paper with its columns of description of the new era, the atomic era, which this colossal slaughter of the innocents has ushered in, is filled with stories covering every conceivable phase of the new discovery. Pictures of the towns and the industrial plants where the parts are made are spread across the pages. In the forefront of the town of Oak Ridge, Tennessee, is a chapel, a large, comfortable-looking chapel benignly settled beside the plant. And the scientists making the first tests in the desert prayed, one newspaper account said.

Yes, God is still in the picture. God is not mocked. Today, the day of this so great news, God made a madman dance and talk who had not spoken for twenty years. God sent a typhoon to damage the carrier *Hornet*. God permitted a fog to obscure vision and a bomber crashed into the Empire State Building. God permits these things. We have to remember it. We are held in God's hands, all of us, and President Truman too, and these scientists who have created death, but will use it for good. He, God, holds our life and our happiness, our sanity and our health; our lives are in His hands.

He is our Creator. Creator.

*   *   *

And I think, as I think on these things, that while here in the Western Hemisphere, we went in for precision bombing (what chance of *precision* bombing now?), while we went in for obliteration bombing, Russia was very careful not to bomb cities, to wipe out civilian populations. Perhaps she was thinking of the poor, of the workers, as brothers.

I remember, too, that many stories have come out of Russia of her pride in scientific discoveries and of how eagerly and pridefully they were trying to discover the secret of life—how to create life (not death).

Exalted pride, yes, but I wonder which will be easier to forgive?

And as I write, Pigsie, who works in Secaucus, New Jersey, feeding hogs, and cleaning out the excrement of hogs, who comes in once a month to find beauty and surcease and glamor and glory in the drink of the Bowery, trying to drive the hell and the smell out of his nostrils and his life, sleeps on our doorstep, in this best and most advanced and progressive of all possible worlds. And as I write, our cat, Rainbow, slinks by with a shrill rat in her jaws, out of the kitchen closet here at Mott Street. Here in this greatest of cities which covered the cavern where this stupendous discovery was made, which institutes an era of unbelievable richness and power and glory for man . . .

Everyone says, "I wonder what the Pope thinks of it?" How everyone turns to the Vatican for judgment, even though they do not seem to listen to the voice there! But Our Lord Himself has already pronounced judgment on the atomic bomb. When James and John (John the beloved) wished to call down fire from heaven on their enemies, Jesus said:

"You know not of what Spirit you are. The Son of Man came not to destroy souls but to save." He said also, "Inasmuch as ye have done it unto one of the least of these My brethren, ye have done it unto Me."

September 1945

IV

Wherever we go there is talk of the atomic bomb. All are impressed with the imminence of death, not only for themselves but for their dear ones, for all about them. Over and over again in history there have been small groups who thought the day of judgment would be next month, or six months from now, and who tried to live accordingly. In the time of the Apostles, there was a widespread feeling that Christ would come again in the twinkling of an eye, at any moment, and that they should be prepared. This feeling was so general that early Christians sold all they had and lived in common those first years after Christ died and rose again.

In contrast to the widespread fear of today, the emotion at that time was of joy. "Who will deliver me from the body of this death?" St. Paul cried out, and this life was looked upon as life in the womb, and the life to come as the bursting out into a glorious day, a release from bondage.

But what sad and fearful times are these for men of little faith, for men of no faith. "Lord, I believe, help Thou mine unbelief!" We must pray, not only for ourselves but for all those who do not believe, who have not been taught, who have not so much as heard that there be a Holy Spirit of love dwelling with us.

The great and glorious cities of the past have fallen: Ur of the Chaldees, Babylon, the cities of the Egyptians, Jerusalem the Golden. And now destruction hangs over New York and London, Moscow and Shanghai.

People are beginning to wonder—how long have we; when should we begin to depart like Lot from Sodom and Gomorrah?

Down in Washington a conference is beginning with Mr. Bevin, Mr. Truman, Mr. King. The great ones of the earth are conferring. The very scientists that brought forth the atomic bomb are the most afraid of all of what is to come. What to do?

We can only suggest one thing—destroy the two billion dollars' worth of equipment that was built to make the atomic bomb; destroy all the formulas; put on sackcloth and ashes, weep and repent. And God will not forget to show mercy. If others go to work to build again and prepare, let them. It is given to man but once to die. (And then the Judgment.)

One of the saints, when asked what he would do if he were told he was to die within the next day, replied that he would go on doing what he was doing. That is the state of mind we must cultivate. It is the only answer.

November 1945

Our Brothers, the Communists

In a slightly humorous reference to the Communist-led Popular Front of the thirties, Peter Maurin once announced the intention of the Catholic Worker to mobilize an "Unpopular Front." It would be composed of "Humanists who try to be human to man; Theists who believe that God wants us to be our brother's keeper; Christians who believe in the Sermon on the Mount; Catholics who believe in the Thomistic Doctrine of the Common Good." Such beliefs, rarely in full season, achieved a new level of unpopularity with the fearful atmosphere of the Cold War.

While congressional committees and grand juries sniffed out un-Americanism in every area of social life, those with a radical past faced the painful choice of jail and the blacklist or the betrayal of their friends and their ideals. If Dorothy Day had lived in Russia at the time, she would undoubtedly have protested the treatment of alleged "capitalist wreckers." But in this country, the victims of the hunt were called Communists. On petitions, platforms, and picket lines, Dorothy made it clear that she would not be counted among the hounds. The title of one editorial proclaimed her position: "We Are Un-American; We Are Catholics."

Women think with their whole bodies. More than men do, women see things as a whole.

Maybe I am saying this to justify myself for my recent protest of the refusal of bail to the eleven Communists, a protest which was published in the *Daily Worker*, the *American Guardian*, and other papers, much to the horror of many of our Catholic fellow workers.

It is necessary to explain if we do not wish to affront people. We sincerely want to make our viewpoint understood.

First of all, let it be remembered that I speak as an ex-Communist and one who has not testified before congressional committees, nor written works on the Communist conspiracy. I can say with warmth that I loved the people I worked with and learned much from them. They helped me to find God in His poor, in His abandoned ones, as I had not found Him in Christian churches.

I firmly believe that our salvation depends on the poor with whom Christ identified Himself. "Inasmuch as you have not fed the hungry, clothed the naked, sheltered the homeless, visited the prisoner, protested against injustice, comforted the afflicted . . . you have not done it to Me." The Church throughout the ages in all its charities, in the person of all its saints, has done these things. But for centuries these works were confined to priests, brothers, and nuns. Pius XI called on everyone to perform these works when he called for Catholic Action. The great tragedy of the century, he said, is that the workers are lost to the Church. All this has been repeated many times.

But I must speak from my own experiences. My radical associates were the ones who were in the forefront of the struggle for a better social order where there would not be so many poor. What if we do not agree with the means taken to achieve this goal, nor with their fundamental philosophy? We do believe in "from each according to his ability, to each according to his need." We believe in the "withering away of the State." We believe in the communal aspect of property, as stressed by the early Christians and since then by religious orders. We believe in the constructive activity of the people, "the masses," and the mutual aid which existed during medieval times, worked out from below. We believe in loving our brothers, regardless of race, color, or creed and we believe in showing this love by working, immediately, for better conditions, and ultimately, for the ownership by the workers of the means of production. We believe in an economy based on human needs, rather than on the profit motive.

Certainly we disagree with the Communist Party, but so do we disagree with the other political parties, dedicated to maintaining the status quo. We don't think the present system is worth maintaining. We and the Communists have a common idea that something else is necessary, some other vision of society must be held up and worked toward. Certainly we disagree over and over again with the means chosen to reach their ends, because, as we have repeated many a time, the means become the end.

As for their alleged conspiracy to overthrow the government by force and violence, I do not think that the state has proved its case. Of course, the Communists believe that violence will come. (So do we when it comes down to it, though we are praying it won't.) They believe it will be forced upon the worker by the class struggle which is going on all around us. This class war is a fact, and one does not need to advocate it. The Communists say it is forced on them and when it comes they will take part in it. In the meantime they want to prepare the ground and win as many as possible to their point of view. And where will we be on that day?

If we spend the rest of our lives in slums (as I hope we will, who work for and read *The Catholic Worker*), if we are truly living with the poor, helping the poor, we will inevitably find ourselves on their side, physically speaking. But when it comes to activity, we will be pacifists—I hope and pray—nonviolent resisters of aggression, from whomever it comes, resisters to repression, coercion, from whatever side it comes, and our activity will be the Works of Mercy. Our arms will be the love of God and our brother.

But the Communists are dishonest, everyone says. They do not want improved conditions for the workers. They want the end, the final conflict, to bring on the world revolution.

Well, when it comes down to it, do we of the Catholic Worker stand only for just wages, shorter hours, increase of power for the workers, a collaboration of employer and worker in prosperity for all? No, we want to make "the rich poor and the poor holy," and that, too, is a revolution obnoxious to the pagan man. We don't want luxury. We want land, bread, work, children, and the joys of community in play and work and worship. We don't believe in those industrial councils where the heads of United States Steel sit down with the common man in an obscene *agape* of luxury, shared profits, blood money from a thousand battles all over the world. No, the common good, the community must be considered.

During the first seven months of this year, 412 miners were killed at work. And as for crippling and disabling accidents there were 14,871 during these same months.

What has all this to do with signing protests, advocating bail for convicted Communists?

If people took time to think, if they had the zeal of the C.P. for school and study and meeting and planning, and with it all the thirst for martyrdom, and if Catholics delved into the rich body of Catholic liturgy and sociology, they would grow in faith and grace and change the world.

I believe we must reach our brother, never toning down our fundamental oppositions, but meeting him when he asks to be met with a reason for the faith that is in us. "We understand because we believe," St. Anselm says, and how can our brothers understand with a darkened reason, lacking this faith which would enlighten their minds?

The bridge—it seems to me—is love and the compassion (the suffering together) which goes with all love. Which means the folly of the Cross, since Christ loved men even to that folly of failure.

St. Therese said her aim was to make God loved. And I am sure that we pray to love God with an everlasting love, and yearn over our fellows in desire that He should be loved. How can they hear unless we take seriously our lay apostolate and answer them when they speak to us? We believe that God made them and sustains them. It is easier sometimes to see His handiwork here than in the Pecksniffs and Pharisees of our capitalist industrial system. We must cry out against injustice or by our silence consent to it. If we keep silent, the very stones of the street will cry out.

November 1949

II

When we read in the papers of a captain of a freighter battling the elements and risking his life to save his ship in a ferocious sea, or the killing of a salesman in Brooklyn, or the death of a little child from beating and starvation, our hearts are torn. We have a fatalistic sense of taking part in a gigantic tragedy, a fearful adventure. Our life is charged with drama, about which we can do nothing. Our role is already written for us.

The war in Korea in which we are engaged takes on that great simplicity. We are at war because of our sins. All the suffering, the misery of the needy and the groaning of the poor, is part of the world's suffering which makes up the suffering of Christ.

Most of us try to forget and look for what joy we can: "Eat, drink, and be merry." Even the great St. Teresa was said to have remarked, as she danced during a recreation hour to the scandal of the other nuns, "One has got to do something to make life bearable."

One of the reasons I am writing a life of St. Therese of Lisieux, the

Little Flower, is because she was determined to do something about it, even though she was imprisoned, for all intents and purposes, in a small French convent in Normandy, unknown to all the world.

Because she was a saint, her words were scattered profligately. Books about her are read, her autobiography has gone into many editions. But the social implications of her teachings are yet to be studied. The significance of our smallest acts! The significance of the little things we leave undone! The protests we do not make, the stands we do not take, we who are living in the world!

I'm not trying to say that the Little Flower would have gone out on picket lines and spoken on Communist platforms or embraced her Protestant neighbors, if there were any in the town of Alençon. She was a product of her environment, bourgeois, middle class, the daughter of skilled workers, comfortable, frugal people who lived apart from the world with their eyes on God. She wanted everything, she said, every apostolate. And she used the means at her disposal to participate in everything, to increase the sum total of the love of God in the world by every minute act, every suffering, every movement of her body and soul, done for the love of God. She used the spiritual weapons every one of us has at our disposal.

All this is by way of preamble for the stands we have taken, the protests we have made during the month. I have spoken at Carnegie Hall against the Smith and McCarran Acts, with Communists and "fellow travelers"; others of us have walked on picket lines protesting the payment of income tax; lastly there have been four days of picketing the Spanish consulate in New York in protest against the execution of five Spanish trade unionists. On this last picket line, a young Negro girl, commenting on our presence, said to a fellow radical, "These Catholic Workers will demonstrate with anybody."

Perhaps it was meant as an insult (we Catholics are very sensitive to insult), but one could also understand it to mean that, in St. Paul's words, we were trying to be all things to all men, and also, in Peter Maurin's words, that "we have no party line."

In making this open confession of our collaborations, I forgot to mention that we filed a protest in the Rosenberg case.

We are in favor of life. We are trying to work here and now for the brotherhood of man, with those minorities, those small groups of "willful men" who believe that even the few can cry out against injustice, against the man-made suffering in the world, in behalf of those who are hungry and homeless and without work, in behalf of those who are dying.

We may be considered guilty of an emotional approach, but what about that story that Jesus told of the prodigal son, an illustration of the folly of love if anything ever was. To have faith that God loves us all, Communists and Socialists and I.W.W.'s, Protestants and Catholics, colored and white, Jew and Gentile, because we are all made in His image and likeness. He is life, and if He withdrew from us His hand, we would collapse into nothingness. He sustains our fellow picketers, as He sustains us.

"Go to the poor," the Holy Father has said. "Go to the man in the street," Peter Maurin used to say, and he did it literally—as we are doing when we go out behind picket signs in this way. We learn many things. We hear the voice of the suffering on the other side of the world. We hear the hostility at home from the masses who do not know the Church and fear and hate her.

We know there will be no utopias, that we will always have the poor. If the Communist economy succeeds, there will still be the poor; if the anarchist way of Kropotkin and Francisco Ferrer should ever succeed, there will still be the poor. There is always the fact of the Fall, as well as the fact of our Redemption.

We knelt in the library to say the rosary this noon. Slim turned down the radio and covered his eyes while he waited for us to finish, and Catherine ceased her crossword puzzle, and Shorty and California George sat and their lips moved soundlessly. And I knelt there, and looked at their feet, at the holes in Shorty's socks, which exposed his bony ankles; and the mismatched socks on George, too long, too stylish, and ripping at the seams. They are the meek; they epitomize the poor. They do not cry out.

But we are the articulate and we must speak and write for them. And we have no party line.

April 1952

III

At eight o'clock on Friday, June 19, the Rosenbergs began to go to death. That June evening the air was fragrant with the smell of honeysuckle. Out under the hedge at Peter Maurin Farm, the black cat played with a grass snake, and the newly cut grass was fragrant in the evening air. At eight o'clock I put Nickie in the tub at my daughter's home, just as Lucille Smith was bathing her children at Peter Maurin Farm. My heart was heavy as I soaped Nickie's dirty little legs, knowing that Ethel Rosenberg must have been thinking with all the yearning of her heart of her own soon-to-be-orphaned children.

How does one pray when praying for "convicted spies" about to be electrocuted? One prays always of course for mercy. "My Jesus, mercy." "Lord Jesus Christ, Son of the living God, have mercy on them." But somehow, feeling close to their humanity, I prayed for fortitude for them both. "God let them be strong, take away all fear from them; let them be spared this suffering, at least, this suffering of fear and trembling."

I could not help but think of the story of Dostoevsky's *Idiot*, how Prince Myshkin described in detail the misery of the man about to be executed, whose sentence was commuted at the last moment. This had been the experience of Dostoevsky himself, and he had suffered those same fears, and had seen one of his comrades, convicted with him, led to the firing line, go mad with fear. Ethel and Julius Rosenberg, as their time approached and many appeals were made, must, in hoping against hope, holding fast to hope up to the last, have compared their lot to that of Dostoevsky and those who had been convicted with him. What greater punishment can be inflicted on anyone than those two long years in a death house, watched without ceasing so that there is no chance of one taking one's life and so thwarting the vengeance of the state. They had already suffered the supreme penalty. What they were doing in their own minds, no doubt, was offering the supreme sacrifice, offering their lives for their brothers. Both Harold Urey and Albert Einstein, and many other eminent thinkers at home and abroad, avowed their belief in the innocence of these two. They wrote that they did not believe their guilt had been proved.

Leaving all that out of account, accepting the verdict of the court that they were guilty, accepting the verdict of the millions of Americans who believed them guilty, accepting the verdict of President Eisenhower and Cardinal Spellman, who thought them guilty—even so, what should be the attitude of the Christian but one of love and great yearning for their salvation?

"Keep the two great commandments, love God and love your neighbor. Do this and thou shalt live." This is in the Gospel; these are the words of Jesus.

Whether or not they believed in Jesus, did the Rosenbergs love God? A rabbi who attended them to the last said that they had been his parishioners for two years. He followed them to the execution chamber reading from the Psalms, the Twenty-third, the Fifteenth, the Thirty-first. Those same psalms Cardinal Spellman reads every week as he reads his breviary, among those hundred and fifty psalms which make up not only the official prayers of the Church, but also the prayers which the Jews say. We used to see our Jewish grocer on the East Side, vested for prayer, reciting the Psalms every morning behind his counter when we went for our morning supplies. I have seen rabbis on all-night coaches praying thus in the morning. Who can hear the word of God without loving the word? Who can work for what they conceive of as justice, as brotherhood, without loving God and brother? If they were spies for Russia, they were doing what we also do in other countries, playing a part in international politics and diplomacy, but they indeed were serving a philosophy, a religion, and how mixed up religion can become. What a confusion we have gotten into when Christian prelates sprinkle holy water on scrap metal, to be used for obliteration bombing, and name bombers for the Holy Innocents, for Our Lady of Mercy; who bless a man about to press a button which releases death on fifty thousand human beings, including little babies, children, the sick, the aged, the innocent as well as the guilty. "You know not of what Spirit you are," Jesus said to His Apostles when they wished to call down fire from heaven on the inhospitable Samaritans.

I finished bathing the children, who were so completely free from preoccupation with suffering. They laughed and frolicked in the tub while the switch was being pulled which electrocuted first Julius and then his wife. Their deaths were announced over the radio half an hour later, jazz music being interrupted to give the bulletin, and the program continuing immediately after.

The next day, *The New York Times* gave details of the last hours, and the story was that both went to their deaths firmly, quietly, with no comment. At the last, Ethel turned to one of the two police matrons who accompanied her and, clasping her by the hand, pulled her toward her and kissed her warmly. Her last gesture was a gesture of love.

July–August 1953

Visiting The Prisoner

On June 15, 1955, New York City conducted its first annual air-raid drill. According to the Civil Defense Act, all city residents were required, at the sound of a warning siren, to take shelter for at least ten minutes, thus "simulating" the reaction to a nuclear attack on the city. The climate of opinion which tolerated such a ludicrous exercise may be judged by the newspaper account which appeared the following day in the New York *Mirror*:

"As 679 warning sirens wailed, millions of New Yorkers took shelter in the city's greatest air raid drill—an exercise marred only by 29 arrests and, in spots, by errors, lethargy and defiance, but hailed nonetheless as a 'complete success' by authorities.

"An imaginary H-bomb fell at the corner of N. 7th St. and Kent Ave. in Brooklyn, 'wiping out' vast areas of the city and claiming 2,991,185 'fatalities'! Another 1,776,899 men, women and children were listed as 'injured' as imaginary flames roared through the area. Robert Condon, City Civil Defense Director, called the drill 'a complete success as far as public reaction goes.' "

Those twenty-nine persons who, by their non-compliance with the law, had "marred" the verisimilitude of this imaginary holocaust included Dorothy Day, Ammon Hennacy, Judith Malina Beck of the Living Theater, and various other representatives of the small pacifist community. In setting bail at $1,500, a judge denounced the protesters as "murderers" who "by their conduct and behavior contributed to the utter destruction of these three million theoretically killed in our city." Despite the gravity of the charge (theoretical homicide, no less), the twenty-nine spoilers were later released with suspended sentences.

Arrested in two succeeding years, Dorothy served jail sentences of five and thirty days. She described the second occasion in several articles, from which the following account is compiled.

The ethics of Dorothy's action were vigorously debated in the Catholic and liberal press. As for the civil defense drills, they were discontinued after 1961, when the annual protest drew a crowd of thousands to City Hall Park.

Whenever I am invited to speak at schools around the country and receive praise for talking about the problems of destitution in this rich country, I feel guilty. We live in the midst of destitution in a rich country, and when we sit down to eat, we know that there is a line waiting at the door so long that the house cannot hold them. When we pass men lying on the streets at night, see them huddled around a fire while we go into our House of Hospitality, a house where men are sleeping on the floor (because all the beds are taken), and we go to our own warm and comfortable bed, once again we cannot help but feel guilty.

It is hard to comfort ourselves with the reflection that if we did not get rest and food we would not be able to do the work we do. We can reflect that some of the poverty we profess comes from lack of privacy, lack of time to ourselves. We can list instances of sights and sounds, smells and feelings that one can never get used to nor fail to cringe from. Yet God has blessed us so abundantly, has provided for us so constantly over these twenty-five years that we are always in the paradoxical position of rejoicing and saying to ourselves, "It is good, Lord, to be here." We feel over-whelmed with graces, and yet we know we fail to correspond to them. We fail far more than seven times daily, failing especially in our vocation to poverty.

For this reason, as well as for the reason that we are pacifists, we refused to take part in the war maneuvers, if you can call them that, the compulsory civil defense drills of the past three years. We were, frankly, hoping for jail. Perhaps jail, we thought, would put another compulsion on us, of being more truly poor. Then *we* would not be running a House of Hospitality, *we* would not be dispensing food and clothing, *we* would not be ministering to the destitute, but would be truly one with them. We would be truly among the least of God's children, sharing with them their misery. Then we could truly say in the prayers at the foot of the altar, "poor banished children of Eve, mourning and weeping in this valley of tears." How hard it is to say it, surrounded by material and spiritual benefits as we are!

And so on three occasions we have been imprisoned. Each time we have gone through the grueling experience of torturous rides in the police van, sitting for long hours in prison cells awaiting booking or trial. In the first year, we had only an overnight experience of jail (which necessitated, however, the examinations for drugs, the humiliations of being stripped and showered and deprived of clothing and belongings). The second year the sentence was five days, and this last summer it was thirty days (with five days off for good behavior). . . .

Commonweal, December 27, 1957

II

I had not expected that when I came out of jail I would feel so exhausted mentally, physically, and spiritually. The impact of the world and its problems is crushing, numbing, and painful at the same time. It is hard to rise in the morning to the "duties of one's state in life," as the spiritual writers put it.

One comes out from jail into a world where everyone has problems, all but insoluble problems, and the first thing that strikes me is that the world today is almost worse than jail. Looking at newspapers, listening to the radio, even watching the activities of children, and thinking fearfully of what they have to look forward to in the way of education, work, and war, I am appalled.

If we who think are sensitive to this, the average ex-prisoner is sensitive in a different way. He comes out a marked man, with the eye of the law upon him. One prison official, at a recent meeting to discuss prison problems, said that most prisoners today are serving life sentences "on the installment plan."

One looks at one's children and thinks, "How easy for them to get caught in this net."

I still think that the only solution is the land, and *community*, a community which is unjudging and which forgives "seventy times seven," as Jesus Christ said. We who think in terms of community at least have the assurance, the conviction, that we are on the right path, going in the right direction, taking the right means to achieve the goal of increased love of God through an increased and proven love of our brothers. So many in these days have taken violent steps to gain the things of this world—war to achieve peace; coercion to achieve freedom; striving to gain what slips through the fingers. We might as well give up our great desires, at least our hopes of doing great things toward achieving them, right at the beginning. In a way it is like that paradox of the Gospel, of giving up one's life in order to save it.

That, in effect, is what we did when we went to jail. It was part of it. We were setting our faces against the world, against things as they are, the terrible injustice of our capitalist industrial system which lives by war and by preparing for war; setting our faces against race hatreds and all nationalist strivings. But especially we wanted to act against war and the preparation for war: nerve gas, guided missiles, the testing and stockpiling of nuclear bombs, conscription, the collection of income tax—against the entire military state. We made our gesture; we disobeyed a law. . . .

Liberation, September 1957

III

At the Women's House of Detention, five doctors are in attendance, as well as nurses and nurse's aides. First, preliminary tests and examinations, X rays, cardiographs, blood tests, smears, and so on are taken. Every morning for the duration of one's stay, the shout "Clinic!" reverberates through the corridors. Girls leave their workshops or their cells to vary the monotony of their days by waiting in line for an aspirin, heat-rash lotion, gargle, eyewash, or other innocuous remedies. In addition, they have the refreshment of a visit with inmates from other floors.

The four of us arrested for violating the civil defense law had cells next to each other. We were two in a cell, on the most airless corridor, with the darkest cells. We had a dim twenty-five-watt bulb in ours, Judith Beck and

I, until the last week, when a tall young Negro woman climbed on the cot and took out a fifty-watt bulb from another cell just vacated. Our cells faced north, looking out over the old Jefferson Market Courthouse. We felt that we had been put there because the picketing meant to call attention to our imprisonment was going on along the south side of the jail—from the other corridors we might have seen the line. Our windows were small, and there was no cross-ventilation. Opposite us the showers steamed with heat. One of the captains said she was putting us in a good corridor, next to each other. She said she thought she was doing us a favor, but it was so obviously the least desirable, the most airless and dark corridor, that I do not see how she could honestly have thought that. Perhaps she did. I do know that from the time one is arrested until the time one leaves a prison every event seems calculated to intimidate and to render uncomfortable and ugly the life of the prisoner.

How entirely opposite is the work of the Good Shepherd nuns, who care for delinquent girls after they have been sentenced by the state. Their Mother Foundress said that her aim was to make the girls happy, comfortable, and industrious; she surrounded her charges with love and devotion and with the expectation of good.

"Here we are treated like animals," one girl said to me, "so why shouldn't we act like animals?" I can only hint at the daily, hourly repetitive obscenity that pervades a prison. Shouts, jeers, defiance of guards and each other, expressed in these ways, reverberated through the cells and corridors at night while, rosary in hand, I tried to pray. Noise—perhaps that is the greatest torture in jail. It stuns the ear, the mind. After I came out it took me at least a week to recover from it. The city itself seemed silent. Down the corridor from me was a strong, healthy Polish woman who should have used her great vitality rearing children instead of dissipating it in prostitution and drugs. Often she held her head in her hands and cried. Even to her the noise was torture. Yet she herself was one of the worst offenders. When she started screeching her ribald stories at night, her voice reverberated from cell to cell. "But this place was not made to live in," she complained, pointing to the iron bars, the cement and tiled walls. "The ceilings are low, the sounds bounce around."

Everything *was* exaggeratedly loud. Television blared from the "rec" room on each floor in the most distorted way. One heard not words or music but clamor. The clanging of gates—seventy gates on a floor—the pulling of the master lever which locked all the cells of each corridor, the noise of the three elevators, the banging of pots and pans and dishes from the dining room, all these made the most unimaginable din, not to mention the shouting of human voices.

The guard (one to a floor) had to have strong lungs to make herself heard. Ours was one who could. She looked like a stern schoolteacher; she seldom smiled and never "fraternized." The women respected her. "She's an honest cop," one of them said of her. "She's just what she is and doesn't pretend to be anything else." A "good" officer had to know just how far to go in severity; just how firm to be and just how much to put up with, to overlook. I saw one guard trying to hasten a prisoner's exit from the auditorium, where the inmates had just put on a show, with what we took to be a friendly push. The prisoner turned on her viciously, threateningly. On such occasions the officers do not press the point. They realize they are sitting on a volcano. They know when to back down. But a number of times, witnessing the officers' humiliation, I was ashamed for them. Helpless as the prisoner may seem to be, she knows that she has the superior numbers on her side, that she can start something if she wants to. She knows, too, the worst she has to expect. In many cases the worst has already happened to her. She has undergone the "cold turkey cure."

While in prison I received a letter inviting me to speak on television. It had already been opened by the censor and commented on all over the House of Detention. The girls came to me and begged me to plead their case to the world: "You must tell how we are put here for long terms, and about the cold turkey cure, too; about how we are thrown in the 'tank' and left to lie there in our own vomit and filth, too sick to move, too sick even to get to the open toilet in the cell."

"I know," one girl added, "because I had to clean out those places." These cells are called tanks, I suppose, because they are so bare of furnishings they can be hosed out. The "cooler," on the other hand, is the punishment cell; there are several of them on various floors. Here a recalcitrant prisoner is kept in solitary for brief periods, until she "cools off."

I heard stories of padded cells; of cells with only ventilating systems— no window, no open bars—in which a girl sits in the dark; of cells where water can be turned on in some kind of sprinkler system to assist the process of cooling off. I heard of girls being thrown naked in these cells on the pretense that they might use some article of clothing to make a rope to hang themselves. I heard of girls breaking the crockery bowls and using the shards to cut their throats or their wrists. I heard of girls trying to hang themselves by their belts. But I know none of these things of my own knowledge. From the open elevator door, as we journeyed to and from clinic or workshop, I saw only the gruesome steel-plated doors, ominous indicators of the presence of these punishment cells.

Most cells for the five hundred or so prisoners, or girls held in "detention," are cemented and tiled halfway up the front, and then barred to the ceiling; about ten bars across the front of the cell, perhaps five bars to the gate, which is so heavy one can hardly move it. It is the crowning indignity for the officer to shout, "Close your gates!" and to have to lock oneself in. The open bars at the top enable one to call the guard, to call out to other prisoners, to carry on some friendly intercourse. The cooler is meant to be a place of more severe punishment than the cell, or course, so it is completely closed in.

"*Tell how we are treated*," they cried out to me. I can only tell the things that I have seen with my eyes, heard with my ears. The reports of the other prisoners will not be considered credible. After all, they are prisoners; why should they be believed? People will say, "What! Do you believe self-confessed thieves, prostitutes, drug addicts, criminals who are in jail for assault, for putting out the eyes of others, for stabbing and other acts of violence?"

Perhaps it is a little too much to believe that twenty girls have died in the House of Detention from the cold turkey cure these last two years, as one inmate charged. But there have been ominous stories in the *New York Times* and other New York papers. I heard one young drug addict tell the story of a girl who died in the cell, after her "cellie," as the roommate is called, had cried out over and over again for the officer to come and minister to the sick girl. When the doctor finally came hours later, after the cells were unlocked, she was dead. Two prisoners assaulted the doctor and kept her head poked down the open toilet while another prisoner kept flushing it in an attempt to drown her. "Her head shook from that time on, as though she had palsy," one of the girls said, with grim satisfaction.

I repeat, these are tales I heard told and repeated. They may be legends, but legends have a kernel of truth.

Ill treatment? How intangible a thing it sometimes is to report! Whenever I was asked by the officers and captains and the warden himself how I was making out, how I was being treated, I could only say that everything was all right as far as I was concerned. After all, I was only there for twenty-five days, what with the five days off for good behavior. I had no complaint to make against individuals, and yet one must complain about everything—the atmosphere, the attitude, the ugliness of it all. "After all, we don't want to make this place glamorous," the guards protested.

Listening to the prisoners talk about the kick they got out of drugs, I saw how impossible it was for them to conceive of themselves as "squares"—those who go out to work every day—and how hopelessly they regarded the world outside, which they nevertheless longed for hourly. They made me feel, too, that without a "community," in the early Christian sense, to return to, their future was indeed bleak.

But in the attempt to keep the place "unglamorous" there need not be so many small indignities heaped on each prisoner. Why cannot they be treated as they are in the Good Shepherd Homes (where they are sentenced for two years or more), as children of God, and made happy and comfortable? The very deprivation of freedom is punishment enough. For the prisoners the breaking of the habits of vice is difficult enough.

On one occasion in the chapel, the catechist said to Deane, "Just look at that wonderful electric fan! How good they are to you. Such luxury in a prison!" She was speaking lightly, of course, but a prisoner resents such lack of understanding.

In the past I have received letters from *Catholic Worker* readers who have been prison officers and officials which showed the same lack of understanding, and I could only think: What if *they* were treated as prisoners? What if *they* were crowded into a bullpen, a metal cage, awaiting trial, then transported in a sealed van, with no springs, where they are tossed from seat to ceiling in imminent danger of broken bones and bruised spines; or stripped naked, lined up, and prodded rudely, even roughly, in the search for drugs; or dressed in inadequate garments coming only to the knees, and then, with every belonging from rosary to prayer book to Testament taken away, led off to a permanent cell and there locked behind bars? Envisaging our critics, our chaplains, our catechists under such circumstances, seeing *them* also shivering nakedly, obeying blindly, pushed hither and yon, I could not help but think that it is only by experiencing such things that one can understand and have compassion for one's brother.

How many priests and nuns around the world have had these experiences in Russia, Germany, and Japan in our generation? In the face of the suffering of our time one is glad to go to prison, if only to share in some small way these sufferings.

Of course, our friends and readers will remind us of the torture, the beatings, the brainwashings in the prisons of Russia and Germany. As for beatings, third degree methods are generally accepted in our own land—in practice, if not in theory. I have read of them, heard of them from parole officers as well as from prisoners. In the case of sex offenders, offenses against little children, brutality is repaid with brutality and with a righteous indignation to justify it. One prisoner, a drug addict, told me that she had been so beaten by members of the narcotic squad trying to force her to tell where she had gotten her drugs that they were unable to arrest her for fear they themselves would be held criminally liable for her condition.

Over a year ago the magazine section of the *New York Times* carried a long article on the treatment of drug addicts in Great Britain. There they are regarded not as criminals but as patients and are so treated, through clinics and custodial care. Here they are made into criminals by our "control" methods, which make the drug so hard to get that the addict turns to crime to get it. The girl who told of the beating and other ill treatment started to use drugs when she was twelve, and became a prostitute at that time also. She had been in prison sixteen times since then and now she was twenty-two.

As for the problem of prostitution, most of the girls openly admitted it. "I'm a pross," they would tell us. "I was money hungry. I wanted a car," or "I wanted drugs." They felt the injustice of the woman being arrested and not the man, and they despised the tactics of the plainclothesmen who solicited them in order to trap them. The grossest misconception held not only by prostitutes but also by some pious people is that were it not for the lowly prostitute there would be far more sex crimes. I heard this statement made by Matilda, one of the girls down the corridor, one evening when she was in an unusually quiet and philosophical mood. Matilda pointed out that jaded men, in their demands on prostitutes, wished to explore every perversion, to the disgust of what society considers the lowest of women, whores and dope fiends. These are not pretty words nor are they pretty thoughts. But everything comes out in the open in jail. "The more I see of men," one girl said, "the more I'd prefer relations with a woman." And another pretty girl added wistfully, "I've got to get used to the idea of men, so that I can have a baby. I would love to have a baby."

Cardinal Newman once wrote that not even to save the world (or to save good women and children) could a single venial sin be committed. When I lay in jail thinking of these things, thinking of war and peace, and the problem of human freedom, of jails, drug addiction, prostitution, and the apathy of great masses of people who believe that nothing can be done—when I thought of these things, I was all the more confirmed in my faith in the little way of St. Therese. We do the minute things that come to hand, we pray our prayers, and beg also for an increase of faith—and God will do the rest.

One of the greatest evils of the day is the sense of futility. Young people say, "What can one person do? What is the sense of our small effort?" They cannot see that we can only lay one brick at a time, take one step at a time; we can be responsible only for the one action of the present moment. But we can beg for an increase of love in our hearts that will vitalize and transform these actions, and know that God will take them and multiply them, as Jesus multiplied the loaves and fishes.

Next year, perhaps, God willing, we will again go to jail; and perhaps conditions will be the same. To be charitable we can only say that the prison officials do the best they can, according to their understanding. In a public institution they are not paid to love the inmates; they are paid to guard them. They admit that the quarters are totally inadequate, that what was built for a House of Detention for women awaiting trial is now being used for a workhouse and penitentiary.

When the girls asked me to speak for them, to tell the world outside about "conditions," they emphasized the crowded and confined surroundings. "We are here for years—to work out our sentences, not just for detention!" Shut in by walls, bars, concrete, and heavy iron screening so that even from the roof one's vision of the sky is impeded—mind and body suffer from the strain. Nerves clamor for change, for open air, more freedom of movement.

The men imprisoned over on Hart Island and Riker's Island can get out and play ball, can work on the farm or in the tree nursery. They can see around them water and boats and seagulls and breathe the sea air coming from the Atlantic. The women have long been promised North Brother Island as a companion institution for them. But there are seemingly insuperable obstacles in the way. Money figures largely. There is money for civil defense drills, for death rather than for life, money for all sorts of nonsensical expenditures, but none for these least of God's children suffering in the midst of millions of people scarcely aware of their existence. "Nothing short of a riot will change things," the warden told us. Was he perhaps suggesting that we pacifists start one?

If those who read this will pray for the prisoners—if our New York readers, when they pass the Women's House of Detention, will look up, perhaps wave a greeting, say a prayer, there will be the beginning of a change. Two of the women, Tulsa and Thelma, said that they never looked out through those bars; they could not stand it. But most of the other prisoners do, and perhaps they will see this gesture; perhaps they will feel the caress of this prayer, and a sad heart will be lightened, and a resolution strengthened, and there will be a turning away from evil, and toward the good. Christ is with us today, not only in the Blessed Sacrament and where two or three are gathered together in His Name, but also in the poor. And who could be poorer or more destitute in body and soul than these companions of our twenty-five days in prison?

September 1957

IV

One of the peculiar enjoyments I got out of jail was in being on the other side for a change. I was the one working in a laundry, ironing uniforms of jailers. I was the one sitting in the sewing room turning the collar and mending the uniform of an officer. It gave me a chance to tell the other prisoners about Tolstoy, and how he said the first move toward reform was to do one's own work. Everyone regarded the officers as members of the parasite class, though they would not use that word. How much more respect they would have had for the officers, and for the work they themselves had to do, if they had seen the officers sitting mending their own clothes. If they had seen them working to help their fellows. Perhaps it would have meant a beginning of the philosophy of work which Peter Maurin used to say was so sadly lacking today. If prisoners and officers had worked together to make the prison a happier place, what a change there might have been in the hearts of those confined.

The officers sat all day at their desks, watching, directing, always expecting the worst, always looking for some small infraction, always seeing the women as criminals. They did not see that which is of God in every person, as the Friends put it. St. John of the Cross said, "Where there is no love, put love, and you will find love." The officers looked for the criminal and found the criminal.

The women got away with what they could. They fought, they lied, they stole when they could. While working in the laundry I saw a girl put a folded dress, which she wanted for herself, up between her legs, under her skirt. When she spoke of it afterward to some of the other prisoners on our corridor, they jeered. "That's nothing," one said, "I've seen girls who worked in the kitchen get away with a turkey or a ham." Judith made us all hilarious by immediately getting up and trying to impersonate a girl walking out of the kitchen with a turkey or ham held thus.

Looking back on these last paragraphs, I see that I have gone from the sublime to the ridiculous, even to the vulgar and, for some, the revolting. But beauty and joy often spring from the dungheap.

I have said that I enjoyed being on the other side for a time. People come into the Catholic Worker in such numbers: 800 a day for food; hundreds of men, women, and children coming in for clothes. When all the beds in the house are full we often give out "flop" money, the fifty cents a night it costs to sleep on the Bowery. All that we give is given to us to give. Nothing is ours. All we have to give is our time and patience, our love. In the movie *Monsieur Vincent,* the saint tells a young nun that she has to love the poor very much for them to forgive her the bread she gives them. How often we have failed in love, how often we have been brusque, cold, and indifferent. "Roger takes care of the clothes; you'll have to come back at ten o'clock." Or "Just sit in the library and wait." "Wait your turn, I'm busy." So it often goes. And now I was getting pushed here and there, told what I could or could not do, hemmed in by rules and regulations and red tape and bureacracy. It made me see my faults, but it also made me see how much more we accomplish at the Catholic Worker in our own direct way, by not asking questions or doing any investigating, but by cultivating a spirit of trust. The whole experience of jail was good for my soul. I realized again how much ordinary kindness can do. Graciousness is an old-fashioned word but it has a beautiful religious tradition. "Grace is participation in the divine life," according to St. Peter.

Most of the time we were treated like dumb beasts—worse, because it was with indifference and contempt. "You'll be back" was the common farewell to the prisoner. It was, in effect, wishing her not to fare well. There was no *goodbye, "God be with you,"* because there was not enough faith or hope or charity to conceive of a forgiving and loving God being with anyone so lost in vice and crime as prostitutes, drug addicts, and other criminals are supposed to be.

One great indignity is the examination given all women for drugs. There is certainly no recognition of the fact of political imprisonment. All of us were stripped and searched in the crudest way—even to the tearing of tissues so that bleeding resulted. Then there is the matter of clothing— the scanty garments, the crude wrappers which scarcely wrap around one, the floppy cloth slippers which are impossible to keep on! In Russia, in Germany, and even in our own country, to strip the prisoner, to humiliate him, is a definite part and purpose of a jail experience. Even in the Army, making a man stand naked before his examiners is to treat him like a dumb beast or a slave.

A great courtesy accorded us was a visit from the warden himself. Never had anything like that happened before, one of the girls assured us. He wanted to know about our demonstration, why we had done it. He was a

Hungarian Catholic; so perhaps it was easy to understand his confusion about our pacifism. What man does not wish to resist a foreign aggressor, to defend his home and family? But the problem of the means to an end had never occurred to him. Nowadays it is pretty generally accepted that the end justifies the means. To his mind, one just could not be a pacifist today. It was an "impossible" position.

As to our attitude toward the prison and the prisoners, he could not understand our love for them, our not judging them. The idea of hating the sin and loving the sinner seemed foreign to him. Of course, he did not hate the sinner but he had to look upon them as evil; otherwise his job would be meaningless. When we talked of the good we found there, in spite of perversion, prostitution, and drugs, he looked at us strangely and wanted to know if we were Christian Scientists. At least he did not call us Communists. He was too intelligent for that. But we seemed to him to be denying the reality of evil, because we were upholding the prisoner. The evil was there, all right, frank and unabashed. It was inside and also outside the jail.

We feel definitely, not that the prisoners should be coddled, but that those in authority should provide them with healthy surroundings, not just a huge block of a building in the heart of the city. The House of Detention is a living testimonial to the inefficiency and wastefulness of our prison administration. So much food wasted, poured out in ashcans—bread, stew, powdered milk, cereal, even huge containers of marmalade and jam. If the women had a penitentiary on North Brother Island or some other rural spot, where they could raise their own food, or help provide it; if they could bake their own bread, milk cows, tend chickens, engage in healthy and creative activity, share in the responsibility of the institution, it could become a better place, it could become in its own way a community. I read of an experiment in the Suffolk County jail where the men are farming (some of them) at Yaphank; and not only the jail but the county home for the aged receives vegetables and milk from the farm without charge. They call it a "mutual aid program." A place out of the city would provide more room for shops, for school, and for recreation.

When we first went in, Judith used to say ardently, "When the peaceable revolution comes, we will abolish all prisons, throw wide all doors." Several serious young prostitutes asked her when this would be. "Do you mean there is no need for prisons?" "Do you mean I ought not to be here? You know I killed five people" (it was in an auto accident). Deep down in themselves they felt they were on a wrong path, but did not know how to find a right one. Certainly beginnings can be made now, here and now, and even the most powerless, humblest officer or attendant can begin—not by the drastic act of resigning, as Ammon Hennacy might suggest, but by each man's being good and kind himself and spreading that atmosphere wherever he is. The "means to the end" begins with each one of us.

Liberation, October 1957

V

When we were locked in that first night in a narrow cell meant for one but holding two cots, we had just passed through an experience which was as ugly and horrifying as any I may ever experience. We had been processed, and as we got off the elevators on the seventh floor to be assigned to our cells, clutching our wrappers around us, we were surrounded by a group of young women, black and white, who first surveyed us boldly and then started making ribald comments. Deane Mowrer and I are older women, but Judith Malina Beck is young and beautiful. She is an actress, one of the leaders of the Living Theater group, which means that she carries herself consciously, alert to the gaze of others, responding to it. That night her black hair hung down around her shoulders and her face was very pale, but she had managed to get some lipstick on before the officers took all her things away from her.

"Put her in my cell," one of the roughest of the Puerto Rican girls shouted, clutching at Judith. "Let me have her," another one called out. It was a real hubbub, ugly and distracting, coming as it did on top of hours of contact with prison officials, officers, nurses, and so on.

I had a great sinking of the heart, a great sense of terror for Judith. Was this what jail meant? We had not expected this type of assult—and on the part of women. With the idea of protecting Judith, I *demanded,* and I used that term, too, for the only time during my imprisonment, that she be put in my cell or Deane's, even if we had to be doubled up because of crowding. "I will make complaints," I said very firmly, "if you do not do this."

The jeering and controversy continued, but the officer took us to our respective cells, putting Judith and me in one and Deane in another.

We felt a great sense of separation from the other prisoners, and as we were locked in that first night, I thought of a recent story by J. D. Salinger I had read in *The New Yorker.* It is about the impact of the Prayer of Jesus, famous among pilgrims in Russia, on a young girl from an actor's family.

The prayer is: "My Lord Jesus Christ, Son of the Living God, have mercy on me a sinner." Sometimes the prayer is shortened: "My Lord Jesus, have mercy on me a sinner."

Franny, the girl in Salinger's story, has become entangled in this prayer and is in such a state that her mother is about to get the advice of a psychiatrist. But the brother, who, with his sister, has been educated by an older brother who is something of a mystic, accomplishes his sister's release from her compulsion in a long conversation which makes the tale more a novella than a short story. He finally convinces her that she is looking for a shortcut to religious experience, that fundamentally she scorns other people and is turning to God to escape contact with humankind; he reminds her of a piece of advice given by the older brother. When she was acting in a radio play, she was to remember the fat lady sitting on her porch rocking and listening to the radio. In other words, "Jesus Christ is the fat lady," and she is to act with all her heart and love directed to the fat lady.

Part of the impact of the story is the contrast between the reverence of the prayer and crude truth. The language—including a compulsive use of the name of God—is often shocking. But the profound Christian truth the story expresses has been repeated over and over again by the saints. In the words of St. Catherine of Siena: "I have placed you in the midst of your fellows that you may do for them what you cannot do for Me, that is to say . . . that you may love your neighbors without expecting any return from them, and what you do to them I count as done to Me."

We were locked in our cells, and all the other five hundred women in the House of Detention were locked in theirs. The lights would go out at nine-thirty. The noise, the singing, the storytelling, the wildly vile language would go on until then. We were stunned by the impact of our reception and the wild, maniacal spirits of all those young women about us. The week's work was finished, it was Friday night, and here were two days of leisure ahead.

I thought of this story of Salinger's and I found it hard to excuse myself for my own immediate harsh reaction. It is all very well to hate the sin and love the sinner in theory, but it is hard to do in practice. By my peremptory rejection of the kind of welcome we received, I had of course protected Judith, but there was no expression of loving friendship in it toward the others. Lying there on my hard bed, I mourned to myself, "Jesus is the fat lady. Jesus is this unfortunate girl, Jackie, who is making advances. Jesus is Baby Doll, her cellmate."

Jackie was released the next week; she had finished her six months, or her year, or her two years, or whatever it was. From a window I watched Jackie, handsome and well dressed, hover a moment on the corner of the Avenue of the Americas and Tenth Street, then disappear into a bar. A week later we saw in the *Daily News* (which can be purchased by the inmates) that Jackie had attempted suicide and had been taken to Bellevue psychiatric prison ward. And a week after that she was back in the House of Detention on another floor.

The other prisoners certainly did not harbor any hostility to us or take offense at the openness of my judgment. It was my interior fear and harshness that I was judging in myself.

We had not been issued clothing, and the officers were not going to allow us to go to the chapel in our wrappers. So our kind fellow prisoners, sensing our keen disappointment, gathered together clothing, underwear, socks and shoes, and dresses, so that we could go to Mass and receive Communion. Prostitutes, drug addicts, forgers, and thieves had more loving-kindness toward us than our jailers, who had no sense of the practice of religion being a necessity to us, but acted as though it were a privilege which they could withhold.

Remembering Salinger, and Dostoevsky's Father Zossima, and Alyosha and the Honest Thief, and reading Tolstoy's short stories, made me feel again that I had failed. We had the luxury of books—our horizons were widened, though we were imprisoned. We certainly could not consider ourselves poor. Each day I read the prayers and lessons from my daily missal and breviary to Judith, and when I told her stories of the Fathers of the desert, she told me tales of the Hassidim. On the feast of St. Mary Magdalene I read:

> On my bed at night I sought Him
> Whom my heart loves—
> I sought Him but I did not find Him.
>
> I will rise then and go about the city;
>   in the streets and crossings I will seek
> Him whom my heart loves.
> I sought Him but I did not find Him . . .
>
> Oh, that You were my brother,
>   nursed at my mother's breasts!
> If I met You out of doors, I would kiss You
>   and none would taunt me.

I would lead You, bring You in
   to the home of my mother . . .

Rejoice with me, all you who love the Lord, for
I sought Him and He appeared to me. And while I
   was weeping at the tomb, I saw my Lord,
   Alleluia.

Yes, we fail in love, we make judgments and we fail to see that we are all brothers, we all are seeking love, seeking God, seeking the beatific vision. All sin is a perversion, a turning from God and a turning to creatures.

If only our love had been stronger and truer, casting out fear, I would not have taken the stand I did, I would have seen Christ in Jackie. Suppose Judith *had* been her cellmate for the night and suppose she had been able to convey a little of the strong, pure love the pacifists feel is the force which will overcome war. Perhaps, perhaps . . . But this is the kind of analyzing and introspection and examination of conscience the narrator in *The Fall* indulged in after he heard that cry in the dark, that splash in the Seine, and went his way without having helped his brother, only to hear a mocking laughter that followed him ever after.

Thank God for retroactive prayer! St. Paul said that he did not judge himself, nor must we. We can turn to Our Lord Jesus Christ, who has already repaired the greatest evil that ever happened or could ever happen, and trust that He will make up for our falls, for our neglects, for our failures in love.

Commonweal, December 27, 1957

This Money Is Not Ours

A principle, Dorothy believed, remains abstract until it costs us something. In 1961, she welcomed the opportunity to test the value of one of her convictions in a gesture of disarming originality. The cost was $3,579.39.

For years *The Catholic Worker* had repeated Peter Maurin's defense of the medieval ban on usury. The acceptance of the belief that value resides in currency rather than labor, he believed, was a turning point in the transition from a functional to an acquisitive society. The Catholic Worker could not single-handedly reverse this process, but it could at least issue a solitary protest, and make what Peter would call a "point."

The Catholic Worker
39 Spring Street
New York 12, N.Y.
July 1960

Treasurer
City of New York

Dear Sir:

We are returning to you a check for $3,579.39 which represents interest on the $68,700 which we were awarded by the city as payment for the property at 223 Chrystie Street which we owned and lived in for almost ten years, and used as a community for the poor. We did not voluntarily give up the property—it was taken from us by right of eminent domain for the extension of the subway which the city deemed necessary. We had to wait almost a year and a half for the money owed us, although the city permitted us to receive two-thirds of the assessed valuation of the property in advance so that we could relocate. Property owning having been made impossible for us by city regulations, we are now renting and continuing our work.

We are returning the interest on the money we have recently received because we do not believe in "money lending" at interest. As Catholics we are acquainted with the early teaching of the Church. All the early councils forbade it, declaring it reprehensible to make money by lending it out at interest. Canon law of the Middle Ages forbade it and in various decrees ordered that profit so obtained was to be restored. In the Christian emphasis on the duty of charity, we are commanded to lend gratuitously, to give freely, even in the case of confiscation, as in our own case—not to resist but to accept cheerfully.

We do not believe in the profit system, and so we cannot take profit or interest on our money. People who take a materialistic view of human service wish to make a profit but we are trying to do our duty by our service without wages to our brothers as Jesus commanded in the Gospel (Matthew 25). Loaning money at interest is deemed by one Franciscan as the principal scourge of civilization. Eric Gill, the English artist and writer, calls usury and war the two great problems of our time.

Since we have dealt with these problems in every issue of The Catholic Worker since 1933—man's freedom, war and peace, man and the state, man and his work—and since Scripture says that the love of money is the root of all evil, we are taking this opportunity to live in practice of this belief, and make a gesture of overcoming that love of money by returning to you the interest.

Insofar as our money paid for services for the common good, and aid to the poor, we should be very happy to allow you to use not only our money without interest, but also our work, the Works of Mercy which we all perform here at the headquarters of *The Catholic Worker* without other salary or recompense than our daily food and lodging, clothes, and incidental expenses.

Insofar as the use of our money paid for the time being for salaries for judges who have condemned us and others to jail, and for the politicians who appointed them, and for prisons, and the execution chamber at Sing Sing, and for the executioner's salary, we can only protest the use of our money and turn with utter horror from taking interest on it.

Please also be assured that we are not judging individuals, but are trying to make a júdgment on *the system* under which we live and with which we admit that we ourselves compromise daily in many small ways, but which we try and wish to withdraw from as much as possible.

Sincerely yours,
Dorothy Day, Editor

September 1960

II

It is not easy, having acted upon principle, to explain it in ways acceptable and understood by others. An instance is our recent sending back of the interest on the money given us for St. Joseph's House on Chrystie Street.

During the course of the month we have received a few letters, not very many, of criticism of our act. One letter, from a generous benefactor who had given us a large sum when her father died, pointed out that if her parent had not invested his money wisely she and her mother would not have had anything left to live on; also that we probably received many donations which came from dividends, interest, etc.

I only try to answer as best I can. But sometimes one confuses others the more by trying to answer objections. When we wrote our letter to the city, and published it in the paper, we also printed some excerpts from the teaching of St. Thomas Aquinas on interest and money-lending. We used some of Peter Maurin's easy essays on the subject, and an article by Arthur Sheehan on credit unions, which, however, ask for a small interest on their loans. How can this be reconciled with the "gesture" we made of returning to the city the large check which represented the interest for a year and half on the money paid us for our property on Chrystie Street? First of all, we asked with Chesterton: Whose money is this interest which the city was paying us? Where did it come from? Money does not breed money; it is sterile.

To answer our correspondent: Of course we are involved, the same as everyone else, in living off interest. We are all caught up in this same money economy. Just as "God writes straight with crooked lines," so we too waver, struggle on our devious path—always aiming at God, even though we are conditioned by habits and ancestry, etc. We have free will, which is our greatest gift. We are free to choose, and as we see more clearly, our choice is more direct and easier to make. But we all see through a glass darkly. It would be heaven to see Truth face to face.

We are publishing a paper in which ideas are discussed and clarified, and illustrated by act. So we are not just a newspaper. We are a revolution, a movement, as Peter Maurin used to say. We are propagandists of the faith. We are the Church. We are members of the Mystical Body. We all must try to function healthily. We do not all have the same function, but we all have a vocation, a calling. Ours is a "prophetic" one, as many priests have said to us. Pope John recently cited the courage of John the Baptist as an example for today. Prophets made great gestures, did things to call attention to what they were talking about. That was what we did; we made a gesture, when we returned the money to the city. It was calling attention to a great unsolved problem in which we are all involved, Church, State, corporation, institution, individual.

There is no simple solution. Let the priests and the economists get to work on it. It is a moral and an ethical problem. We can work on the lowest level, the credit union in the parish, for instance. Through the credit union families have been taught to resist the skillful seductions of the advertising men and by doing without many things, to attain to ownership, homes, workshops, tools, small factories, and so on. These things have happened in Nova Scotia, in missions throughout the world, and this is one way to combat what the bishops call the all-encroaching State. It is the beginning of the decentralist society.

So primarily, our sending back the money was a gesture. It was the first time we had to do so with so large a sum of money. We were being reimbursed by the city—and generously, as far as money went—for the house and our improvements on it. (They had taken over the property by the right of eminent domain because a subway extension was going through.) One can argue that the value of the property went up, that the city had the eighteen months' use of our money, that money purchases less now, and so on. The fact remains that the city was doing what it could to pay off each and every tenant in the two tenement houses from which they were being evicted, giving bonuses, trying to find other lodgings, though these were usually unacceptable, being in other neighborhoods or boroughs.

We agree that slums need to be eliminated, but that an entire neighborhood, which is like a village made up of many nationalities, should be scattered, displaced—this is wanton cruelty, and one of the causes of the juvenile delinquency of our cities. Also, it is terribly bad and ruthless management on the part of the city fathers.

Is Robert Moses responsible? He is the planner. But he deals recklessly with inanimate brick and cement at the expense of flesh and blood. He is walking ruthlessly over brokenhearted families to make a great outward show of a destroyed and rebuilt city. He has been doing what blockbusters and obliteration bombing did in European and British cities. Right now an entire neighborhood just south of Tompkins Square where some of our poor friends live is being demolished and the widows and fatherless are crying to heaven. The city fathers try to recompense them, try to give them bonuses to get out quickly. But what good does the money do them when there is no place to go? They do not want to go to another neighborhood or even to another block. Actually, as piled-up furniture on the streets testifies, many cling to their poor homes until the last moment, and probably forfeit the two or three hundred dollars they are offered, rather than be exiled. That money means as much to them as the two or three thousand did to us.

There is talk about doing things economically, yet money is poured out like water in all directions and scandals are always being unearthed of cheating and graft in high places. This extends down to the smallest citizen, too, trying to get in on the big deal and get his—from the building inspector who expects to be tipped, to the little veteran around the corner who is speculating in the real estate by buying and improving and renting and then selling back his property to the city at exorbitant prices. "It doesn't matter if it is going to be torn down in a year or so," he assured us. "Rent out all the apartments and stores and then you can ask more from the city." Big deal! Everyone is trying to get in on the Moses big deal.

So to put it on the natural but often most emotional plane of simple patriotism, love of country or city, this feeling, too, prompted us to send back the interest. We do not want to participate in this big deal. "Why are there wars and contentions among you? Because each one seeketh his own."

We considered this a gesture, too, toward peace, a spiritual weapon which is translated into action. We cannot talk about these ideas without trying to put them into practice, though we do it clumsily and are often misunderstood.

We are not trying to be superior, holier than thou. Of course we are involved in paying taxes, in living on money which comes from our industrial capitalist way of life. But we can try, by voluntary poverty and labor, to earn our living, and not to be any more involved than we can help. We, all of us, partake in a way in the sin of Sapphira and Ananias, by holding back our time, our love, our material resources even, after making great protestations of "absolutism." May God and you, our readers, forgive us. We are, in spite of all we try to do, unprofitable servants.

November 1960

A Revolution near Our Shores

By 1961, the Catholic Worker's sympathetic response to the Cuban Revolution had become a cause for perplexity and anger among many friends of the movement as well as among its critics. Were not the Communists in power avowed atheists? Had they not already expropriated extensive Church property and placed restrictions on religious education? Furthermore, how could the Catholic Worker reconcile its pacifism with a movement which attained its aims through violence? Dorothy's attempt, over the next year, to answer these questions served to intensify the controversy.

The problem, she charged, was really the failure of Christians to live by their faith, to embrace poverty, to hunger after justice, to lay down their lives in service to their neighbors. How much was said about the atheism of the Communists and how little about the scandal of those churchmen who cried "Lord, Lord," while at the same time denying Christ in His poor. Sadly, she acknowledged the fact that, given the commitments of many wealthy Christians, she might find herself, sometimes, on the side of those who were called enemies of the Church.

If her arguments seem, in retrospect, to romanticize the Castro government, her position would anticipate the crisis of conscience through which the Latin American Church would pass in subsequent decades, leading to the Nicaraguan hierarchy's support for the Sandinist Revolution, the martyrdom of Archbishop Romero in San Salvador, and the declaration by the Latin American bishops in 1979 of the Church's "preferential option for the poor."

Each day there is some new word about Cuba and the revolution going on there, and we have had many letters from our readers asking us to clarify our position. This is extremely difficult to do, since we are religious in our attitude, with a great love for Holy Mother Church; and we are also revolutionaries, in our own fashion.

No matter what we say, I am afraid we will not be able to make ourselves clear. I shall write from my own point of view, from my own experience, which is a long one, among the poor, the workers, organized labor, and throughout a long series of wars, "imperialist wars," class wars, civil wars, race wars. Shall I say that it is almost fifty years of struggle since at fourteen I began to read the class-conscious fiction of Upton Sinclair and Jack London.

A good part of this will probably be written in church, where I'll be groaning and sweating, trying to understand and clarify my ideas to present them so that our 70,00 copies of the paper will be read and understood. I won't say 70,000 readers, since libraries and schools get copies and many read them. Who knows who reads the paper or who will be so influenced by the paper that they will try to see things in the light of the faith, in the light of the history of the Church, and the history of the poor, who are the first children of the Church.

I have not been in Cuba, but I was in Mexico City during the persecution of the Church in the twenties, when the churches had just reopened in 1929. The laws of the state against the Church are still on the books in 1961, though the Church is functioning as normally as it can in our materialist civilization. While I was in Mexico, at the same time the Church was being persecuted and Mexico was being denounced by the Catholic press as Communistic, my friend Tina Medotti was being arrested and other Communists were going into hiding. When I interviewed General Sandino, the Nicaraguan leader who was opposing United States troops in his country, he stated clearly that he was a communist for his own country, not for Russia, that he was a communist because he was for the poor.

It is hard, too, to say that the place of the Catholic Worker is with the poor, and that being there, we are often finding ourselves on the side of the persecutors of the Church. This is a tragic fact. It is hard, too, to be writing from New York, where one is not in danger. It is hard to write this way when I know that were I in Cuba and I heard a mob shouting outside a church for the blood of the priests and worshippers within, I would then be on the side of the "faithful." Of course, persecution is deserved and undeserved. What is more, it is promised us. "The servant is not above his master and if they have persecuted Me they will persecute you also." If we are not being persecuted there is something wrong with us. And this is not having a persecution complex.

One could weep over the tragedy of the denial of Christ in the poor. The Church is the Cross on which Christ is crucified, Guardini has written, and one does not separate Christ from His Cross. Christ has left Himself to us in the bread and wine on the altar; He has left Himself to those who gather together, two and three in His name; He has left Himself to us in the poor: "There I am in the midst of you." Saul was imprisoning and putting to death those who walked in the Way, and Christ cried out on the road to Damascus, "Saul, Saul, why persecutest thou Me?"

Fidel Castro says he is not persecuting Christ, but churchmen who have betrayed Him. He says that he differentiates between Christ and the clergy, the Church and the clergy. He reassures the people that they can administer the sacrament of Baptism themselves, that a marriage is consummated by the act of marriage and is blessed by the priest. The fact that he has to make these things clear to his people shows how deeply religious they are, that they need reassuring. He asked the clergy to remain and to teach when he took over the schools and nationalized Church property. God knows he needs teachers to send out all over the island. But their reply, according to our diocesan press, was that priests and nuns would not teach Communism to their students. And Castro in his turn taunted them with the fact that all they thought of was money and property.

A few months ago I came back from the West Coast, where I saw the hierarchy silent in the face of the slavery and exploitation of the bracero and the agricultural worker. There had been a lettuce strike in the Imperial Valley, where thousands of braceros, imported from Mexico, were harvesting the crop. The Agricultural Workers Organizing Committee and the Packinghouse Worker's Union held meetings at the entrance to the fields urging the workers to come out on strike and not to take the jobs of their brothers. There were many arrests and some of the organizers were put in prison. Some sympathetic priests came to speak at the meetings and were rebuked by their diocesan officials, some of whom even went so far as to say that some Communists masquerading as priests had appeared at the union meetings.

Only a few days after I returned to New York, I was on my way up Second Avenue to go to Nativity Church, in the heart of the slums, where Puerto Ricans are crowded together, where storefront churches abound, and where some of the worst gangs of the city hang out. At night the streets are alive with children. They cannot go to bed until they are ready to drop with exhaustion because the rooms are too crowded. Their parents go out to the hardest and least-paid labor.

A convent built in the slums for twelve nuns at a cost of $85,000. A family of twelve Puerto Ricans living in a two-room tenement apartment. These things should not be. Billions of dollars in buildings, plants, as they have come to be called, including church, school, convent, and rectory, and nothing spent on the family, on youth.

St. Teresa of Avila prayed that before her nuns became rich and lived in fine buildings, the walls would fall upon them and crush them. Yet she accepted money from her brothers who went to the New World to make their fortunes. Those fortunes were made by robbing the native population, enslaving them, even wiping them out completely (after baptizing them and anointing them first, perhaps). Hard not to be cynical, hard not to judge. Father John J. Hugo said that one could go to hell imitating the imperfections of the saints. He also said that we love God as much as the one we love the least. What a hard and painful thing it is to love the exploiter. . . .

So here we have the problem. The education of the people. Fifty percent of Cuba's millions were illiterate. No wonder Castro had to talk for so many hours at a time, giving background and painting a picture of what they were aiming at, for a multitude who could not read. He has pleaded for peaceful coexistence, and he has said that the Church has endured under the Roman Empire, under a feudal system, under monarchies, empires, republics, and democracies. Why cannot she exist under a socialist state? He has asked the priests to remain to be with their people, and a goodly number of Jesuits, God bless them, have elected to remain and do parish work instead of run schools.

The world "socialism" has many meanings. In Russia it is understood as Marxist socialism as opposed to utopian socialism. And "atheism is an integral part of Marxism," according to Lenin. If this is the type of socialism which will be taught in the schools which are springing up all over Cuba, of course we are against it. But there is an atheistic capitalism too, and atheistic materialism, which is more subtle and more deadly. The former editor of *Osservatore Romano* has called attention to this cancer on our social body. Certainly we have kept God out of our own school system here in the United States. What is worst of all is *using* God and religion to bolster up our own greed, our own attachment to property, and putting God and country on an equality.

We are certainly not Marxist socialists, nor do we believe in violent revolution. Yet we do believe that it is better to revolt, to fight, as Castro did with his handful of men, than to do nothing.

We are on the side of the revolution. We believe there must be new concepts of property, and that new concept is not so new. There is a Christian communism, and a Christian capitalism, as Peter Maurin pointed out. We believe in farming communes and cooperatives and will be happy to see how they work out in Cuba. We are in correspondence with friends in Cuba who will send us word as to what is happening in religious circles and in the schools. We have been invited to visit by a young woman who works in the National Library in Havana and we hope sometime we will be able to go. We are happy to hear that all the young people who belong to the Sodality of Our Lady in the United States are praying for Cuba and we, too, join in prayer that the pruning of the mystical vine will enable it to bear much fruit. God bless the priests and people of Cuba. God bless Castro and all those who are seeing Christ in the poor. God bless all those who are seeking the brotherhood of man, because in loving their brothers they love God, even though they deny Him.

We reaffirm our belief in the ultimate victory of good over evil, of love over hatred, and we believe that the trials which beset us in the world today are for the perfecting of our faith, which is more precious than gold.

"Be glad in the Lord, and rejoice you just and be jubilant all you upright of heart." Because "all the way to heaven is heaven, for He has said, 'I am the Way.' "

July–August 1961

II

This last month I have been reading a lot of Chekhov, beginning with an article by Thomas Mann in which he quotes Chekhov as saying continually, "Am I not deceiving my readers, in not being able to answer their most important questions?" "No other utterance," writes Mann, "ever had such impact on me; in fact it prompted my close study of Chekhov's biography." That question which Chekhov brings out in all his stories is: "What is to be done? What is life for?" Chekhov's conclusion is that we are here to work, to serve our brothers. He himself was a doctor, and wrote on the side in order to support himself through medical school, and to support also his father, mother, and brothers.

Not to be a parasite, not to live off of others, to earn our own living by a life of service—this answered the question for him. And we have, too, that sureness of an answer: We must try to make that kind of a society in which it is easier for people to be good.

Man needs work, the opportunity to work, the tools, the strength, the will to work. And when we see Castro dealing with the problem of unemployment and poverty and illiteracy, we can only say, "We will see this good in him, that which is of God in every man," and we will pray for him and for his country daily.

I once heard Bishop Sheen tell the story of the two sons in the Gospel, a story which Jesus himself told. There were two sons and the Father told them both to go out and do certain tasks. The one son said, "I will," and then failed to do the work assigned him. The other said, "I won't," and yet went away and did the Father's will. And which of the two sons found favor with the Father?

Marjorie Hughes was reminded of the parable in the Gospel of the man born blind who answered his questioners, after he had been hectored and badgered by men who said, " 'Give glory to God. We ourselves know that this man is a sinner.' He therefore said, 'Whether he is a sinner, I do not know. One thing I do know, that whereas I was blind, now I see.' "

The Cuban people are in that state now, and so are the poor and oppressed of all of Latin America. One thing they know, and that is that work and schooling, land and bread are being provided, and that the Colossus whom they feared and hated, the Yankee of the North, has been defied.

We are not going to win the masses to Christianity until we live it.

December 1961

III

Last month the National Council of Catholic Men, with the consent of the Bishops of the United States, was making a documentary on the Catholic Worker movement. One of the questions asked of a group of the editors was: "Do you agree with everything that is written in *The Catholic Worker?*" As I remember it, all of them answered "No," and I would have given the same answer myself, if I had been asked.

Of course we are not in agreement with the most basic and fundamental point of view expressed by our friend Mario Gonzales in his letter on

Cuba.* We are not Marxist-Leninists. At the same time we admit to being fascinated by the lives of both Marx and Lenin. To be interested in a Garibaldi, a Napoleon, a Castro, is to be interested in men who have made and are making history, and to be inspired furthermore by their zeal, their study, their hard labors, and to say again and again that until we ourselves as followers of Christ abjure the use of war as a means of achieving justice and truth, we Catholics are going to get nowhere in criticizing men who are using war to change the social order. Too often, as Cardinal Mundelein once said, we will find ourselves on the wrong side.

We agree, of course, with the letter's utter condemnation of the Cuban invasion of a year ago, and the deception of the American people by both President Kennedy and Adlai Stevenson, who had too much conscience and not enough ruthlessness to be all-out villains and make a thorough job of it. So it failed, as it was bound to fail in the long run even if it had been successful at once. There are all manner of ways of resisting the enemy in an occupied country, and I am not talking about sabotage and destruction either. I am talking about the resistance the Christian ought to give, to be trained to give, with nonviolence, with Christian love.

What if men are stripped of their goods? "If a man takes your cloak give your coat too." It is good to be compelled to practice poverty (not destitution), which is the ideal of the Christian life and most in conformity with the life of Jesus Christ. There is many a young priest throughout the world, and old ones, too, caught in the System, going along with building laws, state requirements, involved with building operations, financing, interest, debts—wearing their lives away building ever bigger buildings and institutions while the institutions of the family and the poor are left to the state to care for. There is too little personal contact with the poor.

Helen C. White's book *To the End of the World* is about the French Revolution, but she confessed to me that she wrote it for our time. In that book there were priests and bishops who fled to other countries and tried to stir up armed intervention. And there were those who stayed, who went to prison. The head of the Sulpicians sat in jail and said, "Now I have the time to study St. Thomas!"

In our own day the persecution in Mexico was overcome by nonviolence

*Mario Gonzales, a young Cuban intellectual, wrote several letters to *The Catholic Worker* expressing his enthusiasm for the revolution. In one letter he wondered what Dorothy Day would do if she were in Cuba. "Some plutocratic servants feel that she would be in jail, but I think she might be working in some cooperative or helping the bearded rebels teach the socialist morality of generosity and sacrifice."

and civil disobedience. The Church cannot be destroyed, the gates of hell cannot prevail against it. At the same time we recognize the fact that in England the Catholic religion was wiped out so that only a remnant remained. All the bishops but one went with the state at that time.

Over and over again we hear that such techniques as nonviolence, voluntary poverty, suffering, prayer, and fasting are too heroic weapons to expect the laity to use. And yet in our time they are *compelled* to use them, and without the training and preparation necessary for such heroism. In the life of the family heroic virtue is expected, in accepting from the hand of God each child sent or accepting continence or celibacy within marriage. The teaching of the Church in regard to marriage and its indissolubility demands over and over again heroic sanctity, and in both cases without the help of the teaching of voluntary poverty and the mutual aid which maternity guilds and credit unions in the parish could give.

Mario Gonzales writes that parochial schools are all closed and the clergy have no newspapers and magazines in which to express themselves.

To speak frankly, this is a wonderful opportunity for the Catholic press to practice the silence of the Trappist, using another spiritual weapon. Baron von Hügel, a great Catholic layman and theologian, said once that he was in danger of losing his faith if he read the diocesan press. I can understand such a remark when I read some of the hymns of hate and the Hearst-like editorials in some of the papers.

What has not been done voluntarily has now been done with the revolution, by force of arms, by confiscation, though the Castro regime has offered to pay, over the years, for the property nationalized. (Little attention has been paid to such offers.)

I must assure Mario Gonzales that were I in Cuba I would not be teaching "socialist morality of generosity and sacrifice," but would certainly try to speak always in terms of the generosity and sacrifice of Jesus Christ, our Brother and our God.

As for the bitterness of soul expressed by Mario, I confess that I, too, have felt that bitterness, but at the same time felt self-judged. I, too, am immersed in comforts, in luxury even, with enough food to eat, a roof over my head, even the means to travel, thanks to people who pay my way. I know that people look at me and judge me with the same harshness as the clergy are judged. "How hard it is to be what you want the other fellow to be," as Peter Maurin used to comment when criticisms were hurled about.

I must confess that righteous wrath as well as any kind of wrath wearies me. Rebellion, too, I find exhausting. To grow in love, to rejoice, to be happy and thankful even, that we are living in such parlous times and not just benefiting unwittingly by the toil and suffering of others—rejoicing even that there is every sign that we are going to be given a chance to expiate here and now for our sins of omission and commission—and so to help the revolution and convert the revolutionaries. This is a dream worth dreaming, and the only kind of vision powerful enough to stand side by side with the Marxism-Leninism which, with its vision, is working out in our day the Legend of the Grand Inquisitor.

July–August 1962

IV

So now I am going to take our readers with me to Cuba, those who wish to read about it, even those who read with doubts as to whether I am going to be truthful, or see the whole picture. I'm afraid there will be plenty of readers who will say I am only going to see what "they" wish me to see. Others will say I am only going to see what I myself wish to see.

I have been thinking about this, because I do wish to be truthful. But the trouble is, if you have only managed to survive the filth, the misery, the destitution of our American skid rows by seeing Christ in the people thereon, you've got yourself pretty well trained to find the good, to find concordances, to find that which is of God in everyone. The trouble is that our country has severed relations with Cuba, a country the size of Pennsylvania, ninety miles from Florida. I am afraid that I can only look upon this original breach of friendly relations as a cold war over possessions. When the revolution, which we cheered at first, turned out to be very radical, getting to the roots of the troubles of our day, and when a start was made to build a new social order, then the trouble began. The history of it is in all our journals, the history of the past as well as the present.

The fact of the matter is that Cuba is now a socialist republic, and we are supposed to have no relations with her. To get permission to visit Cuba I wrote to the State Department and also to the Czechoslovakian Embassy, which is representing Cuba in Washington. If I wish to be in touch with my own country in Cuba, I must go to the Swiss Embassy there.

To get back to my initial paragraphs and amplify them—of course I am going to see what I want to see, and that is the farming communes, whether they are state farms or collectives. I want to see how far they have gotten in diversified farming. I want to see how the family fits into the new economy, what the school situation is, what the Church is permitted to do in giving religious instruction, whether any new churches are being built in the country districts or on the new collectives. I want to see a country where there is no unemployment, where a boy or a man can get a job at any age, when he wants it, at some socially useful work. "There is nothing better for a man than to rejoice in his work." (Ecclesiastes)

Of course I know that the island is an armed camp, that all the people make up the militia. It is too late now to talk of nonviolence, with one invasion behind them and threats of others ahead. And according to traditional Catholic teaching, the only kind Fidel Castro ever had, the good Catholic is also the good soldier.

Several of our old editors have accused us of giving up our pacifism. What nonsense. We are as unalterably opposed to armed resistance and armed revolt from the admittedly intolerable conditions all through Latin America as we ever were. We are against capital punishment, whether it takes place in our own country or in Russia or Cuba. We are against mass imprisonments, whether it is of delinquents or counterrevolutionaries.

No one expects that Fidel will become another Martin of Tours or Ignatius and lay down his arms. But we pray the grace of God will grow in him and that with a better social order, grace will build on the natural good, and the Church will be free to function, giving us the Sacraments and the preaching and teaching of the Man of Peace, Jesus.

An assignment like this is interesting, but also presents the greatest difficulties. I am most of all interested in the religious life of the people and so must not be on the side of a regime that favors the extirpation of religion. On the other hand, when that regime is bending all its efforts to make a good life for the people, one cannot help but be in favor of the measures taken.

The motive is love of neighbor, and we are commanded to love our neighbor. If religion has so neglected the needs of the poor and of the great mass of workers and permitted them to live in the most horrible destitution while comforting them with the solace of the promise of a life after death when all tears shall be wiped away, then that religion is suspect. Who would believe such comforters of Job? On the other hand, if those professing religion share the life of the poor and work to better their lot and risk their lives as revolutionists do, then there is a ring of truth about the promises of the glory to come. The Cross is followed by the Resurrection.

Orwell said that one of the tragedies of the present day was the loss of a sense of personal immortality. But are those to be believed who see their brothers in need and do not open their hearts, their doors, their purses to them? Whatever we have over and above what we need belongs to the poor, we have been told again and again by the Fathers of the Church and the saints, up to the very present day. But how much does a man need to cultivate the talents God has given him? To raise his family and educate them and to take care of his older ones? How much land does a man need?

September 1962

V

Dorothy embarked for Cuba on September 5, 1962. Her brief trip resulted in several long articles in which she offered a generally positive account of the Cuban government's efforts in the areas of education, health, housing, and employment. Throughout her travels she maintained her practice of receiving daily Communion, and made a deliberate effort to seek out the views of Catholics.

Among the Catholics I met there was complete freedom of speech, and there was criticism as well as praise of the regime. It was in the field of education that parents were in a quandary. "How can we let our children go to schools where Marxism-Leninism is taught?"

I spoke to many Catholics and it was hard to answer such a question. I could only say as Father Ignacio Biain, a Franciscan, said: "Have more faith in Divine Providence." And in one's own courage, in the effectiveness of prayer to build up courage. I told them of our own American Negro families who brought their little children with heroic courage through lines and mobs of jeering, insulting, and threatening whites in an effort to integrate the schools, and urged them to build up that same courage in their own children. And to find concordances, as our own Holy Father has urged, rather than to seek out heresies; to work as far as one could with the revolution, and always to be ready to give a reason for the faith that is in one.

There is the singing of the *Internationale,* for instance, most of whose verses can be joined in with enthusiasm. "Arise, poor of the world—on your feet, slaves without bread—and let us shout all together—All united, Long live the International. . . Let us remove all shackles that tie humanity—Let us change the face of the earth, burying the bourgeois empire." The third verse is the one where I would recommend that children sit down. It is: "No more Supreme Saviours, no Caesar, no bourgeois, no God. We ourselves have our own redemption." There are three more verses.

This is the rough translation given to me by a Catholic mother, who said wistfully, "We could well sing the other verses. We ourselves have been ashamed of our position in the face of poverty and ignorance, of not having done more about it."

Father Matteo once said that the churches could all remain open in a persecution of the Church, provided that religion was strong in the home. Groups should keep meeting together to discuss not their oppositions with the revolution, but Scripture, social justice, theology. The main thing was to have courage, to stand fast in one's faith, and find out every way in which one could lawfully participate.

One example of courage was that of a young family man, a lawyer, who was asked by the security police on his block to work with them in prosecuting "counterrevolutionaries," a request which he refused. To be put in the position of a spy on people he might know, and to inform and be a party to their prosecution—this he could not do. When later he himself was persecuted by a woman member of the security police, he complained to the authorities, perhaps to Castro himself, and was upheld. The persecutions ceased and he attended block meetings, continued his work in the teaching field, and gave an example of a man of principle.

In Santiago de Cuba I visited the shrine of Our Lady of Cobre, an hour up in the mountains in the little mining town of Cobre (copper), and there I found a Sister Mercedes, one of the Social Service Sisters, who was as serene and calm as though it were the most natural thing in the world to live under a Marxist-Leninist government. The Sisters ran a guest house, and it would have been a lovely place to stay and make a retreat. Retreats were still going on in Havana. The priests at the shrine were still offering Mass each day.

I talked with one young woman, a devout Catholic, who up to the time of the March 13 speech* had been most fearful about the revolution and its attitude toward religion. She wears a medal of the Blessed Virgin, and is a good and conscientious worker in the field of education, which Fidel considers the most important branch of the revolution. But she feels the pressures of her fellow Catholics who tell her she is cooperating with Communism by working for the government. This woman told me that there are four churches open in her city, not a large one, that at the cathedral of the province there are four Masses and at the other churches three and two a day, that in the eastern part of the state of Matanzas there are ten Canadian priests and twelve Sisters teaching catechism.

---

*A speech by Castro on March 13, 1962, seeming to guarantee freedom of religion, was received hopefully by Cuban Catholics.

But if they do not teach together with their catechism an acceptance of voluntary poverty, manual labor, a devotion to the common good, the works of mercy as worked out by the government in housing, agriculture, clothing factories, hospital work, care of children in nurseries, harvesting of crops, studying to become literate and to cultivate their talents, catechism becomes principle divorced from practice.

Man is a creature of body and soul, and he must work to live, he must work to be co-creator with God, taking raw materials and producing for human needs. He becomes God-like, he is divinized not only by the Sacrament but by his work, in which he imitates his Creator, in which he is truly "putting on Christ and putting off the old man." He must be taught those words of Jesus to St. Catherine of Siena, "I have left Myself in the midst of you, so that what you cannot do for Me, you can do for those around you."

November 1962

V I

One of our readers, and a very dear friend, asked me after I came home, "Is there no criticism you can make about Cuba? Is everything so wonderful there, can't you find anything against it?"

Of course one could find plenty wrong. It is a country racked by war, boycotted by its nearest neighbor, and without many of the amenities of life. I could tell of water supplies breaking down, pumps not functioning in the big apartment houses, so that the tenants are forced to carry water from the first floor to fill the tanks of their toilets, the bathtubs, and many pails for cooking. . . .

Life is not easy in Cuba these days and the people are undergoing great hardships in every way. They are getting enough food to survive, but certainly not the kind of food they wish. They are just getting by, and undoubtedly food shortages make tempers short too. There is a great shortage of the professional classes, teachers, doctors, and so on. There is a shortage of drugs necessary to save lives.

But just the same, there are widespread efforts toward health and education and work for all, and the crisis has united the people so that there are not the problems of delinquency, and violence, drug and drink addiction, lack of work for young and old.

Before the revolution, less than three-tenths of one percent of the population was Communist. Those who were, were highly trained and few.

They had not been in favor of the Castro revolution, but when it succeeded they threw themselves into the work of building up the country, with the help, of course, of their fellow Communists in the U.S.S.R. and other socialist countries. What help the United States withheld was given them by others. So now Cuba is the first socialist state in the Western Hemisphere. What to do about it? How to live with it? How to learn from it?

As I came through Mexico, spending ten days there on the way home, I spoke to the Maryknoll nuns in Mexico City, who are still forbidden to wear their own garb, as are all nuns, and so wear plain skirts and blouses like laywomen. They told me that no religion is permitted in the Mexican schools where they teach, no crucifix is allowed in the schoolroom, and all religious instruction must be given outside of class, as in our own public school system. But in addition they have government textbooks which they are forced to use, and there is one in particular which they have protested. It is only now, this year, that they have been permitted to teach from their own text (together with the text of the government, which must also be used). It seems to me the Catholics in Cuba must learn from the Catholics in Mexico how to deal with and survive in a godless state and show the same courage the Catholics in Mexico have shown. The Catholic, the Christian, must outdo in zeal, in self-sacrifice, in dedication, in service for the common good those who are following the teachings of Marxism-Leninism. So let us learn our lessons, and continue the struggle with that joy which Léon Bloy says is the sure sign of the life of God in the soul.

December 1962

We Go on Record

As one method of withholding consent from the State's preparation for war, the Catholic Worker has always urged nonpayment of federal income tax. Dorothy's position had been well known to the government since at least the late 1950's, when she was summoned by the Internal Revenue Service to give an accounting. After submitting patiently to a long discourse on personal responsibility and the Fathers of the Church, a young I.R.S. employee asked Dorothy to estimate her personal income for the previous ten years. "I'll tell you what," she is reported to have answered. "You estimate my income for the past ten years, and you estimate what I owe you, and I won't pay it! How's that?"

The subject was not raised again until 1972, when a suit from the Internal Revenue Service threatened to put the Catholic Worker out on the street. Refusing to contest the issue in court, Dorothy trusted instead in her "spiritual weapons." Girded with prayer, she rose with confidence to meet the challenge head on.

The Catholic Worker has received a letter from the Internal Revenue Service stating that we owe them $296,359 in fines, penalties, and unpaid income tax for the last six years. As the matter stands right now, there might be a legal battle with delays and postponements which may remind us of Dickens' *Bleak House*. Or, since we will not set up a defense committee to campaign for funds, it may terminate swiftly in the confiscation of our property and our bank account (never very large). Our farm at Tivoli and the First Street house could be put up for sale by government agents and our C.W. family evicted.

Perhaps no one here at St. Joseph's House realizes the situation we are in right now as keenly as I do, having seen so many evictions in the Depression—furniture, clothes, kitchen utensils piled up on the streets by landlords' marshals. The Communists used to demonstrate and forcibly move the belongings of the unfortunate people back into the tenements, but our Catholic Worker staff, a handful of us, begged money and rented other apartments for eight to fifteen dollars a month and moved the evicted families there. What a job! It exhausts me to think of it.

I can only trust that this crisis will pass. Just as we believe that God, our Father, has care of us, I am sure that some way will be found either to avert the disaster or for us to continue to care for our old, sick, helpless, hungry, and homeless if it happens.

One of the most costly protests against war, in terms of long-enduring personal sacrifice, is to refuse to pay federal income taxes which go for war. The late Ammon Hennacy, one of our editors, was a prime example of this. He earned his living at agricultural labor, always living on a poverty level so as not to be subject to taxes, though he filed returns. Another of our editors, Karl Meyer, recently spent ten months in jail for what the I.R.S. called fraudulent claims of exemption for dependents. He ran the C.W. House of Hospitality in Chicago for many years, working to earn the money to support the house and his wife and children. Erosanna Robinson, a social worker in Chicago, refused to file returns and was sentenced to a year in prison. While in prison she fasted and was forcibly fed. It will be seen that tax refusal is a serious protest. Wars will cease when we refuse to pay for them (to adapt a slogan of the War Resisters International).

The C.W. has never paid salaries. Everyone gets board, room, and clothes (tuition, recreation included, as the C.W. is in a way a school of living). So we do not need to pay federal income taxes. Of course, there are hidden taxes we all pay. Nothing is ever clear-cut or well defined. We protest in any way we can, according to our responsibilities and temperaments.

(I remember Ammon, a most consistent, brave, and responsible person, saying to one young man, "For the love of the Lord, get a job and quit worrying about taxes. You need to learn how to earn your own living. That is most important for you.")

We have to accept with humility the fact that we cannot share the destitution of those around us, and that our protests are incomplete. Perhaps the most complete protest is to be in jail, to accept jail, never to give bail or defend ourselves.

In the fifties, Ammon, Charles McCormack (our business manager at the C.W.), and I were summoned to the offices of the I.R.S. in New York to answer questions (under oath) as to our finances. I remember I was asked what happened to the royalties from my books, money from speaking engagements, etc. I could only report that such monies received were deposited in the C.W. account. As for clothes, we wore what came in; my sister was generous to me—shoes, for instance.

Our accounts are kept in this way: Contributions, donations, subscriptions that come in daily are entered in one book. The large checkbook tells of bills paid, of disbursements. Since we send out an appeal once or twice a year, we have to file with our state capital, pay a small fee, and give an account of monies received and how they were spent. We always comply with this state regulation because it is local—regional. We know such a requirement is to protect the public from fraudulent appeals and we feel our lives are open books— our work is obvious. And of course our pacifism has always been obvious—a great ideal of nonviolence to be worked toward.

Christ commanded His followers to perform what Christians have come to call the Works of Mercy: feeding the hungry, giving drink to the thirsty, clothing the naked, sheltering the harborless, visiting the sick and the prisoner, and burying the dead. Surely a simple program for direct action, and one enjoined on all of us. Not just for impersonal "poverty programs," government-funded agencies, but help given from the heart at a personal sacrifice. And how opposite a program this is to the works of war which starve people by embargoes, lay waste the land, destroy homes, wipe out populations, mutilate and condemn millions more to confinement in hospitals and prisons.

On another level there is a principle laid down, much in line with common sense and with the original American ideal, that governments should never do what small bodies can accomplish: unions, credit unions, cooperatives, St. Vincent de Paul Societies. Peter Maurin's anarchism was on one level based on this principle of subsidiarity, and on a higher level on that scene at the Last Supper where Christ washed the feet of His Apostles. He came to serve, to show the new Way, the way of the powerless. In the face of Empire, the Way of Love.

And here in small groups we are trying to talk of these things in the midst of the most powerful country in the world, during wartime, with the imminent threat of being crushed by this government, all because of principle, a principle so small and so important! It is not only that we must follow our conscience in opposing the government in war. We believe also that the government has no right to legislate as to who can or who are to perform the Works of Mercy. Only accredited agencies have the status of tax-exempt institutions. After their application has been filed, and after investigation and long delays, clarifications, intercession, and urgings by lawyers—often an expensive and long-drawn-out procedure—this tax-exempt status is granted.

As personalists, as an unincorporated group, we will not apply for this "privilege." We have explained to our donors many times that they risk being taxed on the gifts they send us, and a few (I can only think of two right now) have turned away from us. God raises up for us many a Habakkuk to bring his pottage to us when we are in the lion's den, or about to be, like Daniel of old.

Frankly, we do not know if it is because the government considers us a danger and threat that we are faced by this crisis. I beg the prayers of all our readers, whether they are sympathetic to us or not. I'm sure that many will think me a fool indeed, almost criminally negligent, for not taking more care to safeguard, not just the bank account, but the welfare of all the lame, halt, and blind who come to us.

Our refusal to apply for exemption status in our practice of the Works of Mercy is part of our protest against war and the present social "order" which brings on wars today.

May 1972

II

Last month, I wrote of the crisis we found ourselves in when we received a letter from the Internal Revenue Service stating that we owe them $296,359 in fines and penalties and unpaid income tax for the years 1966 through 1970. This was a very impressive bill, and we wondered what it would be if they started figuring out what they thought we owed them for the years from 1933, when we started, up to 1966!

There is no real news at the moment, nor will there be until I appear before a federal judge on July 3 to explain why the C.W. refuses to pay taxes, or to "structure itself" so as to be exempt from taxes. We are afraid of that word "structure." We refuse to become a "corporation."

Perhaps it is a *structure* which makes for such a scandal as the story which appeared in the press all over the country of a famous charity for children which had millions of dollars in reserve, money which could have been used either for expansions in the work or in working to bring about conditions in housing and education which would make so much "charity" unnecessary. "Charity" becomes a word which sticks in the gullet and makes one cry out for justice!

We repeat—we do not intend to "incorporate" the Catholic Worker movement. We intend to continue our emphasis on personal responsibility, an emphasis we were taught from the beginning by Peter Maurin.

I would like to be able to say to our readers, our family (as I like to think of them), that I am not at all worried about all this mishmash and the outcome. But of course one becomes intimidated in the awesome presence of a judge—not to speak of stenographers, and swearing "to tell the truth, the whole truth and nothing but the truth, so help me, God," and maybe not being allowed to finish a sentence or to explain. Anyone who writes as much as I do is not a "woman of few words." The older I get, the more I have to study and learn—there is no end to it. Of course, the Gospel tells us that when we are called before judges we should not worry about how to answer, what to say. I'll have to do a good deal of praying, doing what in the quaint terminology of the Church was formerly called "making acts of adoration, contrition, thanksgiving, and supplication." A.C.T.S. Easy to remember. Easy to do in those crises in which every family, without exception, finds itself.

O God, make haste to help me. Hear my prayer. Let my cry come unto Thee.

Besides praying, it is also good to distract the mind. In Tolstoy's *War and Peace,* which I read again recently (part of the distraction), Nicolai advises the fearful sixteen-year-old soldier never to think of the battle ahead, or of previous fears.

Actually our tax situation and the threats which hang over us involve nowhere near as much suffering and heartbreak as the moral, physical, and mental illnesses of so many who are dear to us.

It is then that I turn most truly for solace, for strength to endure, to the Psalms. I may read them without understanding, and mechanically at first, but I do believe they are the Word, and that Scripture, on the one hand, and the Eucharist, the Word made Flesh, on the other, have in them that strength which no power on earth can withstand. One of Ammon Hennacy's favorite quotations was "All things work together for good to those who love God."

As Sonya said at the end of *Uncle Vanya,* "I have faith, Uncle. I have fervent, passionate faith."

June 1972

III

Dear fellow workers in Christ,

Good news! On July 11 we received absolution from the U.S. Government in relation to all our tax troubles. We have related the story of the notice we had received—that we owed the government nearly $300,000 in back income taxes including penalties for "late filing and negligence." The examining officer of the Manhattan District had arrived at these figures through the reports we had obediently made to Albany on our appeals for funds. We had accepted this compromise with our local state because we are decentralists (in addition to being pacifists). When we first thought about federal income taxes, most of which go for war or "defense," we simplistically considered ourselves exempt because we had no income; no salaries are paid at the Catholic Worker, nor ever have been since we started in 1933.

But with growing tax resistance throughout the United States the government has become concerned. Telephone calls and official visits made us realize that trouble was impending.

Now we are happy to report the outcome. In a conference in late June with William T. Hunter, litigation attorney from the Department of Justice, one of the Assistant Attorneys General of the United States, we reached a verbal settlement couched in more human and satisfactory terms than the notice we later received.

"They" were willing to recognize our undoubtedly religious convictions in our conflict with the state, and were going to drop any proceedings against us. They had examined back issues of *The Catholic Worker,* they had noted the support we had from the press (the editorials of the *New York Times* and the *New York Post*), and had come to this conclusion that ours was a religious conviction. They had come to the further conclusion that it was not necessary that the federal government seek any other kind of a "conviction" against us.

The conference took place in a law office in Manhattan, 9:30 of a Monday morning. John Coster, our lawyer, Mr. Hunter and Ed Forand, Walter Kerell, Patrick Jordan, Ruth Collins, and I attended. There were no hostilities expressed. As peacemakers we must have love and respect for each individual we come in contact with. Our struggle is with principalities and powers. We cannot ever be too complacent about our own uncompromising positions because we know that in our own way we, too, make compromises. (For instance, in having a second-class mailing privilege from the government we accept a subsidy, just as Mr. Eastland does in Mississippi!)

It was Jesus who said that the worst enemies were those of our own household, and we are all part of this country, citizens of the United States, and share in its guilt.

I think Mr. Hunter (our opponent) shared with us the conviction that you could not kill an idea, and that we would continue to express ourselves and try to live the Catholic Worker positions as best we could, no matter what steps were taken against us by government. To *resist* and to *survive*— these are the growing convictions amongst the best of our youth. Harder for the aged and ill, but many of those among us have had a background of practice through the Depression, unemployment, and war.

It was a good confrontation we had for those three or four hours with the lawyers. We left to celebrate with a lunch at the Automat before we returned to office and work.

Yes, we would survive, I thought to myself, even if the paper were eventually suppressed and we had to turn to leafleting, as we are doing now each Monday against the I.B.M. Wall Street offices, trying to reach the consciences of all those participating in the hideous and cowardly war we are waging in Vietnam.

July–August 1972

ON PILGRIMAGE: TWENTY YEARS

The selections in this chapter are excerpted from Dorothy Day's regular column in *The Catholic Worker*.

The Fear of Our Enemies

Last week, I stayed awake until 4 a.m. after reading too stimulating an article by Thomas Merton, "The Pasternak Affair in Perspective." In it, Merton not only analyzes the Communist concept of man, but goes on to talk of the attitudes of the West. The concluding paragraphs of the article were what caused my happy sleeplessness. Merton writes:

> [Pasternak] is just as likely to be regarded as a dangerous writer in the West as he is in the East. He is saying that political and social structures as we understand them are things of the past, and that the crisis through which we are now passing is nothing but the full and inescapable manifestation of their falsity. For twenty centuries we have called ourselves Christians, without even beginning to understand one-tenth of the Gospel. We have been taking Caesar for God and God for Caesar. Now that "charity is growing cold" and we stand facing the smoky dawn of an apocalyptic era, Pasternak reminds us that there is only one source of truth, but that it is not sufficient to know the source is there—we must go and drink from it, as he has done.
>
> Do we have the courage to do so? For obviously, if we consider what Pasternak is saying, doing, and undergoing, to read the Gospel with eyes wide open may be a perilous thing!

It was not only Merton's article but also Anne Fremantle's *Desert Calling*, her biography of Charles de Foucauld, that kept me awake. It is a wonderful book, and the more I read it, the more I get from it. How utterly and completely Brother Charles tried to follow in the footsteps of Jesus, and how little we ourselves do to rejoice in mockery and contempt and misunderstanding. As a matter of fact, how fearful most of us are! Just a few Sundays ago, Judith Gregory and I were coming from eleven o'clock

Mass at our parish church, St. Patrick's old cathedral on Mott Street, and as we walked down Mulberry Street we suddenly felt objects whizzing past our ears. I thought it was snowballs thrown by the small boys, because we had had snow the week before and there was still a little in the corners of buildings. But as I turned, another missile flew past and Judith said, "Those are meant for us, all right." She went to investigate the broken mass where it had struck against a garage door, and found it to be bits of hard-boiled egg. Two had been flung at us as we passed, and I was literally afraid to turn and look, for fear some would hit me in the face. I should have been delighted, as Charles de Foucauld was when he was pelted in the streets of Nazareth, but my feeling was one of fear, just as it was when I was shot at at Koinonia.* It was fear in the flesh, the fear of the flesh, and I am glad I have it because it helps me to understand the fear that is eating at the hearts of people in the world today. No one is safe. We are no longer protected by oceans separating us from the rest of the warring world. Yesterday the Russians fired a rocket 7,760 miles into the central Pacific which fell less than one and a quarter miles from its calculated target. The U.S. Defense Department confirmed the shot's accuracy.

Anywhere, at any time, we can be reached. Leaders of governments say that none but a madman would launch a war today. But there are madmen, human senses are faulty, men may think they see and hear approaching planes, bombs, rockets, and the button may be pushed to set off a counter-offensive. Everything depends on the human element.

There are all kinds of fear, and I certainly pray to be delivered from the fear of my brother, I pray to grow in the love that casts out fear. To grow in love of God and man, and to live by this charity, that is the problem. We must love our enemy, not because we fear war but because God loves him.

Mike Wallace asked me that question: Does God love murderers, does He love a Hitler, a Stalin? I could only say, "God loves all men, and all men are brothers."

There is so little time on a broadcast, in an interview, so little time to answer or to think. I could have said, "Christ loved those who crucified Him. St. Stephen loved those who stoned him to death. St. Paul was a murderer. We are all murderers."

---

*Koinonia, an interracial Christian community in Americus, Georgia, was subjected, through-out the fifties, to intense segregationist violence. In April 1957, Dorothy traveled to Koinonia to lend her support. On Easter Eve, while she and another member of the community did sentry duty at the entrance gate, their parked station wagon was suddenly peppered by a shotgun blast, fired from a passing car. No one was injured in the attack.

Deane Mowrer and I knelt by the side of women who were charged with murder and who were awaiting trial, the last time we were in prison in New York, put in the corridor with those awaiting trial, because we would not give bail. There were four homicide cases on that corridor: one a very young girl, one a somber, dark Negro who, it was said, had hired someone to kill her husband, and, just opposite us, a sad Puerto Rican woman nearly forty, mother of many children, who had been beaten by a drunken husband so many times that on the last occasion as he held her choking over the kitchen table, she reached behind her for a knife and struck at him any place she could so that he would release his strangle grip upon her throat. How many of us would not do the same? Thank God for our guardian angels, thank God for all the evil we are delivered from. And oh, how close we need to be in pity and in love to such a woman, thrown into jail, separated from her children for many months.

But of course Mike Wallace was not talking of such murderers, of whom we may feel no fear. He was speaking of the Hitlers and the Stalins and of such men as those accused of putting bombs in airplanes to collect insurance.

What to do about them? I remember asking Father Roy how God could love a man who came home and beat up his wife and children in a drunken rage (there was one such in our midst), and Father Roy shook his head sadly and said, "God loves only Jesus, God sees only Jesus." A hard lesson to take, to see Jesus in another, in the prodigal son, or members of a lynch mob. Have we begun to be Christians?

February 1960

A Family

No one has given a realistic description of our new headquarters, St. Joseph's House at 175 Chrystie Street, and everyone who comes there is shocked at how miserable our surroundings are. If the loft on Spring Street was inadequate and dingy, though spacious, the new site is dingier and smaller. There is a cellar, half of which the landlord uses. When the cellar door fell in, we paid for a new one, seventy-five dollars, so he allows us to use the back of the cellar. Our rent is $275 a month. The ground floor is cemented, and impossible to keep clean with hundreds of people tramping in and out each day. We cannot seat more than twenty at a time and the others sit on benches toward the front of the store, or go up the one short flight to the "sitting room" floor where the clothing rooms are. On the third floor are offices, and the floors slant, and every time anyone walks across the room the boards shake. From the interstices of the metal ceiling, the rain pours in, so that on rainy days we have had three large metal wastepaper baskets filling up with water over and over again. Tarring the roof around the skylight does not seem to have helped much.

Even with all this, given the money for materials, a few skilled workers could effect a change, but the clutter and filth would remain the same. It is not just books and papers and overflow of desks all over the place. All Catholic Workers feel their desk is their home, and all have demanded one, save Peter Maurin alone, who made his knees his desk, and his pockets his bookcases.

The filth comes from a packrat we have with us, a most lovable guy whom we have known for many years and who is evicted over and over and always returns with more and more clutter, boxes upon boxes of trash, garbage, old papers, books, bits of furniture, piled in every corner, hallway, toilet, cellar, and roof. He rooms in an apartment with two other men, and he has surrounded himself there also in the same way with this inconceivable quantity of trash which it is impossible to get him to move without all the moral and physical force one can command. And if one is anarchist-pacifist to the unreasonable degree that so many around the Catholic Worker are, an Augean stable is the result of this respect for man's freedom.

Authority and freedom, reason and faith, personalism and communitarianism—all these were the subjects of Peter Maurin's discussion. But if you asked him what to do about Kichi Harada or Roy Bug, he would give you a few essays on the Thomistic Doctrine of the Common Good to read and digest, to help you solve your problems and come to your own decision. Peter having died in 1949, such problems are left for me to solve when I return home from a trip.

So far Hercules has not arrived to solve this problem for us. The thing to do is hire a truck, find out if we can bring it down to the river to load on one of the garbage barges to be taken off to some far-off dump where it may be used as fill, or burned, or both. We have lost some beautiful swampland, once a game preserve where even wild orchids grew, by such city efficiency. But this line of thought would lead one to give up, wander away, and become a desert father, and we are a family, which includes Roy Bug, and must stick together. The only thing is to be ruthless and energetic and start afresh. Is there anyone ruthless and energetic around the C.W.?

But this outward show of destitution is nothing compared to the destitution suffered by those whose plumbing is out of repair, whose toilets overflow, who have no sixty dollars to call a Roto-Rooter to unstop the pipes and drains.

And of course there are always the problems of lice and dirt in slum tenements with neither bath nor shower. Such is our life in the city, and it is a gigantic effort for the destitute to try to live decently, a Herculean effort.

The Catholic Worker headquarters remains in the city because our work is here, and it is where people can find us. Visitors abound to the extent that it is hard to get work done. Mail piles up that needs to be answered, and there are meetings each Friday night. There is a mysterious attraction in the great city for the young. So we remain in the cities, the gutter sweepers of the diocese, working yet beggars, destitute yet possessing all things; happy because today the sun shines, there is a symphony on the radio, children are playing on the streets, there is a park across the way and a church around the corner where we receive our daily Bread.

June 1961

Snowed In

December 25: "The brightness of Your glory has made itself manifest to the eyes of our mind by the mystery of the Word made flesh, and we are drawn to the love of things unseen through Him whom we acknowledge as God, now seen by men." (From the Preface in the Christmas Mass.)

"What have I on earth but Thee and what do I desire in heaven beside Thee?"

It is joy that brought me to the faith, joy at the birth of my child, thirty-five years go, and that joy is constantly renewed as I daily receive Our Lord at Mass. At first, I thought that following the prayers of the Mass would become monotonous and something for the priest to continue day after day, and that was why people were silent and bookless. A Quaker going to Mass with me once said, "Now I know what the Mass is—it is a meditation." But it is an act, a sacrifice, attended by prayers, and these prayers repeated daily, of adoration, contrition, thanksgiving, supplication, are ever there. One or another emotion may predominate, but the act performed evokes the feeling of "performing the work of our salvation."

December 28. Vermont (Tamar's farm). Feast of the Holy Innocents. From early morning till late at night the house is riotous—Tamar's nine, and two guests, an eight-year-old and a fifteen-year-old.

Today we are snowed in. "What shall we feed thirteen people for dinner?" Tamar muses, and then remembers the four pounds of ground deer meat which a hunter sent her for holding his stray dog until he returned for it. There are two sacks of potatoes, plenty of squash, pumpkin, turnips, onions, bread, and cake. There are two jars of hard candies, and some apples. All the homemade cider has turned to vinegar.

One can only try to keep the kitchen orderly, and find a quiet corner to read, write, tease or card some wool for a comforter.

A goodly amount of spun silk and a great deal of cotton thread for the loom had come in at Chrystie Street. Tamar wove a silk scarf, and is going to set up the loom in cotton to make some material which she can afterwards dye. Weaving is her "tranquilizer." Knitting generally is mine, though I never get beyond scarves. I have made socks for the children, and once in a while achieved a good pair for an adult. One monstrosity I made which would match nothing and was due to be ripped out was seized by Anne Marie as an amusing gift for a worker priest. I hope by now some friendly soul has reknit it for him.

As I washed and teased wool for the comforter I had finished last month, I thought of God's goodness and the sacramentality of things. . . .

January 1962

War Without Weapons

Danville, Virginia. Before leaving New York last month to fill a speaking invitation here, I was told by Bob Gore, an organizer for CORE, that in all the country the police of Danville were the most terrible. And on July 12 I heard Martin Luther King tell a mass meeting in Danville that he had seen brutal things done by the police elsewhere in the South, "but seldom, if ever, have I heard of actions as vicious and brutal as those done by the police here."

This is what had happened the week before:

A group of demonstrators, which included prominent ministers and their wives, parishioners, and many young ones, were driven by deputized police into an alley between a parking lot and the City Hall and there the fire hoses were turned on them with such force that they were thrown to the pavement and in one case a woman's clothes were ripped off her. Women taking refuge under parked cars were dragged out and beaten with clubs and kicked. Arms were broken by the force of the blows. Men, women, and children were all beaten unmercifully and deliberately. It was fear run riot.

"Deliver me from fear of their fear," I prayed as I listened, using the words of St. Peter which had been part of the Epistle of last Sunday's Mass, thinking of the hysterical fear of guilty whites, fear of the past, of the future.

I had been invited to speak at a mass meeting in the High Street Baptist Church. The meeting began with songs and hymns and the singing was hearty and beautiful. The invocation was surely a crying out to the Lord, a singing and a sobbing of a prayer, rhythmical, so that it became almost a litany. Rev. James Dixon prayed with all his strength.

And then there were the Freedom songs, many of them composed in jail, coming from the heart, from the suffering, from the open bleeding wounds of a people who have known indignity and sorrow for generations.

There were many speakers, but they were brief. William Canada told with complete lack of emotion how he had spent nineteen days in jail. Authorities kept denying he was there; he was sought for by his family in hospitals and there was no knowing where he was until he was released. Despite beatings, he had been put to work in the quarry.

Bob Zellner talked of Moses and how he had led his people out of Egypt and how tired people got of the struggle so that they wanted to go back to bondage; it was forty years before they saw the Promised Land. And he compared the nonviolent struggle of the Negro to the clamorous attack made on the walls of Jericho, which, he reminded them, had come tumbling down.

Claudia Edwards of Arkansas, one of the task force of CORE, urged the mothers to join me in a picket line in the downtown area the next morning.

There were speakers urging registration for the vote, so that next morning forty-seven went to the polls and registered, going together so that they would not be intimidated. There was only one woman, very nervous, to register them, so it took a long time, and many could not join our picket line at the noon hour. The rule is that at first registration one pays not only the year's poll tax but for three years previous, and this added burden keeps many from registering.

I was the main speaker of the evening and I do not know whether I would have had the courage to speak, outsider that I was, had not the singing lightened my own heart, dissolved my own fear, so that I could tell them of the Women's Pilgrimage for Peace and the Pope's encyclical *Pacem in Terris*.

There was no end to what one could say about the encyclical. There was the part where he said, "He who possesses certain rights has likewise the duty to claim those rights as marks of his dignity, while all others have the obligation to acknowledge those rights and respect them."

There was much to quote from Pope John: what he had to say about the rights of conscience; about unjust laws; about the place of women, the part they had to play in the world.

And I told my listeners, too, that after so many years of work in the Peace Movement, I had come to the conclusion that basic to peace was this struggle of the colored for education, job opportunity, health, and recognition as human beings; that while we talked of averting war, we were in the midst of one of the strangest wars in history—the side which had declared the war was using no weapons but those of suffering. They were praying; they were marching; they were doing without (by boycott); they were in a way offering their own flesh, their suffering, their imprisonment, for their brothers. "A new *commandment* [not a counsel] I give to you, that you love each other as I have loved you." And that commandment of Jesus means laying down of life itself for one's brother, colored and white.

It is the Negro who is leading the way, and it is among the Negroes that the ranks of the martyrs are increasing. They are uncounted, unknown, many of them. Medgar Evers leads them, going down as he did with foreknowledge of his doom. He fell, and his brother is taking his place. Others are unknown, unsung heroes. Something is happening in our midst that we do not recognize. We have eyes and see not, ears and hear not. The last are becoming the first. "He hath put down the mighty from their seat and hath exalted the humble."

It is hard to feel that the color of our skin in a way separates us from this mass of people whom we have injured. It is with too little and too late that we are engaging ourselves. But even if it is at the eleventh hour that we are called to serve, we can respond.

We can pray too that we may be "counted worthy to suffer," a fact the Apostles rejoiced over when they put up their nonviolent struggle for the Faith, and were imprisoned and beaten. I felt that I had not been counted worthy when I learned that the Danville police have been imprisoning all the pickets since I left, besides all those who have been engaged in sit-ins. The jails have been filling up. . . .

There is time to talk about these things in prison, in meeting halls, in times of unemployment and tension. We each have our vocation—the thing to do is to answer the call. We each have something to give.

July–August 1963

The Mystery of the Poor

On Holy Thursday, truly a joyful day, I was sitting at the supper table at St. Joseph's House on Chrystie Street and looking around at all the fellow workers and thinking how hopeless it was for us to try to keep up appearances. The walls are painted a warm yellow, the ceiling has been done by generous volunteers, and there are large, brightly colored ikon-like paintings on wood and some colorful banners with texts (now fading out) and the great crucifix brought in by some anonymous friend with the request that we hang it in the room where the breadline eats. (Some well-meaning guest tried to improve on the black iron by gilding it, and I always intend to do something about it and restore its former grim glory.)

I looked around and the general appearance of the place was, as usual, home-like, informal, noisy, and comfortably warm on a cold evening. And yet, looked at with the eyes of a visitor, our place must look dingy indeed, filled as it always is with men and women, some children too, all of whom bear the unmistakable mark of misery and destitution. Aren't we deceiving ourselves, I am sure many of them think, in the work we are doing? What are we accomplishing for them anyway, or for the world or for the common good? "Are these people being rehabilitated?" is the question we get almost daily from visitors or from our readers (who seem to be great letter writers). One priest had his catechism classes write us questions as to our work after they had the assignment in religion class to read my book *The Long Loneliness.* The majority of them asked the same question: "How can you see Christ in people?" And we only say: It is an act of faith, constantly repeated. It is an act of love, resulting from an act of faith. It is an act of hope, that we can awaken these same acts in their hearts, too, with the help of God, and the Works of Mercy, which you, our readers, help us to do, day in and day out over the years.

On Easter Day, on awakening late after the long midnight services in our parish church, I read over the last chapter of the four Gospels and felt that I received great light and understanding with the reading of them. "They have taken the Lord out of His tomb and we do not know where they have laid Him," Mary Magdalene said, and we can say this with her in times of doubt and questioning. How do we know we believe? How do we know we indeed have faith? Because we have seen His hands and His feet in the poor around us. He has shown Himself to us in them. We start by loving them for Him, and we soon love them for themselves, each one a unique person, most special!

In that last glorious chapter of St. Luke, Jesus told His followers, "Why are you so perturbed? Why do questions arise in your minds? Look at My hands and My feet. It is I Myself. Touch Me and see. No ghost has flesh and bones as you can see I have." They were still unconvinced, for it seemed too good to be true. "So He asked them, 'Have you anything to eat?' They offered Him a piece of fish they had cooked which He took and ate before their eyes."

How can I help but think of these things every time I sit down at Chrystie Street or Peter Maurin Farm and look around at the tables filled with the unutterably poor who are going through their long-continuing crucifixion. It is most surely an exercise of faith for us to see Christ in each other. But it is through such exercise that we grow and the joy of our vocation assures us we are on the right path.

Most certainly, it is easier to believe now that the sun warms us, and we know that buds will appear on the sycamore trees in the wasteland across from the Catholic Worker office, that life will spring out of the dull clods of that littered park across the way. There are wars and rumors of war, poverty and plague, hunger and pain. Still, the sap is rising, again there is the resurrection of spring, God's continuing promise to us that He is with us always, with His comfort and joy, if we will only ask.

The mystery of the poor is this: That they are Jesus, and what you do for them you do for Him. It is the only way we have of knowing and believing in our love. The mystery of poverty is that by sharing in it, making ourselves poor in giving to others, we increase our knowledge of and belief in love.

April 1964

A Prayer for Peace

In the fall of 1965, the Second Vatican Council in Rome entered its final session: a discussion of the Church's role in the modern world, including such problems as war and peace and the formation of conscience. It was Dorothy's hope that from this discussion would issue a clear condemnation of the means of modern war. In late September, she joined a group of twenty women in Rome who had come from various countries to fast for ten days and keep a vigil of prayer as the Council Fathers addressed these vital issues. The fast was organized by Lanza del Vasto and his wife Chanterelle, founders of the Ark, an ecumenical pacifist community in France.

Rome. The fast of the twenty women, which I had come to join and which was the primary reason for my visit to Rome during the final session of the Council, began on October 1, a Friday. That morning I checked out of my hotel and proceeded to the great square in front of St. Peter's to wait for Barbara Wall and Eileen Egan at the end of the Colonnade. We were going to Mass together on that First Friday morning.

Without tickets we could not have got in, since all the Masses which preface the meetings of the Council are packed to the doors. The laity receive Communion not at the main altar but at a side altar. All around there were confessionals, frequented, I was edified to see, by bishops and cardinals, their scarlet and purple robes billowing out behind them. They took as long, I noticed, as nuns, who I always thought were scrupulous indeed, judging by the length of their confessions.

But I was able to go to confession on that last visit I paid to St. Peter's, and I felt with joy and love that warm sense of community, the family, which is the Church. How the Council has broken down barriers between clergy and laity, and how close the bishops seem to us when they are together from all parts of the world, at home in Rome, and not set apart alone and distant on episcopal thrones and in episcopal palaces!

The Mass that morning was in the Syriac rite and was sung, so it was not until ten that I arrived at the Cenacle on Piazza Pricilla on the other side of Rome. There we gathered in the garden, twenty women, and a few of the male members of the Community of the Ark, including Lanza del Vasto, whose wife, Chanterelle, had initiated the fast. He led us in the prayers that we would say each morning as we gathered together after Mass: the Our Father, the peace prayer of St. Francis, and the Beatitudes. Afterward, the trained members of the community sang. Then we went to our rooms, which were on the third floor of the old convent, looking out on gardens and sky.

Each day we followed a schedule. There was Mass at seven-fifteen and then prayer together. From nine to twelve we kept to our rooms in silence, reading, writing, or praying. During the day and night there was always one of us keeping vigil. At noon we went to the garden and read together. Readings included a book by Martin Luther King and an account of the work of Father Paul Gauthier, who founded the Companions of Jesus the Carpenter, in Nazareth. Most of us had some sewing or knitting to do. The wicker chairs were comfortable, the garden smelled of pine trees and eucalyptus and sweet herbs, and every day the sun was warm. Other members of the Ark, who were running an exhibit on nonviolence, came and told us news of the visitors to the exhibit and of the Fathers of the Council they had talked to.

At four in the afternoon there were lectures by priests, and at six a French doctor came daily to see how everyone was getting along. Two of the women were ill during the fast and had to keep to their beds, so the lectures were held in Chanterelle's room. Prayers again at seven or eight, and then silence and sleep—for those who could sleep.

As for me, I did not suffer at all from the hunger or headache or nausea which usually accompany the first few days of a fast, but I had offered my fast in part for the victims of famine all over the world, and it seemed to me that I had very special pains. They were certainly of a kind I have never had before, and they seemed to pierce to the very marrow of my bones when I lay down at night. Perhaps it was the hammock-shaped bed. Perhaps it was the cover, which seemed to weigh a ton, so that I could scarcely turn. At any rate, my nights were penitential enough to make up for the quiet peace of the days. Strangely enough, when the fast was over, all pains left me and I have not had them since. They were not like the arthritic pains which, aggravated by tension and fatigue, are part of my life now that I am sixty-eight. One accepts them as part of age and also part and parcel of the life of work, which is the lot of the poor. So often I see grandmothers in Puerto Rican families bearing the burden of children, the home, cooking, sewing, and contributing to the work of mother and father, who are trying so hard to make a better life for their children. I am glad to share this fatigue with them.

But these pains which went with the fast seemed to reach into my very bones, and I could only feel that I had been given some little intimation of the hunger of the world. God help us, living as we do, in the richest country in the world and so far from approaching the voluntary poverty we esteem and reach toward.

On the night of the 10th of October, the fast, those ten days when nothing but water passed our lips, was finished. Hard though it was, it was but a token fast, considering the problems of the world we live in. It was a small offering of sacrifice, a widow's mite, a few loaves and fishes. May we try harder to do more in the future.

November 1965

II

The happy news on the radio this morning is that the Vatican Council has passed with an overwhelming majority the Schema on the Church in the Modern World, included in which is an unequivocal condemnation of nuclear warfare. It was a statement for which we had been working and praying.*

As to the questions this condemnation will raise in the hearts and minds of all men, Catholic or otherwise—I can only feel that such questions and the attempts to answer them will lead to more enlightened knowledge, more enlightened conscience on the part of all. It will lead, as Peter Maurin was always fond of saying, to clarification of thought, a state of mind which should precede all action. I am sure that he thought our action very often trod on the heels of thought too quickly and so was very imperfect. But I always felt, with St. Francis of Assisi, that we do not know what we have not practiced, and that we learn by our actions, even when those actions involve us in grave mistakes, or sin. God brings good out of evil, that evil which has come about as a result of our free will, our free choice. We learn, as the saying is, the hard way. But the promise remains: "All things work together for good to those who love God," or who want to love Him, who seek to love Him. In other words, the promise is there: "Seek and you shall find, knock and it shall be opened to you." And to repeat again,

---

*The declaration which caused Dorothy's rejoicing was the following: "Any act of war aimed indiscriminately at the destruction of entire cities or of extensive areas along with their population is a crime against God and man himself. It merits unequivocal and unhesitating condemnation." (*Pastoral Constitution on the Church in the Modern World*, Ch. 5, paragraph 80)

since there is no time with God, the promise, the finding, and the seeking go together. Even when one is following a wrong or ill-informed conscience.

For me, this answers the question as to whether we, at the Catholic Worker, think that a man is in the state of mortal sin for going to war. I have been asked this question so often by students that I feel we must keep on trying to answer, faulty and obscure as the answer that each one of us makes may seem to be. To my mind the answer lies in the realm of the motive, the intention. If a man truly thinks he is combating evil and striving for the good, if he truly thinks he is striving for the common good, he must follow his conscience regardless of others. But he always has the duty of forming his conscience by studying, listening, being ready to hear his opponents' point of view.

Whenever this question of conscience comes up, the question of obedience immediately follows, obedience to Church and State, even when commands are not personally directed at us lay people, nor obedience exacted of us, as it is of the clergy. We have pointed out again and again the freedom *The Catholic Worker* has always had in the Archdiocese of New York. We have been rebuked on occasion—when we advised young men not to register for the draft; when we spoke of capitalism as a cancer on the social body, as did Count della Torre, former editor of *Osservatore Romano;* and, on only one occasion, for our use of the name *Catholic.* This last reproach came up again in a news report recently, and we can only repeat what I said to our former chancellor, Monsignor Gaffney (God rest his soul), that we have as much right to the name *Catholic* as the Catholic War Veterans do.

As to my oft-quoted remark that if the Cardinal asked me to stop my writing on war, I would obey, which has been brought up quite a number of times recently, I will try to clarify: First of all, I cannot conceive of Cardinal Spellman's making such a request of me, considering the respect he has always shown for freedom of conscience and freedom of speech. But in the event of so improbable a happening, I have said that I would obey. "What becomes of your obligation of conscience to resist authority? You have quoted St. Peter's saying that we must obey God rather than men."

My answer would be (and it is an easier one to make now that the Council has spoken so clearly) that my respect for Cardinal Spellman and my faith that God will right all mistakes, mine, as well as his, would lead me to obey. We have been a troublesome family to the chancery office, and I am sure that there are plenty of bishops around the country who are glad we are not in their dioceses. It is fitting, of course, that the Christian revolution (it has scarcely begun in its pacifist-anarchist aspects) should struggle on in New York as it has these last thirty-three years. Let us pray that it continues.

As to what change will be brought about by the pronouncements of the Council? None immediately, just as there was none when Pope Pius XI spoke out against Fascism in Italy. Popes speak out, as Paul VI did recently at the United Nations, but wars go on. There are cheers and rejoicings, and seeming assent to what they say, but action does not seem to be influenced, *that is, immediately*. But in the long run, these words, these pronouncements, after much blood has been shed, influence the course of history, which progresses more and more toward a recognition of man's freedom, his dignity as a son of God, as made in the image and likeness of God, whether he is Communist or imperialist, Russian or American, North or South Vietnamese. All men are brothers, God wills that all men be saved, and we pray daily, *Thy will be done, on earth as it is in heaven.*

A Jesuit priest from Madras, India, came in the office to visit us the other afternoon. When he spoke of the war in Vietnam he spoke as one nearer to it than we were, and he reiterated the familiar argument: If Vietnam is lost to the Communists, all Asia goes too.

But from the Christian point of view (and in this case from the Jesuit point of view), when he asked, "What are we to do?" I could only point to the example of St. Ignatius, who first of all laid down his arms, then went to support himself by serving the poor in hospitals, and then went back to school to study.

When a mother, a housewife, asks what she can do, one can only point to the way of St. Therese, that little way, so much misunderstood and so much despised. She did all for the love of God, even to putting up with the irritation in herself caused by the proximity of a nervous nun. She began with working for peace in her own heart, and willing to love where love was difficult, and so she grew in love, and increased the sum total of love in the world, not to speak of peace.

Newman wrote: "Let us but raise the level of religion in our hearts, and it will rise in the world. He who attempts to set up God's kingdom in his heart, furthers it in the world." And this goes for the priest too, wherever he is, whether he deals with the problem of war or with poverty. He may write and speak, but he needs to study the little way, which is all that is available to the poor, and the only alternative to the mass approach of the State.

As Pope John told the pilgrimage of women, Mothers for Peace, the seventy-five of us who went over to Rome to thank him for his encyclical

Pacem in Terris, just the month before his death, "The beginnings of peace are in your own hearts, in your own families, schoolrooms, offices, parishes, and neighborhoods."

It is working from the ground up, from the poverty of the stable, in work as at Nazareth, and also in going from town to town, as in the public life of Jesus two thousand years ago. And since a thousand years are as one day, and Christianity is but two days old, let us take heart and start now.

December 1965

If Your Brother Stumbles

This morning I was inspired to preach a strong sermon against drink, the curse of so many of those we live with and sit at the table with. St. Paul talks of abstaining from what causes your brother to stumble. We concede, of course, that wine is good and lightens the heart of man, as Scripture says, but we live in the midst of the tragedy drink has caused, and so ought to use the most difficult but the only potent means to help: inflict suffering on ourselves by sacrificing this little enjoyment, put to death that bit of self that demands this indulgence and justifies it as being harmless. We had just received a letter from the mother of a young man who, with his wife and unborn child, was killed in an auto crash caused by two young drunken drivers, also killed. And there was the drinking and perhaps drug addiction on the part of three teen-agers which led to the brutal beating and murder of our friend Al Uhrie last month, on East Fifth Street, a young man who was one of the gentlest and most consistent pacifists in his daily life that we ever knew. His wife and five-month-old baby are now living with us in Tivoli. When one is surrounded by many sorrows, one's own are lightened a little, leveled off a bit perhaps by the way people try to take care of one another. I cannot believe that people are so captivated by drink that they will not give up their own harmless indulgence for the sake of others around them. It must be that they do not have faith in the weapons of the spirit or recognize that power. How to explain it, or make it clear? St. Ignatius said love is an exchange of gifts. St. Teresa said that we could only show our love for God by our love for our brothers. Jesus said for us to pray thus: *Our Father.* So we can say, Father, I love my brother and I love

You. I want to offer You a sacrifice, and beg You in return to send Arthur or Louis the grace to overcome the most dangerous failing they suffer from. Give us this day our daily bread of strength to suffer for each other these little ways of sacrifice, as well as the daily pinpricks of daily living which can become a martyrdom in a family and grow into hate and violence.

I thought these things at Mass this morning, and I had to say them when I encountered someone for whom I thought the words important.

September 1966

"In Peace Is My Bitterness Most Bitter"

It is not just Vietnam, it is South Africa, it is Nigeria, the Congo, Indonesia, all of Latin America. It is not just the pictures of all the women and children who have been burnt alive in Vietnam, or the men who have been tortured, and died. It is not just the headless victims of the war in Colombia. It is not just the words of Cardinal Spellman and Archbishop Hannan It is the fact that whether we like it or not, we are Americans. It is indeed our country, right or wrong, as the Cardinal said in another context. We are warm and fed and secure (aside from occasional muggings and murders amongst us). We are among nations the most powerful, the most armed, and we are supplying arms and money to the rest of the world where we are not ourselves fighting. We are eating while there is famine in the world.

Scripture tells us that the picture of judgment presented to us by Jesus is of Dives sitting and feasting with his friends while Lazarus sat hungry at the gate, the dogs, the scavengers of the East, licking his sores. We are Dives. Woe to the rich! *We* are the rich. The Works of Mercy are the opposite of the works of war, feeding the hungry, sheltering the homeless, nursing the sick, visiting the prisoner. But we are destroying crops, setting fire to entire villages and to the people in them. We are not performing the Works of Mercy but the works of war. We cannot repeat this enough.

When the Apostles wanted to call down fire from heaven on the inhospitable Samaritans, the "enemies" of the Jews, Jesus said to them, "You know not of what Spirit you are." When Peter told Our Lord not to accept the way of the Cross and His own death, He said, "Get behind me, Satan. For you are not on the side of God but of men." But He also had said "Thou art Peter and upon this rock I will build my church." Peter denied Jesus three times at that time in history, but after the death on the Cross, and the Resurrection and the Descent of the Holy Spirit, Peter faced up to Church and State alike and said, "We must obey God rather than men." Deliver us, O Lord, from the fear of our enemies, which makes cowards of us all.

I can sit in the presence of the Blessed Sacrament and wrestle for that peace in the bitterness of my soul, a bitterness which many Catholics throughout the world feel, and I can find many things in Scripture to console me, to change my heart from hatred to love of enemy. "Our worst enemies are those of our own household," Jesus said. Picking up the Scriptures at random (as St. Francis used to do), I read about Peter, James, and John who went up on the Mount of Transfiguration and saw Jesus talking with Moses and Elias, transfigured before their eyes. (A hint of the life to come, Maritain said.) Jesus transfigured! He who was the despised of men, no beauty in Him, spat upon, beaten, dragged to His cruel death on the way to the Cross! A Man so much like other men that it took the kiss of a Judas to single Him out from the others when the soldiers, so closely allied to the priests, came to take Him. Reading this story of the Transfiguration, the words stood out, words foolishly babbled, about the first building project of the Church, proposed by Peter. "Lord, shall we make here three shelters, one for You, one for Moses and one for Elias?" And the account continues, "for he did not know what to say, he was so terrified."

Maybe they are terrified, these Princes of the Church, as we are often terrified at the sight of violence, which is present every now and then in our Houses of Hospitality, and which is always a threat in the streets of the slums. I have often thought it is a brave thing to do, these Christmas visits of Cardinal Spellman to the American troops all over the world, Europe, Korea, Vietnam. But oh, God, what are all these Americans, so-called Christians, doing all over the world so far from our own shores?

But what words are those he spoke—going against even the Pope, calling for victory, total victory? Words are as strong and powerful as bombs, as napalm. How much the government counts on those words, pays for those words to exalt our own way of life, to build up fear of the enemy. Deliver us, Lord, from the fear of the enemy. That is one of the lines in the Psalms, and we are not asking God to deliver us from enemies but from the fear of them. Love casts out fear, but we have to get over the fear in order to get close enough to love them.

There is plenty to do, for each one of us, working on our own hearts, changing our own attitudes, in our own neighborhoods. If the just man falls seven times daily, we each one of us fall more than that in thought, word, and deed. Prayer and fasting, taking up our own cross daily and following Him, doing penance, these are the hard words of the Gospel.

As to the Church, where else shall we go, except to the Bride of Christ, one flesh with Christ? Though she is a harlot at times, she is our Mother. We should read the Book of Hosea, which is a picture of God's steadfast love not only for the Jews, His chosen people, but for His Church, of which we are every one of us members or potential members. Since there is no time with God, we are all one, all one body, Chinese, Russians, Vietnamese, and He has *commanded us to love one another.*

"A new commandment I give, that you love others *as I have loved you,*" not to the defending of your life, but to the laying down of your life.

A hard saying.

Love is indeed a "harsh and dreadful thing" to ask of us, of each one of us, but it is the only answer.

January 1967

Martin Luther King

Just three weeks ago Martin Luther King was shot as he stood on the balcony of a motel in Memphis, Tennessee. I was sitting in the kitchen of one of the women's apartments on Kenmare Street watching the television when the news flash came. I sat there stunned, wondering if he was suffering a superficial wound, as James Meredith did on his Mississippi walk to overcome fear, that famous march on which the cry "Black Power" was first shouted. Martin Luther King wrote about it in his last book, *Where Do We Go from Here?*—a book which all of us should read because it makes us understand what the words "Black Power" really mean. Dr. King was a man of the deepest and most profound spiritual insights.

These were the thoughts which flashed through my mind as I waited, scarcely knowing that I was waiting, for further news. The dreaded words were spoken almost at once. "Martin Luther King is dead." The next day was Good Friday, the day commemorated by the entire Christian world as the day when Jesus Christ, true God and true Man, shed His blood.

"Unless the grain of wheat fall into the ground and die, it remains alone. But if it die it produces much fruit." Martin Luther King died daily, as St. Paul said. He faced death daily and said a number of times that he knew he would be killed for the faith that was in him. The faith that men could live together as brothers. The faith in the Gospel teaching of nonviolence. The faith that man is capable of change, of growth, of growing in love.

Cynics may say that many used nonviolence as a tactic. Many may scoff at the outcry raised at his death, saying that this is an election year and all candidates had to show honor to a fallen Black hero. But love and grief were surely in the air those days of mourning, and all that was best in the country—in the labor movement, the civil rights movement, and the peace movement—cast aside all their worldly cares and occupations to go to Memphis to march with the sanitation union men, on whose behalf, during whose strike, Martin Luther King had given himself; and to Atlanta, where half a million people gathered to walk in the funeral procession, to follow the farm cart and the two mules which drew the coffin of the dead leader.

Always, I think, I will weep when I hear the song "We Shall Overcome," and when I read the words "Free at last, Free at last, Great God Almighty, Free at last."

April 1968

The Business of Living

Sometimes our hearts are heavy with the tragedy of the world, the horrible news from Vietnam, Brazil, Biafra, the Israeli-Arab war. And here it is Advent and Christmastime again, and with it the juxtaposition of joy and sorrow, the blackness of night, brightness of dawn. What saves us from despair is a phrase we read in *The Life of Jesus* of Daniel-Rops, "getting on with the business of living." What did the women do after the Crucifixion? The men were in the upper room mourning and praying, and the women, by their very nature, "had to go on with the business of living." They prepared the spices, purchased the linen clothes for the burial, kept the Sabbath, and hastened to the tomb on Sunday morning. Their very work gave them insights as to *time,* and doubtless there was a hint of the peace and joy of the Resurrection to temper their grief.

"The past year has been difficult," one of our friends writes, "particularly in dealing with the problems of relevancy. To many in the peace-resistance movement, feeding and sheltering the poor is looked upon as non-revolutionary and a mere Band-Aid applied to a cancerous world. To many, only when the American giant is confronted at its jugular vein is it worthwhile. So our involvement and work has really been put into question. Perhaps we attempted to justify ourselves too much or spent too much time attempting to answer the question. But it seems clearer (now), and it can never be completely clear: we must continue with our work and look upon it as a practical response to a revolutionary gospel. The fact remains that while we slay the giant, the wounded have to be cared for. Perhaps those who come by can see the necessity of caring for one another and recognizing the importance of community."

Actually, we here at the Catholic Worker did not start these soup lines ourselves. Years ago, John Griffin, one of the men from the Bowery who moved in with us, was giving out clothes, and when they ran out he began sitting the petitioners down to a hot cup of coffee or a bowl of soup—whatever we had. By word of mouth the news spread, and one after another they came, forming lines (during the Depression) which stretched around the block. The loaves and fishes had to be multiplied to take care of it, and everyone contributed food, money, and space.

All volunteers who come, priests and lay people, nuns and college students, have worked on that line and felt the satisfaction of manual labor, beginning to do without, themselves, to share with others, and a more intense desire to change the social order that leaves men hungry and homeless. The work is as basic as bread. To sit down several times a day together is community and growth in the knowledge of Christ. "They knew Him in the breaking of bread."

We have said these things many times in the pages of *The Catholic Worker,* but it is to reassure these dear friends that I write this again. Perhaps it is easier for a woman to understand than a man. Because no matter what catastrophe has occurred or hangs overhead, she has to go on with the business of living. She does the physical things and so keeps a balance. No longer does the man sit as a judge at the gate, as in the Old Testament where the valiant woman is portrayed. Now there is neither bond nor free, Greek nor Hebrew, male nor female—we are a little nearer to the heavenly kingdom when *men,* as well as women, are feeding the hungry. It is real action as well as symbolic action. It is walking in the steps of Jesus when He fed the multitude on the hills, and when He prepared the fire and the fish on the shore. He told us to do it. He did it Himself.

December 1969

A Little Kinder

I wonder how many of our readers have read Knut Hamsun's book *Hunger*. Or remember the incident in James Baldwin's *Another Country* where a young lad almost sells himself for a hot meal and a place to sleep.

There is a statue on top of my bookcase given to me by a young boy whom we took care of some years back. He had lived this life of the streets. To prevent such things, even for a time, is something. I. F. Stone in his recent *Weekly,* commenting on the bomb tragedy on Eleventh Street, said, "Man himself is obsolete unless he can change. That change requires more altruism, more kindness, more—no one need be ashamed to say it—more love."

Love shows itself in gentleness, in tenderness, and manifests itself physically in serving and accepting service from another. Hans Tunnesen, our Norwegian seaman cook, uses the word "gentle" as his highest form of praise. When he says a man is gentle, he makes us all realize how good a word that is.

We are, too, a community of need, rather than what sociologists call an "intentional community." When people ask us how long people stay with us, meaning "the poor" (although we are all poor), we say, "For life." One of the Works of Mercy is burying the dead, and we remember them all as we say Compline in the country, and Vespers in the city, each night.

One must write about these things now when in the last few weeks three young people were blown to bits in a house on Eleventh Street, just off of Fifth Avenue, reportedly in an attempt to make bombs to blow up banks, department stores, the offices of giant corporations, all those impregnable homes of high finance in this affluent society. One can only use clichés to express these things, it seems. That is one reason perhaps for the use of those four-letter words which shock by their contempt and hatred almost for life itself, for the ecstatic act which is part of the beginning of new life on earth.

"Anarchism" and "nihilism" are two words familiar to the young and now attractive to them. They do not believe in building a new society within the shell of the old. They believe that the old must be destroyed first. That is nihilism. In a way, it is their denial of the "here and now."

Perhaps St. Paul defined the Catholic Worker's idea of anarchism, the positive word, by saying of the followers of Jesus, "For such there is no law." Those who have given up all ideas of domination and power and the manipulation of others are "not under the law" (Galatians 5). For those who live in Christ Jesus, for "those who have put on Christ," for those who have washed the feet of others, there is no law. They have the liberty of the children of God.

But, my God, what a long and painful process this is—and yet how powerful! How long-enduring!

"If there is no law," I have been asked many times, "then why are you a member of the Roman Catholic Church, the authoritarian Church?"

I can only quote Newman in answer to this, and strangely enough, in a most peculiar context. I believe it was during a time of war for England and he was asked at a banquet whether he would go against his country if the Pope called a war unjust. He answered that if he were asked to drink a toast it would be to conscience first, and then to the Pope.

During the Second Vatican Council it was again affirmed:

In the depths of his conscience man detects a law which he does not impose on himself but which holds him to obedience. . . . For man has in his heart a law written by God. To obey it is the very dignity of man. According to it he will be judged. . . . Conscience is the most secret core and sanctuary of man. There he is alone with God whose voice echoes in his depths. In a wonderful manner conscience reveals that law which is fulfilled by love of God and neighbor.

One must follow one's own conscience first before all authority, and of course one must inform one's conscience. But one must follow one's conscience still, even if it is an ill-informed one. All those young ones, and older ones, who are committing themselves to violent revolution as the only way to overcome evil government, imperialism, industrial capitalism, exploitation—in other words, evil—are not only following their consciences but also following tradition.

All Men Are Brothers, that Chinese classic which inspired Mao, and the Buddhist and Hindu classics as well, tell of the gigantic struggle between good and evil with profound faith in the eventual triumph of the good. Even that fool for Christ, Don Quixote, setting out on his donkey with lance in hand, was trying to overcome evil, to right wrongs. It is all another concept of the Incarnation—an acting out in flesh and blood, and in the shedding of blood, man's hope against despair, the belief that physical activity, violence, the pitting of all one's life forces, is the only path that is open to us today. This is the way young people are reasoning. To do otherwise is to betray one's brothers, they believe, to leave them to slow and agonizing death in war or by cold, hunger, and disease.

So we cannot judge the young. But we are challenged to answer.

Jesus said, after He had washed the feet of His disciples, "What I have done, you shall do also."

No one coming into contact with this Man fails to be affected by Him. The French Communist Roger Garaudy writes in a recent journal:

About the time of the reign of Tiberius, no one knows exactly where or when, a person whose name was unknown made a breakthrough in man's horizon. He was neither philosopher nor tribune, but one who lived in such a way that his life signified that every one of us can, at every moment, begin a new future.

In order to proclaim the good news to the very end, it was necessary that he announce that every limitation, even the supreme limitation, death itself, had been conquered. Thus his resurrection.

Various scholars are able to challenge every fact of this existence, but that changes nothing in regard to the certainty which changes life. A fire had been lighted.

This fire was first of all a rising of the poor, without which, from Nero to Diocletian, the "Establishment" would not have persecuted to the extent it did. With this man, love was to be militant, subversive; if it weren't he would not have been crucified. . . . His death was like the birth of a new man.

I look on that cross, and I think of all those who have expanded man's horizons—John of the Cross, who teaches us by dint of having nothing; Karl Marx, who has shown us how we can change the world; Van Gogh—these and others who have made us realize that man is too great to be sufficient unto himself.

You, the receivers of the great hope that Constantine stole from us, you men of the Church, restore him [Christ] to us. His life and his death are for us also, who have learned from him that man has been created a creator.

The power to create, the divine attribute of man, is there—it is, my friends. It is present every time something new is born to augment the human form: in the most passionate love, in scientific discovery, in poetry, even in revolution.

During the Civil War in Spain, the story is that the workers draped a statue of the Sacred Heart in a public square with the printed inscription on the Red Flag: *He is ours. You cannot take him from us.*

The justification for a Christ who urges militant action is the story in the New Testament of how He drove the money changers out of the temple. Over and over again, when I am speaking in colleges and universities, this incident is brought up. There are also many strong denunciations of the oppressor, the hypocrites, the whited sepulchers, the lawyers, of all those who put heavy burdens on men's shoulders and do nothing to share or lighten them.

I can only answer in these other words of His: "Let him who is without sin among you, cast the first stone."

The most effective action we can take is to try to conform our lives to the folly of the Cross, as St. Paul called it.

May 1970

Strength to Endure

It is certainly borne in upon us, day after day, how little it is that we do, or can do. But we are not alone. I remember that sense of shame at turning to God, as I lay in a cell at Occoquan, Virginia, so many years ago. I wanted to stand on my own feet. I thought there was something ignoble about calling for help in my despair, at my first taste of real destitution, of utter helplessness in the face of the vast sufferings of the world. I read the Scriptures, as Ammon Hennacy did. It was the only book we were allowed in jail. But I was ashamed and turned away in the pride of youth for another dozen years. Then it was in gratitude that I turned to Him again, for my own happiness, for the beauty of the sea and the sand, for the smallest shell, the tiniest creature, the gulls, the sky and clouds. It is easier to praise God then, to thank Him, to call upon Him, and to learn that He does indeed answer.

But when we are able to bear some small share of the sufferings of the world, whether in pain of mind, body, or soul, let us thank God for that too. Maybe we are helping some prisoner, some Black or Puerto Rican youth in the Tombs, some soldier in Vietnam. The old I.W.W. slogan "An injury to one is an injury to all" is another way of saying what St. Paul said almost two thousand years ago. "We are all members of one another, and when the health of one member suffers, the health of the whole body is lowered." And the converse is true. We can indeed hold each other up in prayer. Excuse this preaching. I am preaching to myself too.

January and February are those months when winter seems interminable and vitality is low. In the face of world events, in the face of the mystery of suffering, of evil in the world, it is a good time to read the Book of Job, and then to go on reading the Psalms, looking for comfort—that is, strength to endure. Also to remember the importunate widow, the importunate friend. Both are stories which Jesus told. Then to pray without ceasing as Paul urged. And just as there was that interpolation in Job— that triumphant cry—"I know that my Redeemer liveth," so we, too, can know that help will come, that even from evil, God can bring great good, that indeed the good will triumph. Bitter though it is today with ice and sleet, the sap will soon be rising in those bare trees down the street from us.

February 1971

Priest and Prophet

Dear Father Dan Berrigan,*

I woke up thinking of you this morning with love and regret at not having been at the First Street meeting to see you. With love, and gratitude too, for all you are doing—for the way you are spending yourself. Thank God, how the young love you. You must be utterly exhausted too, yet you keep going. I feel this keenly because I've been really down and out since August, what the doctor calls a chronic cough and a "mild heart failure," and I chafe at my enforced absence because of a nervous exhaustion which

---

*Daniel Berrigan, the Jesuit priest and poet, was paroled in February 1972 after serving seventeen months in prison for his part in the destruction of draft files in Catonsville, Maryland. His brother Philip, a Josephite priest, convicted of the same offense, was paroled the following December, and soon after announced his decision to leave his order. Both brothers had long been associated with the Catholic Worker, and Dorothy looked upon their heroic witness with maternal pride. At the same time, however, she was concerned that some young members of the "Catholic Left" seemed inclined to a casual attitude toward tradition, the Sacraments, and Church authority. Typically, she used the occasion of this affectionate "letter" to Father Berrigan to emphasize to her readers the conservative basis of her own faith and practice. Dorothy lived to see the Berrigans arrested again, in September 1980, two months before her death. They were apprehended while hammering on the nose cones of nuclear missiles—so that Scripture might be fulfilled: "And they shall beat their swords into plowshares; nation shall not lift up sword against nation, neither shall they learn war any more."

I realize you must often feel, though you are a generation or more younger than I.

But thank God, you are truly bearing the Cross, giving your life for others, as Father Phil is in cramped cell and enforced idleness, away from all he must crave day and night to do, surrounded by suffering, enduring the clamor of hell itself—he too is giving his life for others.

I cannot tell you how I love you both, and see more clearly how God is using you, reaching the prisoners and reaching the young. They all call you "Dan" and "Phil," but I call you Father Dan and Father Phil because always you are to me priests and prophets.

I feel that, as in the time of the Desert Fathers, the young are fleeing the cities—wandering over the face of the land, living after a fashion in voluntary poverty and manual labor, seeming to be inactive in the "peace movement." I know they are still a part of it—just as Cesar Chavez and the Farm Workers' Movement are also part of it, committed to nonviolence, even while they resist, fighting for their lives and their families' lives.

Meanwhile, up and down on both sides of the Hudson River, religious orders own thousands of acres of land, cultivated, landscaped, but not growing food for the hungry or founding villages for families or schools for the children.

How well I understand that biblical phrase "In peace is my bitterness most bitter." How to reconcile this with Jesus' new commandment of loving others, forgiving others seventy times seven—forgiving and loving the enemies of our own household? Yes, "in peace is my bitterness most bitter." Yet the bitterness subsides and the peace in my heart grows, and even a love and some understanding grows of these "enemies of our own household."

I must tell little stories, as Jesus taught us to do, in trying to teach. They call it "reminiscing," when you are old. The story is this.

We had a mean pastor once long ago who was always blasting women in his sermons for sitting around gossiping, not cleaning their houses, and spending their husband-soldiers' pay on beer and movies. It was during the Second World War. And there was a man in our House of Hospitality arrested for indecent exposure. The parish neighbor who told me this called it "insulting a child," and I had thought she said "assaulting" and nearly fainted with fear and trembling. With no one else to turn to, I went to the pastor, the rigid and cranky one, and asked him to go to the jail, visiting the prisoner being one of the Works of Mercy. With no comment at all but with the utmost kindness and the delicacy of few words, he did as I requested and even interceded for this man off the road and got him a lighter sentence of sixty days. When this happened once again some years later, another priest, a saintly, well-spoken one, was appealed to. He responded, "Too bad they don't give him a life sentence!" You never can tell!

I hope we do not lose many subscribers because of my writing so frankly about matters seldom referred to. But nowadays when there are no longer lines at the confessionals in our churches there surely is an overflowing of public confession. In our newspapers, reviews, advertisements, and novels "nothing is hidden, it seems, that has not been revealed." It is as though the fear of death and judgment has made people rush to tell all, to confess to each other, before the Dread Judge shall tell all to the universe. Poor, fearful creatures that we are, is it that in this strange perverse way of confessing we are seeking Christ, even those who deny Him? Jesus Christ is our truth. By telling the truth, or one aspect of the truth, perhaps we are clinging to the hem of His garment, seeking to touch it like the woman with the "issue of blood," so that we may be healed.

I am not wandering, in writing this way. I am meditating. I am thinking of what I have come to think of as fundamental to our search for peace, for nonviolence. A flood of water (and Christ is living water) washes out sins—all manner of filth, degradation, fear, horror. He is also the Word. And studying the New Testament, and its commentators, I have come in this my seventy-sixth year, to think of a few holy words of Jesus as the greatest comfort of my life.

"Judge not."

"Forgive us our trespasses as we forgive those who trespass against us."

"Forgive seventy times seven times."

All words of Our Lord and Saviour. I "have knowledge of salvation through forgiveness of my sins," as Zacharias sang in his canticle.

And so, when it comes to divorce, birth control, abortion, I must write in this way. The teaching of Christ, the Word, must be upheld. Held up though one would think that it is completely beyond us—out of our reach, impossible to follow. I believe Christ is our Truth and is with us always. We may stretch toward it, falling short, failing seventy times seven, but forgiveness is always there. He is a kind and loving judge. And so are 99 percent of the priests in the confessional. The verdict there is always "not guilty" even though our "firm resolve with the help of His grace to confess our sins, do penance, and amend our lives" may seem a hopeless proposition.

I believe in the Sacraments. I believe Grace is conferred through the Sacraments. I believe the priest is empowered to forgive sins. Grace is defined as "participation in the divine life," so little by little we are putting off the old man and putting on the new.

Actually, "putting on Christ."

P.S. (to our readers). The day after I finished this letter I received a letter from Father Phil—a good and loving letter. He is not *dis*couraged but is strong *in courage*. He will be released on parole on December 20, so let us all pray daily, and every time we hear and see a reference to "the Berrigans" let us pray, even if it is only the briefest "God be with them"—those words so familiar in our liturgy, to which the answer is, "And with you"—and us, too.

And dear Dan, Father Dan, please excuse my wandering like this.

December 1972

All Souls

This month when we celebrate the feast of All Souls it is good to write about heaven as well as death. Someone is always putting a book or article in my hands that I need just at that moment, and the other night, when we gathered for Vespers in our office–library–stencil room, Mike Kovalak handed me a little book, ninety pages long. The first paragraph of the first chapter gave me the definition of heaven I needed.

> There we shall rest and we shall see;
> We shall love and we shall praise;
> Behold what shall be in the end and shall not end.

It is St. Augustine, of course, speaking with his mother just before she died.* It is Scripture also speaking to us, of a future life where we will know as we will be known. The very word "know" is used in Genesis again and again as the act of husband and wife which brings forth more life: Abraham knew Sara, and she conceived and bore a son.

An Evangelist who sends me his comments on the Bible once referred

---

*Dorothy was mistaken. These words are not from the *Confessions* but from the conclusion to St. Augustine's *City of God*.

to death as a "transport," an ecstasy. And indeed we are transported, in this passover to another life.

Jacques Maritain, our beloved friend whose death this year we are also commemorating, said once that the story of the Transfiguration is a feast we should surely meditate on. Three of the Apostles, sleeping as they often do even to this day, awoke to see Jesus standing with Moses and Elias, transfigured and glorified. It is a glimpse, Maritain commented, of the future, of life after death, of the dogmas contained in the creed—in the "resurrection of the body and life everlasting."

And Peter, the rock upon which Christ said He would build His Church, was confused, as popes have been many a time since, and wanted to start to build! But let's forget about criticism of Peter and find always concordances, as Pope John, the beloved, told us to do.

I had the great privilege of standing by my mother's bed, holding her hand, as she quietly breathed her last. So often I had worried when I was traveling around the country that I would not be there with her at the time if she were suddenly taken.

And now I have seen my little four-year-old great-granddaughter worrying about me. It was just after Rita Corbin's mother's death (another member of our family to remember this month). After Carmen's death and burial in our parish cemetery, my little Tanya came and sat on my lap. It was after one of my weeks-long absences from the farm, and stroking my cheek, she said anxiously, "You're not old—you're young."

Sensing her anxiety, I could only say, "No, I'm old too, like Mrs. Ham, and someday, I don't know when, I'm going to see my mother and father and brother too." And as she was accustomed to my absences, I am sure she was comforted. How wonderful it is to have a granddaughter and her little family living with us. A House of Hospitality on the land can indeed be an "extended family."

Meanwhile, in the joys and sorrows of this life, we can pray as they do in the Russian liturgy for a death "without blame or pain." May our passing be a rejoicing.

October—November 1973

Holy Fools

Why do I go around speaking where I am invited when there is so much to do at home? This question was very much in my mind as I woke at 4 a.m. this morning (not quite as early as the Trappist monks). I often wake thus troubled, but my bedside books are at hand—a missal, Julian of Norwich, and this particular Sunday morning, St. Francis de Sales, a paperback given me yesterday by a young girl at the annual Anarchist Conference at Hunter College, here in New York.

My missal opened at yesterday's Epistle, which begins, "The priests and elders were amazed as they observed the self-assurance of Peter and John and realized the speakers were uneducated men of no standing." This immediately gave me comfort. "Go where you are invited," Father McSorley, my first spiritual adviser, once told me. He was a man who listened, who never criticized. He knew instinctively that as a woman, as a convert, I was filled with uncertainties, always coming away from speaking engagements with the feeling that I was inadequate, had said what I had not intended to say, had talked too long about irrelevancies, had not "made my point," as Peter Maurin would say.

Today I must go up to a convent, an Academy of the Sacred Heart, and, at the Liturgy of their annual reunion, give a ten-minute homily. What an impossible assignment.

How could I in those few minutes deliver the message—give what was in my heart? "Thy will be done" is the topic assigned me. And "God's will is that all men be saved." *All men.* All the unworthy poor, the drunks, the drug-ridden, the poor mentally afflicted creatures who are in and out of our C.W. houses all day. And yet Jesus told us what we were to do—feed the hungry, clothe the naked, shelter the homeless, "worthy or unworthy." Oh, how much could be done if there were a House of Hospitality in every neighborhood, in every parish! Lowering the tone of the neighborhood? We have heard this everywhere. In some cities we have been driven from pillar to post by it, forced to move many times. A long history could be written—Detroit, Rochester, etc., etc.

"Those who have the substance of this world and close their hearts to the poor . . ." Am I going to make this kind of a judgment today on Fifth

Avenue, I, who have so much of the substance—books, radio, heat and hot water, food and clothing? (I *could* complain of crowding, of too much of the substance of this world all around me in shopping bags, clothes, suitcases, under the bed, over the bed on shelves, sometimes hardly a passage through a dormitory to my own cluttered room which is office, library, and guest room, too, when I am away.)

Can I talk about people living on usury, on the interest accruing from stocks and bonds, living on the interest, "never touch the principal," not knowing in what ways the infertile money had bred more money by wise investment in God knows what devilish nerve gas, drugs, napalm, missiles, or vanities, when housing and employment, honest employment for the poor were needed, and money could have been invested there?

To talk economics to the rich and Jesus to the anarchists gathered in convention these two days (and have to write this column) is a job. Besides, I did not "talk Jesus" to the anarchists. There was no time to answer the one great disagreement which was in their minds—how can you reconcile your anarchism with your faith in the monolithic, authoritarian Church which seems so far from Jesus, Who "had no place to lay His head," and Who said "sell what you have and give to the poor"?

Because I have been behind bars in police stations, houses of detention, jails, and prison farms (whatsoever they are called) eleven times, and have refused to pay federal income taxes, and have never voted, they accept me as an anarchist. And I, in turn, can see Christ in them even though they deny Him, because they are giving themselves to working for a better social order for the wretched of the earth.

God wills that *all* men be saved. A hard saying for us to take and believe and hold to our hearts to ease its bitterness. St. John of the Cross wrote, "Where there is no love, put love, and you will find love." He was in jail too, put there by his own brethren.

I will write about my pitifully brief jail experiences one day, God willing. Such brief episodes, compared to the time spent by c.o.'s or Martin Sostre.* Even the Berrigans' imprisonment seems light compared to so many Blacks who are serving long terms. So many of us are holy fools in the eyes of our friends and readers because we share their sufferings or try to.

But the term has a special meaning in Russian literature and is used to

---

*A radical Black activist who spent eight years in prison after an arrest for what he claimed was a frame-up charge of selling heroin. He was recognized by Amnesty International as a prisoner of conscience, and in 1975 he was granted executive clemency by the governor of New York.

describe Myshkin in *The Idiot,* a truly Christ-like figure. I was glad to see it used again in relation to Solzhenitsyn in an article in *Newsweek* last month. Every day *The Daily World* is filled with vituperation for Solzhenitsyn, which just goes to show how important he has become in the eyes of the Soviet bureaucracy, and how much he must have meant to other writers and scientists who were being harassed or imprisoned.

Teilhard de Chardin writes: "Someday, after mastering the winds, the waves, the tides and gravity, we shall harness for God the energies of love, and then for the second time in the history of the world, man will discover fire."

May 1974

The Third Part

Buddhists teach that a man's life is divided into three parts: the first part for education and growing up; the second for continued learning, through marriage and raising a family, involvement with the life of the senses, the mind, and the spirit; and the third period, the time of withdrawal from responsibility, letting go of the things of this life, letting God take over. This is a fragmentary view of the profound teaching of the East. The old saying that a man works from sun to sun but woman's work is never done is a very true one. St. Teresa wrote of the three interior senses, the memory, the understanding, and the will. So even if one withdraws, as I am trying to do, from active work, these senses remain active.

I am, however, leaving everything to the generous crowd of young people who do the editing and getting out of *The Catholic Worker,* seeing visitors, doing the work of the Houses of Hospitality, and performing, in truth, all the Works of Mercy. Day and evening and even nights are filled with "unprogrammed" work. One never knows what crisis is going to arise, what emergency is coming up next. Living in our slums is like living in a war-torn area.

And here I am living on the beach, writing, answering some letters, and trying to grow in the life of the spirit. I feel that I am but a beginner.

I remember a young woman who came to help us years ago who, after her first, early enthusiasm had worn away, used to sigh wearily and say, "What's it all about?" I am sure many of our friends and readers also pose, more seriously, the same question. For instance, what are Ernest and Marion Bromley all about? Why is this frail, elderly man in jail right now for "disorderly conduct," that is, for distributing leaflets about the nefarious workings of the Internal Revenue Service and their ways of penalizing people for advocating tax refusal. Remember, it is the federal taxes paid by each of us that supply the arms that are keeping wars going.

What I want to bring out is how a pebble cast into a pond causes ripples that spread in all directions. And each one of our thoughts, words, and deeds is like that. Going to jail, as Ernest Bromley has done, short though his stay may be, causes a ripple of thought, of conscience among us all. And of remembrance, too.

Ernest Bromley is sharing, in his (we hope) brief jail encounter, the sufferings of the world. And we hope, like the Apostles, he rejoices in having been accounted "worthy to suffer."

"What is it all about—the Catholic Worker movement?" It is, in a way, a school, a work camp, to which large-hearted, socially conscious young people come to find their vocations. After some months or years, they know most definitely what they want to do with their lives. Some go into medicine, nursing, law, teaching, farming, writing, and publishing.

They learn not only to love, with compassion, but to overcome fear, that dangerous emotion that precipitates violence. They may go on feeling fear, but they know the means, they have grown in faith, to overcome it. "Lord, deliver us from the *fear* of our enemies." Not from our enemies, but from the fear of them. In jail, too, there is a very real sense of fear.

To be a prisoner, whether for a weekend or a month, as many of us have, is never again to forget those walls, those bars, those brothers and sisters of ours behind them.

March–April 1975

Psalms of Rejoicing

I had a mild heart attack in September, pains in my chest and arms and a gasping need of fresh air. It is certainly frightening not to be able to breathe.

My orders were bed rest for four weeks here at Tivoli. I am sitting outside in the sun to write this (after the fourth week), with healing beauty all around. St. Bruno, who founded the Carthusians, advocated for his monks beauty of surroundings as a help to contemplation. He also provided them each with a little house and walled-in garden. We do not have that privacy unless we flee to the woods and build our own.

Stanley Vishnewski and I get a great excitement over weather. "The wind is rising. The tide will be high tonight," and sure enough there were hurricane warnings one day and tornado warnings the next. I sat in the chapel and contemplated the trees tossing wildly, especially the hemlock outside the window, the roots of which burrow under the house. If it were uprooted, one could imagine the house being uprooted with it, the trees being higher than our two-story house. The maples and sumac are brilliant in red, yellow, and green, and they are stubbornly hanging on to their leaves.

There is unanimous agreement here that no one is "in charge." The expression "Who has the house?" started at First Street. And the one who "has the house" is responsible, whether at First Street or Third Street (I would prefer, of course, "St. Joseph House" and "Maryhouse," but the young are afraid of religiosity or pietism). To be responsible means to be able to recognize situations and how to handle them, how to get someone to the hospital, or just to sit him or her down to a bowl of soup or toast or tea.

Three ginkgo trees on First Street have been uprooted by a maniacal drunk, and innumerable windows broken by others. We have experimented with unbreakable glass (very expensive). Peter Maurin was always talking about the Thomistic Doctrine of the Common Good, so our young people know when to be firm and keep a troublemaker out of the house. Charles Butterworth, who "had the house" a great deal in some of our most troublous times, used to take the "disorderly" one for a walk until he found a more stimulating companion for him amongst his Bowery friends.

All this talk about who is "responsible" is to hint, rather broadly, that many letters, inquiries, requests for "clarification of thought" could well be sent to our young and healthy editors in New York.

Today is Thursday and I began thinking this morning how the psalms on this day in the old breviary reflect such tremendous joy. Thursday is, after all, the night the Eucharist was celebrated on Holy Thursday, when Christ washed the feet of His Apostles and gave them the bread and wine which was to be their strength and nourishment. All the Thursday psalms are psalms of rejoicing.

One line of a psalm is: "Be still and know that I am God." You hear things in your own silences. The beauty of nature, including the sound of waves, the sound of insects, the cicadas in the trees—all were part of my joy in nature that brought me to the Church. I don't think we can over-emphasize the importance of song. Psalm 96 begins: "Sing to the Lord a new song . . . Sing joyfully to the Lord, all you lands; break into song; sing praise . . . Let the sea and what fills it resound, the world and those who dwell in it. Let the rivers clap their hands, the mountains shout with them for joy."

The other thing I thought a good deal of this morning, in my six o'clock meditation, is the lack of love and the irritation at others in the community. Father Henri Nouwen has written about hospitality and hostility. It will certainly mean for me an increase of bodily health as well as mental and spiritual health to get rid of some of this irritation in me, this lack of hospitality and love. I must try working at it very hard.

Since I have been forbidden speaking and traveling by my doctor, the column this month is a pilgrimage of another sort.

I must not omit from mention the articles on death and dying which solicitous friends have sent me, God bless them. Catherine of Genoa, whose biography was written by Baron von Hügel, said that Purgatory is the next-happiest place to Heaven. A cheering note—we all acknowledge the need for purging.

October–November 1976

"Eye Hath Not Seen . . ."

Staten Island. It is low tide on a dull, gray day, after a week of glorious weather, a good time to settle down to writing my column. How rich we are, we who profess voluntary poverty as a foundation for our work as agitators, to be able to take a ferry ride and be, within an hour, in a rural area which is still part of New York City. Staten Island is not as fashionable as Long Island, its beaches are not clean and sandy, but rocky, often strewn with driftwood and debris. But my conversion took place here.

I am writing this in the early morning and a mourning dove is mak-ing doleful sounds in one of the beautiful mimosa trees which abound hereabouts. Tamar, my daughter, intends to transplant some tiny mimosa seedlings. No matter how small these seedlings are, they close up their fern-like leaves if you touch them.

Rita Corbin is here too, and all day she has been carving a woodcut of Sacco and Vanzetti, the fiftieth anniversary of whose death we are commemorating in this issue.

I, too, wish to write about these two anarchists, because that is the word or label which confuses many of our readers (especially the bishops?), and "clarification of thought" is the first plank in the Catholic Worker program. I add my contribution to the recalling of Sacco and Vanzetti, because I was very much alive when their execution took place, and will never forget that day of grief. We spent the day in mourning, and Tamar's father lay with his face to the wall, almost unconscious with shock and grief.

To us at the Catholic Worker, anarchism means "Love God and do as you will." "For such, there is no law." "If anyone asks for your cloak, give him your coat too." One could go on with these scriptural teachings of Jesus.

*   *   *

"Faith is the substance of things hoped for, the evidence of things not seen. . . . If, in this life only, we have hope in Christ, we are of all men the most miserable. Eye hath not seen, nor ear heard the things which God hath prepared for those who love Him." What samples of His love in Creation all around us! Even in the city, the changing sky, the trees, frail though they be, which prisoners grow on Riker's Island, to be planted around the city, bear witness. People—all humankind, in some way.

"In the beginning God created heaven and earth." Looking out over the bay, the gulls, the "paths in the sea," the tiny ripples stirring a patch of water here and there, the reflections of clouds on the surface—how beautiful it all is.

Alone all day. A sudden storm in the night. Vast, dark clouds and a glaring, lightning flash with thunder. No rain. Reading Dr. Zhivago a second time.

*   *   *

Stormy day. Woke at 5:30 a.m. Reading Scripture: Genesis and Psalms. Today I will begin with the Ascension and read Acts.

A letter came reproaching me for my love for Solzhenitsyn, claiming he is a warmonger.

*   *   *

Very cool. Woke up with great feelings of joy and gratitude to God for His great gifts of the Holy Spirit. "Ask and you shall receive."

Reading this morning from Ezekiel: "These bones shall rise again."

"Consider all things but dung compared to the love of Christ." St. Paul certainly went to an extreme in expressing himself. Father Hugo, too, did not hesitate to quote this. He ended his famous retreats with "You are dead and your life is hid with Christ in God."

July–August 1977

Fall Appeal 1977

Dear Friends,

We are all poor in one way or another, in soul, mind, and body, in exterior or interior goods. Yet even the widow gave her mite and the little boy his loaves and fishes, and the Lord will see to it that they are multiplied to cover our needs.

All through the year, we take what comes to us from day to day, to keep our three houses going in this area, and sometimes clothes come in, sometimes bread, and, last week, a whole carton of frozen ice cream sticks! It is only once a year that we imitate most truly the poverty of Christ and come to you to beg. There is a story of St. Francis, how, when he was a guest in the house of Cardinal Ugolino, he did not eat the food offered, but went out to beg, saying, playfully, "I have shown you honor by giving honor to a greater Lord in your home, for the Lord takes great pleasure in poverty, especially in the form of voluntary begging."

Individually, in our houses, we beg from the one who holds the purse, and that purse is only filled by you, our readers. In return, we give what we have, *The Catholic Worker,* its articles and reviews, to you, and our services, as your stewards, to the destitute who come to our doors.

Sometimes, I think the purpose of the Catholic Worker, quite aside from all our social aims, is to show the providence of God, how God loves us. We are a family, not an institution, in atmosphere, and so we address ourselves especially to families, who have all the woes of insecurity, sin, sickness, and death, side by side with all the joys of family. We talk about what we are doing, because we constantly wonder at the miracle of our continuance.

This work came about because we started writing of the love we should have for each other, in order to show our love of God. It's the only way we can know we love God.

For forty-four years we have maintained St. Joseph House of Hospitality in the city. The daily soup line still goes on there. Now, seventy-five people share St. Joseph House on First Street and Maryhouse on Third Street, and about fifty are at the farm in Tivoli. Just the heating bill for these places is appalling. No use trying to be businesslike. None of us has that talent. The paper sells for a cent a copy, and the printing bill is big. But no salaries are paid to anyone, so there is not that overhead. Besides, we want far more than a weekly wage. We want God to teach us love. Without it, we are sounding brass and a tinkling cymbal.

The main thing, of course, is to love, even to the folly of the Cross. In the Book of Hosea in the Old Testament, the picture of God's love is the picture of the prophet loving his harlot wife, and supporting not only her but her lovers. What foolish love, what unjudging love! And the picture of God's love in the New Testament is of Christ, our Brother, dying for us on the Cross, for us who are ungrateful, undeserving. Let us love God, since He first loved us. And let us show our love for God by our love for our neighbor.

Our Lord said, "To him who asks of thee, give, and from him who would borrow of thee, do not turn away." And so again we beg, in the name of St. Francis, and in the name of St. Therese, whose desire was to make Love loved.

> Gratefully yours in Christ,
> Dorothy Day

Sunrise

Here at the Catholic Worker we have been rejoicing in our new pope, Holy "Father" to us all. St. Catherine of Siena used to call the pope of her time her "dear sweet Christ on Earth." Peter Maurin admired St. Catherine very much, and wanted me to emulate her and advise the bishops and cardinals, one and all, to start hospices or Houses of Hospitality in every diocese, or, if necessary, in every parish.

*   *   *

At exactly 8:05 a.m., the morning sun gilds the upper floors of the buildings across the street, creeping from the gray one to the red brick one. A lovely sight. Pigeons fly from the roofs. Looking up, I see squirrels on the roof edge. The ailanthus tree (maybe it's a sycamore) stirs in the cold east wind, the sky is a cloudless blue—and now one side of the tree, reaching the third floor of those once-luxury tenements, is all gilded, as the sun spreads rapidly around. Young people are on their way to work, but the children are not yet on their way to school. "My" tree is now radiant with sun!

*   *   *

Woke up this morning thinking of a bitter saying which was used about the Catholic Worker: "The gold is ejected but the dross remains."

Help me, dear Lord, to do my little daily tasks with "ease and discretion, with love and delight." I do not know where that quote comes from. It just popped into my head.

*   *   *

I must cultivate holy indifference. I should rejoice that I am "just an old woman," as the little boy said at the Rochester House of Hospitality long ago. He said, "All day long they said, 'Dorothy Day is coming,' and now she's here and she's just an old woman!"

*   *   *

"I know not ugliness, it is a mood which has forsaken me." Where does that quote come from? Suddenly, these words had come into my mind this morning while I enjoyed watching the rays of the sun rising over the East River, touching up the withered leaves on the little tree across the street.

*   *   *

Thank you, all our readers, for the loving-kindness shown us all, for all the cards, gifts, and remembrances.

December 1978

"And Again I Say, Rejoice"

Woke up this morning with these lines haunting me: "Joyous, I lay waste the day." "Let all those that seek Thee be glad in Thee, and let such as love Thy salvation, say always, the Lord be praised."

This afternoon I listened to *Tosca* on the radio.

* * *

Sad news of my great-grandson, little Justin Haughton's death (struck by a car) in Vermont. I, too, feel prostrated. Grief is numbing.

* * *

Beautiful cards are sent in with donations. One came from an Eskimo cooperative in Canada. I have been keeping the card as a bookmark in my Bible. "The world will be saved by beauty," Dostoevsky wrote.

* * *

From the Psalms: "They shall give thanks unto Thy Name, which is great, holy, wonderful."

* * *

We had hard baked potatoes for supper, and overspiced cabbage. I'm in favor of becoming a vegetarian only if the vegetables are cooked right. (What a hard job cooking is here! But the human warmth in the dining room covers up a multitude of sins.) Another food grievance: onions chopped up in a fruit salad, plus spices and herbs! A sacrilege—to treat foods in this way. Food should be treated with respect, since Our Lord left Himself to us in the guise of food. His disciples knew Him in the breaking of bread.

* * *

Watched Gene O'Neill's *Ah, Wilderness* on television—his one happy play. My memory is so bad—old age is certainly trying. Friends are too solicitous for my health.

*   *   *

Movies on television are a great temptation, but also a good distraction in time of sorrow. Tamar and I watched *The African Queen,* with Katharine Hepburn and Humphrey Bogart. Unbelievable, but interesting. Tamar enjoyed it.

*   *   *

There was a mini-earthquake in Brooklyn, Staten Island, and New Jersey. Why was not Manhattan Island affected? What a thought! Unimaginable to think of those two, fantastic World Trade Center towers swaying with a sudden jarring of what we have come to think of as solid earth beneath our feet.

Yet I sat one day in a rocking chair, fifty years ago, nursing my tiny daughter in front of a large mirror which hung on the wall in my beach bungalow on Staten Island, and suddenly saw the mirror begin to quiver, as though a train or truck (neither of which could have been within miles of us) had suddenly passed the little house, making it tremble.

*   *   *

I woke up this morning with a tune running through my head—"He has the whole world in His hands. He has the whole, wide world in His hands." So why worry? Why lament? "Rejoice," the psalmist writes, "and again I say, rejoice."

February 1979

Postscript

We were just sitting there talking when Peter Maurin came in.

We were just sitting there talking when lines of people began to form, saying, "We need bread." We could not say, "Go, be thou filled." If there were six small loaves and a few fishes, we had to divide them. There was always bread.

We were just sitting there talking and people moved in on us. Let those who can take it, take it. Some moved out and that made room for more. And somehow the walls expanded.

We were just sitting there talking and someone said, "Let's all go and live on a farm."

It was as casual as all that, I often think. It just came about. It just happened.

I found myself, a barren woman, the joyful mother of children. It is not easy always to be joyful, to keep in mind the duty of delight.

The most significant thing about the Catholic Worker is poverty, some say.

The most significant thing is community, others say. We are not alone anymore.

But the final word is love. At times it has been, in the words of Father Zossima, a harsh and dreadful thing, and our very faith in love has been tried through fire.

We cannot love God unless we love each other. We know Him in the breaking of bread, and we know each other in the breaking of bread, and we are not alone anymore. Heaven is a banquet and life is a banquet, too, even with a crust, where there is companionship.

We have all known the long loneliness and we have learned that the only solution is love and that love comes with community.

It all happened while we sat there talking, and it is still going on.

The Long Loneliness

Index

A NOTE ABOUT THE EDITOR

Robert Ellsberg was a member of the Catholic Worker
community in New York City from 1975 to 1980, and
managing editor of *The Catholic Worker* newspaper from
1976 to 1978. Born in Jacksonville, North Carolina, he
graduated from Harvard College and now lives in
Cambridge, Massachusetts.

A NOTE ON THE TYPE

The text of this book was set in a film version of a type face
named Perpetua, designed by the British artist Eric Gill
(1882–1940) and cut by The Monotype Corporation, London,
in 1928–1930. Perpetua is a contemporary letter of original
design, without any direct historical antecedents. The shapes
of the roman letters basically derive from stonecutting, a
form of lettering in which Gill was eminent. The italic is
essentially an inclined roman. The general effect of the type
face in reading sizes is one of lightness and grace. The larger
display sizes of the type are extremely elegant, and form
what is probably the most distinguished series of
inscriptional letters cut in the present century.

Composed by Centennial Graphics, Inc.,
Ephrata, Pennsylvania

Printed and bound by R. R. Donnelley & Sons,
Harrisonburg, Virginia

Typography and binding design
by Dorothy Schmiderer

29820166

DATE DUE